INTRODUCTION TO CYBER-WARFARE

INTRODUCTION TO CYBER-WARFARE

A Multidisciplinary Approach

PAULO SHAKARIAN

JANA SHAKARIAN

ANDREW RUEF

Foreword by

SUSHIL JAJODIA

ELSEVIER

AMSTERDAM • BOSTON • HEIDELBERG • LONDON
NEW YORK • OXFORD • PARIS • SAN DIEGO
SAN FRANCISCO • SINGAPORE • SYDNEY • TOKYO

Syngress is an Imprint of Elsevier

SYNGRESS.

Acquiring Editor: *Chris Katsaropoulos*
Development Editor: *Benjamin Rearick*
Project Manager: *Malathi Samayan*
Designer: *Mark Rogers*

Syngress is an imprint of Elsevier
225 Wyman Street, Waltham, MA 02451, USA

Notices
Knowledge and best practice in this field are constantly changing. As new research and experience broaden our understanding, changes in research methods or professional practices, may become necessary. Practitioners and researchers must always rely on their own experience and knowledge in evaluating and using any information or methods described herein. In using such information or methods they should be mindful of their own safety and the safety of others, including parties for whom they have a professional responsibility.

To the fullest extent of the law, neither the Publisher nor the authors, contributors, or editors, assume any liability for any injury and/or damage to persons or property as a matter of products liability, negligence or otherwise, or from any use or operation of any methods, products, instructions, or ideas contained in the material herein.

Library of Congress Cataloging-in-Publication Data
Application submitted.

British Library Cataloguing-in-Publication Data
A catalogue record for this book is available from the British Library.

For information on all Syngress publications visit our website at http://store.elsevier.com

ISBN: 978-0-12407-814-7

Working together
to grow libraries in
developing countries

www.elsevier.com • www.bookaid.org

Contents

II

CYBER ESPIONAGE AND EXPLOITATION

7. Enter the Dragon: Why Cyber Espionage Against Militaries, Dissidents, and Nondefense Corporations Is a Key Component of Chinese Cyber Strategy

8. Duqu, Flame, Gauss, the Next Generation of Cyber Exploitation

9. Losing Trust in Your Friends: Social Network Exploitation

10. How Iraqi Insurgents Watched U.S. Predator Video—Information Theft on the Tactical Battlefield

III

CYBER OPERATIONS FOR INFRASTRUCTURE ATTACK

11. Cyber Warfare Against Industry

12. Can Cyber Warfare Leave a Nation in the Dark? Cyber Attacks Against Electrical Infrastructure

13. Attacking Iranian Nuclear Facilities: Stuxnet

Preface

Since Stuxnet emerged in 2010, "cyber warfare" has truly entered into public discourse. But what is cyber war and what do we really know about it? Much has been written about the topic that has taken a solely information assurance perspective or a purely policy perspective. The former tends to focus on low-level technical details that are already described extensively in computer security books, whereas the latter emphasizes high-level policy decisions that most readers can do little to affect. All the while, details of the highly interesting cyber incidents are often overlooked. As a result of this omission, the current literature leaves a very basic question unanswered: "how have human beings conducted cyber-warfare"?

In this book, we seek to close the gap and provide the reader with numerous case studies highlighting what we felt were some key aspects of cyber war. Our interdisciplinary approach includes plenty of technical information assurance details, although these are not the sole focus of the book. In each case study, we also attempt to highlight relevant military, policy, social, and scientific issues at play. We hope that reading this book is a great learning experience for the reader—as writing it certainly was for the authors.

Paulo and Jana would like to thank all of their friends and coworkers who supported them throughout the writing of this book as well as their dog Sage who loudly assures them of how lively the neighborhood is.

Andrew would like to thank his wife, Alice, for her love and support. He would also like to thank his friends and coworkers, for years of education and experience.

All the authors would like to thank all reviewers (including the anonymous[1] ones), supportive employers, and the good people at Syngress—who helped make this book possible. In particular, we would like to thank (in no particular order) Steve Elliot, Ben Rearick, Pat Moulder, Sushil Jajodia, Gerardo I. Simari, Roy Lindelauf, Jon Bentley, Eugene Ressler, J. Scot Ransbottom, Dan Guido, Dino Dai Zovi, T.J. O'Connor, Charles Otstott, V.S. Subrahmanian, and Greg Conti.

Paulo Shakarian
Jana Shakarian
Andrew Ruef

[1]Note that the "a" is lowercase.

Foreword

The concept of cyber warfare has now become a regular part of public discourse. It dominates the contents of popular technical outlets such as *Wired* and *SlashDot*; it often appears in the more general media such as CNN, it has become a political priority in the United States, and a major concern for militaries around the world. But what do we know about this new dimension of conflict? There are many pundits that would have you believe that cyber warfare has put the world on edge—at any moment, the world's computer systems can be sent into chaos by a clever teenager at a keyboard. On the other extreme, there are those who think that cyber warfare is overhyped—a minor issue exaggerated by computer security firms and defense contractors to line their pockets. As with many issues, the real answer lies somewhere in between. While it is true that cyber weaponry can potentially cause great damage, we must also understand that when these weapons are used to further political means, the actors in question operate under certain constraints—and cannot wield these hi-tech instruments without encountering various consequences. So then the question becomes how are cyber warriors using these weapons in a political conflict? This suggests the need to study a history of sorts. Such a "history of cyber" is exactly what is presented in this book.

This book is a one-of-a-kind anthology of cyber case studies. As the cyber domain of warfare is very technical in nature, such details, mainly regarding information assurance, are a must. However, as the Internet has grown in a way where it touches many facets of our lives, studying cyber warfare in the vacuum of information assurance would lead us to place the incidents out of context. As this domain evolves, so must cyber warriors—and these warriors will need to look at problems in this area from many dimensions. Paulo, Jana, and Andrew are truly an interdisciplinary team, and this is reflected throughout this book. Relying on Paulo's computer science background and military experience, Jana's expertise in the social sciences and violent conflict, and Andrew's industry experience as a security practitioner, this book weaves together the requisite interdisciplinary threads to allow the reader to appreciate the tapestry that is cyber warfare.

"Cyber" is a hot area today and will continue to be so for the foreseeable future. As society's dependence on technology is a given, its dependence on *secure* technology is a must. Better understanding when, why, and how cyber war happens is the goal of this book—and there are already many individuals in industry, academia, policy, and the military who need this understanding. How should a firm's computer security personnel adjust their posture in the time of an international conflict? What are the important research questions that, if solved, will have a great impact on the cyber domain? What is the relationship between political decisions and technical reality? How can cyber operations augment traditional military ones? These are questions that will be asked by a variety of players and are explored throughout the chapters of this book.

So, if I have convinced you to read this book because of its importance, that's good, but reading a book because it is interesting is even better. The good news here is that this book is both—solid coverage of an important topic presented in an interesting way. Some of the stories described here you may have heard, but you will be surprised as to how much of these "old" stories you haven't. How the poisoning of Russian journalist relates to a DDoS attack or what a Tibetan learned about Chinese cyber exploitation while detained are nuggets of information that make this book thought provoking.

So I invite you to read this book and learn why this new domain is significant, as well as what can and cannot happen in it. I promise that you will learn something new. Despite my two plus decades of cyber experience, I certainly did!

Sushil Jajodia
Professor and Director of Center
for Secure Information Systems
George Mason University

Introduction

It is 2006. An American businessman sits down at his computer to check his e-mail. A mysterious message from an "Israel cyber-terrorist hunter" claims that Hezbollah has hijacked one of his company's IP addresses in order to disseminate their propaganda on the Internet.[1] Not taking it seriously, but just to be sure, he calls his IT office. A few hours later, they confirm the scary truth; the Israeli sender was correct— one of the world's most fervent insurgent groups had used his IT infrastructure for their strategic communication.

Two years later. The political situation between Georgia and Russia becomes nerve-wracking as tensions rise over Georgia's recent hostilities with South Ossetia. Reports indicate that Russian armor formations are amassing near the border poised to invade the Western-friendly Caucasus state. Suddenly, Georgia is hit with a massive distributed denial of service attack (DDoS) against their main Internet servers[2]—just about severing their ability to communicate to the outside world. The Georgians, now unable to tell their story to the rest of the world, are faced with an unencumbered Russian military crossing the border one day after the cyber attack.

It is 2009. Iranian scientists at the Natanz Fuel Enrichment Plant have been scratching their heads for months. Even though they have nearly doubled the number of centrifuges, the amount of enriched Uranium produced has been stagnant—and worse, they are running out of ideas on how to fix the problem. Tests ruled out mechanical and electronic failure. Further, the Siemens Step 7 software reports that the controller cards are receiving the proper instructions. The scientists are mystified. Then a small Belarusian security firm discovers a piece of malware hidden on a USB drive of the computer that hosts the controller software. As it turns out, this stealthy piece of software, named "Stuxnet," has been tampering with the Iranian machinery for months.[3]

Still in 2009. In the neighboring country of Iraq, U.S. soldiers tasked with counter-insurgency operations raid a house inhabited by a member of a Shi'ite insurgent group. In addition to finding weapons and Shi'ite insurgent propaganda, they confiscate a computer. Booting it up, they discover scores of Predator videos[4]—the insurgent had somehow been able to see everything the mightiest unmanned aircraft was looking at—in real time.

It is 2010. The Tunisian government has just been hacked and numerous sensitive e-mails are published on the Internet for the world to see[5]—imposing a twenty-first century version of *Glasnost* on the North African country. The responsible hackers, though savvy, are not affiliated with a government or traditional organization. They are simply an agglomeration of self-selected individuals who refer to themselves as "Anonymous." The posted documents do not endear the population to the government. The already tense situation builds up. When a despaired local street vendor sets himself on fire in December, Tunisians take to the streets. Thus starts the first revolution of a series of upheavals in Arab countries around the Mediterranean Sea, which would become known as the "Arab Spring."

It is 2012. In the United Kingdom, several senior British military officers receive a Facebook friend request from the NATO commander—their boss.[6] Wanting to be on good terms with one of the most senior military officers in Europe, they click "accept the request" providing their new "friend" with access to their personal profiles and communication—only to find out a few days later that the request was a hoax and they unwittingly exposed their private profile data to an unknown third party.

In recent years, the authors of this book have become fascinated with the idea of cyber war. From the Russian invasion of Georgia to the employment of Stuxnet and Duqu, the hacking of Tibetan exiles by GhostNet, to the international cyber-espionage ring known as the Shadow Network and others, cyber war has moved to the forefront of many national agendas. In trying to wrap our heads around this fascinating new dimension of warfare, we examined the available literature. Much seemed to be a re-hash of information assurance—covering important, but already well-documented, topics in computer network security. Other work seems to take a much broader view of the topic—exploring cyber warfare from a high-level policy view—discussing the possibilities of legal accountability and the effects on international relations. While works of these types are useful, they are not addressing cyber war from an operational and tactical perspective. We wanted to understand how cyber war was currently being conducted, what type of cyber operations seemed to be useful in a conflict, and under what circumstances nation-states and nonstate actors engaged in these operations. We wanted to go beyond information assurance, without marginalizing its importance. Cyber warfare is more than just information assurance and more than just policy. In this book, we make an effort to highlight military, sociological, and

scientific aspects of cyber war as well. It turns out that all of these factors significantly affect how cyber warfare is conducted. None of the existing literature adequately explores cyber war in this way.

In analogy to the way military art is being taught at the U.S. Military Academy, the structure of this book is centered on case studies. At West Point, military art is explored through actual historical battles and wars rather than through weapon systems. Hence, we wanted to explore what were the major actions of the cyber conflict; under what circumstances did they occur; and what tactics, techniques, and procedures were used. In our representation of the case studies, we relied solely on open sources—specifically reports of computer security firms, academic journal and conference papers, and media reports. As cyber warfare is inherently linked to the evolution of science and technology, we included several scientific experiments among our case studies. These experiments (particularly "Robin Sage" and the DoE "Aurora Test" found in Chapters 9 and 12, respectively) were conducted under such conditions that their real-world replicability is apparent. Further, throughout the book, we often comment on scientific developments that, when considered in conjunction with the incidents in a given case study, lead to important considerations for the future. Additionally, it has recently been noted that many major corporations desire a more "military style" approach to cyber security.[7] This book is based on such an approach.

We also look at military, sociological, and policy implications of the various case studies we present. For instance, militarily, we discuss how the targeting process is leveraged in cyber espionage in Chapter 7 as well as how intelligence gathering plays a key role in cyber operations in Chapter 13. We perform an in-depth description of the infamous hacking group Anonymous and its affiliates in Chapter 6. Sociology is also important in discussing the interplay between cyber warfare and social networking—we have dedicated an entire chapter to this topic as well. Policy is another thread that runs through the book—nation-states and nonstate actors employing cyber operations clearly go through a decision-making process before they employ such attacks. This particularly comes into play when we explore how Israel, Hamas, and Hezbollah use cyber attacks to augment their information operations and their implications on world opinion (Chapter 4). But policy is also important in regard with the Chinese development of a national cyber strategy in the 1990s (which manifested in the 2000s—see Chapter 7).

We organized this book into three parts. In the first part of the book, we explore how cyber attacks are used to achieve political objectives. This includes support to conventional military operations—particularly as a component of information warfare. Another area where we explore politically motivated cyber attacks is in the case of internal strife: when a state takes action against dissidents. In some cases, large and capable, politically motivated hacker organizations direct these cyber maneuvers with the full knowledge of the government (albeit often maintaining plausible deniability). We avoid the term "computer network attack" (CNA) as it implies a more narrow information assurance-related concept. We view a "cyber attack" as an attack launched using one computer system against another as part of a cyber-warfare operation.

In the second part of the book, we study cyber espionage and cyber exploitation. Again, we use these terms instead of the expression "computer network exploitation" (CNE) in order to highlight the newly arisen implications of these problems. We view cyber espionage and cyber exploitation as attempts to steal data from target information

systems through the use of technology. In this part of the book, we study Chinese-attributed cyber espionage, the hacking of unmanned aerial vehicles, social network exploitation, and high-end malware specifically designed for exploitation.

Finally, in the third part of the book, we discuss the use of cyber operations to attack various kinds of physical infrastructure. These operations aim to cause damage in the physical world, although they are initiated on a computer system. We explore topics such as industrial control systems, the power grid, and the most famous example of a cyber-based infrastructure attack to date, Stuxnet.

So, welcome to *Introduction to Cyber Warfare*. This book is designed to be read by information technology and military practitioners in addition to policy makers, historians, as well as everybody who is just curious about this new phenomenon. The chapters do not necessarily have to be read in order—most of the requisite knowledge is contained in a given chapter (or it is explicitly mentioned where else in the book to look for more background). Finally, as we mentioned in the preface, we learned a great deal in writing this book; we hope that the reader learns as much in reading it.

References

1. Hylton H. How Hizballah Hijacks the Internet. *Time*; August 8, 2006.
2. Bumgarner J, Borg S. *Overview by the US-CCU of the Cyber-Campaign Against Georgia in August of 2008.* US Cyber Consequence Unit Special Report; http://www.registan.net/wp-content/uploads/2009/08/US-CCU-Georgia-Cyber-Campaign-Overview.pdf August 2, 2009 [accessed April 23, 2013].
3. Shakarian P. Stuxnet: cyberwar revolution in military affairs. *Small Wars Journal*. http://smallwarsjournal.com/jrnl/art/stuxnet-cyberwar-revolution-in-military-affairs; April 2011 [accessed April 11, 2013].
4. Gorman S, Dreazen YJ, Cole A. $26 software is used to breach key weapons in Iraq; Iranian Backing Suspected. *Wall Street Journal*. http://online.wsj.

com/article/SB126102247889095011.html; December 17, 2009 [accessed March 17, 2012].

5. Al Arabiya. Wikileaks might have triggered Tunis' revolution. http://www.alarabiya.net/articles/2011/01/15/133592.html; January 15, 2011 [accessed April 11, 2013].

6. Lewis J. How spies used Facebook to steal Nato chiefs' details. *The Telegraph.* http://www.telegraph.co.

uk/technology/9136029/How-spies-used-Facebook-to-steal-Nato-chiefs-details.html; March 10, 2012 [accessed June 21, 2012].

7. Kelly S. Executives advocate a military approach to cyber security. *CNN.com.* http://security.blogs.cnn.com/2012/08/13/executives-advocate-a-military-approach-to-cybersecurity/; August 13, 2012 [accessed September 14, 2012].

Biography

Paulo Shakarian, Ph.D. is a Major in the U.S. Army and a computer scientist who actively conducts research in the areas of cyber security, social networks, and artificial intelligence. He has written over 20 papers published in scientific and military journals. Relating to cyber warfare, he has written the paper "Stuxnet: Cyberwar Revolution in Military Affairs" published in *Small Wars Journal* and "The 2008 Russian Cyber-Campaign Against Georgia" published in *Military Review*. His scientific research has also been well received, featured in major news media such including *The Economist*, *WIRED*, and *Nature*. Paulo holds a Ph.D. and an M.S. in computer science from the University of Maryland, College Park, a B.S. in computer science from West Point, and a Depth of Study in Information Assurance also from West Point. Paulo has served two combat tours in Operation Iraqi Freedom and has held a variety of military duty positions. Currently, he is an assistant professor at West Point where he teaches classes on computer science and information technology. His military awards include the Bronze Star, Meritorious Service Medal, Army Commendation Medal with Valor Device, and Combat Action Badge. Paulo's Web site is http://shakarian.net/paulo.

Jana Shakarian is an independent researcher studying cyber warfare, terrorism, and violence from a social science perspective. Previously, she has worked as a research assistant at Laboratory for Computational Cultural Dynamics at the University of Maryland where she extensively studied terrorist groups in southeast Asia in addition to other research initiatives at the intersection of social and computational science applied to military and security problems. She has also worked as a consultant for the West Point Network Science Center. Jana has written numerous papers in addition to coauthoring the book *Computational Analysis of Terrorist Groups: Lashkar-e-Tabia*. Jana holds an M.A. in cultural and social anthropology as well as sociology from the Johannes Gutenberg University, Mainz, where her thesis was on "new war" theory. Jana's Web site is http://shakarian.net/jana.

Andrew Ruef is a senior systems engineer at the firm Trail of Bits (New York, NY) where he conducts information security analysis. Andrew has nearly a decade of industry experience in computer network security and software engineering, working on various projects including reverse engineering of malware, analysis of computer network traffic for security purposes, system administration, and development of secure software products. Andrew has also written numerous white papers on information security and has spoken at various conferences including a recent conference talk at the Dagstuhl computer research center in Germany. A sampling of some of Andrew's technical work can be found here: http://www.kyrus-tech.com/tag/andrew-ruef/.

The opinions in this book are those of the authors and do not necessarily reflect the opinions of the U.S. Department of Defense, the U.S. Army, or the U.S. Military Academy.

Cyber Warfare: Here and Now

INFORMATION IN THIS CHAPTER

- What is Cyber Warfare?
- The growing importance of cyber warfare
- Attribution in cyber war
- Basic topics in information assurance

What is Cyber Warfare? Is it a credible threat? How should we study it? Before we start to present some case studies, we felt these questions need to be addressed first. Granted, our answers to these questions are only tentative: cyber warfare is and will be evolving. In this chapter, we attempt to define cyber war, discuss why it is important, and outline some techniques that can help us study it. We also address the issue of attribution and examine an information assurance-based framework that helps to better grasp some of the more technical issues.

WHAT IS CYBER WAR?

Many have sought to answer this question during the last decade as the Internet emerged as a new battlefield in conflict. It is tempting to simply define cyber war as when a nation state engages in cyber operations. However, a definition that restricts actions to a nation state is likely incomplete. As we note throughout the book, extra governmental organizations—from the more traditional actors such as Hamas and Hezbollah to newer organizations such as Anonymous and LulzSec—continue to play an increased role in conflict. However, in extending the range of actors in cyber warfare beyond nation states, where do we draw the line? It would not make sense to include every two-bit criminal sending out spam e-mails and high-school kids conducting Web defacements as cyber warriors. On the other hand, we cannot make an arbitrary decision based on the size of the organization conducting the attacks. This book is littered with examples of major cyber operations conducted by a handful of individuals.

Clearly, cyber war is difficult to pin down with a definition. In this book, we first take on Clausewitz's definition of war: "an extension of policy (or politics) by other means."[1] Based hereon, we can create a corollary for cyber war: "an extension of policy (or politics) by actions taken in cyber space." But we also want to avoid considering every politically motivated Web site defacement as an act of cyber war. Perhaps we should also account for capability and add the condition that the actions pose a "serious threat" to national security. However, we still cannot account for cases in which a state uses cyber operations against nonstate actors. Eventually, we resolved to use the following definition of cyber war:

> Cyber war is an extension of policy by actions taken in cyber space by state or nonstate actors that either constitute a serious threat to a nation's security or are conducted in response to a perceived threat against a nation's security.

Most certainly, the debate on what (does not) constitutes cyber war is far from over. However, we found the above-mentioned definition a helpful guidance for this book and the case studies we present are good illustrations of the current state of cyber war.

IS CYBER WAR A CREDIBLE THREAT?

With our definition of cyber war, the reader may wonder if it is even *possible* for a cyber operation to pose a serious threat to national security. Based on the stories in this book, we (the authors) are convinced that cyber warfare can pose a serious threat to national security. Further, cyber operations, in general, can aide other military operations such as intelligence gathering and information warfare. Hence, cyber warfare can potentially make conventional conflict more potent as well. However, there are many that in the past have disagreed with cyber war posing a serious risk to national security.

About a decade ago, many analysts felt that cyber war was not a serious threat. In 2002, James Lewis of the Center of Strategic and International Studies (CSIS) dismissed cyber warfare as a serious threat—referring to cyber weapons as "weapons of mass annoyance."[a;2] The idea of cyber war was further downplayed in 2004 by noted security expert Marcus Ranum, who refers to it as "hype" arguing that cyber war is not cost-effective and lacks high-level expertise.[3] Putting the analysis of Lewis and Ranum in context, their reports were created at a time when cyber warfare was not known to be well practiced by nation states. Further, Ranum cites the late 1990s as a period of mass speculation in popular media about the mere possibilities of cyber war. Back then, actual acts of cyber warfare were insignificant. Without major, publically known incidents of cyber war, analysts such as Lewis and Ranum were quick to ask "why is this important"?

However, in the decade since the term "weapons of mass annoyance"[4] was coined, there have been numerous instances of cyber warfare that we view as significant threats to security. Here is a sampling of some of the operations described in this book.

- In 2006, the armed group Hezbollah hijacked IP addresses in order to circumvent Israel shutting down its Web page during the July War (Chapter 4).
- In 2007, the U.S. Department of Energy conducted an experiment that resulted in a real power generator being destroyed by cyber attacks alone (Chapter 12).
- In 2008, Russian cyber attacks against Georgia during the initial phases of its conventional operation prevented Georgian new media from reaching the rest of the world as Russian armor formation entered the Caucasus nation (Chapter 3).
- In 2008, the Iraqi militant group Kata'ib Hezbollah was successfully able to steal the video feeds of Predator drones (Chapter 10).
- In 2009, security researchers discovered that many Tibetan Government-in-Exile computer systems were hacked into and monitored (likely by the Chinese government) for periods as long as 2 years (Chapter 7).
- In 2010, the Stuxnet worm was discovered. The Iranian government later made statements indicating that the worm had infected and caused damage to its Uranium Enrichment Facilities (Chapter 13).
- In 2010–2011, hacktivists from the group Anonymous played a major role in conducting DDoS attacks against government computers in various countries in the Middle East as part of the "Arab Spring" (Chapter 6).

These and other cyber events have changed the public discourse on the topic. Even Marcus Ranum now seems to concede (at least partially)—particularly in the wake of Stuxnet.[5]

---

[a] Note that in the paper, Lewis attributes the term "weapons of mass annoyance" to Stewart Baker. However, it was Lewis who assessed cyber war to not be a major threat to national security.

However, some individuals during the era of insignificant activity on the field of cyber warfare had a better intuition of what the future would hold. The computer science department at the U.S. Military West Point then headed by Colonel Gene Ressler, in particular, prepared future officers for serious cyber threats. With several undergraduate initiatives, including the "cyber defense exercise"—a competition to protect a computer network against a team of hackers supplied by the National Security Agency, the program formed the avant-garde in taking the possibilities of new technologies surrounding the Internet seriously. Students going through the exercise and associated classes were awarded an additional "Depth of Study in Information Assurance" in addition to their Bachelor's degree. These initiatives were started in 2001 and helped ensure that the U.S. Army had a group of well-trained cyber warriors when Army Cyber Command was stood up nine years later.

ATTRIBUTION, DECEPTION, AND INTELLIGENCE

As we will describe in this book, cyber warfare is a complicated matter due to a large variety of issues—we have already touched on a few on a more abstract level in the section "Introduction." One problem that seems to stand apart is the question of *attribution*—determining the creator and origin of a given cyber operation. To understand why this is so difficult, let us consider (at a coarse-grain level) how a security analyst examines the consequences of an adversary's cyber operation. The key item that (s)he studies is the cyber weaponry—the software used to conduct the attack—which is transmitted through the Internet (or through some closed network). To conduct any type of attribution in the aftermath of an attack, security analysts basically look at three things:

1. Where (from what IP address) the software came from (origin)?
2. How, when, and by whom was the software constructed (structure)?
3. What was the software designed to do (purpose)?

Origin

Suppose that a security analyst can work through the obfuscations employed by a cyber warrior to hide information regarding the software's origins and find a source address (an Internet Protocol or IP address). Even if she or he can successfully reverse engineer the software, the analyst still faces the problem that the source IP address can be faked and rerouted through many different physical locations. Further, the source IP address of a given piece of malicious software (malware) may even be computer, which itself was compromised. Hence, an analyst can never be quite certain that she or he correctly determined from where in the world the software originated.

Structure

Scrutinizing the structure of the malware often proves tricky as well as this analysis poses its own unique set of challenges. Essentially, everything within a piece of software could potentially be designed to deceive the analyst. Normal techniques of investigation, such as determining when the software was compiled, what natural language (i.e., English, Arabic, Russian) was used on the computer upon which it was created, and so on, can all be forged at an extremely low cost.

Purpose

The third lead in the attempt to find who is responsible for the cyber attack is in many ways the most promising, since it is difficult to obscure its purpose. For instance, malware used to target a Uranium fuel enrichment plant is likely created by a very different group of individuals as malware designed to steal credit card numbers. But often the mission of the malware may be deceitful too as criminal activities may be employed to hide the primary objective. Throughout this book, we highlight several instances of cyber warfare where criminal cyber infrastructure is leveraged for a politically motivated attack. The botnet attacks against Georgia (Chapter 3) and some of the actions against dissident groups (Chapter 5) come to mind. Hence, even this simplistic test yields unclear results.

Knowing exactly who conducted a cyber operation is impossible to determine with 100% certainty unless the attacker simply claims responsibility. However, we note that many of the techniques described above are not always used and in fact suggest elaborate technical skills. Another way to approach the issue of attribution is not to look for *evidence*, but rather *intelligence* that indicates who *could* have created the malware. *Intelligence* differs from evidence in that it is not something that can be used in a court of law. However, it can still help us paint the picture of what is happening.

In studying artifacts of malware, intelligence relieves us from the task of knowing exactly who conducted an attack. But how can we account for the possibility of the cyber warrior attempting to mislead the analyst? Intelligence allows for considerations in regard to the origins of malware that lie beyond actionable evidence found in its structure. It also makes room to account for potentially employed deception tactics. Intelligence takes background and context information into account in an attempt to learn from actual, historical conflicts. It thoroughly examines the capabilities of known adversaries as well as the likelihood of potential deception operations. In this regard, intelligence gathered in the wake of an adversary's cyber operation is no different than intelligence gathered in other conflict situations.[6] In a deception operation, an adversary exploits the biases held by his opponent, "feeding" intelligence that may confirm preexisting beliefs. The opponent becomes willing to accept the deceiving intelligence as it is in line with his preconceptions and thus appears plausible. For example, an adversary may launch a cyber attack from a hijacked server located in a country that is already an established foe of the targeted nation. In the eyes of the analysts of the victim country, it seems reasonable to look for the culprit there. In another scenario, the attacker may include hints in the malware's source code that point to a certain organization—either revealing or referring responsibility.

If we are considering the possibility of an adversary using deception, we should consider a "deception hypothesis" that corresponds with every piece of intelligence that attributes a cyber operation to a certain source. By definition, the deception hypothesis is difficult to prove—as the adversary is assumed to make every effort to hide his/her identity, location, and intentions. However, some considerations aide in creating an intelligence estimate that attributes a cyber attack to a certain group. In the guidelines listed below, suppose that security analysts studying cyber operation X have produced intelligence Y by analyzing the traffic of the malware. Y seemingly identifies organization Z as the perpetrator of the cyber attack. Considering a deception, the analysts should also consider the following points:

1. Does organization Z have the capability to conduct operation X?
2. Does organization Z have a reason to conduct operation X?
3. How likely is it that organization Z would have left intelligence Y indicating its responsibility?
4. What other intelligence causes the analyst to believe that organization Z conducted cyber operation X?
5. Is there another organization (Q) that has the capability to conduct operation X?
6. Is there another organization Q that would have a reason to conduct operation X and benefit from misguiding the analyst into believing that Z was responsible?
7. Is there another organization Q that would be savvy enough to plant intelligence Y indicating that organization Z was responsible?
8. Is there another organization Q for which there exists some other intelligence (Y') indicating that it conducted cyber operation X?

Items 1-4 deal with determining the likelihood that a given piece of intelligence is accurate. Items 5-8 deal with determining the likelihood of a deception hypothesis. Again, we note that using such techniques can only lead us to indicate who may have done the attack, but does not provide hard evidence. However, in the case of cyber *warfare* (as opposed to the study of cyber *crime*) often all we need is a good intelligence assessment as opposed to actual evidence.

INFORMATION ASSURANCE

In the final part of this chapter, we review a popular model for studying information assurance that is prevalent in the literature—the *extended* McCumber model.[b,7] This model was then extended adding a fourth dimension 10 years later by Maconachy and his colleagues[8]:

1. *Information States*: In a computer system, information is found in one of three states: storage, processing, or transmission.
2. *Security Services*: A truly secure information system will guarantee the user of five security services: availability, integrity, authentication, confidentiality, and nonrepudiation.
3. *Security Countermeasures*: In order to maintain the security of an information system, technology, operations, and people must be considered—vulnerability in any one of these areas could lead to the entire system becoming vulnerable.

---

[b]The *original* McCumber model for information assurance was introduced in 1991.

4. *Time*: Temporal elements of the other three dimensions need to be considered. The state of information changes from one form to another in a system. Security services must adapt to a constantly changing environment as new software and new requirements are put in place within an organization. Likewise, countermeasures also need to be updated as the threat is dynamic—new malware and enemy tactics, techniques, and procedures (TTPs) are constantly introduced.

As this book is primarily about *cyber warfare* and not *information assurance*, we will focus on the first two dimensions because they allude to offensive cyber warfare (more purely defensive operations tend to fall into the realm of information assurance).

The *state* of information is an important concept as it often dictates what type of TTPs an attacker may use when evaluating a target. As stated above, there are three such states: *Storage* refers to the state when the information is written to a disk. *Transmission* refers to the information being transmitted across a network. Finally, *processing* refers to the information being loaded in the temporary memory (RAM) of a computer. The state of the information becomes most important in the second part of this book where we explore cyber espionage and exploitation. For example, in Chapter 10, we describe how Kata'ib Hezbollah (KH) was able to successfully steal the video feeds of Predator drones. KH stole this information while it was being transmitted from the drone to a ground station. By contrast, Operation Aurora, described in Chapter 7, hackers, likely from China, stole sensitive intellectual property from Google—pilfering it from file servers. The information in question was in the storage state.

The second point listed above (*security services*) is discussed throughout the book. One of these services is *availability*. This crucial service ensures that users are able to access the information they seek. For instance, if a Web server is down, it is not *available* to provide information. Distributed denial of service (DDoS) attacks—as described in every case study in the first part of this book—target this specific security service as they are designed to bring down computer systems, thereby denying individuals access to the information contained in those systems.

Another service informs about the authenticity of the data. If the data have *integrity*, a user can be sure that a third party did not alter it. Many of the attacks seen in the first part of this book were designed to cause users to question data integrity—specifically, Web site defacements of groups like Hamas (Chapter 4) and Anonymous (Chapter 6). In the second part of this book, the integrity of the data was violated by virtue of a third party obtaining unfettered access to a target system. The break-in of the Tibetan Government-in-Exile (Chapter 7) and the cutting-edge malware known as Duqu (Chapter 8) come to mind. Integrity violations can affect industrial equipment as well. We give examples in Chapter 11 where we describe how the integrity of the Maroochy water facility was compromised. In Chapter 13, we present how Stuxnet manipulated the hardware and software that controlled Iranian centrifuges—hence, violating the overall integrity of the system.

The next security service is *authentication*. We primarily see examples where authentication is violated in Chapter 7 when we describe several case studies of cyber espionage attributed to Chinese hackers. Authentication was also a missing component in the unencrypted Predator drone feeds that we will discuss in Chapter 10. Another role played by this security service is in industrial control systems—as many of these systems use protocols that rely on implicit trust relationships (Chapters 11–13).

Confidentiality is a security service that ensures that the communication between two parties is not "overheard" by others. This service primarily comes into play in the second part of this book on espionage and exploitation—particularly in Chapters 7 (Chinese-attributed espionage) and 9 (KH tapping into Predator drone feeds).

Finally, *nonrepudiation* refers to the assurance that the sender of the data is provided with proof of delivery and the receiver is provided with proof of the sender's identity.[9] Perhaps the best example of this service being violated is in Stuxnet's man-in-the-middle (MITM) attack against Siemen's Step 7 software (described in Chapter 13) where the user is issued a false report about the software uploaded to a controller card.

Now with a basic understanding of what this book is attempting to study, we shall examine several case studies. First, we look at what constitutes perhaps the first cyber warfare event to really capture the imagination of the general public: the 2007 Russian cyber attacks against Estonia—possibly the first significant cyber assault in history launched by one state against another.

References

1. On War, Indexed Edition, Carl von Clausewitz, translated by Michael Eliot Howard and Peter Paret. Princeton University Press, Princeton NJ, 1989.
2. Lewis JA. Assessing the risks of cyber terrorism, cyber war and other cyber threats, Washington, DC: Center for Strategic and International Studies; 2002. http://csis.org/files/media/csis/pubs/021101_risks_of_cyberterror.pdf.
3. Ranum MJ. CyberWar: reality or hype? Vanguard security conference, 2004, Reno Nevada; 2004. http://www.ranum.com/security/computer_security/archives/myth-of-cyberwar.pdf.
4. Ibid., Lewis.
5. Ranum M. Cyberwar, critical infrastructure protection. *SearchSecurity*. http://searchsecurity.techtarget.com/video/Marcus-Ranum-on-cyberwar-critical-infrastructure-protection; July 9, 2011 [accessed July 5, 2012].
6. Johnson M, Meyeraan J. *Military deception: hiding the real—showing the fake. Joint Forces Staff College*. http://www.au.af.mil/au/awc/awcgate/ndu/deception.pdf; 2003.
7. McCumber J. Information systems security: a comprehensive model. Proceedings of the 14th national computer security conference. Baltimore, MD: National Institute of Standards and Technology; October 1991.
8. Maconachy WV, Schou CD, Ragsdale D, Welch D. A model for information assurance: an integrated approach, Proceedings of the 2001 IEEE workshop on information assurance and Security United States Military Academy, West Point, NY; June 5–6, 2001.
9. Ibid., Maconachy *et al.*

PART I

CYBER ATTACK

Information has become an important aspect in modern life. Banks, businesses, and media rely on a constant flow of information to operate. In a conflict, information is used to provide commanders situational awareness as well as to allow propaganda artists to provide their viewpoint on the conflict to the rest of the world. In a *cyber attack*, a combatant seeks to reduce the effect of information by taking computer systems offline, or at least somehow blocking access. A key example of this is when Russian hackers denied the Georgian media an outlet to the world as the Russian army invaded the Caucus state in 2008. Alternatively, when a combatant is able to weather a cyber attack and leverage information technology to broadcast their message, they may gain an informational advantage. For instance, in the case of the July War of 2006, Hezbollah was able thwart Israel's best efforts and still reach their worldwide diaspora on the Internet. Many considered Hezbollah as the victor in this incident.

In this first part of the book, we start out by studying one of the first observed cyber-warfare incidents that involved politically-motivated cyber attacks originating from one state directed against another: the case of the 2007 Russian cyber attacks against Estonia (Chapter 2). We then explore how the Russians used cyber attacks during a conventional conflict in 2008 against Georgia (Chapter 3). In Chapter 4, we explore how cyber operations were used to support broader information operations in two conflicts in the Middle East: the 2006 Israel-Hezbollah war and the 2008 Israel-Hamas war. This is followed by a discussion of how certain states leverage cyber attacks internally against dissident groups (Chapter 5)—specifically citing case studies from Russia and Iran. Finally, in Chapter 6, on the example of Anonymous and some of its collaborators we study how non-state actors conduct politically motivated cyber attacks (hacktivism).

Political Cyber Attack Comes of Age in 2007

INFORMATION IN THIS CHAPTER

- Cyber attacks as political expression
- Denial-of-service attacks in Estonia, 2007
- Political behavior regarding cyber attacks
- The global information infrastructure

As discussed in Chapter 1, throughout the 1990s, it was unclear whether attacks against computer systems would constitute a serious political statement. The possibility of a group to carry out a massive, effective, and meaningful attack in order to achieve a political goal seemed remote at that time. However, when Russian hackers decided to take a stand as the Estonian government moved a Soviet-era statue of a Russian soldier, conventional wisdom shifted dramatically. Though there were instances of cyber warfare prior to 2007, the attacks against Estonia were large enough in scale to garner worldwide attention—demonstrating to the global community that cyber warfare would add a new dimension to international relations.

In this chapter, we discuss how disruption of information infrastructure can pose a significant threat and how relatively simple means such as denial of service attacks can be an effective method to attack such. We explore denial of service, related techniques, and issues in this chapter as well as describe the 2007 cyber attacks against Estonia and the response.

RELIANCE ON INFORMATION AS A VULNERABILITY

Edward Waltz in *Information Warfare* describes the concept of the Global Information Infrastructure (GII), a service and network providing communications and control services worldwide. The GII would quickly and efficiently carry voice communications for phone systems, commercial data traffic, and would connect the intranets of large global organizations via virtual private networks.[1] The GII is an idealized concept of how humans will someday share information in a streamlined manner. Access to such an infrastructure would be essential for modern life. Today, this vision is not fully realized. However, the Internet is considered by many as the current *de facto* GII.[2]

Access to and the availability of the Internet in today's GII are essential for the function of many first-world services, such as banking, personal communications, and logistical coordination. Estonian government officials have compared denial of access to the GII to closing a nations sea ports.[3] Without access to the communications infrastructure, the ability for businesses to communicate and transfer data would be significantly impeded. For instance, business-to-business communication and logistical coordination are highly dependent on communication. Further, some businesses rely on network connectivity for their entire operation.

Denial and disruption of the GII can then serve two powerful goals. First, it can cause a real-world disruption to the operations of businesses and governments. Second, it can also invoke the feeling of weakness or vulnerability in the victim because their systems and lives can indeed be disrupted in this way. As discussed in Chapter 1, availability is a key aspect of information assurance. Attacks that disrupt the availability of network and computing resources are commonly referred to as DoS attacks.[4]

RUDIMENTARY BUT EFFECTIVE: DENIAL OF SERVICE

If availability is important, the disruption and denial of availability become a powerful and desirable capability to any adversary. Denial of service attacks, commonly abbreviated as DoS or sometimes simply "dos," are a well-known form of aggression on the Internet. The essence of a denial of service attack is to flood the target of the attack with an abnormally large amount of legitimate traffic to the effect of rendering it inaccessible to other users, though more subtle forms of this attack exist.[5] When numerous systems are involved in the DoS attack (hence amplifying its effects) it is often referred to as a "Distributed Denial of Service" or DDoS.

Data are carried over the Internet within a sequence of packets. Each packet can be thought of as an envelope, with some information on the outside describing where the packet is from and where it is going. Inside this "envelope" are the data carried by the packet. A packet flood denial of service attack entails one computer on the Internet sending another computer an unregulated and continuous stream of packets. Computers on the Internet, and the routing infrastructure that carry packets on the Internet, are required to examine every packet they transmit or receive. There is no obvious indicator in a packet whether it is part of a denial of service attack, or simply part of a file download or otherwise legitimate request of a server.

Other forms of denial of service attacks are more subtle. Denial of service attacks ultimately hinge on an attacker's ability to exhaust or monopolize computing resources of a server or network. For example, the Secure Socket Layer (SSL) protocol provides a mechanism for two computers to transmit data without allowing an eavesdropper to read the data. It does this by using encryption. Using legitimate features of the SSL protocol, attackers are able to convince servers that support SSL into performing spurious computation, denying the usage of the servers to legitimate users.[6]

These more subtle forms of DDoS attacks can carry individual markers that can allow network defense software to block or reject requests that would cause a denial of service condition. For example, the Low Orbit Ion Cannon (LOIC) tool, used by the Anonymous hacktivists,[a] contained an identifying string that differentiated it from connections from benign Web browsers. Web servers could use this string to determine whether or not a client was the malicious LOIC tool or a Web browser, and could then deny all connections to the LOIC tool. In the event where attackers were able to coordinate a sufficient number of hosts running the LOIC tool, the amount of bandwidth consumed by maintaining each individual connection could be sufficient for a DDoS attack of its own. Also, mitigatory technologies that perform this kind of discrimination can themselves become bottlenecks that are targets of DDoS attacks.[7]

In the attacks against Estonia in 2007, posts were made on pro-Russia message boards inciting members and readers of those message boards to conduct a packet flood denial of service attack against Estonian computer systems. The posts contained a very simple program that users could download and run on their computers. The program would use commands that are present on all Windows computers, namely the "ping" command, to flood Estonian computers with traffic. "Ping" is normally used as a diagnostic utility to troubleshoot networking issues; however, when used *en masse* by a large group of people, the "ping" command can generate enough traffic to cause a packet flood DoS attack.[8]

While performing a denial of service attack, it is very easy for the attackers to assess the effectiveness of their attack. If the Web site is reachable, then the attack is not working and the parameters of the attack need to be adjusted. This rapid feedback of information allows attackers conducting denial of service attacks to adapt quickly to changes that system administrators make.

---

[a]We further discuss the Low Orbit Ion Cannon, including its legitimate uses, in Chapter 6.

LEAVING UNWANTED MESSAGES: WEB SITE DEFACEMENT

Defacement shares many characteristics with denial of service. Defacement usually applies to Web sites that people view in their browsers, and usually are carried out against Web servers owned by the organization that the attackers have a grievance with.

Web site defacement usually results from a Web server with an exploitable vulnerability. The attacker uses this vulnerability to compromise the Web server and modify its content (i.e., Web pages). As long as the exploitable vulnerability remains present, the attacker can enter at will and change the contents of the Web page to any message they choose.

Web site defacement has the same overall effect as a denial of service in that the intended users of a service cannot use it. It has an additional effect in that it communicates a message of the attackers' choice to all of the intended users as long as the defaced message remains on-line. Usually, defacements are relatively easy to remove, but if the original vulnerability is not also mitigated, the attacker can continue to alter the content of the Web server. This can be an even more potent message to the users of a Web site.

Web site defacements used to be quite popular and they have been archived on the Internet.[9] However, if attackers can compromise a Web server, they can also access any information that Web server has, which could include valuable information such as usernames and passwords. Where previously, sites would be exploited and defaced, recently, this seems to have been eclipsed by silent compromises of Web sites followed by a gloating disclosure, weeks after the fact, including lists of compromised usernames and e-mail addresses. Typically these disclosures are made on third party Web sites such as pastebin.com or e-mail lists (see Chapter 6 for more details on how hacking groups such as Anonymous use sites such as pastebin.com to publicize stolen information). Another reason for the stealthy compromise of information is to gather intelligence. We discuss this in more detail in Part 2 of this book.

TOOLS FOR DENIAL OF SERVICE

Packet floods are considered unsophisticated because they are relatively easy to perform. Though custom software is required to carry out a packet flood denial of service attack, this software is extremely basic, usually just a few hundred lines of code at most. Writing a tool to execute a packet flood denial of service attack requires only a basic knowledge of Internet communications.

Packet floods usually target servers and routers on the Internet. Packets used in a packet flood are identical to packets that servers and routers process normally. Servers and routers are designed to process many packets, so for a flood to be successful, it has to exceed the amount of packets that a server or router was designed to process. This is hard for an individual computer to accomplish, we can think of it like a four-door sedan in a tractor pull against a bulldozer.

Packet flood attacks can gain momentum by having more computers send floods at the same time. Attackers who conduct denial of service attacks have a few options for expanding the scope of their attack, but ultimately they must run a program on many other computers.

Some attackers entice other users to download and run denial of service programs as in Estonia in 2007 and the Anonymous hacker group in 2011 with the "LOIC" program.

Other attackers make use of "botnets." A botnet is a collection of compromised computers controlled by the same entity. Usually, the owners of the compromised computers are unaware that their computers are being remotely commanded. Botnets are maintained by "bot herders," individuals who compromise computers by a variety of means and monetize the compromised systems in the botnet.

Attackers who wish to perform denial of service attacks can rent the services of botnets from bot herders. The services of botnet rental are quite affordable.[10] Performing denial of service attacks via botnets is often an included feature of the bot software. Some botnets are known to be rented out for use by vengeful video gamers, the packet flood attack from the botnet are used to deny network connectivity to other gamers in competitive online video games.

Computers are compromised globally, so a botnet for sale would have bots in many countries around the world. Some countries are more compromised than others. This is thought to be a function of the rate of software piracy in those countries. Pirated Microsoft products cannot receive updates for security issues. However, the originating country is not a sufficient discriminator to use when responding to denial of service attacks as small numbers of compromised computers in countries with fast network connections (the United States, the United Kingdom, etc.) can be more effective than a larger number of computers in countries of poorer reputation with slower network connections.

THE DIFFICULTY OF ASSIGNING BLAME: WHY ATTRIBUTION IS TOUGH IN A DDoS ATTACK

As described in Chapter 1, conclusive attribution of a denial of service attack can be extremely difficult and often impossible. Messages sent as part of a denial of service attack can enter the Internet from any location. The source addresses assigned to packets as part of a packet flood can be falsified, and it is infeasible for the Internet service providers (ISPs) that carry data in the GII to trace a packet backwards through its network.

Communication between two computers on a network can often be described as either *connectionless* or *connection oriented*. In connectionless communication, the information sent between the two computers is parceled into packets. These packets include enough address information to ensure that they can be transmitted from computer "A" to computer "B" independently. On the other hand, in connection-oriented communication, a connection between computers "A" and "B" is first established before the data are sent between the two. In reality, computers on the Internet often use both modes together in a multifaceted method of communication often referred to as a "protocol stack." For instance, in the TCP/IP protocol stack, TCP is connection oriented, while IP is connectionless. Both TCP and IP work together to establish communication among computers on the Internet.

While some denial of service attacks are connectionless, relying on sheer volume of packets, others are connection oriented, such as the denial of service attack against SSL. To carry out these attacks, an attacker cannot falsify the address information in packets sent to the server. Therefore, in connection-oriented attacks, the source of the attack can be determined as far as the computer that ran the denial of service program, where that computer is identified by its IP address.

If messages can be sourced accurately, they could be part of a botnet that has been rented from its original owner for the attack. For example, a person sitting in St. Petersburg can command a computer that is in France to carry out a denial of service attack against another computer in Estonia.

If the attack is grassroots and generated by posting inflammatory messages on Web sites, the attribution of the attack hinges on accurately identifying the author of the messages. This identification can often be impossible, as described in Chapter 1.

Identifying the true source of a Web site defacement attack is as difficult as correctly identifying the author of a public blog or forum post. Web site defacements usually arise from vulnerabilities in Web sites or the servers that host them. Attackers can use co-opted proxy servers (systems that exist solely to relay application level traffic) or open proxy servers on the Internet to mask the source of their attack. Other uses of proxy servers are discussed in Chapter 5.

Sometimes an attacker will ransom the target of the denial of service attack. The target will receive a communication claiming responsibility for an ongoing or very near future attack and ask for payment to stop the attack. In these instances, attribution is at least a little easier, as the blackmailer will probably be very closely tied to the attack.

ESTONIA IS HIT BY CYBER ATTACKS

On April 27, 2007, the Estonian government completed long-running plans to relocate a national monument. This monument was originally installed by the USSR in 1944 to honor Soviet soldiers who died during the Second World War. The government's plan to move the monument was opposed by the ethnic Russian population of Estonia. The relocation of the monument triggered a wave of protest both in Tallinn and on the networks of Estonia that would last until May 18 (Figure 2.1).

The ethnic Russian population of Estonia, who views the monument as a symbol of Russian sacrifice and victory in its fight against Nazi Germany,[11] took to the street in protest of the statues relocation.[b] There were violent altercations between security forces and rioters that lasted for days. At the beginning of the protests on April 27, a post was made to an Internet forum that gave instructions for participating in a distributed denial of service attack against Estonian government systems.

By April 29, the riots in the streets of Tallinn had been calmed. On the Internet, a multifaceted campaign of denial and disruption was under away against Estonia's electronic infrastructure. Inspired and directed by posts on the Internet, thousands of users in Russia simultaneously transmitted network packets at Estonian computer systems. The attacks came in four major forms: grassroots network packet flood, rented network packet flood, Web site defacement, and junk e-mail.

[b]In contrast, the majority of ethnic Estonians interprets the monument as a symbol of Russian occupation which merely replaced the oppressive Nazi-regime, emplaced in 1939 when Stalin and Hitler divided Europe with the Molotov-Ribbentrop Act.

FIGURE 2.1 The Bronze Soldier of Tallinn. The relocation of this statue, which commemorates the Russian victory against Nazi Germany in World War II, led to massive cyber attacks against the Baltic State by Russian hackers. (For color version of this figure, the reader is referred to the online version of this chapter.) *Source: Petri Kohn via Wikimedia Commons.*[23]

E-mail servers on the Internet are used to receiving unsolicited messages at continuous but moderate pace. They use techniques from machine learning to classify incoming messages as spam or not spam. The purpose of this classification is entirely to lessen the irritation to human users of unsolicited messages. E-mail severs exist entirely to process incoming messages; therefore, if they are sent an overwhelming quantity of e-mail, they are generally unprepared to deal with this in a graceful way. Which messages are part of the flood, and which messages are illegitimate? The system would not know until it reads them all, and since computing power is finite, the availability of e-mail servers can be negatively impacted by sending it a very large number of messages.

On April 29, a flood of messages made the e-mail servers of the Estonian parliament unavailable. This system would remain off-line for 12 h. What direct impact this had on the government's response both to the computer-based attacks and to the preceding riots is unknown. It is not difficult to imagine that the unavailability of e-mail significantly impacted the situation, especially given the lack of direct action that the government could take to restore availability (Figure 2.2).

This is a difference between electronic disruptions and physical disruptions: the source and means of a physical disruption can be identified. If protestors impede the availability of a road, clearing the protestors will restore access to the road. In the face of a flood of messages sent to an e-mail server, what means has the administrators of this server at hand to restore its availability? The source of the messages can be distributed across the entire Internet.

FIGURE 2.2   Toompea Castle in the upper town of Tallinn is the home of the Estonian Parliament. A Denial of Service attack in April 2007 caused the Parliament's e-mail servers to become unavailable, delaying the Estonian government's response to countrywide cyber attacks at the time. (For color version of this figure, the reader is referred to the online version of this chapter.) *Source: CIA World Fact Book.*

Some hackers were able to compromise the security of the Web servers of Estonian political parties. They used their new access to these servers to deface them, replacing legitimate content provided by the government with content mocking the government. One such defacement added a moustache to a picture of the prime minister. Another placed a false apology letter from the prime minister.

The Estonian Government's Response

In the face of a massive and distributed denial of service attack, options are generally limited. Some Internet service providers offer a "DDoS protection" service or plan; however, efficacy of these services can be limited. In the face of a single remote host sending large amounts of data, an effective mitigation would be to stop talking to the host. Two complicating factors in the presence of a distributed denial of service attack are, firstly, the attacking computers will be numerous and will change over time, and secondly, the source addresses (IP addresses) of the attacking computers can be forged.[12]

A denial of service attack can lead to panic and confusion among IT staff, so a critical element of the reaction to a denial of service attack is a swift and meaningful response by IT security. The Estonian government had a very capable computer emergency response team (CERT) that was able to both identify that an attack was taking place against their infrastructure and mobilize experts to help counter the attacks.[13]

The Estonian CERT was able to contact other national CERTs in Europe, such as the German, Finnish, and Slovenian CERTs. Together, this collection of expertise was able to identify the nature of the attack against Estonian systems as well as the general location in the network of the systems that were generating the traffic for the attack. The security responders were able to identify networks that were originating attacks destined for Estonia, and could direct network operators to block those systems from reaching Estonia.

The critical disruption with a DDoS is separating a business or organization from its customers or beneficiaries. By making a Web site for banking customers or citizens unavailable, the attackers deprive the customers/citizens of the ability to carry out some critical action or receive some potentially critical information. In the Estonian case, the attacks originated from outside the country while the customers resided in the country. With this realization, Estonian network operators and businesses could block all traffic from outside the country and maintain service for citizens inside the country. This is an option not available for many companies who are the victims of a DDoS, as their customers are spread across the globe and the attack source could be immediately adjacent to a customer who needs access to the site.[14]

The End of the Attacks

In the weeks following the Estonian government's responses to the DDoS attacks, the DDoS attacks lessened over time and eventually stopped. These DDoS attacks were generally incited by individuals and carried out by either individuals or individuals commanding a botnet, and they did not gain any financial rewards, which shows that the incentive to continue the attacks arose purely from personal interest. As the efficacy of the attack faded, and as the anger from the "Bronze Soldier of Tallinn" incident diminished, the staying power of the attack also dwindled.[15]

About 2 years after the attacks, a leader from a pro-Kremlin youth group known as the "Nashi" (translated "ours") named Konstantin Goloskokov claimed that he and other members of the youth group orchestrated the cyber attacks against Estonia.[16] While on the surface, the Nashi seems to be well supported among Russian youth, there are some who allege that the Kremlin often pays members to attend events such as protests and youth rallies.[17] More recently, a group referring to itself as the "Russian Wing of Anonymous"[c] posted e-mails that it claimed belong to those who lead the Russian youth movements—specifically the head of the Federal Youth Agency Vassily Yakemenko and its spokeswoman Kristina Potupchik. The e-mails revealed that the youth groups are often used as a tool for pro-Putin propaganda.[18] We revisit the Nashi in Chapters 3 and 5, as they are believed to be involved in the 2008 cyber campaign against Georgia as well as cyber attacks against independent media outlets in Russia. Hence, it is probable that the attack claims are at least somewhat accurate. However, the question that remains unanswered is to what extent were the Nashi involved in the attacks as compared to other possible players—such as organized crime and the Russian government.

---

[c]We discuss the hacking collective *Anonymous* more in detail in Chapter 6.

If the claims of the Nashi are correct, then it is likely that the groups' leadership arranged to leverage the computing resources of Nashi members to generate the traffic against Estonia—which caused the DoS. However, in general, DDoS attacks that arise from inciting a large number of people to generate mass amounts of traffic toward an individual Web site are difficult to sustain over time. Eventually, either the individual participants in the attack will become exhausted and lose interest, and/or the network operators that are hosting the attacks will discover the compromised or subverted systems that are participating in the attacks and wall them off or shut them down. Historically, these kinds of responses may take weeks, but it does set an upper limit on the lifetime of a particular DDoS attack. When the attack begins, the victim can reason that, in the best case, the attack will last only a few hours before mitigating efforts take effect, and in the worst case, the attack will last a few weeks before the attackers lose interest or ability.[19]

GENERAL RESPONSE TO DDoS

DDoS is incredibly effective against small organizations. As a DDoS is a simulation of sorts of an extremely trafficked Web site, a Web site that is able to be used by millions of people worldwide is also generally a Web site that is resilient to DDoS. By taking a Web site's content and making it available via a content delivery network (CDN), the ability for that Web site to be taken off-line is greatly diminished. Content delivery networks must serve high volumes of data to the global Internet constantly, and even a large DDoS against them would be dwarfed by the amount of legitimate traffic they receive and process.

Movement of content in a CDN has been made more widely available since the Estonia DDoS. If a similar event happened, attackers would most likely be thwarted much speedier as resources are now available to quickly take a Web site and place it in a CDN. At present, services exist that make use of CDNs for the purpose of mitigating denial of service attacks. One example for a company presently providing this service is CloudFlare, which—like its competitors—transparently makes static content accessible via CDN.[20]

The threat of DDoS attacks has generally been mitigated by the astute use of large-scale network architectures and CDNs. Organizations and companies with enough resources to deploy a significant presence on the Internet and the ability to support a large volume of traffic (e.g., Akamai, CloudFlare, Amazon) are not threatened by DDoS attacks. However, many local or state government and some federal government Internet resources are not supported by such large-scale architectures due to lack of funds, lack of awareness, or a regulatory restriction on where their data may be stored. Those systems, like the Estonian government's systems, are at a greater risk.[21,22]

For individuals, maintaining a large-scale network architecture is economically infeasible, hence the utility of companies providing CDNs. Purchasing the support of a CDN is a little like buying insurance: for a small premium, a buyer's systems are protected by the CDN's large-scale network architecture, and in the (hopefully) unlikely event that those systems come under a DDoS attack, the CDN/insurer will pay out in the form of bandwidth and other mitigating efforts.

SUMMARY

The attacks against Estonia demonstrated that computer-enabled demonstration against government resources was not fiction and within the reach of individuals on the Internet. This should not have come as a surprise to any informed observer, as these types of DDoS attacks have been carried out against individual and corporate entities in the past (Chapter 6 discusses several attacks of this type). The efficacy of the attacks, however, may foreshadow the role of DDoS in future conflicts that include a computerized element. However, the cyber attacks against Estonia were really only the start of politically motivated cyber warfare. In Chapter 3, we shall see how politically motivated cyber attacks against Georgia contributed to conventional military operations in the Caucus nation.

SUGGESTED FURTHER READING

Edward Waltz was one of the few in the 1990s, who had some foresight into what the future of cyber warfare would hold. His seminal work, *Information Warfare*, published in 1998 was one of the first to look at how information could be targeted and weaponized—particular paying attention to commercial and military information systems.

For more information on DDoS, in general, we recommend Subramani Sridhar's SANS paper entitled *Denial of Service attacks and mitigation techniques: Real time implementation with detailed analysis*. This chapter studies various types of DDoS attacks, detecting such attacks, and mitigation strategies.

For more on the Russian hacker cyber attack on Estonia in 2007, we recommend Merike Kaeo's presentation *Cyber Attacks on Estonia—Short Synopsis* produced by Double Shot Security. This presentation provides a detailed technical analysis of the DDoS attacks against the Baltic state.

References

1. Waltz E. Information warfare principles and operations. Norwood, MA: Artech House Inc.; 1998.
2. Global Information Infrastructure. *SearchCIO*. Retrieved December 18, 2012 from http://searchcio.techtarget.com/definition/global-information-infrastructure.
3. Landler M, Markoff J. *Digital Fears Emerge After Data Siege in Estonia*. Retrieved June 4, 2007, from nytimes.com: http://www.nytimes.com/2007/05/29/technology/29estonia.html?pagewanted=all; May 29, 2007.
4. Sridhar S. *Denial of Service attacks and mitigation techniques: real time implementation with detailed analysis*. Retrieved 8 18, 2012, from SANS.org: http://www.sans.org/reading_room/whitepapers/detection/denial-service-attacks-mitigation-techniques-real-time-implementation-detailed-analysi_33764; 2011.
5. Rogers L. *What is a distributed denial of service (DDoS) attack and what can i do about it?* Retrieved August 16, 2012, from CERT.org: http://www.cert.org/homeusers/ddos.html; February 10, 2004.
6. Bernat V. *SSL computational DoS mitigation*. Retrieved August 16, 2012, from Disruptive Ninja: http://vincent.bernat.im/en/blog/2011-ssl-dos-mitigation.html; November 1, 2011.
7. Johnson J. *What is LOIC?* Retrieved August 16, 2012, from Gizmodo: http://gizmodo.com/5709630/what-is-loic; December 8, 2010.
8. Nazario J. *Politically Motivated Denial of Service Attacks*. Retrieved August 16, 2012, from Security to the Core: http://www.ccdcoe.org/publications/virtualbattlefield/12_NAZARIO%20Politically%20Motivated%20DDoS.pdf; August 12, 2008.

9. Preatoni R. *Zone-H*. Retrieved August 16, 2012, from Zone-H: http://www.zone-h.org; March 9, 2002.

10. Franklin J, Paxson V, Perrig A, Savage S. In: An inquiry into the nature and causes of the wealth of internet miscreants. CCS 2007. New York: ACM; 2007, p. 375–88.

11. Ibid.

12. Sridhar S. *Denial of Service attacks and mitigation techniques: Real time implementation with detailed analysis*. Retrieved 8 18, 2012, from SANS.org: http://www.sans.org/reading_room/whitepapers/detection/denial-service-attacks-mitigation-techniques-real-time-implementation-detailed-analysi_33764; 2011.

13. Franklin J, Paxson V, Perrig A, Savage S. In: An inquiry into the nature and causes of the wealth of internet miscreants. CCS 2007. New York: ACM; 2007, p. 375–88.

14. Davis J. Hackers take down the most wired country in Europe. Wired Magazine 2007.

15. Kaeo M. *Cyber Attacks on Estonia Short Synopsis*. Retrieved August 16, 2012, from Double Shot Security: http://www.doubleshotsecurity.com/pdf/NANOG-eesti.pdf; June 3, 2007.

16. Shachtman N. Kremlin kids: we launched the Estonian Cyber War. *Wired*. Retrieved October 28, 2012 from http://www.wired.com/dangerroom/2009/03/pro-kremlin-gro/; March 11, 2009.

17. Rodgers J. Putin's next generation make their mark. *BBC News*. Retrieved October 28, 2012 from http://news.bbc.co.uk/2/hi/europe/6624549.stm; May 4, 2007.

18. Hackers and the Kremlin: Nashi Exposed. *The Economist*. Retrieved October 28, 2012 from http://www.economist.com/blogs/easternapproaches/2012/02/hackers-and-kremlin; February 9, 2012.

19. Sridhar S. *Denial of Service attacks and mitigation techniques: real time implementation with detailed analysis*. Retrieved 8 18, 2012, from SANS.org: http://www.sans.org/reading_room/whitepapers/detection/denial-service-attacks-mitigation-techniques-real-time-implementation-detailed-analysi_33764; 2011.

20. Pathan A-MK, Buyya R. A taxonomy and survey of content delivery networks. Parkville: University of Melbourne; 2007.

21. Pathan A-MK, Buyya R. A taxonomy and survey of content delivery networks. Parkville: University of Melbourne; 2007.

22. Glotzbach M. *Google Apps and Government*. Retrieved August 16, 2012, from Official Google Enterprise Blog: http://googleenterprise.blogspot.com/2009/09/google-apps-and-government.html; September 15, 2009.

23. Kohn P. *Image-File: Tallinn Bronze Soldier—May 2006—029.jpg*. Retrieved October 7, 2012: http://en.wikipedia.org/wiki/File:Tallinn_Bronze_Soldier_-_May_2006_-_029.jpg; 2006.

How Cyber Attacks Augmented Russian Military Operations

INFORMATION IN THIS CHAPTER

- The use of cyber attacks to augment Russian military operations in Georgia, 2008
- Russian DDoS techniques
- Botnets used in the conflict
- The political and military goals of coordinated cyber attacks
- The potential for integrating cyber warfare with conventional military operations

In August 2008, the Russian Army invaded Georgia with the mission of expelling the latter from South Ossetia. The military campaign was accompanied by numerous coordinated cyber attacks. This represents the first instance of a large-scale cyber attack conducted in tandem with major ground combat operations. While there is no direct connection to the Russian government, these cyber attacks had a significant informational and psychological impact on the Georgians as they effectively isolated the Caucasus state from the outside world. This chapter describes the Russian-Georgian cyber conflict, analyzes the campaign, and draws conclusions on how to better prepare for a cyber-capable adversary in the future.

THE 2008 RUSSIAN CYBER CAMPAIGN AGAINST GEORGIA

The Russian cyber campaign against Georgia can be divided into two phases as earlier identified by security experts from a private, nonprofit organization known as the "US Cyber Consequence Unit." The first phase commenced on the evening of August 7[1] when Russian hackers primarily targeted Georgian news and government Web sites. Head of the Russian Military Forecasting Center, Colonel Anatoly Tsyganok, describes these first actions as a response to Georgians hacking South Ossetian media sites earlier in the week.[2] Note that the alleged counter-attacks occurred only one day prior to the commencement of the ground-campaign. This has led many security experts to suggest that the hackers at least knew about the date of the invasion beforehand.

The types of attacks launched by the Russian hackers in the first phase were primarily Distributed Denial of Service (DDoS) attacks. The DDoS attacks during this phase were primarily carried out by *botnets*.[3] Criminal organizations like the Russian Business Network (RBN) use and lease botnets for various purposes.[4] The botnets used in the onslaught against Georgian Web sites were affiliated with Russian criminal organizations, including the RBN.[5]

In this first phase, the attacks were aimed primarily at Georgian government and media Web sites. The Russian botnets relied on a brute force DDoS when actioning these targets.[a,6] The Georgian networks, due to their fragile nature, were more susceptible to flooding than the Estonian networks attacked by Russian hackers a year earlier (described in the last chapter).[7]

While Georgian media and government Web sites continued to receive DDoS, the Russian cyber operation in the second phase sought to inflict damage upon an expanded target list including financial institutions, businesses, educational institutions, western media (BBC and CNN), and a Georgian hacker Web site[8] (Figure 3.1). The assaults on these servers not only included DDoS, but defacements of the Web sites as well (e.g., pro-Russian graffiti on government sites such as a picture likening Georgian President Mikheil Saakashvili to Adolf Hitler). In addition, several Russian hackers utilized publically available e-mail addresses of Georgian politicians to initiate a spam-e-mail campaign.[9]

In order to carry out Web site defacements, the Russian hackers resorted to another type of attack known as an *SQL injection*. This particular tactic exploits a common vulnerability in Web applications. SQL refers to "structured query language," currently the most popular way to program queries for a database. In an *SQL injection*, SQL code is entered into the

---

[a] The Russian botnets in this phase particularly focused on a vulnerability in the protocol known as a TCP SYN exploit.

FIGURE 3.1   The Georgian President's Palace in Tbilisi, the country's capital. Georgia was the subject of massive cyber attacks during the initial phases of the Russian invasion of that country in 2008. (For color version of this figure, the reader is referred to the online version of this chapter.) *CIA World Fact Book photo.*

Web form from an untrusted source and passed to the back-end database of the application either changing the content in the back-end database or dumping the database (normally, a common SQL database—hence the name). A system susceptible to this type of vulnerability essentially gives the hacker total access to the database—including anything from list user login IDs, financial transactions, or Web site content[10].

In this phase of the operation, much of the cyber activity shifted to the recruitment of "patriotic" Russian computer users—often referred to as "hacktivists."[11] According to postings on some Russian hacker Web sites, many "hacktivists" were thought to be members of Russian youth movements—specifically, the Nashi described in Chapter 2.[12] The recruitment was primarily done through various Web sites, the most infamous of which was StopGeorgia.ru, which went online on August 9.[13] One hacktivist notes that the instructions provided were very accessible, even for a novice user.[14] For example, StopGeorgia.ru provided easy-to-use tools and instructions to launch DDoS from private machines. It even featured a user-friendly button called "FLOOD" which, when clicked, deployed multiple DDoS on Georgian targets. Although many of the hacktivist assaults relied on a different specific vulnerability than the botnet actions, they still aimed to overload Georgian servers by a brute force DDoS.[b;15] The tools provided were also very versatile. For instance, some could assail

---

[b] The DDoS attack conducted using such tools differed somewhat from the DDoS attacks by the botnets. Where the botnets used TCP SYN attacks, which exploit the underlying network protocol, many of the tools employed by the "hacktivists" relied on flooding servers with HTTP requests. Basically, this attack worked by requesting a given web site more times than the webserver can handle.

.

up to 17 Georgian servers simultaneously. These hacktivist Web sites also featured target lists of Georgian systems—including specifications whether it was accessible from Russia or Lithuania[16] and known vulnerabilities, including susceptibility to SQL injection.[17] It is also noteworthy that some security experts have linked StopGeorgia.ru to Russian organized crime.[18]

Another interesting aspect of the Russian hacker Web sites is the level of their administrators' professionalism. Not only did they provide novice hacktivists with timely advice, they also policed their sites very well. During the conflict, administrators of Russian hacker site XAKEP.ru promptly responded to port-scans by the US-based open-source security project called "Project Grey Goose" by temporarily blocking all US Internet Protocol (IP) addresses. There was also evidence of them quickly cleaning up the server, in one instance, removing a post containing the keyword "ARMY" in a matter of hours.[19] The precautions of the administrators were well founded as one security organization identified a fake tool uploaded to a Russian hacker Web site described to launch attacks against Georgian targets. However, this particular piece of software turned out to actually target Russian systems. The experts concluded that Georgian hackers uploaded the software in an effort to launch a cyber counterattack, although there was no evidence that this tool caused significant damage.[20]

The Georgian reaction to the Russian attacks first consisted of filtering Russian IP addresses, but the Russian hackers quickly adapted and used nonRussian servers or spoofed IP addresses. The Georgians then moved many of their Web sites to servers out of the country (mainly to the United States). But, even these offshore servers were still susceptible to the flooding exploits due to the extremely high volume of the Russian brute force assault.[21]

WHAT IS INTERESTING ABOUT THE RUSSIAN CYBER CAMPAIGN

Objectives of the Attack

Kenneth Corbin wrote that the goals of the Russian cyber attacks were to "isolate and silence" the Georgians.[22] The assaults had the effect of (1) silencing the Georgian media and (2) isolating the country from the global community. The reports on the event and the target lists provided on the Russian hacker Web sites give credence to Corbin's hypothesis. Furthermore, the Georgian population was dealt with a significant informational and psychological defeat as they were unable to communicate what was happening to the outside world.

While careful not to attribute the cyber attacks to the Russian government, the head of the Russian Military Forecasting Center, Colonel Anatoly Tsyganok, describes the Russian cyber campaign as part of a larger information battle with Georgian and western media.[23] This is also echoed by Russian journalists Maksim Zharov, who describes cyber warfare as only a small part in a larger information campaign that also included bloggers and media outlets.[24] At one point, Russian sympathizers even flooded a CNN/Gallup poll with over 300,000 responders stating that the Russian cause was justified.[25] In Chapter 4, we shall see similar actions by the pro-Israeli groups in the 2006 Israel-Hamas war.

Many analysts believe that the primary goal of the first phase of the Russian cyber attack was to prevent Georgian media from telling their side of the story.[26] This seems to align with the Russian emphasis on information warfare.[27] This goal of isolating Georgia from the outside world also may explain the attacks on Georgian banks that occurred during the second phase of cyber operations. At this time, several banks were flooded with fraudulent transactions. International banks, wanting to mitigate the damage, stopped banking operations in Georgia during the conflict.[28] As a result, Georgia's banking system was down for 10 days.[29] Russian hackers targeting of Georgian business Web sites, also during the second phase, may have aimed to cause similar economic damage.

It should also be noted that the objectives of "isolate and silence" were limited in scope. Cyber attacks causing permanent damage to Georgian networks and on Industrial Control Systems (ICS) and Supervisory Control and Data Acquisition (SCADA) targets were generally avoided.[30] Such systems are designed for real-time data collection, control, and monitoring of critical infrastructure, including power plants, oil/gas pipelines, refineries, and water systems.[31] Obviously, disruption to these systems would have serious implications for the Georgian infrastructure. As the Russian hackers most likely had the capability to action these targets, it is feasible to assume that some restraint was exercised to make sure they were avoided. Further, Georgia's physical connection to the Internet remained largely unaffected. At the time of the attacks, Georgia was connected to the Internet by landlines through Turkey, Armenia, Azerbaijan, and Russia. No evidence points to an attempt to sever these connections in either the physical or virtual world—including the connections running through Russia.[32] This could suggest that the Russian aggressors did not intend to inflict permanent damage on Georgia's Internet infrastructure, but rather target particular servers to meet their objectives of "isolate and silence." Such restrictions on warfare are actually quite common in conventional military operations as well. For instance, in the initial campaign of Operation Iraqi Freedom, power and oil infrastructure were spared. It is important to understand that, despite the conflict, Russia and Georgia have deep economic and cultural ties. Hence, permanent damage to the Georgian Internet infrastructure could lead to a negative outcome for both parties.

Coordination with Conventional Forces

The coordination of cyber attack with conventional forces was very limited. While many experts assert that the Russian hackers at least knew when the ground operations would commence, beyond the timing of the cyber attacks, there is little evidence of coordination. Two possible reasons for this are (1) the Russian government wanted to be able to totally disassociate itself from the cyber attack operations (and there is still no hard proof for their involvement) and (2) the Russian military had not embraced jointness to a great extent at the time of the conflict—causing cyber operations to be stovepiped.[33] However, some security experts made observations that would indicate some coordination between cyber and ground forces. For example, media and communication facilities were not targeted by kinetic means (i.e., normal warfare with bullets and bombs)—this may have been due to the success of the Russian cyber attack. Additionally, Russian hackers also attacked a Web site for renting diesel-powered electric generators—an odd target for such an action. However, the attack on this site may have been conducted in support of conventional strikes against the Georgian electrical infrastructure.[34]

Reconnaissance and Preparation

Many security experts[35] believe that the Russian hackers had prepared their operation prior to the initial cyber strikes of August 7. This is due to the speed of the botnet attacks in phase 1 and the availability of target lists and hacking tools—which included known SQL injection vulnerabilities—in phase 2. Simply put, the effectiveness of the cyber attack initiated by the Russian hackers leads us to infer that reconnaissance took place well in advance.

There are other indicators of preparation as well: In July 2008, Georgian servers (including the presidential Web site) were flooded with the message "win + love + in + Russia."[36] These DDoS attacks originated from a botnet known as *Machbot Network*, which is known to be used by various Russian criminal organizations.[37] Some analysts suspect that this early strike may have been a "dress rehearsal" for the August attacks.[38] Another indicator of prior preparation is based on the analysis of the graffiti images used to deface the Georgian Web sites. Security experts discovered that some of these images were created as early as 2006.[39] This could mean that the cyber attacks may have functioned as a contingency operation well before 2008.

Attribution

Many authors (particularly bloggers and news reporters) have pondered the level of involvement of the Russian government in the attacks. Here are a few theories on the level of the Russian government's potential involvement with the cyber attacks against Georgia:

1. *The Russian cyber operations originated spontaneously from patriotic "hacktivists" primarily in response to attacks on South Ossetian Web sites.* While this theory may seem plausible, it also poses some problems. First, there was apparently a great amount of reconnaissance planned and executed in preparation. This most likely occurred well before the attacks on South Ossetian media sites on August 5. Secondly, the majority of cyber attacks during the first phase of the operations were launched from botnets. These assaults were significant and occurred several days before many sites recruiting and supporting the hacktivists went online. The use of botnets suggests the involvement of Russian organized crime—either launching DDoS against Georgia themselves or leasing their botnets to other individuals doing so.

2. *The cyber attacks originated solely from Russian organized crime.* The use of botnets and the fact that many hacktivist Web sites (such as StopGeorgia.ru) have been linked to Russian organized crime makes this hypothesis more credible than the previous one. However, the obvious question is what did the criminal organizations gain from these operations? Supposing that they were not funded or otherwise supported by the Russian government, one theory suggests that the hackers were using the cyber attacks to infiltrate certain Georgian systems for later use (such as the financial institutions attacked in phase 2).

FIGURE 3.2 The Russian Tomb of the Unknown Soldier outside the Kremlin Wall. While there are many indicators in Kremlin involvement or complacency in the cyber attacks against Georgia, it is difficult to attribute the attacks to the Russian government with 100% confidence. (For color version of this figure, the reader is referred to the online version of this chapter.) *Photo from the CIA World Fact Book.*

3. *The cyber attacks originated from Russian organized crime at the request of the Kremlin.*
   This theory has been put forth by several writers, particularly pointing out that organizations such as the RBN have links to Vladimir Putin and the Kremlin.[40] The coordination with conventional military operations addressed earlier and a linkage between StopGeorgia.ru and the Russian GRU are also supporting arguments.[c;41] However, these findings are circumstantial (at the time of this writing, there is no hard proof of Kremlin's involvement; Figure 3.2).

PREPARING FOR A CYBER-CAPABLE ADVERSARY

Cyber as a Battlefield Operating System

Whether or not the Kremlin was involved, the cyber attacks yielded a benefit to the overall Russian operation. As such, perhaps cyber capabilities should be considered as a battlefield operating system (BOS) similar to maneuver, artillery, air-defense, and others. Fully understanding the enemy's cyber capabilities is an important piece of analysis when considering the cyber BOS. We note that the enemy hacker can take various forms—including individuals at government-sponsored labs, uniformed members of cyber units, members of criminal

---

[c]This circumstantial linkage is based on WHOIS registration for servers associated with StopGeorgia.ru. One registration address is located next to the Russian GRU headquarters in Moscow. This analysis was performed by security experts and Project Grey Goose.

organizations, and hacktivists (politically motivated hackers). Often in cyberspace, it is difficult or impossible to distinguish different players. However, understanding which of these cyber soldiers are in a combatant's order of battle (OB) can provide insight into their actions. With the OB established, cyber "doctrinal templates" (DOCTEMP) can then be applied. An example based on the Georgia conflict would include Russian criminal organizations in the OB, even though their precise relationship to conventional forces is not known. Based on their presence in the OB, we can then look at a DOCTEMP associated with the criminals. This may indicate the use of botnets and hacktivists with the mission to isolate and silence the enemy, but not permanently affect the cyber infrastructure or ICS/SCADA.

The Cyber Aspect of the Area of Interest

Another lesson to infer from the Georgian case is that perhaps commanders should consider security issues not only for military networks but also for civilian networks. While generally not focused on military targets, the Russian cyber attacks in Georgia had significant informational and psychological effects. Further, some cyber attacks, such as the July attacks on Georgian government Web sites, may forebode not only larger-scale cyber attacks but also ground operations. In order to help protect the local populace, it may become imperative to ensure the survival of civilian computer networks.

As a result, a commander may want to develop priority information requirements (PIRs) that are cyber in nature. Priority information requirements refer to information that a military commander must be aware of as soon as it is known. Normally, this type of information will cause a military commander to make a decision. As the modern battlefield, it will become necessary for all military commanders to thoughtfully consider how cyber operations affect their overall plan—regardless of what the nature of the current fight is.

Cyber Reconnaissance and Surveillance (R&S)

As described above, smaller cyber attacks may be indicators for larger-scale cyber attack as well as kinetic operations. Additionally, there are other signs of impending cyber attack, the reporting of which may fall on a variety of individuals. For example, suspicious traffic on a computer network may be reported by the computer security personnel for military networks, or a liaison with a host nation government for civilian networks. Bloggers or other posts to hacker Web sites may also hint at an imminent cyber offensive. These could be monitored by personnel tasked with conducting open-source intelligence (OSINT) analysis. Finally, more traditional intelligence reporting such as signals intelligence (SIGINT, information obtained through the interception of electronic signals) and human intelligence (HUMINT, information gained from insiders) should also be tasked and trained to identify indicators of cyber attacks specific to their domain.

In many of the other case studies in this book, we find examples of cyber warriors preparing to conduct operations through their own reconnaissance efforts. A good cyber counterreconnaissance is a must for cyber defenders. We specifically explore this issue with respect to cyber espionage in Chapter 8. It should also be noted that "gaining a foothold" in a computer network through cyber espionage and exploitation is often a prerequisite for cyber attack.

SUMMARY

The Russian cyber campaign on Georgia in August 2008 represents the first large-scale cyber attack occurring simultaneously with major conventional military operations. These cyber operations had a significant informational and psychological impact on Georgia as they reduced the capability to communicate with the outside world not only for media and government but also for the general public. Although the attacks cannot be directly linked to the Russian government, the benefits are clear and probably warrant consideration in future conflicts. Processes such as PIR (priority information requirement) development and R&S (reconnaissance and surveillance) planning should be adjusted to account for a cyber-capable enemy.

SUGGESTED FURTHER READING

Much of this chapter is based on one of the author's (Paulo Shakarian's) journal articles entitled *The 2008 Russian Cyber-Campaign Against Georgia* that was featured in the November to December 2011 issue of *Military Review* where the cyber campaign was explored as a military operation. For more of a policy-oriented view on this cyber conflict, see Stephen Korns' and Joshua Kastenberg's "Georgia's Cyber Left Hook" in the winter 2008-2009 issue of *Parameters.* For technical analyses of Russian cyber operations against Georgia, we recommend John Bumgarner's and Scott Borg's US Cyber Consequence Unit report entitled *Cyber Campaign Against Georgia* as well as Jeff Carr's GreyLogic report entitled *The Evolving State of Cyber Warfare.*

References

1. Bumgarner J, Borg S. *Overview by the US-CCU of the cyber-campaign against Georgia in August of 2008. US Cyber Consequence Unit Special Report*, August 2009, 2.
2. Tsyganok A. Informational warfare—a geopolitical reality. *Strategic Culture Foundation Online Magazine,* http://rbth.ru/articles/2008/11/05/051108_strategic.html; November 5, 2008 [accessed October 10, 2010]. Note that this is an English version of the article provided by the website. South Ossetian News Sites Hacked. *Civil.ge Daily News Online.* http://www.civil.ge/eng/article.php?id=18896; 2008 [accessed October 16, 2010].
3. Nazario J. Georgia DDoS attacks—a quick summary of observations. *Arbor SERT (Security Engineering and Response Team).* http://asert.arbornetworks.com/2008/08/georgia-ddos-attacks-a-quick-summary-of-observations/; August 12, 2008 [accessed October 16, 2010].
4. GreyLogic. *Project Grey Goose Phase II Report: the evolving state of cyber warfare;* May 20, 2009.
5. Corbin K. Lessons from the Russia-Georgia Cyberwar, internetnews.com: real time IT News March 12, 2009; http://www.internetnews.com/government/article.php/3810011/Lessons-From-the-Russia-Georgia-Cyberwar.htm [accessed October 16, 2010].
6. Nazario. August 12, 2008.
7. Bumgarner and Borg, 4.
8. Ibid, 5.
9. Danchev D. Coordinated Russia vs. Georgia cyber attack in progress. ZDNet August 11, 2008; http://www.zdnet.com/blog/security/coordinated-russia-vs-georgia-cyber-attack-in-progress/1670 [accessed October 16, 2010].
10. Ullricha JB, Lamb J. Defacing websites via SQL injection. Netw Security January 2008;2008(1):9–10.
11. Danchev.
12. Ibid., GreyLogic.

13. Ibid., GreyLogic.
14. Morozov E. Army of Ones and Zeros: how I became a soldier in the Georgia-Russia Cyberwar. *Slate*. http://www.slate.com/id/2197514; August 14, 2008 [accessed 16 October, 2010].
15. Bumgarner and Borg, 4.
16. Morozov.
17. Danchev.
18. Ibid., GreyLogic.
19. Ibid., GreyLogic.
20. Bumgarner and Borg, 7.
21. Ibid.
22. Ibid., Corbin.
23. Ibid., Tsyganok.
24. A synopsis of Maksim Zharov's articles at the time of the conflict can be found in: Thomas T. The bear went through the mountain: Russia appraises its five-day war in South Ossetia. *J Slavic Military Studies* 2009;**22**:31–67.
25. Clayifeld M. Attacks on cyberspace preceded Russian tanks. *The Australian*. http://www.theaustralian.com.au/news/attacks-on-cyberspace-preceded-russian-tanks/story-e6frg6to-1111117197354; August 15, 2008 [accessed October 7, 2012].
26. Corbin.
27. Thomas T. Russian information-psychological actions: implications for U.S. PSYOP. Spec Warfare 1997;10 (1):12–9.
28. Corbin.
29. Bumgarner and Borg, 6.
30. Bumgarner and Borg, 5.
31. Fernandez JD, Fernandez AE. SCADA systems: vulnerabilities and remediation. J Comput Sci Coll 2005;20 (4):160–8.
32. Zmijewski E. Georgia clings to the 'Net'. *Reneysys: the Internet Intelligence Authority*. http://www.renesys.com/blog/2008/08/georgia_clings_to_the_net.shtml; August 10, 2008 [accessed October 16, 2010].
33. Bikkvol Tor. Russia's military performance in Georgia. Military Rev 2009;57–62.
34. Bumgarner and Borg, 6.
35. See GreyLogic and Bumgarner and Borg, 6.
36. Thomas T. The bear went through the mountain: Russia appraises its five-day war in South Ossetia. J Slavic Military Studies 2009;2(2):56.
37. Korns S, Kastenberg J. Georgia's cyber left hook. Parameters 2008–2009;38:60–76.
38. Thomas T. The bear went through the mountain: Russia appraises its five-day war in South Ossetia. J Slavic Military Studies 2009;22:56.
39. Bumgarner and Borg, 5.
40. Corbin.
41. GreyLogic.

When Who Tells the Best Story Wins: Cyber and Information Operations in the Middle East

INFORMATION IN THIS CHAPTER

- Cyber operations during the 2006 Israel-Hezbollah war
- The utility of cyber operations in information operations
- IP address hijacking and CYOP
- Cybercortical warfare

In Chapters 2 and 3, the incidents of cyber attack were somewhat one-sided in the virtual world. The Russians attacked Estonia and Georgia with little or no retaliation from the other combatant. However, two other wars that occurred in the same decade saw significant cyber attacks performed by both sides, specifically, the Israel-Hezbollah war in the summer of 2006 ("July War") and the Israel-Hamas war of 2008-2009 ("Operation Cast Lead").

Conventional wisdom on the cyber capabilities of the combatants in these conflicts could lead us to believe that Israel likely is the more formidable cyber force. For instance, it has been long rumored that the Israeli Defense Force (IDF) "Unit 8200" was involved in cyber operations throughout the early 2000s.[1] Anti-Israeli groups were generally less regarded in this respect. The "cyber terrorist" group known as "Team Evil"[2]—predominantly consisting of Moroccan youths[3]—was noted for many hacks, particularly Web defacements, throughout the first decade of the 2000s. However, although numerous, these hacks generally lacked sophistication. The cyber activities of the "July War" and "Operation Cast Lead" moved somewhat beyond these more simplistic attacks. As Israel's conflict with Hezbollah and Hamas is expected to continue for the foreseeable future, we can expect the cyber activities to continue to evolve, perhaps making the Levant one of the fastest developing areas of the world in the field.

HIJACKING NONCOMBATANT CIVILIAN IP ADDRESSES TO HELP THE WAR EFFORT: THE ISRAEL-HEZBOLLAH "JULY WAR" OF 2006

In February 2005, Lebanon was rocked with the assassination of Former Prime Minister Rafiq al-Hariri. This event resulted in mass Lebanese protests ("Cedar Revolution") against occupational power Syria as well as American and French insistence on the withdrawal of Syrian troops from the country. Syria ultimately obliged, leaving the Lebanese to form a new coalition government in April 2005.[4] Many in the West believed that this new government would lead to the demilitarization of Hezbollah. The Iranian-supported Shi'ite militant group operates freely in Lebanon and is listed as a "terrorist group" by the United States. With its role doubted by many in Lebanon, and rumors of an impending Israeli strike on Lebanon, the leaders of Hezbollah decided to take preemptive action against Israel in July 2006. Members of the organization killed three and kidnapped two Israeli soldiers in cross-border raids. Hezbollah proceeded by initiating a series of short-range rocket attacks against the Jewish state. The resulting massive Israeli retaliation caused significant damage to the Lebanese infrastructure and claimed the lives of over one thousand civilians—while failing to dislodge the true culprit, Hezbollah. After about a month of fighting, the Lebanese government announced that it would send 15,000 troops to the South—a move that would potentially escalate the conflict further. However, at this point, both sides sought to end the conflict—which was done by U.N. Resolution 1701, which ordered a ceasefire and practically led to the end of the "2006 Lebanon War."[5]

Though both Hezbollah (Figure 4.1) and Israel declared victory, the fact that Hezbollah was neither destroyed nor disarmed led many to view Israel as having lost the conflict.[6] After all, these were the original goals Israel had stated, while Hezbollah sought to merely survive.

The operations on the ground were accompanied by various cyber war techniques on both sides. Notably, the Israelis conducted a denial-of-service attack on the Web site of Hezbollah's

FIGURE 4.1 Hezbollah insignia (http://www.english. moqawama.org/). (For a color version of this figure, the reader is referred to the online version of this chapter.)

television station, "Al Manar." Israeli civilians, especially the "World Union of Jewish Students" created a piece of software called "megaphone" that alerted users to online polls, discussion forums, and blogs in order to encourage them to post information supportive of the Israeli cause.[7] On the other side, there have been reports of Hezbollah hackers gaining access to networks of Israeli Defense Force (IDF) units stationed on the Lebanese border.[8] If such activities occurred, it was likely for Intelligence gathering as there have been no reports in the open media of DDoS-style attacks against tactical IDF units during this conflict.

The Information Operations of Hezbollah

Perhaps the most noteworthy instance of cyber warfare during this conflict was a tactic to support Hezbollah's information operations (IO). It is feasible that one of the key enablers of Hezbollah's "victory" was their ability to communicate their story faster and more effectively than the Israelis. For example, immediately after the successful missile attack on an Israeli naval vessel, Hezbollah's Secretary General, Sayyed Hassan Nasrallah, was on Al-Manar satellite television station persuading viewers to take a look at the burning Israeli ship. His statements followed footage of the attack and the wreckage. At that point in time, the Israelis had not even confirmed the event.[9]

Hezbollah's integrated approach to information warfare was central to their strategy (Figure 4.2). One of the main components was "cyber psychological operations" (Cyber-PSYOP or CYOP).[10] CYOP is defined as the use of cyber operations to directly attack and influence the attitudes and behaviors of soldiers and the general population. For instance,

FIGURE 4.2 Hezbollah's Secretary General, Sayyed Hassan Nasrallah. Under Nasrallah, Hezbollah embraced the Internet in the 1990s for propaganda purposes and later for cyber warfare activities in support of propaganda (http://www.english.moqawama.org/). (For color version of this figure, the reader is referred to the online version of this chapter.)

CYOP could include the use of "new media"—social networking sites such as Facebook—to spread the message of one of the combatants. Likewise, CYOP can also potentially take the form of a DDoS attack—denying the enemy the ability to spread their message. CYOP is a core component of a new type of strategy adopted by Hezbollah in the early 2000s known as *cybercortical* warfare.[a] In this strategy, a state or nonstate actor uses credible political and military power to command attention and project information power—offensively shaping the information environment in a conflict via the Internet.[11]

Hezbollah's efforts to leverage cyber assets as a key part of their information campaign started as early as 1996 with the launch of "hizbollah.org." Other related Web sites included one for Hezbollah's Al-Manar satellite television station (www.almanar.com.lb) as well as a homepage for Hassan Nasrallah. At the time of writing, the Al-Manar Web site coexists with a Web site of the "Islamic Resistance in Lebanon" (www.moqawama.org). Perhaps most interesting about the early launch of "hizbollah.org" was the lack of Lebanese and Arabic audience. In 1997, there were less than a quarter million Internet users in the Arab world (outside of Israel) and a mere 35,520 users in Lebanon.[12] This small presence, coupled with the fact that Hezbollah maintained their sites in both English and Arabic from the day of their launch, indicates that the militant organization viewed the Internet as a tool to shape their image in (mainly) western eyes. Hezbollah's targeting of worldwide and adversarial media had become a standard practice by the 2006 war with Israel. The organization quickly and accurately reported the tactical situation and created professional media products that were disseminated through a variety of means—their respective Web sites and YouTube. Further, these products were created in a variety of languages, including Hebrew—which again illustrates the strategy's main goal of influencing the opponent's perception.[13]

These reports tended to focus on and emphasize the destruction of civilian infrastructure caused by the IDF. What could be viewed as "collateral damage" Hezbollah understood to exploit for its own benefits. It should be noted that in the aftermath of the war the assessed damage was less than reported by the group.[14] Perhaps most infamous in the exaggerated

---

[a]The term *cybercortical warfare* is derived from the idea of *neocortical warfare* that was introduced by Richard Szafranski in the November 1994 issue of *Military Review*. Szafranski defines *neocortical warfare* as a warfare that "strives to control or shape the behavior of enemy organisms, but without destroying the organisms."

reporting of this sort was the case of Reuter's reporter Adnan Hajj who doctored images of destruction. Hajj was ultimately dismissed by Reuters.[15]

Hezbollah Hijacks IP Addresses

In response to Hezbollah's CYOP, many of Israel's allies in the West, such as the United States, banned Hezbollah Web sites such as Al-Manar.[16] There were also reports of the IDF launching unspecified cyber attacks against Al Manar and other Hezbollah sites.[17,18] Unable to rely on their own, legitimate IP address, Hezbollah "hijacked" addresses from corporations worldwide—including the United States, Canada, and India.[19] We will now examine a case study of this sort of hijacking (Figure 4.3): on the Internet, information is transmitted from one location to another through a series of routers. A collection of routers and other network devices under control of a single organization on the Internet is referred to as an "autonomous system" (AS).[20] Each AS has a few routers that are facing the rest of the Internet known as "border gateway routers." These special routers communicate to the rest of the Internet and help ensure that any traffic intended for a computer in a certain AS is directed the right way. For example, if you request to view the Web site of "Company X," your request will be routed through the Internet until it reaches the border gateway router of that company. It is then internally routed though Company X until it reaches their Web server. The routers on the Internet are able to successfully transmit the request to Company X's AS because their border gateway router sends its adjacent routers on the Internet a list of IP addresses that the firm uses. This information is communicated using the "Border Gateway Protocol" (BGP).[21]

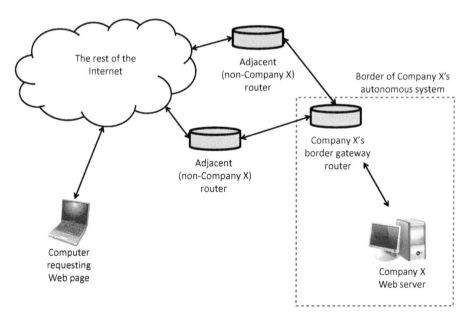

FIGURE 4.3   The role of a border gateway router. (For color version of this figure, the reader is referred to the online version of this chapter.)

In the BGP protocol, there is an implicit trust relationship. The adjacent router receiving the list of IP addresses from the border gateway router assumes that the addresses are valid (which in normal goodwill transactions is the case). However, if the administrator of an autonomous system does not take the proper precautions, and/or misconfigures the border gateway router, then some of the IP addresses allocated to this network could be hijacked. In such a case, a third party advertises a subset of the target system's addresses.[22] As Hilary Hylton of *Time* magazine points out, IP-address hijacking is analogous to adding an extension on a phone line from the victim company. If the target does not detect the hijack, the hijackers would have effectively taken control over that IP address to use for their own purposes. This is what Hezbollah did during the July war. The organization that headed the effort to stop Hezbollah's hijackings was the "Society for Internet Research"—a group that referred to themselves as "freelance counter-terrorists."[23] This informal group of computer security experts monitored Hezbollah's Internet traffic in order to identify the coopted address and alert the target company in order to shut down the Hezbollah IO operations. However, the Society for Internet Research noted that Hezbollah once detected was able to quickly hijack new IP addresses, which caused them to refer to their efforts as "whack-a-mole"—soon after one hijacked IP address was shut down, another one was corrupted.[24]

The Israel-Hezbollah war of July 2006 is significant from a cyber war perspective, because it illustrates the emerging interplay between cyber warfare and information operations. Because of their prior adoption of the strategy of cybercortical warfare, Hezbollah closely linked tactical operations with information operations (IO). The Israeli response of shutting down their opponent's Web sites can be viewed similar to the supposed Russian intent of their 2008 Georgia campaign. However, Hezbollah was able to successfully respond with cyber operations of their own, borne out of and extending their preexisting IO efforts. The repeated hijacking of noncombatant IP addresses allowed Hezbollah to maintain the communication of their strategic message.

CIVILIANS IN THE CYBER MELEE: OPERATION CAST LEAD

Israel learned some difficult lessons from the 2006 war with Hezbollah. Despite the fact that the UN Resolution 1701 was actually more favorable toward Israel, the IO campaign of Hezbollah was able to portray Israel as a paper tiger to the "Arab Street." According to their IO, Hezbollah appeared to be David fending against the Goliath IDF. Hezbollah further painted a picture of the IDF as a force that, despite launching attacks that had serious impact on Lebanese infrastructure, was still unable to achieve the tactical goals of liberating Israeli prisoners and stopping Hezbollah's short-range rocket attacks. As a result, the Israelis entered a period of introspection. The Jewish state established the Winograd Commission to collect the lessons learned from their recent bout with Hezbollah. The commission found that tactically the IDF leadership had become entrenched in the mindset of Low Intensity Conflict (LIC) as exemplified by the al Aqsa Intifada in 2000. Consequently, combined operations that involved armor and tactical aviation became neglected in the years leading up to the 2006 war.[25] The Winograd Commission also made recommendations to improve Israeli IO and subsequently the National Information Directorate was created. This organization—tasked with "hasbara" or "explanation" organized all media activities—from traditional means (i.e. broadcast) to emerging technologies on the Internet.[26] These efforts included outreach to Jewish and Israeli support groups worldwide through social media. This outreach differs from Hezbollah's cybercortical warfare, which is oriented toward the opponent as these Israeli efforts were directed at like-minded audiences to rally support.

IO and Cyber Warfare in the 2008 Israel-Hamas War

In late December 2008, Israel commenced a new operation—"Cast Lead"—with the goal of stopping missile strikes in southern Israel that originated from Gaza. The attack commenced with an air assault that took out 50 Hamas targets on the first day. Israel emplaced a carefully constructed information campaign that actually began simultaneously with the physical conflict. Two days after the initial airstrike, the IDF launched the YouTube channel called the "IDF Spokesperson's Unit." This channel, the brainchild of some IDF soldiers, included a variety of footage of the IDF—everything from video logs ("vlogs") of IDF personnel to gun video of precision strikes and the footage of humanitarian assistance missions.[27] Additionally, the "Jewish Internet Defense Force" played a key role in encouraging the Jewish Diaspora to become active in the "new media" of the Internet. For instance, their Web site included instructions for using various types of social media—including Facebook, YouTube, Wikipedia, and various blogging services. Further, they also directed efforts against the "new media" of the opposing force as they also claimed to be responsible for shutting down several pro-Hamas YouTube channels.

Hamas and the inhabitants of Gaza responded to Israel's IO campaign with its own content documenting the devastation of the Israeli attack. Leveraging mobile phones, Twitter, digital images, and blogs, the Gazans were able to tell their story to the world.[28] They responded to the attempts to shut down their YouTube channels with the creation of paltube.com—a site dedicated to Hamas videos.

Not only did Hamas and its supporters fight Israeli IO with their own information campaign, and conducted a series of hundreds of defacements of Israeli Web sites. Though some Web site defacements were high profile enough to gain the attention of mass media,[29] the actual damage (likely economic) is presumed to have resulted from the sheer number of these actions carried out by pro-Hamas hackers. Typically, the pro-Hamas groups conducted some rudimentary vulnerability scanning of targeted Israeli Web sites, often with the Web server software. Upon obtaining access to parts of the server, the pro-Hamas hackers would deface the Web sites with anti-Israeli graffiti.[30]

Perhaps the most notable hacking group for these Web site defacements was known as "Team Hell." One member, known as "Cold Zero," was responsible for over 2000 defacements of Israeli Web sites, nearly 800 of which were carried out during the 2008 war. He allegedly conducted defacements of high-profile sites such as Israel's Likud Party and the Tel Aviv Maccabis basketball team.[31] Upon his arrest in early January 2009, "Cold Zero" was found to be a 17-year-old Palestinian male Israeli-Arab who worked with accomplices in other Islamic countries.

In addition to Web site defacements, Hamas supporters also leveraged DDoS attacks on a small to medium scale. Pro-Hamas hacker, Nimu al-Iraq, who is thought to be a 22-year-old Iraqi Mohammed Sattar al-Shamari, modified the hacking DDoS-tool known as al-Durrah for use in the 2008 Gaza war. This software is similar to that the DDoS software used by the Russian hacktivists in the Georgian conflict (as described in Chapter 3): both allowed novice users to easily participate in DDoS attacks during the conflict without giving up control of their own computer. An al-Durrah user would enter the addresses of targeted Israeli servers into al-Durrah's interface, which he/she would obtain from a pro-Hamas hacker forum, and the software would proceed to flood the targeted server with requests eventually taking it offline.[32]

Israeli hacktivists also had DDoS tools of their own. A pro-Israeli group known as "Help Israel Win" created a tool called "Patriot" which was designed to attack pro-Hamas Web sites during the conflict. This software has been referred to as a "voluntary botnet" as the users of this software would then be connected to a command-and-control server, which uses the URL "defenderhosting.com" which would then direct the Patriot user's computer in attacks. Unlike al-Durrah, the tools used by the Russian hacktivists (see Chapter 3), or the low-orbit ion cannon (LOIC) of Anonymous (Chapter 6), Patriot is not configurable by the user—allowing defenderhosting.com to completely control the cyber attack actions of its volunteered host.[33]

As the 24-day conflict passed its initial days, the tide of the IO war shifted from Israel, who initially was telling the more dominant story, to Hamas. The pictures of devastation in Gaza spread through the news media like a virus. What led to this shift? The likely explanation is the fact that several months prior to the outbreak of the conflict Israel started limiting media access to Gaza. In doing so, they hoped to limit the images of collateral damage to infrastructure and civilian casualties that would undoubtedly be reported by Hamas and the Gazans. By limiting the output of such reports, the international community would be slower to call for a resolution to stop the hostilities—thereby giving Israel more time to accomplish its tactical objectives. In this regard, their plan worked—the IDF was generally successful in achieving its tactical goals (as opposed to the 2006 conflict with Hezbollah). However, the side effect was that all the reporting from within Gaza came from Hamas and the Gazans. As a result, the story told from within Gaza was one-sided. By not letting independent media in the area, the Israelis effectively denied the opportunity for a disinterested party to refute the claims of the Gazans.[34] Though there were some successful Israeli hacking operations, such as the IDF's hack of the Hamas television station and attempts by Israeli supporters to hack pro-Palestinian Facebook accounts,[35] the Israeli efforts in cyberspace were insufficient to stop Hamas from delivering an effective message to the world. Further, the presence of Arab news media reporters from Al Jazeera, who stayed in Gaza since before the IDF started to curb media access, ensured that the Gazans' story was told to the entire (Arab) world.[36]

The Israel-Hamas war of 2008 illustrates the importance of social media in modern information operations during conflict and both sides' attempts to integrate cyber operations to support them. However, unlike Hezbollah's use of IP address hijacking, which directly contributed to the success of their IO in 2006, neither Israel nor Hamas were able to make highly effective use of cyber tactics to support their respective public relations in 2008. The Israelis, despite DDoS attacks against a pro-Hamas Web site and the shutting down of pro-Hamas YouTube channels, was ultimately unsuccessful in stopping Gazans' story from reaching the world. While the Hamas supporters may have successfully leveraged some IT knowledge, as in the case of setting up paltube.com, they did not seem to conduct successful, sophisticated cyber operations—as their cyber attacks appeared to be limited to Web site defacements and small-/medium-scale DDoS. Likely, this is due to a lack of technical expertise in their organization—something Hezbollah clearly had in 2006. This could potentially reflect a lack of prioritization on cyber within Hamas in 2008.

SUMMARY

The armed conflicts between Israel and Hezbollah in 2006 as well as Israel and Hamas in 2008 illustrate how combatants attempt to use cyber operations to support their information campaign. These conflicts clearly illustrate that the use of social media such as Facebook and Twitter, along with the ease of uploading digital images from mobile phones, adds a new dimension to an otherwise conventional conflict. As a result, cyber operations—to both enhance and diminish the adversary's use of social media—become an attractive option to military commanders and civilians alike to support the war effort. Hezbollah showed how an organization can become resilient by cleverly hijacking IP addresses to convey their message. Israel, in 2008, sought to use cyber attacks to prevent Hamas from telling their story—at least long enough to complete tactical objectives. Hacktivism by all parties will likely increase in future conflicts as civilians—both in the conflict area and members of global communities backing one side or the other. For example, Chapter 6 describes how members of Anonymous enabled and supported the protestors in Tunisia, Egypt, and other countries experiencing the upheaval of the so-called Arab Spring.

SUGGESTED FURTHER READING

Cybercortical Warfare, which is viewed as central part of the Hezbollah strategy, is discussed by Maura Conway in an article entitled "Cybercortical Warfare," which was presented in 2003 at the *European Consortium for Political Research*. This concept is closely related to the idea of "CYOP" introduced by Timothy Thomas in his paper "Hezbollah, Israel, and Cyber PSYOP" published in *IO Sphere* in 2007. Cyber operations of the Israel–Hezbollah war are discussed in the *ACM WebSci'11* conference paper "Asymmetric Cyber-warfare between Israel and Hezbollah: The Web as a new strategic battlefield," by Sabrine Saad *et al.*

The information operations of the Israel-Hamas confrontation are discussed in detail in the *Military Review* paper "Learning to Leverage New Media: The Israeli Defense Forces in Recent Conflicts" by LTG William Caldwell and others. Cyber operations during that conflict, though limited, are explored along with an analysis of pro-Hamas hacking groups, in a paper published in 2009 by *GreyLogic* security firm entitled "Project Grey Goose Phase II Report: The evolving state of cyber warfare."

References

1. Katz Y. IDF admits to using cyber space to attack enemies. The Jerusalem Post June 3, 2012; http://www.jpost.com/Defense/Article.aspx?id=272503&R=R9.
2. See "Case study: a cyber-terrorism attack, analysis, and response" by Damari K, Chayun A, and Evron G and "The return of SIMBAR: cyber terrorism methodology" by Damari K and Oboler A published by Beyond Security. http://www.beyondsecurity.com.
3. Mor G, Kinan E. Major Israeli websites hacked, YNet News June 2006; [accessed January 2, 2013]. http://www.ynetnews.com/articles/0,7340,L-3268449,00.html.
4. Nakhleh HT. The 2006 Israeli war on Lebanon: analysis and strategic implications, *Master's Thesis*, U.S. Army War College; 2007.
5. Ibid.
6. Inbar E. How Israel bungled the second Lebanon war. The Middle East Quarterly 2007; vol. XIV, 57–65.
7. Saad S, Bazan S, Varin C. Asymmetric cyber-warfare between Israel and Hezbollah: the web as a new strategic battlefield. Proceedings of the ACM WebSci'11, Koblenz, Germany, June 14–17, 2011; 2011.
8. Ibid.
9. Rohozinski R. *New media and information effects during the 33 day war*, The SecDev Group; 2008.
10. Thomas TL. Hezballah, Israel, and cyber PSYOP. IO Sphere Winter 2007;30–35.
11. Conway M. Cybercortical warfare: the case of Hizbollah.org. European Consortium for Political Research, Edinburg, UK, March 28–April 2, 2003; 2003.
12. Ibid.
13. Ibid., Rohozinski.
14. Ibid.
15. Ibid., Thomas.
16. Hylton H. How Hizballah hijacks the Internet. Time August 8, 2006.
17. Ibid., Saad.
18. Peri S. IDF hacks Nasrallah's TV channel. yNetNews.com July 31, 2006; http://www.ynetnews.com/articles/0,7340,L-3283866,00.htm [accessed September 2, 2012].
19. Ibid., Hylton.
20. For a more precise definition, see Hawkinson J. *Guidelines for creation, selection, and registration of an Autonomous System (AS), RFC 1930.* http://tools.ietf.org/html/rfc1930; March 1996 [accessed January 2, 2013].
21. Rekhter Y, Li T. *A border gateway protocol 4 (BGP-4), RFC 1771,* http://www.ietf.org/rfc/rfc4271.txt; March 1995 [accessed January 2, 2013].
22. Ballani H, Francis P, Zhang X. A study of prefix hijacking and interception in the internet. SIGCOMM '07, Kyoto, Japan, August 27–31, 2007; 2007.
23. Ibid., Hylton.
24. Ibid., Hylton.
25. Johnson DE. Military capabilities for hybrid war: insights from the Israel defense forces in Lebanon and Gaza. Santa Monica, CA: RAND Corporation; 2010.
26. Caldwell W, Murphy D, Menning A. Learning to leverage new media: the Israeli defense forces in recent conflicts. Military Rev., May-June 2009;2–10.
27. Ibid., Caldwell *et al.*
28. Ibid., Caldwell *et al.*
29. Ibid., Caldwell *et al.*
30. GreyLogic. *Project grey goose phase II report: the evolving state of cyber warfare;* May 20, 2009.
31. Ibid., GreyLogic.
32. Ibid., GreyLogic.
33. Ibid., GreyLogic.
34. Ibid., Caldwell *et al.*
35. Ibid., GreyLogic.
36. Ibid., Caldwell *et al.*

Limiting Free Speech on the Internet: Cyber Attack Against Internal Dissidents in Iran and Russia

INFORMATION IN THIS CHAPTER

- Attacking domestic dissidents via cyber warfare
- Types of attacks available to governments to use against its citizens
- Attacks against protestors in Iran
- Attacks against independent media in Russia
- The rise of the Iranian Cyber Army and Cyber Police after the 2009 Presidential elections

In Chapter 4, we saw how Israel attempted to use cyber attacks to limit the use of social media by Hamas during their war in 2008. An aspect of this incident that makes it different from other scenarios we discussed so far (e.g., Estonia, Georgia, and Lebanon) is that Hamas is a group whose members live in the Palestinian territories occupied by Israel.[a] Therefore, we can look at Israel's use of cyber attacks against Hamas as a means to quell a dissident group residing within the state. This raises an interesting question: Do governments and their ardent supporters conduct cyber attacks against dissidents outside of civil conflict? It turns out that dissident groups and independent media outlets are reporting distributed denial of service attacks at an alarming rate—particularly in countries known for limiting press freedom.

Why should a "cyber warrior" study intrastate cyber attacks against dissident groups? It might seem that these attacks would be of lesser importance in a book such as this where the primary focus has been on conflict between nation states or conflict against a foreign armed nonstate organization such as Hezbollah. How do attacks against independent media residing within a state's territory fit in?

First, the tactics, techniques, and procedures (TTPs) used in cyber operations against a dissident group within a state may also be used in an interstate conflict. If a government carries out a certain type of attack against nonconformists, then they clearly have that capability for conflicts involving external actors. If a certain attack against such a group is carried out by a patriotic pro-regime organization, then perhaps we can expect to see that organization on the cyber battlefield of an interstate conflict. For example, consider the actions of the Russian youth groups in the 2008 conflict with the Georgia or the Jewish Internet Defense Force described in Chapter 4—such groups could conceivably conduct cyber attacks against internal as well as external adversaries without discrimination.

A second reason to study cyber attacks by dissident groups is to understand the techniques used to limit the communication within a country. As we saw in Chapter 4, cyber operations can be a key enabler of information operations (IO) as well as a weapon used to counter them. Further, the use of dissident groups, both for propaganda and operational purposes, is quite common in conflict—often these groups tend to continue to exist and operate after a conflict.

The rest of the chapter is organized as follows: first, we discuss some general trends in the use of cyber attacks against dissident groups—in particular distributed denial of service attacks (DDoS). We then describe case studies from two nation states where cyber attacks against dissident groups are well documented: Russia and Iran.

DDoS AS A CENSORSHIP TOOL: WHY DISSIDENT GROUPS ARE INHERENTLY VULNERABLE TO CYBER ATTACKS

In 2010, researchers from the Berkman Center for Internet and Society at the Harvard University conducted a study of independent news media and human rights groups that were targets of DDoS attacks.[1] This section is largely based on their study. Based on a series of Google searches and alerts on open-source information, the group found 329 different attacks against 815 different sites of this type from 1998 to 2010. However, the trend seemed to accelerate: 140 of

---

[a]Gaza and the West Bank are collectively referred to as OPT—Occupied Palestinian Territories.

FIGURE 5.1   Countries where independent media on the Internet is often targeted (though not necessarily by the host nation): USA, Tunisia, Russia, China, Vietnam, Burma, Mexico, Israel, Egypt, and Iran.

those attacks on 280 different sites occurred from September 2009 to August 2010. While it can be expected that these numbers are much lower than the actual number of attacks, they indicate that independent media and human rights groups are significant targets of cyber attack. Further, the researchers noted that sites registered in the USA, Tunisia, Russia, China, Vietnam, Burma, Mexico, Israel, Egypt, and Iran were particularly common—which indicates the global spread of such attacks (Figure 5.1).

In addition to where a dissident group or independent news media outlet hosts its Internet presence, another factor that may account for the likelihood of them being attacked is the size of their Internet service provider (ISP). Such providers are informally categorized into three tiers. Tier 1 are the major service providers (e.g., the American companies AT&T, XO Communications and CenturyLink, as well as German Telekom and Indian Tata Communications), which consist of providers that reach a large number of customers. Tier 1 ISPs exchange Internet traffic with each other without paying transit costs, because the large volume of users such a network services makes it beneficial for the receiving provider to forgo transit costs. Tier 2 providers are peers with some networks, but pay transit costs for others, whereas Tier 3 networks purchase IP transit from all other providers (Figure 5.2). Popular Tier 2 networks are administered by Vodafone, Atrato IP networks, Comcast, and Virgin Media. Unsurprisingly, the security staff of a Tier 1 provider is typically much larger than others, allowing them to be able to rapidly respond to security incidents such as a denial of service attack. Often, Tier 1 networks are pictured as lying near the "core" of the Internet. Among each other, Tier 1 providers typically share information, particularly with regard to security matters. Hence, the security personnel of these large networks are usually very knowledgeable about the latest tactics, techniques, and procedures (TTPs) in the realm of cyber security.

Independent media and human rights groups most typically operate servers that are connected to a Tier 3 Internet provider. The reasons may be manifold—such as budget constraints or the Tier 1 provider in their home country is close to the government which

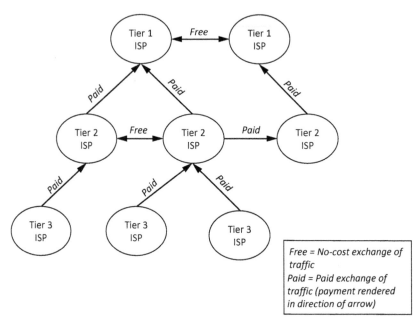

FIGURE 5.2   Fictitious example of the relationship among ISP's of different tiers.

might not support them or which they may oppose. As a result, these servers are located farther away from the Internet "core" and skilled security personnel, and hence face more difficulty in responding to attacks.

The Harvard researchers surveyed 317 independent media and human rights sites concerning cyber attack and received 45 responses. Of the respondents, 72% experienced some sort of filtering at the national level, 62% experienced DDoS attacks, 39% experienced forms of intrusion, and 32% experienced some sort of Web site defacement. It is noteworthy that the Harvard study also found a correlation between sites targeted with DDoS and those targeted with filtering. Perhaps this suggests that respective governments and/or their supporters seek multiple means to inhibit the message of these groups.[2]

Further, at the time of the survey, 2010, the majority of respondents reported an increase in the number of cyber attacks over the previous year. This aligns with broader surveys (i.e., including business, governmental, and private organizations), which also report increases in cyber attacks in more recent years. Another concern of the surveyed organizations that is interesting within the context of this chapter is the fact that 48% reported that they experienced unexplained downtime of their systems for seven or more days a year. Granted, cyber attack is just one possible explanation, but such a noticeable amount of time, in which the networks remain inexplicably unavailable, is noteworthy. All reported incidents highlight the lack of technical expertise small network providers may often experience and which makes them vulnerable to cyber attacks. By contrast, the researchers noted that Tier 1 and 2 providers respond to the majority of cyber assaults in under an hour.[3]

According to the survey, the Tier 3 ISPs appear less than helpful to these organizations once their sites are under attack. Only 36% of respondents reported that their provider was able to successfully defend them from a DDoS attack, whereas 55% stated that their Internet connections were shut down instead. It is possible that smaller Internet providers, with a low profit margin, could view independent media and human rights groups as clients whose political positions potentially lead to higher costs than profitable when it comes to maintaining their Internet presence.

The Harvard researchers also interviewed a dozen of the administrators of sites that had experienced cyber attacks. The interviews show that many assaults take on the form of hybrid attacks, in which DDoS is paired with a different form of attack. For example, in the anonymous survey results of Zuckerman *et al.*, according to one system administrator, a dissident organization experienced a DDoS attack followed by an attempted extortion in which he was pressed to retract a particular story (according to the system administrator, the organization refused to comply). Another interviewee reported the occurrence of not only high-volume multigigabit DDoS assaults but also the harassment of individual users of the site, on which additionally inflammatory information was posted in an effort to trigger government persecution. Another administrator reported a creative style of denial of service, where the attacker had hacked into the system and modified the Web site to display fake antivirus messages to the users in an attempt to scare them from accessing the site. These fake antivirus messages also contained links that initiated the download of malware that conceivably might have comprised Trojans allowing the attacker access to the visiting individual's computer systems as well.[4]

The interviews by the Harvard researchers also showed that the site administrators had a strong belief that their national government was ultimately responsible for the attacks. However, none of those interviewed had any clear evidence indicating that this was the case. Despite the lack of evidence, there are some interesting indicators that their suppositions were right. For instance, an interviewee from Vietnam pointed out a press report of a Vietnamese military official claiming responsibility for the attack. Another Vietnamese administrator reported that his national government often filtered his site, but lifted this measure to constrain traffic just in time for a major DDoS attack to hit the site. He claimed that the assault was later attributed to a botnet. An Iranian administrator reported that a DDoS attack against his Web site was traced back to a site hosting the official government newspaper. It appeared that third-party visitors of the newspaper Web site inadvertently triggered a Javascript (computer code embedded as a part of a Web page) that flooded the opposition group's Web presence with requests and eventually shut it down.[5]

The small size of providers catering to dissident groups and independent media make them particularly vulnerable to DDoS attacks. A cyber-capable government or its skillful supporters can easily take a dissident site offline for a week or more at a time. In the remainder of this chapter, we describe specific case studies of cyber attacks targeting dissident groups, particularly in Russia and Iran.

SILENCING NOVAYA GAZETA AND OTHER RUSSIAN DISSIDENTS

Novaya Gazeta[b] is a Russian newspaper known for its investigations into official corruption, human rights abuses, and illicit government affairs.[6] One of its most prominent staff members

[b] An English-language version of the medium is available under http://en.novayagazeta.ru/.

was the late journalist Anna Politkovskaya, whose assassination was prominently featured in Western media. At the time of writing, former lieutenant colonel of the Moscow police, Dmitry Pavlyuchenkov, confessed to initiating her surveillance as well as procuring the murder weapon.[7,8] Stagnant official investigations into the case repeatedly accuse Chechen government supporters[c] as having perpetrated the murder, but the people who tasked them remain unknown.[9,10] The journalist was known for her sharp criticism of the Kremlin, and her death was widely seen as a repercussion of her work. Politkovskaya's fate was shared by four other *Novaya Gazeta* reporters within the last decade.[11,12] In the summer of 2012, Dmitry Muratov, *Novaya Gazeta*'s chief editor published an open letter to the government describing how Russia's chief federal investigator, Aleksandr I. Bastrykin, threatened the life of his deputy editor about an article implicating corruption within the Russian judicial system.[13] The Moscow-based *Novaya Gazeta* is known for its detailed investigations and publications of power abuse, high-level corruption, and human rights violations in Russia.[14] Other prominent stories include the major smuggling scandal involving the TriKita (three whales) and Grand furniture companies as well as officials of the Federal Security Service (FSB, formerly KGB)[15] as well as other government agencies,[16] investigations into which were unfolding over many years finally concluding in court with a relatively minor case of furniture smuggling.[17] The main witness, then president of the Furniture Business Association, Sergei Pereverzev, was murdered in a hospital where he was hoped to recover from a car accident—just days before his scheduled court appearance.[18] A high-profile investigative journalist and state Duma deputy, Yury Shchekochikhin,[19] working for *Novaya Gazeta* on this case died under circumstances similar to the radiation death of Alexander Litvinenko in summer 2003.[20] In both cases, the individuals rapidly showed signs of abnormal exposure to radiation and were thought to have received a high-end poison that has been described as a "nuclear weapon inside one's body."[21] Shortly before his death, the seasoned journalist claimed to have obtained evidence that the smuggling of goods was linked to practices of money laundering (through the bank of New York) and illegal arms trafficking.[22] The case of his death was eventually referred to the Investigative Committee—headed by Aleksandr I. Bastrykin. This fourth probe into his death was closed in 2009 arguing that another tissue lab test had not substantiated poison as the cause of passing away,[23] while all medical files concerning this case remain classified.[24] Organizations like the Committee to Protect Journalists (CJP) have noted that reporters from the *Novaya Gazeta* often operate at significant personal risk.[25]

In early February 2010, the Web site of *Novaya Gazeta* was the victim of a DDoS attack that peaked at 1.5 million connections per second and lasted over 6 days. The newspaper resorted to using the LiveJournal blogging site to maintain an online presence.[26] It was widely thought that the attack was performed in response to an article by a noted reporter Yulia Latynina, who had recently written an article on rampant corruption in Russia. Previously, Latynina was awarded the U.S. State Department's Freedom Defender's Award for her work to expose human rights violations and corruption (Figure 5.3).[27]

---

[c] As the motivation for Politkovskaya's murder investigators cited her reports on human rights abuses committed by the Chechen government.

FIGURE 5.3 Yulia Latynina receiving the Defenders of Freedom award in 2008. An article by Latynina on the corruption in the Russian government is thought to have led to a massive DDoS on the independent news media outlet Novaya Gazeta in 2010. Picture from U.S. State Department video. (For color version of this figure, the reader is referred to the online version of this chapter.)

Moving to LiveJournal

With the February 2010 attack, and a subsequent DDoS attack in November of the same year,[28] the newspaper increasingly relied on LiveJournal for their online presence. According to the report of Harvard's Berkman Center, moving content to a site such as LiveJournal is a good step to mitigate DDoS. Even though an organization might view posting their information on LiveJournal as less prestigious than using their own Web site, the loss in prestige is countered with increased security. Large Web sites such as LiveJournal are typically more robust and therefore fend off DDoS attacks more easily. This is due to having greater capacity, as well as more dedicated information security personnel.

However, about a year later, in April 2011, several Russian LiveJournal sites were hit with DDoS attacks.[29] According to security expert Alexander Gostev of Kaspersky Lab, the Web site of *Novaya Gazeta* was also targeted during this operation.[30] LiveJournal is extensively used in Russia, with an estimated 4.7 million users during the time of the assault.

A report by Kaspersky Lab indicated that the LiveJournal blog of political activists like Alexey Navalny[d] may have been an intended target of the attack.[31,32] Navalny's Twitter account has almost 40,000 subscribers and his blog and Web site, Rospil.info, are a popular outlet for the opposition in Russia.[33] In 2008, the financial lawyer and political activist started a blog on which he posted allegations of corruption within state-controlled corporations. Since then, the prolific blogger became Putin's worst enemy.[34] In 2012—though lacking the support of the majority of Russians[35]—he was featured as one of *Time*'s most influential people and is described as part of Russia's "data dissidents."[36]

Ahead of the December 2011 parliamentary elections, Navalny urged the readers of his blog to give their vote to parties other than pro-Kremlin party United Russia. Putin's party still won, but with a much lesser majority than expected and under allegations of vote-rigging that lead to mass protests ("March of Millions") in Moscow and other major Russian cities.[37] Similar

---

[d]The address of his English-language blog hosted by LiveJournal: navalny-en.livejournal.com/.

events threw shadows on Putin's win of the presidential elections a few months later. Allegations of corruption were brought against himself by the state of Russia in May 2011, which he calls "thought up, falsified, and fabricated."[38] *The New York Times* cites analysts, who believe the charges are the repercussion of Navalny's public campaign against Aleksandr Bastrykin, whom the activist claims, entertains property and other investments in Europe.[39]

At the same time, Navalny reported that the FSB had collected data on donors to his RosPil Web site and had passed them on to pro-Kremlin youth group, Nashi ("ours").[40] Additionally, his e-mail account was hacked into, and the data were subsequently published.[41] In August 2012, Nashi sought to remove Navalny from the board of directors of Russia's main airline, Aeroflot, to which he was just elected. Their argument in court relies on the mistaken interpretation of Russian law that prohibits lawyers from additional employments, but neglects the fact that the position is gained by election and thus perfectly legal to pursue.[42] In preparation of 2012 presidential elections, the youth group apparently bought Putin support as unveiled in the publication of about 1000 e-mails, hacked and published by Internet hackers associated with the Anonymous collective (see Chapter 6).[43] According to the e-mails, Nashi paid Internet users large amounts of money for comments either in favor of Putin or in denigration of the opposition—the financial means to which are alleged to come from the Kremlin.[44] The pro-United Russia youth group is also rumored to be behind a series of DDoS attacks against the liberal media—among others, the radio *Ekho Moskvy* and election monitoring group *Golos*—ahead of Russia's parliamentary elections in December 2011.[45] But as it appears, DDoS attacks against the online presence of independent media and key opposition figures are a common tool for many years already and—as one blogger complains—the perpetrators are met with impunity.[46,47]

Possible Motivation for the 2011 DDoS

Though the reason for the attack is unknown, as it remains unclaimed, however as pointed out earlier the Russian parliamentary elections occurred in December 2011 and Russians cast their vote for a President on March 4, 2012.[48] Perhaps the attacks were a means to silence the opposition as they started their public campaign against the leadership of the country. For instance, in early 2011, prior to the attacks, *Novaya Gazeta* had launched the "Online Parliament of the RUNET" (RUNET is a term referring to the "Russian Internet"). According to the newspaper, this "online parliament" would serve as "an alternative to incumbent authorities." Additionally, the opposition group known as the *People's Freedom Party* was preparing to publish a report on LiveJournal entitled "Putin. Corruption" during the time of the attacks.[49]

If the Russian government was behind the attacks—as claimed by several opposition leaders—another possible theory is that the Kremlin was becoming increasingly concerned that the "Arab Spring" may spread to the Motherland. Prior to the attacks in 2011, the Egyptians, partly fueled by social media, ousted President Hosni Mubarak. In February 2011, one of Prime Minister Vladimir Putin's deputies leveraged accusations at Google for having a role in the Egyptian uprising.[50] Around the same time, with regard to the situation in the Middle East, Russian President Dmitry Medvedev stated "They have prepared such a scenario for us before, and now more than ever they will try and realize it. In any case, this scenario won't succeed."[51] Additionally, during the time of the attacks, the FSB's Cyber

Center chief, Alexander Andreyechkin stated "Uncontrolled usage of [services like Skype, GMail, or Hotmail] may lead to a massive threat to Russia's security."[52]

Despite the theories of Kremlin involvement, Russian President Dmitry Medvedev's LiveJournal page was also taken offline during the attack.[53] We note that by analyzing the network traffic to the compromised computers launching a botnet attack, security researchers can identify which sites were targeted by a specific botnet during a major cyber offensive as well as how many command and control servers were involved. Based on this knowledge, the botnet launching the attacks against LiveJournal and *Novaya Gazeta* at this time was receiving commands to target one or two specific URL's over a period of a few days.[54] On April 6, there was a surge in the attacks, with the botnet receiving 36 such URLs—which included http://livejournal.com and http://livejournal.ru.[55] These attacks effectively took out all LiveJournal users—including the Russian President. Medvedev made statements condemning the attacks on April 7—after his personal blog was attacked. If the Kremlin was involved in the attacks, the 1-day DDoS against Medvedev's blog site might have been the small price paid to maintain plausible deniability for silencing the opposition at a perceived critical juncture. "RUNET" is, at the time of writing, surprisingly free of censorship compared to more traditional media like newspapers, television and radio, which are harshly censored. The collateral damage experienced by the loss of Medvedev's blog would not inhibit the Russian leadership from communicating their message as they could always resort to traditional media—unlike the opposition. Further, the blocking of Medvedev's blog leads to a counterpropaganda campaign. For instance, on April 7, *Reuters* ran a story entitled "Medvedev criticizes 'illegal' attack on his blog."[56]

Days after the attack, the *Novaya Gazeta* made a formal request to the Russian government to investigate the April 2011 DDoS attack against its Web site.[57] It is unknown if any official action has been taken with regard to this request. In an apparent move to appease the public, in February 2011, Russian President Dmitry Medvedev issued an order to the head of the FSB, Aleksandr Bortnikov, to investigate the November 2010 DDoS against *Novaya Gazeta*. However, at the time of this writing, no investigation was carried out.[58]

The Optima/Darkness Botnet

One botnet known to be involved in the April 2011 DDoS attack was known as the "Destination Darkness Outlaw System"[59] also referred to as "Optima" or simply "Darkness."[60] The creators of this botnet first started renting the use of the botnet—allowing users in the criminal underworld to launch attacks or steal data—in March 2009.[61] However, even though the services of the botnet were advertised for rent at this early stage, the earliest evidence of its use was not discovered by security experts until 2010.[62,63] The willingness of botnet authors to sell its services is not uncommon. It was observed that, during the time of the LiveJournal attack (March 23-April 1, 2011), besides the various Navalny Web sites (rospil.info and navalny.livejournal.com), the Web site of the Northwest arm of the Federal office handling industrial supervision as well as the Web site of a furniture factory, kredo-m.ru, were also targeted.[64] The target of a furniture business might indicate a business-to-business attack occurring at the same time as the politically motivated one.[65] Optima/Darkness was well developed by the time of the attack. At that point, the newest version was at least 8—which indicates rapid development and bug-fixing on the part of the authors who initially released the bot in 2009[66] (at the time of this writing; the current version is 10[67]). SecureList identifies Optima's authors as "Russian-speaking malware writers," which is mainly sold over Russian-language forums.[68] The author also reports about the uncertainty in determining Optima's size due to its highly segmented structure. With such a structure, the botnet owners may rent out parts of the botnet and may have more than one renter at any given time.[69] The segmented nature could also explain why the furniture factory as well as the federal office was targeted at the same time as the Russian opposition, although seemingly unrelated. In 2010, it appeared that there were two C&C servers for Optima/Darkness—greatfull.ru and greatfulltoolss.ru, both registered to smilefrince@yandex.ru. Further analysis of this e-mail address led to advertisements for the botnet.[70] In early 2011, researchers identified 16 C&C sites—likely indicating the growth of the botnet in both size and popularity.[71]

The botnet's DDoS capabilities include flooding via various different protocols including HTTP, ICMP, TCP, and UDP. The HTTP and ICMP protocols are used for Web page delivery and system-level message communication, respectively. TCP and UDP are two of the core protocols that many applications on the Internet leverage for communication. Often, the Optima malware makes use of specific design flaws in these protocols.[72] At the time of the attack, the size of the botnet was assessed to be in the tens of thousands of compromised systems.[73,74] Since its inception, the bots of Optima/Darkness were designed to use 100 threads. The use of "threads" allows a computer to run multiple processes at once (each process is run in a different "thread"). As a result, the software running on the infected computer could actually conduct 100 attacks at the same time.[75] The malware was also configured in a manner to make it appear as if each of the hundred threads was running on a different computer—which allows the botnet to fool some DDoS protection tools.[e] The end result is that an attack performed byOptima/Darkness would be substantially amplified. As early as 2010, the authors of Optima/Darkness claimed that just 30 of their bots could overwhelm most Web sites.[76] Other features of the malware include the ability to steal passwords, files, and log keystrokes of the bots.[77]

The "March(es) of Millions"

On June 12, 2012, on the national holiday, Russia Day, antigovernment protestors swarmed the streets of Moscow. Slogan chanted included "Russia without Putin" and "End KGB rule."[78] The event was known as the "March of Millions" and was the first major protest of Vladimir Putin's new term as president which started about a month prior. A prior attempt at the protest—actually held the day before Putin took office—resulted in clashes in which authorities arrested 700 protestors and injured another 150 of the nonviolent protestors.[79] Authorities estimated approximately 18,000 protestors participated in the protest, while protest organizers estimated over 100,000. It appeared as though the Russian authorities sought to curb the effect as much as the protests themselves. Fines for protest-related property damage were raised. The day prior to the protests, Russian authorities raided the apartments of several key protest leaders, including Alexey Navalny—whose LiveJournal site was among the targeted Web sites

---

[e]This is often referred to as *source address spoofing* as each thread sends packets from a different spoofed source address.

in the prior year. Following the searches, protest leaders Navalny, Sergei Udaltsov, Ilya Yashin, and Ksenia Sobchak were summoned for questioning on the day of the protest.[80,81]

During the earlier "March of Millions" protest on May 6, 2011 in Moscow, webcasting (streaming video) sites Ustream and Bambuser were taken offline by DDoS. Other Web sites experiencing DDoS attacks on that day belonged to newspapers, Ekho Moskva and Novaya Gazeta, and Internet-satellite TV station, Dozhd (Rain).[82] Journalist Markaz Kavkaz noted that Chechen news Web site, Kavkaz Center (kavkazcenter.com), was under attack for almost a week and claimed the KGB successor, the FSB, was the perpetrator.[83] At the time of this writing, the technical details are not available.[84] The fact that the protest turned violent has led some to suspect that the DDoS of streaming video sites may have been part of a larger plan to avoid images and video of violence becoming widespread in the media. At the "March of Millions" the following month, major DDoS attacks were once again leveraged against several Russian independent media sites known for antigovernment reporting—including the Web site of *Novaya Gazeta*.[85] Again, although technical details are currently not available, the occurrence of major DDoS attack in conjunction with opposition protests likely indicates a new TTP emerging in Russia. It is interesting to note that just as the Israelis worked to limit the media before military operation "Operation Cast Lead" (see Chapter 4), the Russians looked to curb video accounts of the "March of Millions" as they prepared antiriot operations. The same could also be said for the cyber attacks that occurred against Georgia prior to the Russian invasion in 2008 (Chapter 3). The employment of cyber warfare as a means to silence an opponent—hence denying them the ability to tell their story—is likely to continue as up-to-the-minute news reporting is highly dependent upon the Internet as communication infrastructure.

The response to dissident groups and independent media—whether by the Russian government itself or by staunch supporters—is indicative of a new trend in the politics of the nation. *Novaya Gazeta* and other liberal and independent media are often attacked in cyberspace due to the content of their publications, attempts to form new organizations (such as the "Online Parliament"), or in advance of major protests. Further, these attacks are taking place outside of civil conflict—so even when dissident do not take up arms the state seems to be in a constant state of cyber and information civil war. Finally, the use of highly effective cyber weaponry, such as the Darkness/Optima botnet—even against well-resourced sites such as LiveJournal, indicates a strong capability for cyber attack possessed by either the Russian government and/or highly capable supporters. As of December 2011, 61.5% of the Russians are registered Internet users.[86] The opposition relies heavily on this medium as more conventional media outlets are (traditionally) subject to the government's censorship. With prolific opposition bloggers like Navalny and a feasible rise in Internet users, it appears that the government—which is so far not filtering the information provided on the Internet—is only beginning to appreciate the opportunities this medium can provide.

IRAN—HOW THE 2009 ELECTIONS LED TO AGGRESSIVE CYBER OPERATIONS

In the past 4 years, two events have shaped the Iranian government's view of cyber warfare: Stuxnet and the 2009 Iranian presidential election. Stuxnet was a computer worm that was designed to sabotage Iranian nuclear facilities and will be discussed in detail in the

"Infrastructure Attack" part of this book (see Chapter 13). The Iranian elections saw widespread use of social media among dissidents—particularly Twitter and YouTube (the access to Facebook is usually blocked by the government)—along with dissident-launched DDoS attacks against government run sites.[87] In this section, we briefly review some of the cyber attacks that occurred in the aftermath of the 2009 election. We will further examine a significant proregime Iranian hacker group known as the "Iranian Cyber Army" that started gaining attention in 2010. Finally, we look at the Iranian government's formal solution to deal with problems arising from the cyberspace: the "Cyber Police."

The 2009 Elections

The 10th presidential election of the Islamic Republic of Iran was held in early June, 2009. In the election, incumbent President Mahmoud Ahmadinejad obtained over 60% of the popular vote—besting political rival Mir Hossein Moussavi.[88] Moussavi was a former Iranian Prime Minister who adopted a "reformist" platform that included a willingness to negotiate with the United States.[89] Immediately following the election, Moussavi's supporters took to the streets in Tehran protesting the outcome of the election—claiming irregularities secured Ahmadinejad's victory.[90]

In the immediate aftermath of the election, Iran seemed to drop off the Internet. There were six providers that connected the Iranian Internet to the rest of the world. All noted that communication between the Islamic Republic and the rest of the world nearly stopped the day after the election.[91] It is unclear what caused the outage, but some suspect that the Iranian government implemented deep-packet inspection (allowing extremely selective blocking of potentially subversive communication) of all traffic entering and exiting the country.[92] Such a measure would slow traffic to a crawl. However, Iranian citizens were able to work around the restrictions imposed by the regime through the use of various proxy servers,[93] including software known as Squid and Tor[94] (Tor is discussed further in Chapter 7). Essentially, a proxy server acts as an intermediary that enables the communication between two computer networks.

Able to work their way around potential government censorship, the Iranian protestors embraced social media—particularly using Twitter—to provide updates about their situation to the outside world.[95] In the immediate aftermath of the elections, they were producing over 100,000 Tweets a day relating to the protests.[96] The U.S. government was encouraged by the anti-Ahmadinejad demonstrations. The State department requested Twitter to postpone upgrades to its software during the time of the protest in order to ensure the communication of the dissidents.[97] Ahmadinejad's supporters were also present on Twitter, but they were significantly outnumbered by the opposition.[98]

Another noteworthy use of the Internet by dissidents was YouTube. On June 20, 2009 apolitical Neda Agha-Soltan was gunned down watching a street protest. A bystander recorded her fate on his phone and posted the video to YouTube. Neda soon became the symbol of the cause of Iranian dissidents around the world.[99,100] Supposedly, her killer was a member of pro-government Basij militia.[101]

Basij-e Mostaz'afin (literally "Mobilization of the Oppressed") is a force of currently estimated 400,000 loyalists, which was founded by Ayatollah Khomeini in 1979 (during the Iran-Iraq war). Barely trained they were deployed in human-wave tactics, in which the mere number of armed assailants is hoped to bring victory in close-range battles. During the Iran-Iraq war, they would clear mine fields for the conventional (trained and thus more costly) armed forces by running over them.[102,103] Today, the "Basij Resistance Force" is the feared auxiliary arm of the Revolutionary Guard and is called upon to disperse antigovernment protests, quell dissident gatherings, and enforce dress codes.[104] During the postelection protests, an estimated seven protesters—among them Neda—are thought to have died at the hands of Basij militants.[105] Basij compounds are dispersed throughout Tehran, which makes them readily available. As incentives to join the militia for mainly lower class Iranians (traditionally predominantly male, but more recently female Basijis take action as well) to serve: money, a seat at a university,[106] and possibly the benefits of a like-minded community. The loyalist paramilitary troops are feared for their swift and brutal actions, the employment of crude weapons (such as clubs, hoses, and other readily available material which allows beating up protesters) as well as kidnappings.[107]

Neda's death became the centerpiece of an information campaign by the dissidents and their supporters—as it is thought to symbolize the excesses and brutality of the current Iranian regime. In protests against the current Iranian regime signs depicting Neda or containing the slogan "I am Neda," feature prominently. In her mother's words: "She's dead but her memory is getting brighter and brighter each day"[108]

During these events in Iran, a semiorganized network of hackers mobilized worldwide to provide activists within Iran proxy servers, anonymizers[f] and any other appropriate technologies that would enable them to circumvent filtering and remain undetectable to Iranian authorities in their communication and organization of protest. The project was called "NedaNet"[g] (www.nedanet.org) named for the slain 26-year old.[h] As described earlier, the Iranian government was suspected to have used "deep-packet inspection" to identify content containing messages they did not want to leave Iran and block them. Proxies that encrypted communications would therefore allow activists to communicate with the outside world. The Iranian government reacted to NedaNet by blocking the Internet addresses of the servers and proxies configured by NedaNet volunteers. This is due to an inherent weakness in a proxy server: the address needs to be advertised for a user to access it in the first place. Unfortunately, such advertising also allows adversaries (in this case the Iranian government) to either monitor or block access to the servers.[109]

The protests and use of social media were also accompanied by some simple cyber attacks against Iranian state-run media conducted by dissidents. As with the hacktivists noted in the 2008 Russia-Georgia war and in the Israel-Hamas conflict, individuals were launching distributed denial of service (DDoS) attacks using a tool that was circulated throughout their online community. However, these DDoS tools were much less sophisticated—mainly consisting of automatic Web page refresh trappings such as Pagereboot.com and some simple

---

[f] Anonymizers are proxy servers that hide the source information (IP address) of the user—hence ensuring an additional layer of privacy while he/she uses the Internet.

[g] It apparently spawned the foundation of IT-company, NedaNET Inc., in Silicon Valley providing computer and network counseling services to small and mid-size businesses (www.nedanet.com).

[h] This is the organization whose public spokesperson was Eric S. Raymond.

customized tools.[110] Despite their simplicity though, these attacks were actually somewhat effective. In an interesting counter-attack, the Iran news site *Fars News* added some code to their home page that would redirect the attack to pro-opposition Web sites. However, it was noted that this did not discourage the dissident attacks.[111] This is possibly the same incident described earlier in the chapter by the Harvard researchers.

The Iranian Cyber Army (ICA)

The Ahmadinejad regime ultimately weathered the storm following the June 2009 election. However, Twitter had caused great international embarrassment to the government as this allowed first-hand information to be reported from the protesters to international news media organizations. Supporters of the Iranian regime were likely interested in seeking some sort of retribution. In December 2009, the proregime element got their chance with a "hack" of Twitter—disabling the service for several hours.[112] The group claiming responsibility is known as the "Iranian Cyber Army" (hereafter, ICA) and had managed to replace Twitter's home page with a Web site stating "THIS SITE HAS BEEN HACKED BY THE IRANIAN CYBER ARMY" followed by some anti-US rhetoric.[113] The truth was that this hacking group had not actually broken into Twitter's server, but conducted a domain name hijacking. All computers connected to the Internet can be identified by their Internet protocol (IP) address. However, to avoid having users remember such addresses, domain name service (DNS) servers act as sort of an "address book" resolving standard Web site hostnames to IP addresses. The ICA managed to change the corresponding IP address for Twitter, directing user's to one of their servers.[114] Though it is unclear how the ICA accomplished this, there are a few ways to hijack a domain name. One straightforward method is to deceive the domain name registrar or register organizations into allowing the hijacker to reassign the site a new IP address. An alternative would be DNS poisoning. In this type of attack, the hackers corrupt the information on the DNS server (by hacking into that system) causing it to send users to an IP address of the hacker's choosing rather than the desired destination. Often, DNS poisoning attacks are limited geographically as the user base of a given DNS server is normally limited in space. Either type of attack requires much less computing resources (from the attacker) than a DDoS, but is somewhat easier to overcome—particularly for a firm like Twitter. It is likely that the ICA wanted to simply grab headlines and give the appearance that they exacted revenge against Twitter. If that was their intent indeed, then they seem to have succeeded.

In another high-profile attack, the ICA targeted the Chinese search engine Web site Baidu.[115] The Baidu attack was similar to the Twitter incident and resulted in a similar outcome—the site was unavailable for several hours.[116] A third site was DNS hijacked at the same time of the Twitter attack—the homepage of the Green Movement—mowjcamp.com. The Green Movement is an opposition group that played a key role in the postelection protests.[117] Unlike Twitter and Baidu, the Green Movement was offline (with respect to its DNS name) for 6 weeks following the attack.[118] The difference is whereas Twitter and Baidu are connected to Tier 1 or Tier 2 ISPs, the Green Movement was more on the periphery of the Internet. As described in the introductory part of this chapter, Tier 3 ISPs are usually lacking the technical expertise and bureaucratic resources of the larger companies, so that the Green Movement was forced to work through the time-consuming bureaucracy encountered with

DNS disputes (when two parties register for the same URL name). The disputing second party in this case was a fictitious individual set up by the ICA. The process of identifying the legitimate owner of the domain name appeared to have been particularly lengthy. Hence, the attack on the Green Movement was a very successful ICA operation.

ICA: Beyond Domain Name Hijacking

In 2010 and 2011, the ICA continued to make headlines with its signature domain name hijacking, perhaps the most notorious of which was the attack on the Web site of the Voice of America (VOA)—the U.S. government's external broadcasting institution (Figure 5.4).[119] However, there was another purpose for these attacks beyond media attention. In investigating the ICA 2010 attack of the Web site *TechCrunch*, researchers found something interesting. The DNS entry redirected users to an ICA server, which—as in the other attacks—contained pro-Iranian regime messages. But this time the ICA server additionally executed a script that caused a Web-browser vulnerability to install malware on users' computer.[120] Security researchers at Seculert analyzed this malware and found that it leverages numerous exploits in the target operating system. They were also able to obtain access to a "control panel" view of the malware that revealed statistics on infected machines. There, the researchers found that over 400,000 computers had been infected. However, noticing that the counter had been reset numerous times, the conclusion was reached that the number of infected computers was much higher—the researchers estimated approximately 20 million infected machines.[121] Based on this analysis, the ICA hypothetically used domain name hijacking to create a botnet—likely for more devastating attacks in the future.[i] It also appears that they intended to use the botnet to raise money for their organization—as the interface uncovered by the researchers allows individuals to rent time on the botnet.[122] Another interesting aspect of such a botnet is that hijacked dissident sites, such as the Green Movements,

FIGURE 5.4 ICA "Defacement" of the Voice of America Web site through DNS hijacking. (For color version of this figure, the reader is referred to the online version of this chapter.) *Thetechherald. com, used with permission.*

---

[i]Botnets are described in more detail in Chapter 2.

are usually visited by dissidents. Most botnets allow the botmaster not only to control the bots for a DDoS but also access to their systems. Hence, the ICA might as well gather information on dissident systems.

Who Controls the ICA?

All that is currently known for sure about the ICA is that they are a pro-Iranian hacker group, which has performed the aforementioned attacks. Though there has been no real evidence showing them to be subordinate to the Iranian government, an Iranian dissident Web site known as "The Green Voice of Freedom" claims that the ICA was created in 2005 as part of the Iranian Revolutionary Guard Corps (IRGC). The "Green Voice" also asserts that the Iranian government forced hackers into the ICA by threatening with imprisonment.[123] An alternate hypothesis ponders that the ICA is actually a Russian group—not Iranian. The Center for Strategic and International Studies (CSIS) rejects this notion, stating that the domain name hijacking efforts are a lower skill-level attack—as opposed to the technical prowess held by Russian hackers.[124] However, the CSIS analysis does not take into account that the organization likely used the domain name hijacking efforts to create a botnet.

Alleged Iranian Botnet Strikes

Whether or not the ICA is affiliated with the Iranian government, one thing is clear: the hacking group launches cyber attacks that align well with the politics of the current Iranian regime. Therefore, if the ICA or other pro-government Iranian hackers were working to build a botnet, we would suspect the targets to be political in nature. In the fall of 2012, botnet DDoS attacks occurred against several major U.S. banks including Bank of America Corp., JPMorgan Chase & Co, Wells Fargo & Co, U.S. Bancorp and PNC Financial Services.[125] Security researchers concluded that the attacks were the work of a botnet.

In late September, a group identifying itself as "The Izz ad-Din al-Qassam Cyber Fighters" posted a declaration on *Pastebin*.[j] They stated that the DDoS attacks against the banks were part of what they called "Operation Ababil" ("Swallow"). The "Cyber Fighters" claimed that the attacks were in response to the low-budget anti-Islamic video "Innocence of Muslims" that stoked the ire of the Muslim world.[126] However, U.S. Senator Joseph Lieberman publically disagreed with this motivation, stating that he believed the attacks to be sponsored by the Iranian government and executed in response to increased economic sanctions against the Islamic Republic.[127]

The attack on the American banks was not the only cyber operation in the fall of 2012 that were claimed by hackers on Pastebin and attributed to Iran. In August, the Saudi Arabian oil firm Saudi Aramco revealed that it was a victim of a cyber attack that led to 30,000 of its workstations becoming disabled. The attack was the result of a piece of malware that erased the master boot record (MBR) of the target systems which would cause them to be unable to start up.[128] The Master Boot Record is the first part of the hard drive that is accessed when a

---

[j]Pastebin is a site used by hacker groups to post unattributed communication. Hackers from the group *Anonymous* often use this site. We discuss this more in Chapter 6.

personal computer starts up. Essentially, it lets the rest of the computer know what the major portions of the hard drive contain. Without this information, the computer cannot start up properly. Shortly after the attack, a group of hackers calling themselves the "Cutting Sword of Justice" owned up to the incident and posted the IP addresses of the hacked computers on *Pastebin.*[129]

Even though neither the Aramco nor the "Cutting Sword of Justice" identified the malware used in the attack, security analysts found that the "Shamoon" malware included a command to erase the MBR at the precise time of the Aramco attack and concluded that it was the cyber weapon used in the incident.[130] Some of the over-written files on the target computers were replaced with images of burning American flags.[131] About a week after the attack, Saudi Aramco chief executive Khalid al-Falih stated that the company had recovered from the attack and pointed out that the attack affected only the computer workstations—not systems controlling oil production.[132]

As with the attacks on the U.S. banks, several analysts pointed to Iran as the perpetrator for the Aramco incident.[133] One interesting aspect of the Aramco attack is the fact that the attackers claimed to be hacktivists yet other than hitherto known hacktivists conduct an attack using a piece of malware—as opposed to a DDoS tool (such as those described already in Chapters 2 and 3 and the LOIC tool described in Chapter 6). This could indicate that the *Cutting Sword* either was somewhat savvier than a typical hacktivist group or were provided the malware by a third party that holds a greater degree of sophistication. It is feasible that this attack too was motivated by the resentment of the recent installment of economic sanctions on Iran as mentioned earlier. Regardless, the Aramco attack, along with the attack against the banks, was significant enough to warrant a statement by the U.S. Secretary of Defense Leon Panetta in October 2012 where he warned the business sector of the perils of such incidents (Figure 5.5).[134]

How do these two incidents illustrate the capabilities of groups such as the Iranian Cyber Army once they have control of a large number of compromised systems? Irrespective of whether or not these attacks were sanctioned by the Iranian government, it is clear that both targets aligned well with the politics of the Islamic state. It is notable that the capability to compromise a large number of computer systems is also useful for intelligence gathering

FIGURE 5.5 The cyber attacks against numerous U.S. banks and Saudi oil interests in the fall of 2012 led U.S. Secretary of Defense Leon Panetta (pictured) to make a public statement regarding these cyber operations in October 2012. (For color version of this figure, the reader is referred to the online version of this chapter.) *DoD photo: http://www.defense.gov/.*

purposes. Groups such as the ICA, the Cyber Fighters, or the Cutting Sword could also possibly target organizations such as the Green Movement for purposes of information theft. The use of DNS hijacking could clearly sever this purpose: dissidents attempting to log on to their group's home page may receive a malware payload as a result of this technique. The malware can then reside on their system, sending information on the users back to the hackers (as we shall see in similar events occurring in China in Chapter 7) or even disabling the systems as in the Aramco attack.

The Iranian Cyber Police

By mid-2010, the Ahmadinejad regime apparently felt a desperate need to showcase the nation's cyber prowess. Not only had they experienced negative repercussions from dissidents' use of Twitter following the 2009 elections, but in June 2010, the Stuxnet worm became known to the general public based on a security report by a small Belarusian firm known as VirusBlockAda.[135] We will discuss Stuxnet more in detail later in the book (Chapter 13), but the political effect within the Iranian regime was very significant. In early 2011, the Iranian government announced the creation of a "Cyber Police" that will handle "Internet crimes." According to Iranian Police Chief Esmaeil Ahmadi Moghaddam, the "Internet crimes" in question include the use of cyberspace for "espionage and riots"—perhaps a reference to Stuxnet and the 2009 postelection protests. Further, he stated that the Cyber Police would specifically focus on dissident groups.[136] The Cyber Police has already been active—making a few headlines in 2012. Specifically, they arrested several Iranian Facebook users from a group called "Daaf and Paaf" that had organized an online beauty contest on Facebook. The chief of the Cyber Police, Kamal Hadian, stated that the group was spreading corruption and immorality.[137] More recently, the Cyber Police announced that they plan to start blocking the illegal use of Virtual Private Networks (VPNs) within Iran.[138] Likely this is because VPNs can allow users to access Web sites outside of the Iranian Internet—avoiding filtered and blocked content. VPN would also prevent the Iranian government from examining the content of the communications of an Iranian user with the rest of the world. In another current development, there are reports that the Iranian government intends to create a "Halal Internet" that imposes what has been termed as an "Electronic Curtain" of monitoring and restriction on Iranian Internet traffic.[139]

The use of social media in the wake of the 2009 Iranian presidential elections, as well as the discovery of Stuxnet led the Iranian government to accelerate and strengthen its cyber efforts. The ICA, with possible connections to the IRGC, has launched several high-profile attacks and at the same time seems to be establishing a sizable botnet. The Cyber Police, on the other hand, appears to be cracking down on the internal use of the Internet in Iran. In one way, the ICA can be viewed as an offensive asset and the Cyber Police as a defensive one.

Both the ICA and Cyber Police are relatively new, and it is feasible we will read more about them in the near future. Another harrowing possibility includes the collaboration of the two bodies: the intelligence gathered by the ICA by breaking into dissident systems could be transmitted to the Cyber Police, which would proceed to arrest the identified dissident. Further, it is certainly possible that these organizations (or others like them) may also start working with tech-savvy Iranian proxies, such as Hezbollah (discussed in Chapter 4) and Kata'ib Hezbollah (discussed in Chapter 9).

SUMMARY

Cyber warfare knows no boundaries. Capabilities developed for interstate conflict can easily be leveraged for civil conflict and vice versa. Further, there are some special considerations for dissident groups that should be kept in mind if they are to be used as a part of an information operation campaign. Perhaps most importantly is that Web sites of the opposition are more susceptible to attack due to their location on the Internet, often obtaining service from a higher number Tier ISP. Additionally, organization similar to Iran's "Cyber Police"—whose stated mission is to curb dissident groups online—will likely appear in other countries as well. Finally, it should be noted that capabilities used for internal government actions can be easily used in interstate conflict as well. For instance, consider the large botnets created by Russian criminal organizations or those of the ICA.

References

1. Zuckerman E, Roberts H, McGrady R, York J, Palfrey J. *Distributed denial of service attacks against independent media and human rights sites.* The Berkman Center for Internet & Society at Harvard University; December 2010.
2. Ibid., Zuckerman *et al.*
3. Ibid., Zuckerman *et al.*
4. Ibid., Zuckerman *et al.*
5. Ibid., Zuckerman *et al.*
6. Committee to Protect Journalists. *Novaya Gazeta deputy editor threatened in Russia.* http://cpj.org/2012/06/novaya-gazeta-deputy-editor-threatened-in-russia.php; June 13, 2012 [accessed October 21, 2012].
7. Assassination in action, Novaya Gazeta October 18, 2012; [accessed October 21, 2012]. http://en.novayagazeta.ru/politics/54995.html.
8. *Committee to Protect Journalists (CPJ). Former police colonel indicted in Politkovskaya murder.* http://cpj.org/2012/07/former-police-colonel-indicted-in-politkovskaya-mu.php; July 16, 2012 [accessed October 21, 2012].
9. Milashina E. *Suspects recycled in Politkovskaya case. CPJ.* http://cpj.org/blog/2011/11/politkovskaya-case-breaks-little-new-ground.php; November 7, 2011 [accessed October 21, 2012].
10. Committee to Protect Journalists (CPJ). *Circle of suspects widens in Politkovskaya case.* http://cpj.org/2010/10/circle-of-suspects-widens-in-politkovskaya-case.php; October 6, 2010 [accessed October 21, 2012]. (CPJ, 10/6/2010).
11. Russian official's death threat, in bold type, New York Times June 13, 2012; http://www.nytimes.com/2012/06/14/world/europe/novaya-gazeta-publicizes-russian-officials-threat-to-editor.html?_r=0 [accessed October 21, 2012].
12. Goguelin R. Human rights defenders live under constant threat, France 24 January 23, 2009; http://www.france24.com/en/20090123-russia-human-rights-threat-contract-killings-moscow-Markelov-Baburova-defenders [accessed June 30, 2012, accessed October 21, 2012].
13. Russian official's death threat, in bold type, New York Times June 13, 2012; http://www.nytimes.com/2012/06/14/world/europe/novaya-gazeta-publicizes-russian-officials-threat-to-editor.html?_r=0 [accessed October 21, 2012].
14. Committee for Protecting Journalists. *Dmitry Muratov, editor of Novaya Gazeta, Russia.* http://cpj.org/awards/2007/muratov.php; 2007 [accessed October 21, 2012].
15. Jamestown Foundation. *Novaya Gazeta remembers Yuri Shechkochikhin.* http://www.jamestown.org/single/?no_cache=1&tx_ttnews%5Btt_news%5D=30050; July 5, 2004 [accessed October 21, 2012].
16. Ukraine related news stories from RFE, Radio Free Europe (RFE)/Radio Liberty (RL) 2003; http://www.infoukes.com/rfe-ukraine/2003/0716.html [accessed October 21, 2012].
17. Shleinov R. How whales were turned into mice, Novaya Gazeta July 11, 2008; http://en.novayagazeta.ru/investigations/8217.html [accessed October 21, 2012].
18. Ukraine related news stories from RFE, Radio Free Europe (RFE)/Radio Liberty (RL) 2003; http://www.infoukes.com/rfe-ukraine/2003/0716.html [accessed October 21, 2012].

19. Obituary: Yuri Shchekochikhin, The Guardian July 9, 2003; http://www.guardian.co.uk/news/2003/jul/09/guardianobituaries.russia [accessed October 21, 2012].

20. Russia's poisoning 'without a poison'. BBC News February 6, 2007; http://news.bbc.co.uk/2/hi/programmes/file_on_4/6324241.stm. [accessed October 21, 2012].

21. Goldfarb Alex, Litvinenko Marina. Death of a dissident: the poisoning of Alexander Litvinenko and the return of the KGB. New York: Simon & Schuster; 2007.

22. Mystery shrouds death of journalist Shchekochikhin, St. Petersburg Times July 4, 2008; http://www.sptimes.ru/index.php?action_id=2&story_id=26446 [accessed October 21, 2012].

23. Прекращено уголовное дело по факту смерти журналиста и депутата Госдумы Щекочихина (Criminal case on the death of the journalist and state Duma Deputy Shchekochikhin), Newsru.com April 9, 2009; http://newsru.com/russia/09apr2009/zakryli.html [accessed October 22, 2012].

24. Committee to Protect Journalists (CPJ) Interview with Dmitry Muratov during CPJ's International Press Freedom Awards Winner Dinner. http://cpj.org/awards/2007/muratov.php; 2007 [accessed October 21, 2012].

25. Committee to Protect Journalists (CPJ). *Murder pushes Novaya Gazeta to request guns.* http://cpj.org/blog/2009/01/murder-pushes-novaya-gazeta-to-request-guns.php; January 23, 2009 [accessed October 21, 2012].

26. von Twickel N. Hacker attack freezes Novaya Gazeta's web site. *The Moscow Times.* Available at: http://www.themoscowtimes.com/news/article/hacker-attack-freezes-novaya-gazetas-web-site/398649.html; February 1, 2010 [accessed June 30, 2012].

27. U.S. Department of State. *Remarks at the 2008 International Human Rights Day Awards Ceremony.* Available at: http://2001-2009.state.gov/secretary/rm/2008/12/112974.htm; December 8, 2010 [accessed June 30, 2012].

28. Rights in Russia. *Novaya Gazeta demands a criminal investigation into DDoS attack.* Available at: http://agora.rightsinrussia.info/scene/hro/novayagazeta-1; April 14, 2011 [accessed July 1, 2012].

29. Website of Russian opposition paper hit in massive web attack. *RIA Novosti.* Available at: http://en.rian.ru/russia/20110408/163433642.html; April 8, 2010 [accessed June 30, 2012].

30. Gutterman G. Medvedev criticizes 'illegal' attack on his blog. *Reuters.* Available at: http://www.reuters.com/article/2011/04/07/us-russia-medvedev-cyberattack-idUSTRE7367GF20110407; April 7, 2010 [accessed June 30, 2012].

31. Namestnikov Y. DDoS attacks in Q2 2011. *SecureList*, Kaspersky Lab. Available at: http://www.securelist.com/en/analysis/204792189/DDoS_attacks_in_Q2_2011; 2011 [accessed June 30, 2012].

32. Russia launches criminal probe of top antigraft activist. *Radio Free Europe/Radio Liberty.* Available at: http://www.unhcr.org/refworld/docid/4dd3cb99c.html; May 10, 2011 [accessed October 22, 2012].

33. Russia launches criminal probe of top antigraft activist. *Radio Free Europe/Radio Liberty.* Available at: http://www.unhcr.org/refworld/docid/4dd3cb99c.html; May 10, 2011 [accessed October 22, 2012].

34. The man Vladimir Putin fears the most. *Wall Street Journal.* http://online.wsj.com/article/SB10001424052970203986604577257321601811092.html; 2012 [accessed October 22, 2012].

35. Profile: Russian lawyer Alexei Navalny, BBC News August 7, 2012; http://www.bbc.co.uk/news/world-europe-16057045 [accessed October 22, 2012].

36. The world's 100 most influential people, Time Magazine April 18, 2012; http://www.time.com/time/specials/packages/article/0,28804,2111975_2111976_2112167,00.html [accessed: October 22, 2012].

37. Profile: Russian lawyer Alexei Navalny, BBC News August 7, 2012; http://www.bbc.co.uk/news/world-europe-16057045 [accessed October 22, 2012].

38. Russia launches criminal probe of top antigraft activist. *Radio Free Europe/Radio Liberty.* Available at: http://www.unhcr.org/refworld/docid/4dd3cb99c.html [accessed 22 October 2012]; May 10, 2011 [accessed October 22, 2012].

39. Russia charges anti-corruption activist in plan to steal timber, New York Times July 31, 2012; http://www.nytimes.com/2012/08/01/world/europe/aleksei-navalny-charged-with-embezzlement.html?_r=0 [accessed October 22, 2012].

40. Russia launches criminal probe of top antigraft activist. *Radio Free Europe/Radio Liberty.* Available at: http://www.unhcr.org/refworld/docid/4dd3cb99c.html; May 10, 2011 [accessed October 22, 2012].

41. The man Vladimir Putin fears the most, Wall Street Journal March 3, 2012; http://online.wsj.com/article/SB10001424052970203986604577257321601811092.html [accessed October 23, 2012].

42. Nashi seeks to oust Navalny from aeroflot board, Ria Novosti August 7, 2012; http://en.rian.ru/russia/20120807/175036455.html [accessed October 23, 2012].

43. Hacked emails allege Russian youth group Nashi paying bloggers, The Guardian February 7, 2012; http://www.guardian.co.uk/world/2012/feb/07/hacked-emails-nashi-putin-bloggers [accessed October 23, 2012].

44. Polishing Putin: hacked emails suggest dirty tricks by Russian youth group, The Guardian February 7, 2012; http://www.guardian.co.uk/world/2012/feb/07/putin-hacked-emails-russian-nashi [accessed October 23, 2012].

45. Polishing Putin: hacked emails suggest dirty tricks by Russian youth group, The Guardian February 7, 2012; http://www.guardian.co.uk/world/2012/feb/07/putin-hacked-emails-russian-nash [accessed October 23, 2012].

46. Hacking blamed on pro-Kremlin youth, Wall Street Journal February 10, 2012; http://online.wsj.com/article/SB10001424052970204642604577213351792676444.html [accessed October 23, 2012].

47. GreyLogic. *Project grey goose phase II report: the evolving state of cyber warfare.* http://www.scribd.com/doc/13442963/Project-Grey-Goose-Phase-II-Report; 2009 [accessed October 24, 2012].

48. Smith DJ. Darkness botnet and Russian corruption. *The Potomac Institute Cyber Center.* Available at: http://pipscyberissues.wordpress.com/2012/02/18/darkness-botnet-and-russian-politics/; 2012 [accessed July 1, 2012].

49. Ibid., Smith.

50. Ibid., Gutterman.

51. Ibid., Smith.

52. Ibid., Smith.

53. Ibid., Gutterman.

54. Bechtholt N. Monthly malware statistics, April 2011. *Kaspersky Lab.* Available at: http://newsroom.kaspersky.eu/fr-be/news/news-article/article/monthly-malware-statistics-april-2011-2/?no_cache=1&cHash=bbde3c2922fc7bbc0897e63a9c43580c; 2011 [accessed June 30, 2012].

55. Ibid.

56. Ibid., Gutterman.

57. Ibid., *Rights in Russia.*

58. Ibid., *Rights in Russia.*

59. Ibid., Namestnikov.

60. Danchev D. A peek inside the Darkness (Optima) DDoS Bot. *Webroot Threat Blog.* Available at: http://blog.webroot.com/2012/03/08/a-peek-inside-the-darkness-optima-ddos-bot/; March 8, 2012 [accessed July 1, 2012].

61. Ibid., Danchev.

62. BlackEnergy competitor—the 'Darkness' DDoS bot. *Shadowserver Foundation.* Available at: http://www.shadowserver.org/wiki/pmwiki.php/Calendar/20101205; December 5, 2010 [accessed July 1, 2012].

63. Ibid., Namestnikov.

64. Securelist. *DDoS Attacks in Q2 2011.* http://www.securelist.com/en/analysis/204792189/DDoS_attacks_in_Q2_2011; August 29, 2011 [accessed October 27, 2012].

65. Garnaeva M. LiveJournal under attack. *SecureList, Kaspersky Lab.* Available at: http://www.securelist.com/en/blog/442/LiveJournal_under_attack_1/; April 6, 2011 [accessed July 1, 2012].

66. The Shadowserver Foundation. *Darkness DDoS bot version identification guide.* Available at: http://www.shadowserver.org/wiki/pmwiki.php/Calendar/20110127; February 8, 2011 [accessed July 1, 2012].

67. Ibid., Danchev.

68. Securelist. *DDoS attacks in Q2 2011.* http://www.securelist.com/en/analysis/204792189/DDoS_attacks_in_Q2_2011; August 29, 2011 [accessed October 27, 2012].

69. Securelist. *DDoS attacks in Q2 2011.* http://www.securelist.com/en/analysis/204792189/DDoS_attacks_in_Q2_2011; August 29, 2011 [accessed October 27, 2012].

70. Ibid., BlackEnergy competitor.

71. Spread of darkness...details on the public release of the darkness DDoS bot. *Shadowserver Foundation.* Available at: http://www.shadowserver.org/wiki/pmwiki.php/Calendar/20110123; 2011 [accessed July 1, 2012].

72. *Darkness (Optima) botnet analysis.* Radware, Inc. Available at: http://www.radware.com/workarea/showcontent.aspx?ID=1629155; 2011 [accessed July 1, 2012].

73. Ibid., Namestnikov.

74. Ibid., Garnaeva.

75. Ibid., Danchev.

76. Ibid., BlackEnergy competitor.

77. Ibid., Danchev.

78. Winning A. Moscow 'March of Millions' protests Vladimir Putin's rule. *Los Angeles Times*. Available at: http://articles.latimes.com/2012/jun/13/world/la-fg-russia-protest-201206131/; June 13, 2012 [accessed July 1, 2012].

79. Derinova A. Russia prepares for second March of Millions. *Waging Nonviolence*. Available at: http://wagingnonviolence.org/2012/06/russia-prepares-for-second-march-of-millions/; June 11, 2012 [accessed July 1, 2012].

80. Moscow police swoop on opposition ahead of anti-Putin march. *RIA Novosti*. Available at: http://en.rian.ru/russia/20120611/173974865.html; June 11, 2012 [accessed July 1, 2012].

81. Human Rights Watch. *Russia: March of Millions*. http://www.hrw.org/news/2012/06/13/russia-march-millions; 2012 [accessed October 27, 2012].

82. Malavika J. *DDoS attacks disable independent news sites during Russian protests*. http://blogs.law.harvard.edu/herdict/2012/06/14/ddos-attacks-disable-independent-news-sites-during-russian-protests/; June 14, 2012 [accessed October 27, 2012].

83. Kavkaz M. Cyber war: DDoS. KGB attacks websites. http://www.muxlima.com/Articles201206/WritersArticles_MarkazKavkaz_0616.htm; June 16, 2012 [accessed October 27, 2012].

84. Tung L. Russian citizens targeted in Ustream DDoS. *iTnews*. Available at: http://www.itnews.com.au/News/300128,russian-citizens-targeted-in-ustream-ddos.aspx?utm_source=feed&utm_medium=rss&utm_campaign=iTnews+All+Articles+feed; May 10, 2012 [accessed July 1, 2012].

85. On Russia day, sites of opposition and independent media attacked by hackers. Rights in Russia. Available at: http://hro.rightsinrussia.info/archive/freedom-of-speech/internet/12-june-2012/ddos; June 13, 2012 [accessed July 3, 2012].

86. InternetWorldStats. *Top 10 internet countries in Europe—December 2011*. http://www.internetworldstats.com/stats4.htm; 2011 [accessed October 27, 2012].

87. McMillan R. With unrest in Iran, cyber-attacks begin. *PC World*. Available at: http://www.pcworld.com/article/166714/with_unrest_in_iran_cyberattacks_begin.html; 2009 [accessed July 3, 2012].

88. Ahmadinejad hails election as protests grow. *CNN.com*. Available at: http://articles.cnn.com/2009-06-13/world/iran.election_1_street-protests-voter-irregularities-iranian-president-mahmoud-ahmadinejad?_s=PM:WORLD; June 13, 2009 [accessed July 3, 2012].

89. The answer to Ahmadinejad. *Spiegel*. Available at: http://www.spiegel.de/international/world/iranian-elections-the-answer-to-ahmadinejad-a-622225.html; 2009 [accessed July 3, 2012].

90. Ibid., Ahmadinejad hails election as protests grow.

91. Labovitz C. Iranian traffic engineering. *Arbor Sert*. Available at: http://ddos.arbornetworks.com/2009/06/iranian-traffic-engineering/; June 17, 2009 [accessed July 3, 2012].

92. Timmer J. Using Tor and Squid to loosen Iranian repression by proxy. *Ars Technica*. Available at: http://arstechnica.com/tech-policy/2009/06/using-tor-and-squid-to-loosen-iranian-repression-by-proxy/; June 30, 2009 [accessed July 12, 2012].

93. Thibodeau P. Iran's leaders fight Internet; Internet wins (so far). *Computer World*. Available at: http://www.computerworld.com/s/article/9134471/Iran_s_leaders_fight_Internet_Internet_wins_so_far_?taxonomyId=16&pageNumber=1; 2009 [accessed July 12, 2012].

94. Ibid., Timmer.

95. Gaffney D. #iranElection: quantifying online activism, In: Proceedings of the ACM WebSci'10, Raleigh, NC, April 26–27; 2010.

96. Ibid., Gaffney.

97. Ibid., Gaffney.

98. Nasr O. Tear gas and Twitter: Iranians take their protests online. *CNN.com*. Available at: http://articles.cnn.com/2009-06-14/world/iran.protests.twitter_1_facebook-president-mahmoud-ahmadinejad-supporters/2?_s=PM:WORLD; June 14, 2009 [accessed July 3, 2012].

99. Fathi N. In a death seen around the world, a symbol of Iranian protests. *New York Times*. Available at: http://www.nytimes.com/2009/06/23/world/middleeast/23neda.html?_r=1&ref=middleeast; June 22, 2009 [accessed July 3, 2012].

100. Profile: Neda Agha Soltan, BBC News July30, 2009; http://news.bbc.co.uk/2/hi/middle_east/8176158.stm [accessed October 27, 2012].

101. DeRoy G. In Iran, one woman—Neda—becomes a symbol. *USA Today*. Available at: http://content.usatoday.com/communities/ondeadline/post/2009/06/68337891/1; June 21, 2009 [accessed July 3, 2012].

102. Profile: Basij Militia force, BBC News June 18, 2009; http://news.bbc.co.uk/2/hi/middle_east/8106699.stm [accessed October 27, 2012].

103. Feared Basij Militia has deep history in Iranian conflict, CNN June 22, 2009; http://www.cnn.com/2009/WORLD/meast/06/22/iran.basij.militia.profile/index.html [accessed October 27, 2012].

104. Profile: Basij Militia force, BBC News June 18, 2009; http://news.bbc.co.uk/2/hi/middle_east/8106699.stm [accessed October 28, 2012].

105. Profile: Basij militia force, BBC News June 18, 2009; http://news.bbc.co.uk/2/hi/middle_east/8106699.stm [accessed October 28, 2012].

106. Feared Basij militia has deep history in Iranian conflict, CNN June 22, 2009; http://www.cnn.com/2009/WORLD/meast/06/22/iran.basij.militia.profile/index.html [accessed October 28, 2012].

107. Feared Basij militia has deep history in Iranian conflict, CNN June 22, 2009; http://www.cnn.com/2009/WORLD/meast/06/22/iran.basij.militia.profile/index.html [accessed October 28, 2012].

108. Neda Aga Soltan: 'she is dead but regime is still afraid of her, The Guardian June 11, 2011; http://www.guardian.co.uk/world/2010/jun/11/neda-agha-soltan-iran-killing [accessed October 28, 2012].

109. NedaNet. http://www.nedanet.org [accessed September 17, 2012].

110. Ibid., McMillan.

111. Ibid., McMillan.

112. Ibid., Zuckerman *et al.*

113. Arringto M. Twitter hacked, defaced by 'Iranian Cyber Army'. *TechCrunch*. Available at: http://techcrunch.com/2009/12/17/twitter-reportedly-hacked-by-iranian-cyber-army/; December 17, 2009 [accessed July 3, 2012].

114. Ibid., Zuckerman *et al.*

115. Baidu hacked by 'Iranian cyber army'. *BBC News*. Available at: http://news.bbc.co.uk/2/hi/8453718.stm; January 12, 2010 [accessed July 2, 2012].

116. Ibid., Zuckerman *et al.*

117. Adhikari R. 'Cyber Army' attacks Twitter, Iran green movement site. *TechNewsWorld*. Available at: http://www.technewsworld.com/story/Cyber-Army-Attacks-Twitter-Iran-Green-Movement-Site-68938.html; December 18, 2009 [accessed July 3, 2012].

118. Ibid., Zuckerman *et al.*

119. Ragan S. Iranian Cyber Army defaces Voice of America and 93 other domains. *The Tech Herald*. Available at: http://www.thetechherald.com/articles/Iranian-Cyber-Army-defaces-Voice-of-America-and-93-other-domains-(Update)/12865/; February 22, 2011 [accessed July 3, 2012].

120. The "Iranian Cyber Army" strikes back. *Seculert*. Available at: http://blog.seculert.com/2010/10/iranian-cyber-army-strikes-back.html; October 24, 2010 [accessed July 3, 2010].

121. Ibid., The "Iranian Cyber Army" strikes back.

122. Ibid., The "Iranian Cyber Army" strikes back.

123. Who are the 'Iranian Cyber Army'? *Green Voice of Freedom*. Available at: http://en.irangreenvoice.com/article/2010/feb/19/1236; December 15, 2010 [accessed July 3, 2012].

124. Lukich A. The Iranian Cyber Army. *CSIS*. Available at: http://csis.org/blog/iranian-cyber-army; July 12, 2011 [accessed July 3, 2012].

125. Menn J. U.S. bank website hackers used advanced botnets, diverse tools, Reuters October 2, 2012; http://www.reuters.com/article/2012/10/02/us-bank-attacks-idUSBRE89119F20121002 [accessed October 20, 2012].

126. Huff S. 'Operation Ababil': Muslim cyber fighters return, take down wells Fargo's website, BetaBeat September 25, 2012; http://betabeat.com/2012/09/operation-ababil-muslim-cyber-fighters-return-take-down-wells-fargos-website/ [accessed October 20, 2012].

127. Puzzanghera J. Iran is behind bank cyber attacks, Sen. Joe Lieberman believes, Los Angeles Times September 26, 2012; http://www.latimes.com/business/money/la-fi-mo-bank-cyber-attack-iran-lieberman-20120926,0,1354311.story [accessed October 20, 2012].

128. Leyden J. Hack on Saudi Aramco hit 30,000 workstations, oil firm admits, The Register August 29, 2012; http://www.theregister.co.uk/2012/08/29/saudi_aramco_malware_attack_analysis/ [accessed October 21, 2012].

129. Perlroth N. Hackers lay claim to Saudi Aramco cyberattack, New York Times Bits August 23, 2012; http://bits.blogs.nytimes.com/2012/08/23/hackers-lay-claim-to-saudi-aramco-cyberattack/ [accessed October 21, 2012].

130. Constantin L. Kill timer found in Shamoon malware suggests possible connection to Saudi Aramco attack, PC World August 23, 2012; http://www.pcworld.com/article/261320/kill_timer_found_in_shamoon_malware_suggests_possible_connection_to_saudi_aramco_attack.html [accessed October 21, 2012].
131. Ibid., Leyden.
132. Saudi oil producer's computers restored after virus attack, New York Times August 26, 2012; http://www.nytimes.com/2012/08/27/technology/saudi-oil-producers-computers-restored-after-cyber-attack.html?_r=0 [accessed October 21, 2012].
133. Baldor LC. Iran may hit U.S. with first cyberattack, The Washington Times October 17, 2012; http://www.washingtontimes.com/news/2012/oct/17/iran-may-hit-us-with-first-cyberattack/ [accessed October 21, 2012].
134. Stewart P. 'Shamoon' virus most destructive ever to hit a business, Leon Panetta warns. Reuters October 12, 2012.
135. Oleg K, Sergey U. *Trojan-Spy.0485 and Malware-Cryptor.Win32.Inject.gen.2 Review.* VirusBlockAda; July 2010.
136. Latif L. Iran announces an Internet police force. *The Inquirer.* Available at: http://www.theinquirer.net/inquirer/news/1939109/iran-announces-internet-police-force; January 24, 2011 [accessed July 3, 2012].
137. Esfandiari G. Iran's cyberpolice detain Facebook-group administrators. *Radio Free Europe Radio Liberty.* Available at: http://www.rferl.org/content/irans_cyber_police_detain_facebook_group_administrators/24468239.html; January 30, 2012 [accessed July 3, 2012].
138. Iran to crack down on web censor-beating software. *Hurriyet Daily News.* Available at: http://www.hurriyetdailynews.com/iran-to-crack-down-on-web-censor-beating-software.aspx?pageID=238&nID=22789&NewsCatID=374; June10, 2012 [accessed July 3, 2012].
139. Farivar C. Security researcher unearths plans for Iran's halal Internet, ars Technica April 17, 2012; http://arstechnica.com/tech-policy/2012/04/iran-publishes-request-for-information-for-halal-internet-project/ [accessed October 29, 2012].

6

Cyber Attacks by Nonstate Hacking Groups: The Case of Anonymous and Its Affiliates

INFORMATION IN THIS CHAPTER

- An overview of nonstate hacking groups
- An analysis of the ideological backgrounds and modi operandi of gray and black-hat hackers
- An introduction to the activities of Anonymous, LulzSec, and others

- An overview of the online culture and expertise that provides the basis for "hacktivism"

Anyone can get on 4chan/7chan/someintegerchan/IRC and propose a raid or operation [. . .] It's hard to say when it's the same people pursuing these different causes or different subgroups entirely. I suppose you could say "this group organized at Anonops.net" or "that one from PartyVan.net," but even those are pretty loose affiliations [. . .] it's hard to say how many people on those sites truly agree on what issues are important. **Adrian Crenshaw**[1]

This chapter introduces the hacker collective Anonymous as a real-world and highly popular case study of hacktivism. While what this collective is accused of may not be new, the scale of the activity and popularity of Anonymous certainly is. Anonymous' roots, structures (or the absence thereof), and history is the tale of a new form of political activism. Anons (activists in the realm of Anonymous) merely need to share a common vision to act together for a cause. Geographical boundaries are nonexistent allowing every human being with access to the Internet to participate in protests of their choosing. In support of the Occupy Wall Street, this new cyber social movement claims to represent the 99% of the nameless world population whose lives are inhibited by more or less oppressive governments and corporations.[2,3] The protest is taken mainly to the Web sites of the targets, which are either defaced or subjected to DDoS attacks. Claiming to defend and uphold the Internet as a forum of free speech to some critics, the action appears to belie the collective's proclaimed cause. The more popular discussions revolve around whether Anonymous' hacks are more than a nuisance. On the following pages, we are trying to portray this elusive collective starting with an outline of its possible internal structure according to the information obtainable through open source media: it appears that about two dozen skilled and experienced hackers, former members of the German Chaos Computer Club constitute the directorate, which makes decisions about the general direction, the ethics and enforces crude accountability thereto on behalf of the members of the collective. Besides announcing campaigns ("operations") that form the frame in which individual attacks are undertaken, the leadership also resolves and plans more prominent and sophisticated attacks. The original Anon used to call the "category b" of the largest English image board *4chan* his second home. On this legendary raucous subsection of the anime-inspired message board, the authors of oftentimes repelling posts and images are allowed to remain anonymous. Increasingly, *b-tards* (those who would identify 4chan's b-board as a main communication device or even living space) would refer to "Anonymous" as if it was a real person. The collective's label thus stands for every (potential) anonymous online commentator as well as a nomer for an issue close to its heart: the protection of an individual's online privacy. 4chan's b-board has nothing to do with hacking and thus the legions of Anons originated here (as well as those who later joined from other forums and IRCs) were often less-skilled hackers. Their activism is for the current select cause; their contribution is their computer power as they provide bandwidth to a larger DDoS attack. However, from this mass of supporters, IRC- and system administrators form an intermediate level in the Anonymous hierarchy. These people are knowledgeable with information technology and often moonlight as hackers. In May 2011, the moderator of an Anonymous IRC channel took control of the servers that hosted the collective's IRC network, redirected some "AnonOps" domain names, launched a denial of service attack against the IRC servers, and published the IP-addresses of everyone connected to those servers.[4] So far, a group of people employing user names like "Owen," "shitstorm," "blergh," "power2all," and "Nerdo" has maintained the servers, paid the bills, registered the domain names, and moderated the IRCs somewhat.[5] Ryan stated his coup was motivated by his concerns over private decision making on the part of "Owen" and the other leaders. Increasingly, it appeared that important operations were decided upon and planned in invite-only chats.[6] Lastly, it can be fathomed that Anonymous, like other social movements, has a considerable amount of sympathizers, who do not spend much time on IRC channels, but share the proclaimed ideals. They may download the LOIC (Low Orbit Ion Cannon) to aid in the DDoS attack against Tunisian government Web sites only, but refrain from any further participation in the future.

The rest of this chapter is organized as follows. After outlining the origins and the "membership" of the collective, we attempt to describe the motivations that drive Anons to act on a certain target as well as their most common modus operandi of a DDoS attack. In the case where self-professed members of the collective find it (for whatever reason) necessary to expose the target or affiliated individuals, they conduct cyber-exploitation operations. These may employ other tools, such as SQL injection, to capture personal or confidential data in order to publish it later on Pastebin. Over time, the collective morphed from the boundary transgressing hive-mind of random actors to an organization that collaborates with hacker groups worldwide—provided they pursue a shared goal. During its history, the Anonymous collective gave birth to smaller entities that emphasize either certain aspects of the original Anonymous motivation or redefined its targets. Eventually, the collective stood to absorb the remnants of these spin offs as their smaller, more structured organization proved to be their weakest point. The chapter will conclude with the account of select examples of Anonymous' hacking activities, which help to illustrate the movement's multifaceted, multifactional character. The study of Anonymous and related groups is likely going to gain importance in the study of cyber warfare. The presence of politically motivated hacking groups with an apparent core of highly skilled IT personnel, in addition to their global distribution and ability to mass computing resources in an attack, make this kind of organization rather formidable. Further, the political motivations and willingness to conduct operations against government and military-affiliated Web sites certainly draws them into the fray of cyber war.

"CHAOTIC" BEGINNINGS: THE CHAOS COMPUTER CLUB, CCC

According to a hacker known as *Commander X*, Anonymous' directorate formed itself from the Chaos Computer Club (CCC).[7] The CCC looks back on a 25-year history and is today the largest European hacker conglomerate with its main headquarters in Hamburg, Germany.[8]

Club members engage in technical research, anonymity, and IT services, and organize conferences, campaigns ("Chaos Kampagnen"), and counsel politicians on information technology. It understands itself as a medium operating in the tensions created between social demands and technical development.[9] Its most famous founder was Herwart Holland-Moritz (Wau Holland), who back in 1981 wrote an article titled "Computer Guerilla" for a German left-wing newspaper ("Die Tageszeitung") when computers and certainly hackers were not commonplace.[10] Shortly thereafter, he established the magazine *"Datenschleuder"* (literally translated: data slingshot, with the subtitle *Scientific Journal for Data Travellers*[11]) for (aspiring) hackers. In 2008, the magazine provocatively featured the finger prints of the (then) German interior minister, Wolfgang Schäuble, and added to the public discussion about privacy infringement by the government.[12] The newly incepted Chaos Computer Club set out to shatter trust in the security of computer systems.[13] Wau Holland,[14] founder of the CCC, was a technician and a writer with political vision and viewed hacking as a cultural service, his slogan being "free access to information for everybody."[15] He never sought to earn money with his skills[a;16] but instead eagerly wandered around teaching.[17] Externally, the Chaos Computer Club describes itself as a part of the "Chaos Family,"[b] which is made up of regional versions of the club (e.g., CCC Berlin, CCC Karlsruhe) and organizations that are close in ideology (e.g., a group of women computer scientists or a club that fights for civil rights and online privacy), and/ or technically (e.g., a club of amateur radio enthusiasts). Internally the Chaos Computer Club features three levels of authority: member assembly, executive board, and advisory board ("Erfa-Beirat").[18] There is an initial and annual fee every member has to pay. The CCC is regionally represented through "experience circles" ("Erfahrungskreise") or regional franchises, throughout almost all of Germany's states and neighboring countries. The club encourages on its Web site local foundations of the most basic and loose form of like-minded get-togethers in the so-called Chaos Meetings ("Chaos Treffs"). The headquarters in Hamburg appears keen to keep track of the various loose group meetings and franchises and organizes annual meetings with Erfa directors, as well as themed congresses, and conferences of its own. Besides the annual Chaos Communication Congress, which had to be moved from Hamburg to Berlin due to the number of attendees, the GPN ("Gulaschprogrammiernacht" or goulash programming night[c]) also has programming and hacking workshops and lectures on social as well as political issues on its agenda. The Chaos Communication Camp is held every 4 years and provoked interest across borders, which established English as primary language of the event. The camp features 30 (in 2007, 70 in 2011[19]) themed tent villages and an area dedicated to the arts. For the event in 2007, the project "Hackers on a Plane" (a nod to the 2006 Samuel Jackson movie "Snakes on a Plane") flew participants in from the DefCon Conference in Las Vegas.[20] The Easterhegg is another annual happening that takes on the form of a conference with calls for papers that address one of the topics of interest: "creative ways to utilize technology," "biometric and genetic data sets," "IT- and network security," "hackerspaces," "energy and the smart-grid," "hacktivism, politics, and lobbyism," "art with and around technology," "government surveillance and data

---

[a]"No hacks for money" was one of his slogans.

[b]http://www.ccc.de/de/club/chaosfamily.

[c]A flyer from the co-organizer can be found here: https://entropia.de/wiki/images/6/69/GPN-Flyer.pdf.

retention," "civil rights in the digital age," "data protection and information freedom," and "open government and open data."[d] The Club also sponsors the SIGINT conference in Cologne every year where hackers and "netizens" discuss societal life in the digital age with emphasis on sociopolitical questions, "utopia," and creative deviance ("Normverletzung")—some might say hacktivism.[21]

The Chaos Computer Club first made headlines when in 1985 members hacked a home terminal system that was then widely used in Germany and transferred DM 134,000 to the Club's bank account from a Hamburg bank,[22] which they returned in a press conference the following day. Bildschirmtext (Btx) was owned by the Deutsche Bundespost (German Federal Mail Service, later privatized it took on the name Deutsche Telekom or German Telekom), which before had asserted it was 100% secure.[23] In 1985, the then 20-year-old Karl Koch[e] is a cofounding member of the Chaos Computer Club Erfa-circle in Hanover.[24] Together with Markus Hess and other hackers, he later became infamous for hacking into various U.S. systems stealing more or less sensitive data to sell it to the KGB (hence the catch name "KGB-hack").[f]

The Chaos Computer Club shares a common ground with Anonymous and its associates: an Internet free of censorship.[g;25] The Wau Holland Foundation, which was established after the death of Wau Holland in 2001 and is "loosely"[26] connected to the Chaos Computer Club, made headlines in 2010 with their funding efforts for WikiLeaks.[27] The nonprofit organization reimburses WikiLeaks' business expenses with the donations they collect for WikiLeaks.[28,29] Christopher Doyon is referring to the existence of "two dozen"[30] people in his interview[30] who act as a guiding and directive instance within the Anonymous-collective, which is often portrayed as some sort of self-organizing co-op, but as Christopher Doyon, self-professed person behind ominous screen name "Commander X" and head of the Anonymous-friendly People's Liberation Front quips "It takes organizers to get things done."[31]

THE ROOTS OF THE ANON—4CHAN, 7CHAN, AND OTHER MESSAGE BOARDS

Borne from the illustrious Anonymous contributors to 4chan's early miscellaneous b-forum who is either too busy or shy to identify him or herself, members of Anonymous today are thought to be script-kiddies,[h] hackers, and those less able but wanting to contribute by

---

[d] Easterhegg 2012—Call for Participation—Crossing the Borders. URL: http://events.ccc.de/.

[e] After Karl Koch's death, the CCC publishes an obituary, which can be found here: http://seti23.org/illuminati/illuframe.html.

[f] The case is described in detail in Clifford Stoll's book "The Cuckoo's Egg."

[g] In an interview with the German magazine, Der Spiegel, Hendrik Fulda, a board member of the Wau Holland Foundation, distances his organization from Anonymous' "Project Payback" stating: "We do not encourage people to take such action, nor do we have anything to do with it." (Der Spiegel, December 13, 2010).

[h] "Script kiddies" are amateur hackers who merely follow instructions for a given hack or exploit—rather than using technology to fully understand or create their own exploits.

leveraging their computer's resources. The ever-elusive Anon springs from message board to message board (4chan/b, 7chan, 888chan.org, 711chan.org32, and the like) in search for pristine ideas and true thoughts.[33]

4chan was created in October 2003 in the likeness of 2channel (2chan.net), an image board highly popular in Japan dedicated to Anonymous postings concerning all walks of life. Here, users could post pictures as well as text. The Anime-themed (Japanese animation) board was what inspired the 15-year-old Christopher Pool (screen name "Moot") to set up an English version, hence 4chan.org was born with different subsections.[i] The random-subject board was dubbed simply /b/ and would eventually make this image board famous. At the time of this writing and according to its own statistics, the page serves 22 million plus impressions to more than one million unique users each day and ranks number six in Google's PageRank.[34] The majority of its users are said to be between 18 and 34 years old and mainly male.[35] Offensive too many, /b/ made 4chan.org one of the largest Web forums in the United States.[36] A visit to the forum is a baffling experience for the uninitiated: repulsive images mingle with funny ones (e.g., a dog wearing false teeth or a horribly mutilated dead body). Pornography appears to be a staple of this online culture, in which at times it appears to serve as currency. /b/ is an image board, where members ("b/tards") post and share pictures of any kind (the only taboo being child pornography). Other users respond to these pictures—popular threads stay at the top. /b/ also is the birthplace of many of the Internet's viral memes like "LOLcat" and "rickrolling." If the origins of the Anons can be traced to any one point, it is this almost lawless online space and other forums like it whose Anonymous community grew to be a shared collective identity.[37] This collective identity used to describe itself as an "Internet hate machine" with members using the online forum to vent real-world troubles by cyber-bullying others or hacking for fun ("lulz," see below) or the challenge.[38] Anonymous utilizes forms of shock humor, including cringe, surreal, and black comedy,[39] to make fun of everybody and everything. This principle is best expressed in the distorted meaning of the nowadays ubiquitous "lol" (laughing out loud), "lulz" referring to the fun derived from another person's misfortune.

HOW WE ARE INFLUENCED BY 4CHAN: MEMES

At this point, a closer look at memes is adamant. Linguistically, "meme" is derived from the Greek word "mimema" ("imitation") and was coined to describe the spread of ideas and cultural phenomena—in our case online. The theoretical concept of memes originates from the philosopher Richard Dawkins,[j] and refers to units of information (e.g., a method to make a clay pot, a painting or a catchy tune—any human expression that is meant to communicate an idea) that propagate through a culture. Memes live from their replication and

---

[i]Read more in Cole Stryker's insightful book "Epic Win for Anonymous—How 4chan's Army Conquered the Web."

[j]Richard Dawkins was the first to publish a book on the subject of memes and memetics called "The Selfish Gene" in 1976.

FIGURE 6.1   A "Caturday" image. Anonymous members would post Saturday images of cats with quotations such as this. (For color version of this figure, the reader is referred to the online version of this chapter.) *Source: M-J, WikiCommons.*[43]

experience variations and changes after their inception and have to withstand the competition with other memes in order to survive.[40] Hence, the term also refers to the jokes, videos, and catchphrases that spread online. More exactly, meme is a popular post and Cole Stryker proclaims in his book that 4chan is *"the* meme factory of the Internet."[41] 4chan was not the first and is not the only Internet forum producing, sharing, and replicating memes,[k] but so far it appears to be the most viral. A self-professed Anon describes memes as the 4chan/b/'s *raison d'etre.*[42] Some memes that originated from or entered the vocabulary of "b-tards" eventually became popular among Internet users in general. *LOLcats* is a meme derived from the 4chan's introduction of Caturdays—on Saturdays, the users would post images of cats complemented with phrases representing the cats' comments (Figure 6.1).[l]

Other memes refer to singers like Tay Zonday, whose original of the song "Chocolate Rain" at the time of writing had over 79 million views on YouTube. Since its first upload by the artist in April 2007 on YouTube and its subsequent posting on 4chan.org (in July 2007), it experienced numerous covers and remixes.[44] Rick Astley experienced a comeback when his 1987 song "Never Gonna Give You Up" featured in a bait-and-switch practice, in which a seemingly relevant link leads to the music video. The Internet user who falls prey to this particular bait-and-switch trap is said to have been "rickrolled."[45] As the domain name suggest, the Web site Know Your Meme.com is generally a go-to source for popular and "dead" memes and associated culture.

Even the term "Anonymous" really is a meme referring to bloggers in 4chan, 7chan, and other image boards and associated with its own mythology and aesthetic. "Every time you've ever posted anything on the Internet without stating your name, you've been Anonymous, and that's all that defines Anonymous," an Anon is quoted in an interview.[46]

---

[k] At the time of writing, there are many Web sites and fora dedicated to memes including knowyourmemes.com, memegenerator.net, quickmeme.com, memebase.com, memecenter.com, and thedailymeme.com.

[l] From here, a now popular Web site dedicated to such postings spiraled out (icanhascheezburger.com).

ANONYMOUS—ON IMAGE, STRUCTURE, AND MOTIVATION

Anyone can get on 4chan/7chan/someintegerchan/IRC and propose a raid or operation
[...] it's hard to say how many people on those sites truly agree on what issues are important. *Adrian Crenshaw*[47]

The meme "Anonymous" refers to a collective of image board users who seek to remain nameless. Postings marked as "Anonymous" on image boards like 4chan (7chan, 711chan, PartyVan.net, Anonops.net) are inclusive and unlimited (everybody can use this identification as often as desired). On message boards posters sometimes jokingly pretend "Anonymous" was a real person. Eventually, the concept of "Anonymous" signifies the term as a placeholder for any and all people to represent an unnamed collective, a shared online identity for everybody posting without giving specific names (logos commonly used to represent the Anonymous collective or parts thereof today can be seen in Figures 6.2 and 6.3). In various public statements, the collective claimed to represent the real-world socioeconomical "99%".[48]

Another 4chan/b viral meme was substantiated by the first posting of the b/- internal character of the Epic Fail Guy in 2006, who—well—fails at everything he sets out to do. The Epic

FIGURE 6.2 The Guy Fawkes mask became a prominent symbol of Anonymous. *Source: Anon News Netherlands Blogspot, May 8, 2012.*

FIGURE 6.3 The headless suit also became a symbol of Anonymous. *Source: sott.net, March 7, 2012.*

Fail Guy popped up in posts depicting him in ever new failure-adventures, one of which had him find a Guy Fawkes mask in a trash bin.[49] Two years later, Anonymous' real world-protest against the Church of Scientology ("Project Chanology") had self-proclaimed Anons wear the Guy Fawkes mask as a visual provocation.[50]

In the open media, Anonymous is described as "loose-knit,"[51] which may either hint at an inclusiveness of the membership (there is no apparent selection as to who may join the forum or at the irregularity of members—there is a large amount of fluctuation among the membership). Other media outlets described Anonymous as "anarchic,"[52] describing the apparent lack of leadership. *Commander X*, "field commander" of the People's Liberation Front (PLF)[m;53] an activist group founded in 1986,[54] in an interview gave insight into the internal structure of Anonymous and he stated that Anonymous' organizational structure features "about two dozen [...] older[n;55] leaders, who were once members of the Chaos Computer Club. They make the decisions about what campaigns to endeavor, and "rein in the 'kids'."[56] Not only is there evidence for an internal hierarchy but Anonymous also engages external liaisons in a very structured and organized way: Commander X describes his PLF as being subservient in their cooperation with Anonymous.[57] Stemming from discussions on the 4chan/b/-board, the community ascribes itself labels concerning the duration of a person's experience in the community or an individual's intention: "Moralfags"[o]—moral beings through and through for whom there are (moral) limits to the ways and means to lulz,[58] such as do-gooders and political activists or "Hatefags"—who some people would say remain most true to the original flavor of the board as the "Internet Hate Machine," trolling the Internet and hacking for the lulz.[59] "Newfags" describe newcomer to the Internet or the Anonymous scene, whereas "Oldfags" refer to people being perceived or perceiving themselves as experienced around this particular scene and its culture.[60,61] Likewise, users who are most active during the summer months causing notable hypes of activity across 4chan's boards are known as "summer fags."[62]

Core "Anons" develop into some sort of leadership through creating a history of permanent or frequent presence and certain activities. Leadership through visibility: Visible "Anons" (such as Sabu[p]) establish themselves through their visibility in IRCs as popularities and become as such (informal) representatives of the movement.[63] The longer a member belongs to a movement the more he or she will recognize other members—not only through faces, but also through names or, in this case, online user names. The individual online handle, as it is being consistently used by a single, person undergoes the same process of establishing an identity within a group as a natural person does in a face-to-face setting.

---

[m] The PLF appears to be a smaller organization that started out as a "traditional" (face-to-face interactions and physical, "real world" engagement to make their convictions known) activist group that always exploited the possibilities of (using the internet for dissemination of information and for publicizing their motivations and actions) and later solely depend on (it appears that the PLF from Operation NetShield in late 2001 on) exclusively employs IT technologies as means of their protest.

[n] Older in reference to the majority of Anons in their late teens and twenties.

[o] Users on 4chan use titles containing a most striking feature of one another and add the suffix "–fags" when referring to each other, e.g., Christians are called "Christfags" (Stryker 2012:72).

[p] (The real) Sabu (Twitter-name @anonymouSabu).

The formation of hacking groups like LulzSec proves this very point as Parmy Olson illustrates in her book on Anonymous[64]:

> There were three people, in three different parts of the world, and they had been invited into an online chat room. Their online nicknames were Topiary, Sabu, and Kayla, and at least two of them, Sabu and Topiary, were meeting for the first time. The person who had invited them went by the nickname Tflow, and he was also in the room. No one here knew anyone else's real name, age, sex, or location. [...] They knew snippets of gossip about one another, and that each believed in Anonymous. That was the gist of it. The chat room was locked, meaning no one could enter it unless invited. Conversation was stilted at first, but within a few minutes everyone was talking. Personalities started to emerge. *Olson (p. 10)*[64]

According to Olson, this was the closed-door meeting that ultimately founded LulzSec, but it shows that—just as in real life—certain people had been selected to form it.

> Tflow, the guy who'd brought everyone here [...] had been with Anonymous for at least four months, a good amount of time to understand its culture and key figures within it. He knew the communications channels and supporting cast of hackers better than most. *Olson (p. 11)*[64]

Similar to real-life interactions, the online handles produced identifiable characters that could be called upon to join together and constitute a group who would meet and interact more often with each other, plotting hacks, or just conversing. Eventually, via their online IP addresses, law enforcement agencies in two countries would put an end to LulzSec. Some Anons participating in the only campaign that had a real-life component so far, the protests against the Church of Scientology, built real-life friendships.[65,66]

The PLF's *Commander X* estimates that there are about 10,000 "Anons" worldwide who are willing to join in Anonymous' campaigns.[67] Other than the leaders, these actors appear "Anonymous" on the screen and represent the whole idea of "Anonymous": everybody could and can be Anon.[q] Anons are everywhere, all the time, underestimated but crucial. Let us think about what this means. Like other new social movements, Anonymous does not have a consistent membership outside of its core group (if there is one). Who participates in an attack depends on the target. Hypothetically, an individual Anon may take action once and never again. Although unlikely, every attack could potentially be orchestrated by ever new members. And it does not stop at attacks. The dilemma that comes with such an elusive organizational structure is highlighted during "Project Chanology," where someone posted a YouTube video in the name of Anonymous threatening to blow up Scientology churches, while other members denied the video was genuine.[68] In December 2011, one group associated with Anonymous, LulzSec, claimed responsibility for the intrusion into the Stratfor system and the theft of personal data and credit card information of thousands of its customers.[69] In the following 2 days, a Pastebin entry denied this claim[70] while another posting confirmed, once again, Anonymous' involvement in the hack.[71]

Anonymous today is an inclusive network of screen names—anybody can sign up and create multiple online user names as publically available accounts on the alleged LulzSec members in the aftermath of the arrest wave suggest. At any given time, Anonymous' physical structure is a network of computers that are online, logged on in respective online forums (e.g., message boards

---

[q]Participants in DDoS attacks using LOIC can legally be identified and arrested through their transferred IP addresses.

and IRCs) if only for communication and information purposes. At the time of this writing, worldwide Anonymous groups with a presence on the Internet include but do not suffice Anonymous Sweden (Twitter @AnonOpsSweden, Facebook: Anonymous-Sweden), Anonymous Mexico (Facebook: AnonMex), Germany (Facebook: OfficialAnonymousGermany, anon-ger. blogspot.com, berlinonymous.wordpress), USA (Facebook: AnonUSA), UK (Anonymousuk. org), Romania (Anonymousromania.com, Facebook: anonro, Anonymous-Romania), and China (Twitter: @AnonymousChina). In Germany, Anonymous has launched a Web site (nazi-leaks. net) exposing donors, as well as emails and personal data of members of the neo-Nazi political party and other politically far-right extremist groups as part of Operation Blitzkrieg.[72]

Some members of the now highly publicized strands of Anonymous appear to be young romantic idealists who set out to protect the Internet—as an arena of true democracy, free speech and information, and transparency. Hence, any institution, be it a government or a religious organization, and any individual whose actions are perceived to counteract these ideals becomes a possible target mainly of DDoS attacks or Web site defacement. Taking much inspiration from popular culture, Anonymous often cites popular culture such as the movie "Fight Club"[73] when described by self-professed members. In an apparent contradiction to what Anonymous has set out to defend and protect—transparency—self-professed Anons hold themselves to a rule resembling the first two rules of "Fight Club"[r]: "Do not talk about Anonymous."[74] The headless suit, a ubiquitous graphic that has come to symbolize Anons, is thought to be adopted from a painting by Rene Magritte.[75] Another popular culture token prevalent with these groups is the Guy Fawkes mask. Wearing Guy Fawkes masks in real-world protests may be inspired by Alan Moore's illustration for the comic book series (and 2005 movie adaptation) "V for Vendetta." The main character in the comic book series, who just calls himself "V" and wears a Guy Fawkes mask at all times, is determined to bring down the totalitarian government of a dystopian near-future Great Britain. While he is portrayed as an anarchic character in the original comic book series, the movie paints him more as a revolutionary and freedom fighter (see figure 6.4 for slogans reminiscent of this cultural reference). The film culminates in the blowing up of the Palace of Westminster in the night of November 5 in reference to the historical Gunpowder Plot in 1605.[76]

The adoption of the mask into the realm of Anonymous—like Anonymous itself—came by way of 4chan's b-board coinciding with the release of the movie, "V for Vendetta," in 2006.[77] In a discussion thread, the mask is found by an existing fictional protagonist[s] who fails at everything he attempts (hence, he is called the epic fail guy). With the first real-world protest in Project Chanology, the masks first appeared worn by protestors to conceal their identity. Combined with a black business suit, white shirt and black tie, the mask has subsequently been identified with the movement. The masks depiction as well as references to the movie, "V for Vendetta," repeatedly appeared in the collective's communication.

In May 2012, Anonymous launched "Operation Mayhem Code Tyler" in obvious reference to the cult movie "Fight Club".[79]

---

[r]The first two rules Fight Club members have to adhere to are: "The first rule of Fight Club is: you do not talk about Fight Club. The second rule of Fight Club is: you do NOT talk about Fight Club" (Chuck Palahniuk. 1996 (2005) "Fight Club", Norton, p. 50).

[s]Like a meme, characters like this appear repeatedly through bloggers posting about them in another context or situation (much like a running gag).

The people should not be afraid of their government.

The government should be afraid of its people.

@ExpectUsCanada

FIGURE 6.4   Inspired by the comic book and film "V for Vendetta," anti-establishment rhetoric, often accompanied by the ubiquitous Guy Fawkes mask, is a staple of the collective. *Source: Twitpic Anonymous Circle.*[78]

The Anonymous slogans vary, but all stress that Anonymous represents The People, everybody, but the establishment: "Anonymous—We Are Everywhere—We Are Legion—We Never Forget—We Never Forgive—Expect Us" or alternatively "We are Anti-Security, We Are the 99%,"[t,80] (Figure 6.5) "We Do Not Forgive, We Do Not Forget, Expect Us!" More focused, Anonymous' and PLFs historically seem to spring into action when their decision makers perceive the freedom of information and expression is curbed. Yet, as mentioned earlier, the motivations are almost as numerous as the number of members: albeit sharing (for the most part) a hazily defined ballpark ideology the Anonymous collective is driven by a number of motivations (in publications Anonymous representatives referred to a "hive-mind"). As described earlier, each act could be viewed as a democratic process in which activists decide on a case-by-case basis whether they render bytes for the cause. Anonymous' motivation appears to be more of a patchwork with the rationalization for each hack (and quite possibly each member) differing.[u] In a few cases, the disparity among the collective's motivation is revealed when claims of responsibility are issued, withdrawn, and reissued from different subsets of the collective.[v] This also throws some light on the structure of the collective and its internal (lack of) communication. Hence, it is very feasible that no Anon could draw a map of his collective and all its subsets and subgroups. Understood as such the collective's name "Anonymous" not only is descriptive of its structure, but also of its (main) motivation and goals, such as protection of online privacy and digital rights, unrestricted usage of the Internet as a forum for the publication and exchange of however skewed ideas. These ideals brought the collective into opposing Stop Online Piracy Act (SOPA) and Anti-Counterfeiting Trade Agreement (ACTA), which intend to bolster copyright law and intellectual property rights, respectively. Although Anonymous' campaigns were graded as "very noisy, low-grade crimes" in a CNN article,[81] it may appear to many that now protests can be executed from the comfort of the members' home.

Like other social movements, Anonymous seeks publicity in order to appeal to a certain audience. The media frenzy started with a Fox News report most famous (now infamous) for its depicting a burning van in support of the claim that Anonymous conspired to blow up football

[t]This phrase is also used by the Occupy Movement (CNN, December 01, 2011).

[u]Where available in open media reports, we noted the stated motivation for each represented hack within the text body as well as in the list of events in Appendix II.

[v]As was the case in the Stratforhack of December 2011 (Pastebin entry by "Guest," December 25, 2011, "Emergency Christmas Anonymous Press Release," URL: http://pastebin.com/8yrwyNkt and Pastebin entry by "Guest," 12/26/2011, "Merry LulzXmas," URL: http://pastebin.com/q5kXd7Fd).

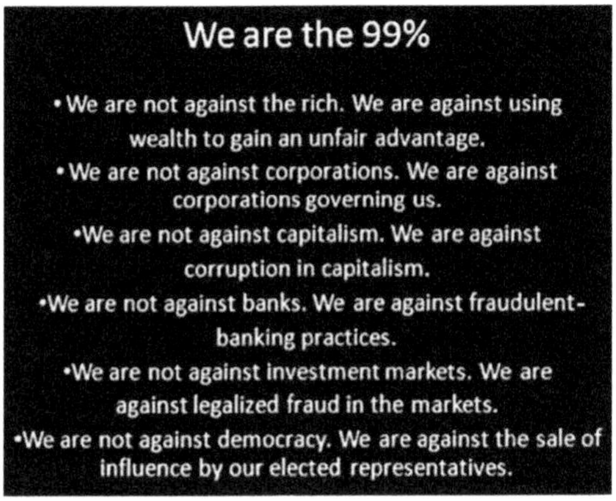

We are the 99%

• We are not against the rich. We are against using wealth to gain an unfair advantage.

• We are not against corporations. We are against corporations governing us.

•We are not against capitalism. We are against corruption in capitalism.

•We are not against banks. We are against fraudulent-banking practices.

•We are not against investment markets. We are against legalized fraud in the markets.

•We are not against democracy. We are against the sale of influence by our elected representatives.

FIGURE 6.5 Often referring to themselves as the "99%," members of the Anonymous collective often would often launch cyber attacks in a stated effort to support online privacy. *Source: Twitpic Anonymous Circle (@AnonCircle).*[82]

stadiums across America.[83] The person responsible for posting these threats on 4chan/b/ (and another 40 Web sites) in fall of 2006 turned himself in.[84] "The report (Fox News) gave us carte blanche. You realized you could get attention," a self-proclaimed member of the collective stated in an interview much later.[85] Whether it matters if this attention is positive or negative is again reflective of the collective's character. People who would call themselves "Anons" differ so much in their motivation; their evaluation of media coverage does so, too. The understanding of what Anonymous is to the individual Anon influences the ways in which this individual participates in Anonymous' attacks and its evaluation in the media. 4chan users who set out to wreak havoc and are dubbed "Internet hate machine" might not mind negative press. Politically aware Anons who see the Internet as a tool to change the world are probably interested in positive media coverage in order to recruit those in the audience who share their view. This part of Anonymous is interested in being viewed as acting in ethical ways (indeed they are called "moralfags" on 4chan) and do not condone the act by its goal: "any illegal act acted out by someone on the Internet is denounced by Anonymous [...] We're not terrorists. We're not bullies,"[86] an Anon from Sydney explains in an interview.

Having in mind the structure of the collective, it is also easy to understand the apparent contradictions in what Anonymous claims to be its goals and ideals and its actions. How is it possible to punish Internet censorship as exercised by regimes and governments with DDoS attacks and Web site defacements while at the same time taking down Web sites and hence rendering them unavailable? How is it reconcilable to fight for privacy in the digital realm and publish huge data files of personal information? Apparently, there are some Anons who are aware of these paradoxes and their effect on the collective's image, who refrain from publishing the personal information they captured and only post censored proof of their hack.[87]

ANONYMOUS—EXTERNAL CONNECTIONS AND SPIN OFFS

Anonymous has declared solidarity with numerous other social movements like the Animal Liberation Movement and the Occupy movement (such as *Occupy Wall Street* or *Occupy London*).[88] It appears that Anonymous takes on the cause of the social movements, expands their action into the realm of the Internet, but also undertakes its own actions dedicated to the specific causes. Self-proclaimed Anons participated in the occasional Occupy protest featuring the iconic mask. Julian Assange, cofounder and chief-editor of the whistle-blowing Web site, WikiLeaks also addressed an Occupy protest in London in October 2011.[89] About a year earlier, WikiLeaks drew ire with the publication of U.S. government cables and lost hosting resources and funding pathways. Anonymous then declared to fully support the organization and its cofounder, which they mainly realized by targeting Amazon, Mastercard, VISA, PayPal, and others who had broken off their business relationship with WikiLeaks with DDoS attacks and data breaches.[90,91] The Stratfor hack in December 2011 officially constitutes the first cooperation of Anonymous with WikiLeaks as the latter published millions of sensitive emails captured in the Anonymous raid.[92] Due to the shared objective of information freedom, Anonymous sources report a personnel crossover between the two entities since the February disclosure of the Stratfor e-mails.[93] Later, hackers with #OpAntiSec and the People's Liberation Front would again turn to WikiLeaks with a huge data trove taken from servers in Syria.[94] Though, the cooperation does not appear to be as smooth as could be expected as can be seen in a row about the release of the Syria data between the author(s) of Anonymous Twitter account (@AnonymousIRC) and the WikiLeaks-tweeter(s).[95] The inauguration of Par: AnoIA, a data dump site set up and run by some Anons, also caused altercations as WikiLeaks apparently perceives the project as competition.[96] In the months leading up the launch of this and another related site (Anonpaste, to be introduced later), doubts arose about the sincerity of the go-to dumping site for Anons, Pastebin.[97]

The People's Liberation Front (PLF) engages in political activism and civil disobedience since 1985[98] and joins in select Anonymous hacks. Gradually, while technical possibilities arose, it shifted its activities from real-world protests to the exclusive use of the Internet. According to its own reporting the PLF started their career in information technologies with phreaking, developing a device ("chinger") that mimicked the frequency of a pay phone after coins were inserted.[99] In their manifesto, the PLF claims to be a "nonviolent group of freedom fighters,"[100] whose foremost interest lies in the protection of the Internet as a source of empowerment to individual freedom.[101] In the same vein, these activists support other groups and organization who share causes among others, and besides select Anonymous operations, Germany's Chaos Computer Club and the Internet Defense League.[102] Fugitive Christopher Doyon is believed to be *Commander X*,[103] the head of the PLF. After his arrest in Santa Cruz, California, on charges of participating in an Anonymous-related DDoS attack on the city's Web site in September 2011,[104] he fled to Canada, where he appears to be still active and entertaining contact with the media.[105]

Famous for its breaches into Manwin-owned pornography Web sites in early 2012,[106,107] *Th3 Consortium* posted subsequently the captured personal information emphasizing especially data pertaining to government employees and military personnel. At the time of writing, there has been no news on the group for 4 months.

A more prominent related hacking group known as *TeaMp0isoN* (read: team poison) is said to have been founded in 2010.[108] The eight members of this group have allegedly accomplished several notable hacks. These include the theft of information from *Research In Motion* (RIM, the makers of the BlackBerry),[109] former British prime minister Tony Blair,[110] the United Nations,[111] the Australian government, and the Panasonic Corporation.[112] In the case of Blackberry, TeaMp0isoN acted to take revenge on the company's attempts to aide authorities in the localization of participants in the London riots.[113] It appears that the hackers mostly breach IT systems in order to steal and later publish personal or confidential information on Pastebin. The online equivalent for stalking is called "doxing" and entails any permissible or illicit action to obtain personal information on the selected person such as names and addresses of family members, their employers, where the children go to school and such.[114] The collected data is then published online mainly to amuse and harass.[115] Members of Anonymous in their protest of Sony suing George Hotz for altering and manipulating his Playstation collected information on the private addresses of Sony executives. Online open sources give away how much in property taxes they pay, how spacious the house, and who the neighbors are.[116] Other sources of dox—the data collected—are often obtained through social engineering. The term was popularized by a famous hacker, Kevin Mitnick, and refers to the practice of manipulating people into unknowingly provide information on or access to the target. Social engineering involves many real world and online tricks found in the toolbox of a theft: a convincing personality is key to obtain confidential information about the company you are working for over the phone by impersonating a coworker or authority figure or to coax the delivery truck to a new address.[117] Social media scams like obtaining access to a Facebook account and subsequently asking friends for money to help out in an alleged dire situation or click jacking scams[w] like the "see who viewed your Facebook profile"—trick that aims at obtaining personal information.[118]

Anonymous members used social engineering against HBGary Federal and CEO Aaron Barr when they engaged in an email conversation claiming that they were HBGary founder Greg Hoglund to obtain access to a simple company account.[119] We describe astonishing cases of online social engineering via social networking sites in Chapter 9.

Besides collecting personal information, hackers might engage in the occasional Web site defacement. Public communication is undertaken via TeaMp0isoN's Twitter accounts, @TeaMp0isoN,[120] and others. In addition to the hacks, TeaMp0isoN members also targeted a British police terrorism hotline[121] and MI6's phone service[122] with automated prank calls.[123] The apparent head of the hacker group, then 18-year-old Junaid Hussain aka TriCk,[124] was arrested in April 2012. Other self-proclaimed members include "Hex0010,"[125] "iN ^SaNe,"[126] and "MLT," who were arrested by British police in May 2011.[127] TeaMp0isoN members in the past claimed their foremost cause is the exposure of wrong doing especially by governments. Like that special benevolent brand of Anonymous, TeaMp0isoN members insist that they are not interested in intruding in ordinary citizens' privacy: "We do not release stuff which causes problems for innocent people, we do it to those who deserve it."[128] But they apparently also dislike "script kiddies" who embarrass skilled hackers and saw LulzSec[129] and Anonymous members as such.[130] Before joining forces with Anonymous, team members set out to reveal identities of LulzSec-members and the progovernment hacker, th3j35t3r (The Jester).[131] According to an interview with Fox News, TeaMp0isoN is officially sympathizing with the Palestinian Mujahideen Hacking Unit and the Pakistan Cyber Army.[132] In operations OpRobinHood, OpCashBack, and OpCensorThis, the merger of TeaMp0isoN with the Anonymous collective formed p0isAnon picked up the fight against corporate banks.[133,134] It is also believed that TeaMp0isoN members participated in the Stratfor hack in December 2011.[135]

---

[w] Clickjacking scam obtains targeted information by duping the victim into clicking certain buttons and links.

But Anonymous is not restricting its reach to the English-speaking world. In April 2012, the outlet, #FreeAnons, published a video declaring Anonymous' support for the Turkish left-wing hacker group, *R3dH4ck* (RedHack).[136] Members of this group hacked into computers of the Turkish police and captured information that they perceive is underlining the claim that the Turkish police are corrupt, using illegal means to further their end, many police departments suffered DDoS attacks.[137] In an attempt to curb *R3dH4ck*, the Turkish authorities arrested seven people, who appear unrelated to the hacker group, which proceeds with intrusion into government affiliated IT Systems as published on their Twitter account (@r3dh4ck).[138] Following the Turkish government's declaration of the group as terrorists, Anonymous launched "OpSupportRedHack"[139] in July 2012 and took down the Web sites of the Turkish Police Directorate (www.egm.gov.tr) and subpages of the Turkish National Intelligence Agency (www.mit.gov.tr).[140]

Out of the turmoil created by LulzSec's and T3amP0ison's demise another hacker group took shape out of the ubiquitous and fluid structure of Anonymous. *Malicious Security* (or *MalSec*) is apparently comprised of Anons who claim to refocus on political activism and that it would avoid harming individuals as they criticize Anonymous for hurting citizens by stealing and publishing confidential information such as credit card details.[141] It is also in contempt with the in-fighting within the Anonymous collective, referring to LulzSec head, Hector Xavier "Sabu" Monsegur, aiding the FBI in arresting other LulzSec members.[142] MalSec makes extensive use of blogs and social media, entertaining presences on Twitter (@malsec), Facebook (Malicious Security) and posting their introductory video on YouTube.[143] Eventually, they hacked into government and government affiliated as well as corporate bank Web sites in Romania, Bhutan, the Philippines, and other countries using SQL injection.[144,145] In late March 2012, the breach into the Web site of Security Centre Ltd. on the Cayman Islands resulted in its defacement and a polite to-do-list on how to fix the security issues that allowed the hack.[146] As it seeks to replicate the structure of the much larger Anonymous collective[147] and avoid the disadvantages of the highly visible and active directorate that brought LulzSec and TeaMP0ison down,[148] it also has to face the accompanying side effects. It will have to be seen, if the fluidity in membership and the decentralized leadership will collide with the proclaimed goals of MalSec.

The possibly most prominent association with hacking groups and Anonymous in 2011 is *LulzSec*, which in its claim that their only motivation and cause to their numerous and highly publicized hacks be amusement appears most contrary to the most vociferous political and ethical hackers within the Anonymous collective (alas at least at the time of writing, in the summer of 2012).

YOUR SECURITY IS A JOKE: LULZSEC

An alleged Anonymous spin off that would later rejoin the collective, Lulz Security (also called itself LulzBoat) announced an end to its "50 day cruise"[150] on Twitter on June 26, 2011 (LulzSec's logo can be seen in Figure 6.6 below). Although one of their slogans, "Laughing at your security since 2011," suggests a longer life-span may have been intended, LulzSec officially lasted only for 50 days. The name is derived from the popular Internet meme "lol" for "Laughing Out Loud" and is meant to represent the group's main motivation: fun.[151] On the

FIGURE 6.6   The LulzSec's logo.[149] (For color version of this figure, the reader is referred to the online version of this chapter.)

contrary, many alleged and confirmed LulzSec hacks were propelled by an ideology close to that of Anonymous (otherwise LulzSec would hardly qualify as actors of hacktivism). As in the hacks of Nintendo and the British National Health Service (NHS), LulzSec members at times present their action as aiding in the discovery of system vulnerabilities.[x;152] LulzSec apparently sees the protection of customer data as a responsibility of an online service. They justified their attack on SonyPictures.com as an exposition of the company's inability to live up to that standard.[153] In other campaigns, LulzSec portrays itself as a defender of human decency and civil rights. In this vein, they accused Arizona law enforcement of racial profiling and corruption.[154]

Since late April, the Anonymous spin-off identified, breached, and circumvented security of computers around the world including Fox News,[155] the U.S. Public Broadcasting System (PBS) television,[156] Sony Corp. compromising more than one million user accounts,[157] the official CIA Web site (www.cia.gov) knocking it offline for a few hours[158,159] as well as the British Serious and Organized Crime Agency (SOCA). Other targets included two Web sites associated with the government of Brazil, an Irish political party, and MasterCard aside several cases in which participation was denied (Sega, UK census 2011). A more complete list of LulzSec events with alleged motivation can be found in Appendix II. The hack of the British tabloid *The Sun* and its sister-newspaper *The Times* posting a story announcing the death of Rupert Murdoch[160] was orchestrated after the disbandment of the group was already announced and could hint at disunity among group members. A week prior to its retirement on June 20, 2011 LulzSec announced its merging with Anonymous in the Operation Anti-Security (also OpAntiSec or #AntiSec), in which government agencies, banks and corporations are targeted in an effort to protest against Internet censorship and surveillance as well as to protect privacy.[161]

---

[x] As will be described later, a few members, including the alleged head of LulzSec have worked as IT professionals specializing in uncovering system vulnerabilities (The Telegraph, June 9, 2011).

LulzSec used Twitter (@LulzSec - The Lulz Boat) to announce its campaigns as well as to celebrate their success in a taunting language.[162] In mid June 2011 a tweet advertised a hotline and encouraged "true Lulz fans" to call in and suggest targets (614 LULZSEC).[163] To communicate with one another a Web site called paste.org was utilized.[164] In their attacks, DDoS and the exploitation of SQL injection vulnerabilities dominate.

The alleged head of LulzSec, (TheReal) Sabu[y] a 28-year-old New Yorker IT consultant, whose real name, Hector Xavier Monsegur, was officially[z;165] revealed after he led law enforcement to the remaining members of the group in early March 2012. As a former member of the defunct IT-security company TigerTeam-Security,[166] he was skilled and trained to find vulnerabilities in computer systems (a hacker with these skills is also called "rooter").[167,168] Monsegur also entertained a private blog on the matter (http://xavsec.blogspot.com). He pleaded guilty to "computer hacking conspiracy" in August 2011 after the FBI closed in on him in June 2011, when several members of Anonymous were arrested. Monsegur's IP address (and eventually physical location) was disclosed as he logged on to an IRC server without using an IP-encoding service.[169] It is possible that rival hacker groups and pro-government hacktivists aided the FBI in identifying Sabu.[170] Monsegur allegedly decided which campaigns to embark upon and famously motivated Anons. Besides computer hacking charges, he also confessed to have sold stolen bank information online and to have used stolen credit card information to purchase car parts for himself among other petty crimes.

With Sabu's help five more LulzSec members were identified and located mainly in Britain and Ireland. Sabu's alleged second-in-command went by the screen name Topiary, who acted as "PR-guy" posting for LulzSec on Twitter.[171] Gregg Housh, who became a sort of a spokesman for Anonymous after his unmasking, stated that a Topiary Gardenslayer was well acquainted with AnonOps, the servers hosting all of Anonymous' communication fori.[172] Jake Davis, who was found to be behind the pseudonym, was arrested in July 2011. The then 19-year-old resident of the Shetland Islands was subject of the "Free Topiary" campaign kicked off by Anonymous after his arrest while part of the collective still insisted the police had arrested the wrong person. The 25-year-old (in 2012) Ryan Ackroyd of Doncaster allegedly used the screen names "Kayla," "lol," and "Lolspoon" and was arrested in summer 2011.[173] His specialty, too, was to identify weaknesses in the targeted computer systems and circumvent their security.[174] Together with Jake Davis, Darren Martyn (aka Pwnsauce, raepsauce, networkkitten),[175] and Donncha O'Cearrbhail, he is charged with the Fox, Sony, and PBS breaches.[176] The latter, known by the screen name "palladium," is additionally accused of eavesdropping on a conference call concerning Anonymous between the FBI and the London police and subsequently posting it on the Internet.[177] Tflow—a 16-year-old London resident, whose name was not revealed due to his young age, was one of the arrested in the summer 2011 international sweep.[178] Much earlier Web designer Sven Slootweg (screen names Joepie91 or Joepie92) was ousted by the then rival hacker group TeaMp0isoN. Not all of these hackers were steady members of LulzSec, but Joepie, Storm, Neuron, and trollpoll were said to have been participating fans or infrequent guests.[179]

---

[y]Other screen names Monsegur used were Xavier Kaotico, Leon, and Xavier de Leon.

[z]A hacker with the pseudonym KillerCube posted Sabu's real name and physical address along with other personal data and affiliations on Pastebin in late June (KillerCube pastebin-entry, June 22, 2011).

LulzSec
☺
Like · Comment · Share · 33 minutes ago · 🌀

🖒 48 people like this.

FIGURE 6.7 LulczSec was sporadically active on Facebook. (For color version of this figure, the reader is referred to the online version of this chapter.)

Another temporary member known by his/her screen name Devrandom ad recursion quit after the FBI hack.[180] The British and Irish nationals arrested in early March 2012 face possible extradition to the United States on charges that range from theft of confidential data to mishandling of computers, computer hacking, as well as conspiracy and if convicted warrant up to 20 years imprisonment.[181]

The Facebook presence of LulzSec appeared to have grinded to a halt after the March-arrests as there were no new posting for about 2 weeks. On March 19, 2012, the status was updated with the post seen in Figure 6.7.

But the group's Facebook activity has since been rather sporadically. Later in spring of 2012, "LulzSec Reborn" (on Twitter as @lulzboatR) claimed the intrusion and theft of data of 170,000 militarysingles.com users.[182]

Another offshoot of Anonymous, *Th3CabinCr3w* ("The Cabin Crew"), experienced a similar fate. In "Operation Pig Roast" Th3CabinCr3w hacked into Web sites of U.S. police departments and other government-affiliated departments with employing SQL injection methods.[183] In response to the Brazilian governments' initiative to control Internet content for their population, members of the CabinCr3w posted captured confidential information in "Operation Satiagraha."[184] Two alleged members, John Anthony Borell III from Toledo, Ohio aka "Kahuna" and Higinio O. Ochoa III aka "w0rmer" or "higochoa" from Galveston, Texas are currently under arrest.[185] The latter published a letter on Pastebin recounting his arrest and the FBI's apparent attempt to recruit him in order to capture the remaining crew members.[186] Following the arrests, the remaining members announced in a post on anonnews.org on April 17, 2012 that they are rejoining the Anonymous collective.[187] The3CabinCr3w ceded their considerable online presence on several social networking and bloghosting sites, such as Facebook,[aa] Scribd,[bb] Twitter,[cc] and Tumblr[dd] in March or April 2012, respectively.

ANONYMOUS' MODUS OPERANDI

I think what is, important about Anonymous is that it works, I don't know how it works but it works *Australian Anon quoted in NineMSN, May 8, 2008*[188]

[aa]https://www.facebook.com/pages/Cabin-Cr3w/200338873391440.

[bb]http://www.scribd.com/CabinCr3w.

[cc]http://twitter.com/CabinCr3w/.

[dd]http://cabincr3w.tumblr.com/.

A video, mostly published on YouTube, announcing a new campaign kicked off many projects in the past.[189] Additionally, every "operation" ("AnonOp") is declared beforehand on Twitter (@YourAnonNews, @Anon_Central), tumblr (youranonnews.tumblr.com), and first-hand Anonymous Web sites, such as anonnews.org and whyweprotest.net. Other commonly used outlets are Pastebin, Pirate Bay,[190] and Facebook (Anonymous News Network).[191] Internet Relay Chats (IRC) and image boards, Internet forums, as well as wikis serve the purpose of online communication and coordination.[ee] These as well as the partyvan.info[192] hosted raid boards and IRCs as well as those run by AnonOps (anonops.ru, anonops.net) are apparently used to garner support for ideas from individual Anons. The Web sites of collaborating hacktivist groups, too, may explain the mission and extend the opportunity to participate to the visitor.[193] One *chan* user might post a call to arms where s/he perceives something is wrong or has potential of being fun. If enough other users agree a date is set on which the operation is launched.[194] If the initial recruiting process was unsuccessful, nothing will happen. Factors that might motivate an Anonymous attack (i.e., further the recruitment process to an individual idea) are the *lulz-potential*,[ff] perceived arrogance of the potential target, and perceived Internet censorship or other ethical or moral challenges.[195] The latter may be secondary or even afterthought for the mere justification of the hacks for the public eye and the decisive moment is the actual possibility to achieve the desired results (although the ensuing real-world consequences may not necessarily have been anticipated fully).[196]

The most often employed tactic in Anonymous & Co.'s campaigns is the distributed denial of service attack (DDoS). As with the some of the other DDoS attacks discussed in previous chapters, the DDoS attacks of Anonymous rely on DDoS tool provided to the hacktivist participants. These tools were somewhat more advanced than the software used by Russian hacktivists in the Georgia cyber campaign (Chapter 3), but unlike the "voluntary botnet" used by pro-Israel supporters against Hamas (Chapter 4) they do not allow a central C&C total control over the user's computer. The creation of such tools allows Anons to participate with virtually no hacking skills—while still contributing their computing resources. The most widely known software of this sort in use by Anonymous includes the Low Orbit Ion Cannon (LOIC) and the RefRef Web script.[197] The latter of which was meant to replace the former in September 2011 since LOIC retains the IP address of the senders, which lead to numerous arrests of Anons.[198] The RefRef Web script is a command-line-based Java site that exploits SQL and Javascript vulnerabilities in order to exhaust the server supporting the Web site.[gg]

[ee]Especially 4chan, 711 chan, Encyclopedia Dramatica, IRC channels, YouTube, and (supported) blogs (e.g., anonops.blogspot.com (by invitation only), Legion News Network and AnonNews.org as news outlets, whyweprotest.net (Anonymous supported website originally in support of operation Chanology, but expanded to service the organization of protest initiatives and campaigns, grass root activism), and Anonywebz.com (Anonymous tool network), social networking services like Twitter and Facebook are used to organize real-world protest.

[ff]According to Adrian Crenshaw ("Crude Inconsistent Threat"), this is what appears to draw the most supporters.

[gg]The tool exploits the fact that most Web sites save the .js file of an incoming request on their own server, since the request is still working the packets bounce back and forth on the target server, exhausting its resources (THN, July 7, 2011).

The low-orbit ion cannon is a legitimate tool to stress test a Web application by sending a large amount of requests to the Web page to see, if it can handle it ("bandwidth raep"). It was written in C#, which is available in three versions (manual, server-controlled, and in JavaScript) and can be found on any major open source code repository. Individual users download the application and opt their computer to become part of the botnet, which is employed in Anonymous' DDoS attacks; one form of membership is thus the mere contribution of computing power to Anonymous' resources. LOIC also features a connection to an IRC channel in order to coordinate the load of packets send from the individual computers. Unbeknownst to a large number of participants in illegal DDoS attacks may be the fact that the LOIC does not encrypt or hide the IP addresses of the senders. The target computer's Web site logs all IP addresses of incoming requests, which in turn can be traced back to a single computer.[199]

Another prevalent Anonymous tactics requiring somewhat more hacking skills, but less computing resources is the SQL injection, which exploits weaknesses in the database of a Web site—previously described in Chapter 3. In its attack on HB Gary Federal and its head, Aaron Barr, a handful of Anonymous and affiliated hackers gathered compromising documents and emails this way. Captured data usually is "dumped," i.e., published on Pastebin or most recently on Anonpaste. More rarely, the obtained data are used for In Real Life (IRL) pranks—the staging of real-world events such as unwanted pizza delivery or using social engineering to have a SWAT team called to the respective residence ("swatting").[200] Other ends through the mean of SQL injection include the defacement of Web sites, in which the original content is substituted by pictures or messages of the intruders or the hijacking and/or redirection of the target Web site. In the latter cases, the Web site would either cease to be under the control of its original authors or redirect to another site as selected by the hacker(s).

TARGETING GOVERNMENTS, CORPORATIONS, AND INDIVIDUALS: NOTABLE HACKS ON ANONYMOUS

Anonymous meanwhile is featured in the media almost every week with either claiming or being found responsible for cyber attacks against selected targets. It would not make any sense to recap a chronology of Anonymous' attacks (for an extensive yet still incomplete list of Anonymous-attributed hacks see the Appendix, which also includes stated motivation for the hacks where available to help form a more complete picture of the ideology behind these actions) as the resulting long list would probably have a lot of holes: the media coverage of Anonymous acts depends either on largesse or on popularity of the target.

Habbo Hotel Raids

Long before Anons engaged in hacks for which the collective know is famous and feared for 4chan's Ur-Anonymous raided their targets. Protesting against Habbo's ban on African-American avatars and accusing Habbo's social moderators of racism the virtual game made a great target for raids. Habbo Hotel raids began in mid-2005 in which avatars looking like a wealthy African-American in a business suit (to some reminiscent of the Samuel Jackson's Pulp Fiction character Jules) obstruct entry to the pool (Figure 6.8). This hack already signifies two important motifs for the collective action of the Anonymous we know today: perceived discrimination as well as the humungous lulz potential.[201]

FIGURE 6.8   During the Habbo hotel raid, members of 4chan protested against the ban on African-American avatars by creating avatars of African-American businessmen who blocked access to the pool. (For color version of this figure, the reader is referred to the online version of this chapter.) *Source: Know Your Meme.*[202]

"Pool's closed" became a catch-phrase for the Habbo raids that resulted in 4chan exercising otherwise rare censorship and moderation. A year later Habbo raids culminated in an unprecedented organized raid across four countries (UK, USA, Germany, and Australia) that resulted in the site being knocked offline. The Habbo raids are also a precedent for the counterproductive actions that bring about what (at least part of) the momentary Anonymous force set out to prevent in the first place and which will form the core of the criticism of Anonymous years later: In the aftermath of the summer 2006 attacks, Habbo Hotel administrators programmed the automatic ban of African-American avatars with afro and suit.[203]

Internet Vigilantism

In December 2007, in an act of Internet vigilantism[204] Anonymous hackers aided the arrest of Canadian Chris Forcand by impersonating teenage girls.[hh;205] He would subsequently be brought to court on charges related to pedophilia.[206] In summer 2012, Anonymous followed up on this initiative against pedophiles in launching the Twitter hashtag "#TwitterPedoRing" to invite pedophiles on the communication network to join. A week later, 190 offenders were arrested by the U.S. Immigrations and Customs Enforcement, though no reference to

---

[hh] The online threads from the perspective of the anonymous collective of b/tards are saved on 4chan's archive here: http://4chanarchive.org/brchive/dspl_thread.php5?thread_id=42828652&x=brb%20church%20-%20chris%20forcand.

Anonymous was made. In August 2012, the Anonymous Twitter account, @YourAnonNews, asked its 615,000 subscribers to report the account "@many501611" spam who had published pornographic pictures of young boys.[207] Other instances in which the propagation of evidence of perceived injustice through the Internet resulted in real-life consequences for the perpetrator include a South Korean girl who refused to clean up after her dog on a subway and whose subsequent harassment brought her on the brink of suicide, the tactless Zhang Ya, whose inhuman remarks on the suffering of the victims of the Sichuan earthquake in 2008 eventually got her arrested, American pioneer spammer, Alan Ralsky, receiving mailbox spam in truck loads, the New York City cop, Patrick Pogan, who attacked an unsuspecting cyclist and would have gotten away with it, if it was not for the video of the incident being spread all over the Internet.[208] Internet vigilantism is neither an invention of 4chan nor the Anonymous collective nor constrained to North America.[ii]

Project Chanology

Anonymous first real-world protest brought thousands donning Guy Fawkes masks onto the streets in numerous cities and countries to protest against the Church of Scientology. Churches experienced real-world pranks, like harassing phone calls, black faxes (in order to waste ink),[209] pizzas and taxis they did not order.[210] as well as letters with what turned out to be harmless white powder.[211] Project Chanology was sparked by the leak of an insider video of an interview with actor Tom Cruise talking about his life in the sect.[212] The subsequent forceful attempts by the Church to retract the video were perceived as a metaphorical example for the general restrictiveness the organization is often criticized for. The initial momentum that kicked of immense headaches for the Church of Scientology was an anonymous post on 4chan/b: "it is time to do something great."[213,214] In January 2008, self-confessed Anons originating from image boards like 4chan, Partyvan.org, and 711chan among others officially launched "Project Chanology" by posting a video on YouTube entitled "Message to Scientology."[215] Besides the real-world protests, Anons rendered the official Web site of the Church of Scientology inaccessible by way of DDoS attacks and captured and published literature for which adherents normally have to pay.[216,217] In the course of 3 weeks, Project Chanology encouraged over 8000 harassing phone calls, 3.6 million malicious emails, 141 million hits against the church Web sites, 10 acts of vandalism, 22 bomb threats, and 8 death threats.[218] The Internet activists employed online tools like JMeter and Gigaloader in DDoS attacks and the exploit of computer security vulnerabilities like Cross-site Scripting.[219] Botnets and the Low Orbit Ion Cannon (LOIC) had their debut as Anonymous' tools in Project Chanology.[220,221] Scientology responded with attempts to obtain restraining orders for their premises and identify the Anons who organized local protests. One of the exposed, Gareth A. Cales of Los Angeles reported legal threats and general harassment by Scientology members.[222] His account also includes details about the organization of the protests associated with Project Chanology. Mark Bunker and other critics of the Church of Scientology released

[ii]Clay Shirky authored an insightful book ("Here Comes Everybody—The Power of Organizing Without Organization") on online group action, which argues that it does not only take new forms of technology but also new forms of behavior.

a video encouraging the protests to remain legal and were surprised that Anons appeared to heed the advice.[223] Four years later, in February 2012, still some protesters wearing Guy Fawkes masks beleaguer Scientology churches.[224] The two-pronged approach showed effect: The resounding response to the Project Chanology not only made the organizers aware of the possibilities of the online organization of a social movement, but it also appears to have refined Anonymous' character. While the majority of the Anonymous collective prior was interested in the lulz potential of an undertaking,[225] with the protest against an enigmatic organization known for its attempts to censor public information about itself, many Anons appear to be spurred by the perceived righteousness of this quest.[226]

Arab Spring

Anonymous targeted government Web sites of countries in North Africa and the Arabian Peninsula as well as Asia Minor that found themselves engulfed in civil uprisings in 2011—the Western world would call it hopefully "Arab Spring." Anons used their computers and knowledge to support the protesters on the ground, whose governments in many cases had resolved to deny them access to social media or the Internet altogether. For each country, Anonymous launched a new "operation." Starting with "Operation Tunisia" and "Operation Egypt" affiliates of the collective and sympathizers took down the governments' computers with DDoS attacks (Figure 6.9).[227]

The PLF's Commander X boasted in a chat-interview that his organization kicked off Tunisia's "Jasmine Revolution" by stealing compromising information on the government and leaking it to WikiLeaks.[229,230] Other media outlets stress the dire living conditions in Tunisia, among others the high unemployment and inflation as well as the lack of political freedom as causes taken to Tunisian streets after the self-immolation of Mohamed Bouazizi on December 17, 2010.[231,232] The press acknowledged Anonymous' support of the protesters on the ground by taking down at least eight government Web sites with DDoS attacks

FIGURE 6.9 2011, Anonymous consequently took up the fight with the Syrian government after it clamped down violently on public protesters. (For color version of this figure, the reader is referred to the online version of this chapter.) *Source: PLF, Operation Syria.*[228]

(including Web sites of the President, Prime minister, the ministries of foreign affairs and industry, as well as the stock exchange)[233] and defacing some of them.[234] Anonymous also provides means and knowledge to activists on the ground to conceal their online identity in order to prevent prosecution and coordinate their activities with the events on the ground.[235] As Commander X stated in regard to their participation in various episodes of the "Arab Spring," besides the admittedly mostly negative attention Anonymous and its collaborators earn with each campaign, the goals are to deny the targets (here: governments) lines of communication and to "encourage the protesters on the ground."[236] The initial motivation to join in the uprising for one Anon was the Internet censorship as exercised by the Tunisian government.[237] Subsequently, a host of Anons identified with the struggles of the revolutionaries in the respective countries and sought to alleviate their plight by doing whatever they could to provide them with avenues for information exchange[238] while at the same time denying them to their opponents. The Tunisian governments attempt to identify political activists by phishing online for their social networking or email accounts[239] was countered by a subdivision of Anonymous, the *Internetfeds*. A greasemonkey script made available to the Tunisian protestors would override the governments' spyware.[240] They also translated and distributed information on how to conceal IP addresses and other techniques to obscure individual identities in French and Arabic.[241] Anonymous' involvement did not stop with the ouster of Zine el Abidine Ben Ali. The new Tunisian Anons proceeded to use online tools to fight alongside the new moderate Tunisian government against the pressure it experienced from Islamist fringe groups.[242] To circumvent Internet censorship in Egypt, Anonymous aided in the restoration of proxies and mirrors in order to guarantee information flow to benefit the revolutionaries.[243] The Egyptian authorities had blocked twitter.com and other social media apparently in order to aggravate communication between protestors.[244] Anons targeted Web sites of the Egyptian government and ministries with DDoS attacks.[245] In both operations, the trickster-natured among the Anons still found pleasure in real-world pranks, like flooding the respective embassies with unwarranted pizza-orders.[246] In August 2011, Anonymous consequently took up the fight with the Syrian government after it clamped down violently on public protesters. The Web site of the Syrian Ministry of Defense was defaced with an encouraging message to the Syrian people.[247]

Besides the above mentioned, the governments of Yemen,[248,249] Algeria,[250] Zimbabwe,[251] and Italy[252] also drew the ire of the online collective, which targeted associated Web sites with more or less extensive DDoS attacks.[253] The predecessor to these diverse operations associated with the "Arab Spring" could perhaps be found in Anonymous' engagement in Iran's post-election crises in 2009. Back then, Anons intercepted the propagation of hit lists depicting protestors distributed by progovernment groups.[254]

HBGary Federal and Aaron Barr

The InternetFeds, an AnonOps spin off of skilled black hat hackers, engaged in what appears to be a "personal" vendetta on Aaron Barr, HBGary's CEO, who had claimed to have identified key actors after infiltrating Anonymous.[255] After mocking Barr online and obtaining all his passwords via SQL injection, the hackers were amused to have him "watch" how they hijacked his email and all Internet social media and stole data from internal company emails he had sent to his coworkers.[256] DDoS attacks brought down hggary.com and hbgaryfederal.com.[257] The latter was breached using SQL injection, which exploited a security flaw in the custom-made content management system (CMS) the company had employed.[258] The so-called rainbow tables appeared to have immensely alleviated the quest to garner the hashed passwords of Aaron Barr and COO Ted Vera.[259] Barr had apparently reused one password over and over, "kibafo33," which allowed access to other company email inboxes, since Barr enjoyed administrator rights.[260] Ultimately, this led to compromising HBGary's founder, Greg Hoglund's rootkit.com Web site by way of hijacking his email account. The hackers then impersonated Hoglund in an email conversation with an associate in order to obtain the last bits of information necessary to gain control over rootkit.com.[261] Besides defacing the Web site, the intruders also resolved to publish the user database.[262] Ted Vera's repeatedly used password enabled the hackers to access the support server that hosted the shell accounts of many HBGary employees and which enabled them to upgrade Vera's personal account through the exploitation of a personal escalation vulnerability, which gave the hackers full access to HBGary's system.[263] Gigabytes of data were now immediately at the hand of the intruders. More than 60,000 company emails were published on the Pirate Bay file-sharing site.[264] Another case apparently motivated by revenge was the hack into Sony's online Playstation store and the DDoS attack against the Playstation Web site.[265] Sony had sued PS3-hacker George Hotz (aka "GeoHot"), who had become famous for unlocking various iPhone versions[266] before he managed to gain administrator rights to the entire system memory and the processor of the PS3 system in early 2011.[267] An abrupt settlement in the case was reached in April 2011 with neither side disclosing the full terms, but on the part of the phreaker/hacker was the deletion of all his information on the PS3-hack from the Internet.[268] Hotz was subsequently hired by Facebook, but found himself just months later with Lady Gaga's start-up social networking site, Backplane.[269]

Straightforward Operations

Anonymous' goals become apparent when looking at those campaigns that aim at institutions that are either held responsible or perceived to embody the objectionable with DDoS attacks. In some cases, sensitive material is published after the successful intrusion of hackers into the target's system. A prominent example is the charge under which attacks against copyright companies were launched. The effort was later extended to also aim at companies that ceased business relation with the whistle-blower, WikiLeaks, after the publishing of sensitive U.S. diplomatic cables (Operation Payback).[270] In this instance, Anonymous officially became a supporter of WikiLeaks, its co-founder, Julian Assange as well as Bradley Manning, a U.S. soldier who had leaked confidential information on America's military campaign in Iraq.

The term "anti-security" refers to a movement conceived in the late 1990s to counteract the cyber-security industry's tactic of provocatively exploiting vulnerabilities in order to increase sales.[271] Apparently, Anonymous joined by LulzSec[272] takes the viewpoint that governments employ similar tactics to justify legislation that monitors Internet behavior and allows censorship and surveillance (Operation AntiSec). In its quest to safeguard online privacy, the hacktivists encouraged the defacement of government Web sites and leaking of data obtained through breaches into the systems government organization, banks, and other institutions deemed to profit from infringements on user privacy.[273] Other digital rights-related reasons for hacks under the AntiSec banner are racial profiling, copyright laws, and the War on Drugs.[274] The attack against the British SOCA presented the debut of AntiSec, followed by the publication of material from the Cyberterrorism Defence Initiative Sentinel program,[275] and the release of private information apparently obtained through SQL injection from sources related to the governments of Brazil, Zimbabwe, and Tunisia. So far, Anonymous attacked U.S. defense contractor Booz Allen Hamilton, U.S. Central Command, U.S. Special Operations Command, U.S. Marine Corps, and the U.S. Air Force in a spree dubbed "Military Meltdown Monday."[276] The December 2011 Stratfor-hack where subscribers' credit card information and emails were stolen and later published on WikiLeaks was also perpetrated by the LulzSec member(s) now working under the Anonymous banner.[277]

Other campaigns launched under the Anonymous banner include Operation Vendetta[278] launched after a wave of arrests of alleged Anonymous-affiliated hackers in March 2012 to help Anons escape the authorities. This campaign is the second one to date that entails a major real-world component in that it aims to set up safe-houses and an "underground railroad"[279] to lead sought-after hackers to countries which do not have extradition treaties with the prosecuting authorities. A popular hacktivist who apparently benefitted from this operation is Christopher Doyon aka Commander X, whose People's Liberation Front had joined forces with Anonymous in this campaign again. After having been arrested in Santa Cruz, California, as the "homeless hacker"[280] who protested against a recent county ban on outdoor sleeping by launching DDoS attacks,[281] Doyon reportedly found an interim sanctuary in Canada.[282]

SOFTWARE FOR THE LEGION: ANONYMOUS PRODUCTS

In early 2012, Anons engaged in the creation of software. Partially in protest to existing applications, such as the social music platform, *AnonTune*, and partially in the quest of opening new avenues beyond hacking as in the launch of its operating system, *Anonymous OS live*. Besides the file-sharing site, AnonPaste, the collective also launched a WikiLeaks-like site in an attempt to control and deepen the public impact of their hacking activity.[283] Both platforms were meant to serve as data dumps.

AnonTune

In April 2012, Anonymous launched a social music platform that provides streaming songs from third party users (e.g., YouTube) for users to compile into playlists and share. Initiated by online discussions the ambitions of an individual, who created and uploaded a prototype, generated the technical support necessary to render AnonTune capable of handling large requests aside from the user interface.[284] It is planned that AnonTune will grant its users anonymity, shielding them from prosecution and copyright law suits while offering a service better organized and less expensive than similar platforms.[285] Upon its launch, AnonTune will be a project borne purely of the Internet. Once more, the creators of this online forum must not have ever been in personal physical contact and may even be spread out over different continents.

AnonPaste

After the operators of PasteBin, hitherto Anonymous' favorite forum to publish captured data, was found to be compromised, Anonymous affiliates associated with Operation Anti-Sec together with the People's Liberation Front launched its own data-sharing Web site, AnonPaste,[jj] in April 2012.[286] Jeroen Vader, owner of PasteBin, announced an increase in censorship of the site.[287] He further admitted that at times he shares his logs—a register of the IP addresses of users—with law enforcement agencies, which drew immediate recognition on the part of Anonymous, which introduced its new Web site with the following comment:

> As a recent leak of private emails show clearly, Pastebin is not only willing to give up IP addresses to governments—but apparently has already given many IPs to at least one private security firm. And these leaked emails also revealed a distinct animosity toward Anonymous *RT.com April 23, 2012*

AnonPaste allows the user to determine when the post is to be deleted at a time increment of his or her choosing. The creators of this new haven for captured data promote a secure forum without advertisements, censorship or connection logs, and which retains only encrypted data.[288] AnonPaste was registered in the New Zealand–administered Tokelau (.tk) which allows everybody to register a free domain. It relies solely on donations as advertisements are not featured.[289]

When WikiLeaks sought to verify the data captured during the intrusion into the intelligence company, Stratfor in December 2011, part of Anonymous was frustrated with the slow release of their bounty and launched Par:AnoIA (Potentially Alarming Research: Anonymous Intelligence Agency). It also appears to be an attempt at solving a problem high-volume Web sites are struggling with everywhere: the sensible organization of humungous amounts of data.[290] The Anons who run the page say their sole task is to present the data others from the Anonymous collective have hacked in a usable format.[291] At the time of writing, neither AnonPaste nor Par:AnoIA were workable Web sites.

Anonymous-OS 0.1/Live

The Ubuntu 11.10-based operating system released for "education purposes,"[292] Anonymous OS Live allegedly performed security checks on Web sites testing for password-security and simulating DDoS attacks.[293] As default search engine, it used DuckDuckGo and it came with a host of preinstalled applications, which included Tor, Slowloris, and AnonymousHOIC.[294] In its initial news release, The Hacker News warned that a genuine source of the operating system is not apparent and that it could be "backdoored" by law enforcement or affiliated hackers.[295] Accompanying the software, a Tumblr and About page provided news and updates and the disclaimer that the user—not the developers—is responsible for any illegal use of the operating system for a screenshot of Anonymous-OS 0.1 see Figure 6.10.[296,297]

In the 4 days following its release, the operating software was downloaded over 26,000 times and enjoyed user ratings of 62%.[299] The free application was quickly marred by doubts about its true origin and the Web site hosting its free download, SourceForge, eventually closed the project site and removed the downloads from its server.[300] Official Twitter accounts, AnonOps, YourAnonNews, and AnonNewsSec warned it was "wrapped in Trojans"[301] while its creators denied it was spyware.[302,303]

[jj]Anonpaste.org, last accessed May 12/2012—no entries.

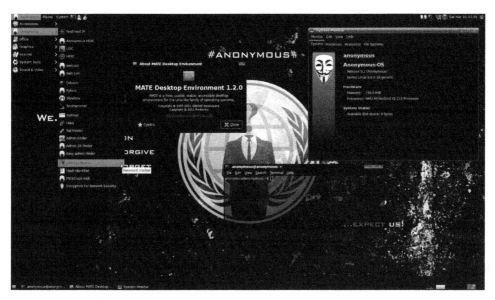

FIGURE 6.10   Screenshot of the Anonymous Operating System—essentially, a Linux distribution. (For color version of this figure, the reader is referred to the online version of this chapter.) *Source: Softpedia, March 16, 2012.*[298]

In July 2012, an effort to represent itself in the media world without the bias other news outlets[304] are accused of carrying took forms in "AnonPR" (anonpr.net, complete with newsletter subscription) and "Anonymous Analytics" (anonanalytics.com, featuring "research" and a mirror of media reports on Anonymous).

SUMMARY

This chapter represents the attempt to outline what the hitherto most notorious hacker collective, Anonymous, might look like on a whiteboard. Publically available hints toward its structure had been followed and explored: the possible initial "directorate" recruited from an idealist veteran hacking group as well as the better known online seedbed, a mingling place for contempt and counterculture. Whatever the beginnings, Anonymous is driven by a set of motivations largely shared by those whose actions are most visible: freedom of information and the right to online privacy. There are a certain number of online arenas that are used to decide upon, plan, and organize a hack—mostly using SQL injection or a related, basic hacker skill that grants access to target systems. Personal, confidential, and otherwise compromising data are later dumped on one or more popular file-sharing sites mainly to give evidence of the intrusion. Mostly after capturing sensitive data, but not requiring this more or less clandestine step a DDoS attack is used to render the target Web site inaccessible. In some cases, Web site defacement prominently displayed the reason and goals of Anonymous' interference. Over its history, the collective experienced dedicated functional spin offs (e.g., LulzSec) or ideological derivatives who sought to be more "pure" (e.g., MalSec) whose history and demise is antidote as well as a defining element of Anonymous' structure. The political hacktivists also encountered like-minded collaborators (e.g., PLF), who probably helped to emphasize this facet of the collective. Finally, this chapter sought to display representative motivations, modi operandi, and tools through the brief description of select hacks. In the wake of Anonymous' refocusing or just the skilled public relation work of a few Anons, the chapter concludes with examples for the nascent stage of products: a music portal, two dumping sites, and a highly controversial, quickly retracted operating system.

Anonymous might be more the history of hacking exploits than a social structure, but in the role of Sabu alone it contradicts its claims of being a legion of countless "everybodies." Sabu organized, motivated, and lead many of the highly popularized hacks in 2011. His absence after the March 2012 arrests was noticeable and it forced LulzSec to reinvent itself. The global wave of arrests in 2011 and especially those in early 2012[305] are perceived by some as crippling for the Anonymous collective,[306] which can only be the case for an organization that is hierarchically structured. Detentions can have effects on the activity-level of a group only, if the arrested individuals were crucial in the organization of the activities. Whether there is or was a handful of people conceiving and directing the politically aware and active Anonymous, the collective appears to be much more than a loosely knit organization now. The collective action presented in its every hack represents an enormous challenge not only to the reader who seeks to wrap her head around this virtual phenomenon but also to the social scientist. Initially self-proclaimed members of the collective without any real-world connection to fellow hacktivists, political Anons may form real local groups with regular meetings and faces, real names. In the virtual meeting spaces (user), name recognition still applies and allows for virtual groups and Anonymous-spin offs to be formed. But the numerical majority of the collective remains elusive with many different levels of possible engagement ranging from sympathizers to participants in DDoS attacks. The world-spanning virtual social network, which conceives, decides, plans, and organizes hacking exploits is what and who Anonymous really is: a number of IRC-channels, blogs and message boards accessed from (at least) several hundred thousand devices all around the globe. 4chan might have been its cradle, but so far it seems Anonymous has risen beyond this tactless, seedy playground with its bored opportunists, tricksters, and hustlers.

So far, it seems the political activists have by and large conquered the movement, though it cannot completely abandon its trickster nature. The Janus-faced character of the collective is reflected in its every aspect from activity, to the motivation and the understanding of itself is due to the myriad of individuals who have used the Anonymous platform for very different reasons. In a handful of interviews some self-proclaimed Anons try to fixate an image for the collective, but due to the elusiveness of its membership it will be difficult to instill and maintain. The political hactivists the Anonymous collective depend on its favorable depiction in the media since the nature of its preferred modus operandi, the employment of the low-orbit ion cannon in DDoS attacks, hinges on a large number of volunteers. The advance in new alleyways with the launches of the Anonymous operating system, the music sharing Web site as well as the data dump sites, albeit with different levels of success, help diversify the collective, but are also evidence of the lack of guidelines for members, that could serve as identity markers.

SUGGESTED FURTHER READING

Parmy Olson's 2012 book, *We Are* Anonymous—*Inside the Hacker World of LulzSec, Anonymous, and the Global Cyber Insurgency*, is a very readable synergy of documentary and novel that explores aspects of the *Anonymous* collective by following the exploits of a fictitious hacker. Some of Olson's story is mirrored in insider Cole Stryker's account of the legendary *4chan* message board in *Epic Win for* Anonymous—*How 4chan's Army Conquered the Web* (2011).

For a more, general perspective on how the Internet has changed social movements, we recommend Clay Shirky's 2008 *Here Comes Everybody—The Power of Organizing Without Organizations*. Finally, one of the best known early computer espionage stories is Clifford Stoll's classic *The Cuckoo's Egg—Tracking a Spy Through the Maze of Computer Espionage*, which provides a first-hand account of the KGB-hack. This was later made into a television documentary entitled *The KGB, the Computer, and Me*.

References

1. Crenshaw A. Crude, inconsistent threat: understanding anonymous. Irongeek.com. http://www.irongeek.com/i.php?page=security/understanding-anonymous; undated [last accessed May 12, 2012].
2. Jeffries A. Anonymous declares war: on October 10 at 3.30p.m., the New York Stock Exchange will be no more [updated]. BetaBeat. Available at: http://betabeat.com/2011/10/anonymous-declares-war-on-october-10-at-330-p-m-the-new-york-stock-exchange-will-be-no-more/; October 4, 2011 [last accessed between December 2012 and February 2013].
3. Twitpic anonymous circle (@AnonCircle). http://twitpic.com/9bzxon, 2012 [last accessed between December 2012 and February 2013].
4. Ars Technica. The hackers hacked: main anonymous servers invaded. http://arstechnica.com/tech-policy/2011/05/the-hackers-hacked-main-anonymous-irc-servers-seized/; May 9, 2011 [last accessed between December 2012 and February 2013].
5. Ars Technica. The hackers hacked: main anonymous servers invaded. http://arstechnica.com/tech-policy/2011/05/the-hackers-hacked-main-anonymous-irc-servers-seized/; May 9, 2011 [last accessed between December 2012 and February 2013].
6. Ars Technica. The hackers hacked: main anonymous servers invaded. http://arstechnica.com/tech-policy/2011/05/the-hackers-hacked-main-anonymous-irc-servers-seized/; May 9, 2011 [last accessed between December 2012 and February 2013].
7. IT World. A conversation with commander X. http://www.itworld.com/internet/137590/conversation-commander-x?page=0%2C0; February 18, 2011 [last accessed between December 2012 and February 2013].
8. Computer Chaos Club Regional. http://www.ccc.de/de/regional [last accessed February 24, 2012].
9. Chaos Computer Club website, main page. http://www.ccc.de/de/ [last accessed March 1, 2012].
10. Tagesspiegel. Wau Holland: Hacken als Kulturleistung. http://www.tagesspiegel.de/zeitung/wau-holland-hacken-als-kulturleistung/245264.html; July 31, 2001 [last accessed between December 2012 and February 2013].
11. German issues of Die Datenschleuder can be found here: http://chaosradio.ccc.de/datenschleuder.html, Die Datenschleuder web site: http://ds.ccc.de/. [last accessed between December 2012 and February 2013].
12. Der Spiegel. Hacker-Club veröffentlicht Schäubles Fingerabdruck. http://www.spiegel.de/netzwelt/web/0,1518,544203,00.html; March 29, 2008 [last accessed between December 2012 and February 2013].
13. Ibid.
14. Der Spiegel. Nachruf auf Wau Holland—Ein ständiger Denkanstoß. http://www.spiegel.de/netzwelt/web/0,1518,147844,00.html; July 30, 2001 [in German]. [last accessed between December 2012 and February 2013].
15. Der Tagesspiegel. Freier Zugang für alle zu allen Informationen; July 31, 2001.
16. Heise online. Hacken als Form der Gesellschaftskritik. http://www.heise.de/tp/artikel/9/9195/1.html; July 30, 2001 [last accessed between December 2012 and February 2013].
17. Ibid.
18. Chaos Computer Club Preamble. http://www.ccc.de/de/club/statutes [last accessed March 1, 2012].
19. c't Magazin. Chaos Computer Club veröffentlicht Flugplan des Sommercamps. http://www.heise.de/ct/meldung/Chaos-Computer-Club-veroeffentlicht-Flugplan-des-Sommercamps-1279300.html; July 14, 2011 [in German]. [last accessed between December 2012 and February 2013].
20. Der Spiegel. Ein Flugzeug voller Hacker. http://www.spiegel.de/netzwelt/tech/0,1518,499247,00.html; August 10, 2007 [in German]. [last accessed between December 2012 and February 2013].

21. SIGINT website. http://sigint.ccc.de/Main_Page [last accessed March 1, 2012].
22. Textfiles presents an article of *Die Zeit*. Bildschirmtext: a blow against the system—a computer club discovers breaches of security in the Bundespost's BTX Program. *Die Zeit*. http://www.textfiles.com/news/boh-20f8.txt; November 30, 1984 [last accessed March 1, 2012].
23. Activism @ suite 101. Hacktivism: what is the chaos computer club? http://joharrington.suite101.com/hacktivism-what-is-the-chaos-computer-club-a387917; September 8, 2011 [last accessed March 1, 2012].
24. A Karl Koch biography. http://www.hagbard-celine.de/main.html [last accessed March 1, 2012].
25. Der Spiegel. German Foundation on Funding WikiLeaks: 'donations were as strong as now'. http://www.spiegel.de/international/world/0,1518,734318,00.html; December 13, 2010 [last accessed between December 2012 and February 2013].
26. Wau Holland Foundation website. http://www.wauland.de/english.html. [last accessed between December 2012 and February 2013].
27. The Local. WikiLeaks sponsor in trouble with the tax man. http://www.thelocal.de/national/20101207-31651.html, a transparency report of the foundation for 2010 can be found here: http://wauland.de/files/2010_Transparenzbericht-Projekt04_de.pdf; December 7, 2010 [in German]. [last accessed between December 2012 and February 2013].
28. Der Spiegel. German foundation on funding WikiLeaks: 'donations were as strong as now'. http://www.spiegel.de/international/world/0,1518,734318,00.html; December 13, 2010. [last accessed between December 2012 and February 2013].
29. *The Wall Street Journal*. How WikiLeaks keeps its funding secret. http://online.wsj.com/article/SB10001424052748704554104575436231926853198.html?mod=WSJ_hpp_MIDDLENexttoWhatsNewsForth; August 23, 2010. [last accessed between December 2012 and February 2013].
30. IT World. A conversation with commander X. http://www.itworld.com/internet/137590/conversation-commander-x?page=0%2C0; February 18, 2011 [last accessed between December 2012 and February 2013].
31. National Post. Insider tells why anonymous might well be the most powerful organization on Earth. http://digg.com/newsbar/Technology/fugitive_hacker_christopher_doyon_or_commander_x_tells_why_anonymous_might_well_be_the_most_powerful_organization_on_earth_news_national_post; May 13, 2012 [last accessed between December 2012 and February 2013].
32. National Post. Online Group Declares War on Scientology. http://web.archive.org/web/20080129063500/http://www.nationalpost.com/most_popular/story.html?id=261308; January 26, 2008 [last accessed between December 2012 and February 2013].
33. LA Weekly. My date with anonymous: a rare interview with the elusive Internet troublemakers. http://www.laweekly.com/2009-02-05/columns/my-date-with-anonymous-a-rare-interview-with-the-illusive-internet-troublemakers/; February 4, 2009 [last accessed between December 2012 and February 2013].
34. Advertise. 4chan.org. http://www.4chan.org/advertise. [last accessed between December 2012 and February 2013].
35. Ibid.
36. *NY Times*. One on one: Christopher Poole, Founder of 4chan. http://bits.blogs.nytimes.com/2010/03/19/one-on-one-christopher-poole-founder-of-4chan/; March 19, 2012 [last accessed between December 2012 and February 2013].
37. Corman J, Martin B. Cognitive dissidents. Building a better anonymous-series. http://blog.cognitivedissidents.com/2012/04/12/building-a-better-anonymous-series-part-5/; 2011 [last accessed between December 2012 and February 2013].
38. Know Your Meme. Internet hate machine. http://knowyourmeme.com/memes/internet-hate-machine; May 1, 2012 [last accessed between December 2012 and February 2013].
39. Corman J, Martin B. Cognitive dissidents. Building a better anonymous-series. http://blog.cognitivedissidents.com/2012/04/12/building-a-better-anonymous-series-part-5/; 2011 [last accessed between December 2012 and February 2013].
40. Stryker C. Epic Win for anonymous—How 4chan's army conquered the Web. New York, Boston, London: Overlook Duckworth; 2011 p. 17–20.
41. Stryker C. Epic win for anonymous—How 4chan's army conquered the web. New York, Boston, London: Overlook Duckworth; 2011 p. 33.
42. NineMSN. The Internet Pranksters who started a war. http://news.ninemsn.com.au/article.aspx?id=459214; May 8, 2008. [last accessed between December 2012 and February 2013].
43. M-J via Wikipedia. File: Lolcat.jpg. http://en.wikipedia.org/wiki/File:Lolcat.jpg. [last accessed between December 2012 and February 2013].

44. Know Your Meme. Tay zonday/chocolate rain. http://knowyourmeme.com/memes/tay-zonday-chocolate-rain; April 2012 [last accessed between December 2012 and February 2013].

45. Know Your Meme. Rickroll. http://knowyourmeme.com/memes/rickroll; February 2012 [last accessed between December 2012 and February 2013].

46. NineMSN. The Internet Pranksters who started a war. http://news.ninemsn.com.au/article.aspx?id=459214; May 8, 2008 [last accessed between December 2012 and February 2013].

47. Crenshaw A. Crude, inconsistent threat: understanding anonymous. *Irongeek.com*. http://www.irongeek.com/i.php?page=security/understanding-anonymous [last accessed May 12, 2012].

48. Montreal Gazette. Christopher Doyon, one of the brains behind anonymous. http://www.montrealgazette.com/technology/Christopher+Doyon+brains+behind+Anonymous/6612381/story.html; May 12, 2012 [last accessed between December 2012 and February 2013].

49. Know Your Meme. Epic fail guy. http://knowyourmeme.com/memes/epic-fail-guy. [last accessed between December 2012 and February 2013].

50. Know Your Meme. Epic fail guy. http://knowyourmeme.com/memes/epic-fail-guy. [last accessed between December 2012 and February 2013].

51. CNet. Anonymous invites CIA, others to its weekend party. http://news.cnet.com/8301-1009_3-57375923-83/anonymous-invites-cia-others-to-its-weekend-party/; February 11, 2012 [last accessed between December 2012 and February 2013].

52. Wired. Par:AnoIA: anonymous launches WikiLeaks-esque site for data dumps. http://www.wired.com/threatlevel/2012/07/paranoia-anonymous/all/and many others; July 13, 2012 [last accessed between December 2012 and February 2013].

53. ITWorld. A conversation with Commander X. http://www.itworld.com/internet/137590/conversation-commander-x?page=0%2C0; February 18, 2011 [last accessed between December 2012 and February 2013].

54. Peoples Liberation Front website. www.peoplesliberationfront.net [last accessed May 15, 2012].

55. ITWorld. A conversation with commander X. http://www.itworld.com/internet/137590/conversation-commander-x?page=0%2C0; February 18, 2011 [last accessed between December 2012 and February 2013].

56. ITWorld. A conversation with commander X. http://www.itworld.com/internet/137590/conversation-commander-x?page=0%2C0; February 18, 2011 [last accessed between December 2012 and February 2013].

57. Peoples Liberation Front Campaigns Archive. http://peoplesliberationfront.net/campaigns.html [last accessed May 15, 2012].

58. Stryker C. Epic Win for anonymous; 2011, p. 72. [last accessed between December 2012 and February 2013].

59. Crenshaw A. Crude, inconsistent threat. *Irongeek*. http://www.irongeek.com/i.php?page=security/understanding-anonymous; undated [last accessed July 16, 2012].

60. Stryker C. Epic Win for anonymous; 2011, p. 72.

61. Crenshaw A. Crude, inconsistent threat. *Irongeek*. http://www.irongeek.com/i.php?page=security/understanding-anonymous; undated [last accessed July 16, 2012].

62. Gawker. A 4channer explains why 4chan's decline is great for 4chan. http://gawker.com/5925847/a-4channer-explains-why-4chans-decline-is-great-for-4chan; July 13, 2012 [last accessed between December 2012 and February 2013].

63. Coleman G. Anonymous. In: Wiedemann C, Zehle S, editors. Glossary of network ecologies, theory on demand. Amsterdam, NL: Institute of Network Cultures; April 2012.

64. Olson P. We are anonymous—inside the hacker world of LulzSec, anonymous, and the global cyber insurgency. New York, Boston, London: Little, Brown and Company; 2012.

65. Jacobson J. We are legion: Anonymous and the war on scientology. http://www.lisamcpherson.org/pc.htm; undated. [last accessed between December 2012 and February 2013].

66. LAist. Church of scientology strikes back—anonymous responds. http://laist.com/2008/03/23/church_of_scien.php; March 23, 2008 [last accessed between December 2012 and February 2013].

67. ITWorld. A conversation with commander X. http://www.itworld.com/internet/137590/conversation-commander-x?page=0%2C0; February 18, 2011 [last accessed between December 2012 and February 2013].

68. Baltimore City Paper. Serious business. http://www2.citypaper.com/columns/story.asp?id=15543; April 2, 2008 [last accessed between December 2012 and February 2013].

69. Zone-h. Anonymous' LulzXmas (video). http://zone-h.org/mirror/id/16416728; December 24, 2011 [last accessed between December 2012 and February 2013].

70. Pastebin entry by "Guest." Emergency Christmas Anonymous Press Release. http://pastebin.com/8yrwyNkt; December 25, 2011 [last accessed between December 2012 and February 2013].

71. Pastebin entry by "Guest." Merry LulzXmas. http://pastebin.com/q5kXd7Fd; December 26, 2011 [last accessed between December 2012 and February 2013].

72. Spiegel. Hackers against neo-nazis—anonymous takes on Germany's far-right. http://www.spiegel.de/international/germany/hackers-against-neo-nazis-anonymous-takes-on-germany-s-far-right-a-806939.html; January 3, 2012 [last accessed between December 2012 and February 2013].

73. Baltimore City Paper. Serious business. http://www2.citypaper.com/columns/story.asp?id=15543; April 2, 2008 [last accessed between December 2012 and February 2013].

74. Baltimore City Paper. Serious business. http://www2.citypaper.com/columns/story.asp?id=15543; April 2, 2008 [last accessed between December 2012 and February 2013].

75. Olson P. We are anonymous—inside the hacker world of LulzSec, anonymous, and the global cyber insurgency. Little, Brown and Company; 2012.

76. Coppens P. V for Vendetta. Available at: http://www.philipcoppens.com/vforvendetta.html; IMDb. Memorable quotes for 'V for Vendetta' (2005). Available at: http://www.imdb.com/title/tt0434409/quotes; undated. [last accessed between December 2012 and February 2013].

77. Olson P. We are anonymous—inside the hacker world of LulzSec, anonymous, and the global cyber insurgency. Little, Brown and Company; 2012.

78. Twitpic Anonymous Circle. @AnonCircle. http://twitpic.com/96aqz7. [last accessed between December 2012 and February 2013].

79. Pastebin entry by "Guest." Anonymous: Project Mayhem 2012// Call to Action—Code Tyler!. http://pastebin.com/SS467cim; May 22, 2012 [last accessed between December 2012 and February 2013].

80. CNN. Inside the offices of Occupy Wall Street. http://news.blogs.cnn.com/2011/12/01/exclusive-inside-the-offices-of-occupy-wall-street/; December 1, 2011 [last accessed between December 2012 and February 2013].

81. CNN. Hacker group anonymous is a nuisance, not a threat. http://money.cnn.com/2012/01/20/technology/anonymous_hack/index.htm; January 20, 2012 [last accessed between December 2012 and February 2013].

82. Twitpic Anonymous Circle. @AnonCircle. http://twitpic.com/9bzxon. [last accessed between December 2012 and February 2013].

83. Anonymous on Fox 11. YouTube. http://www.youtube.com/watch?v=DNO6G4ApJQY&noredirect=1. [last accessed between December 2012 and February 2013].

84. *New York Times*. Man, 20, arrested in Stadium Threat Hoax. http://www.nytimes.com/2006/10/21/us/21stadium.html?_r=1&ex=1185681600&en=6f5000744e8dd0aa&ei=5070; October 21, 2006 [last accessed between December 2012 and February 2013].

85. *LA Weekly*. My date with anonymous: a rare interview with the elusive internet troublemakers. http://www.laweekly.com/2009-02-05/columns/my-date-with-anonymous-a-rare-interview-with-the-illusive-internet-troublemakers/; February 4, 2009. [last accessed between December 2012 and February 2013].

86. NineMSN. The Internet pranksters who started a war. http://news.ninemsn.com.au/article.aspx?id=459214; May 8, 2008 [last accessed between December 2012 and February 2013].

87. C-Net. Anonymous invites CIA, others to it's weekend party. http://news.cnet.com/8301-1009_3-57375923-83/anonymous-invites-cia-others-to-its-weekend-party/; February 11, 2012 [last accessed between December 2012 and February 2013].

88. http://www.peoplesliberationfront.org/ [last accessed February 25, 2012].

89. The Next Web. Julian assange shows up at occupy London wearing an anonymous mask. http://thenextweb.com/uk/2011/10/16/julian-assange-shows-up-at-occupy-london-wearing-an-anonymous-mask/; October 16, 2011 [last accessed between December 2012 and February 2013].

90. Softpedia. Anonymous pledges full support for WikiLeaks and Julian assange. http://news.softpedia.com/news/Anonymous-Pledges-Full-Support-for-WikiLeaks-and-Julian-Assange-170812.shtml; December 6, 2010 [last accessed between December 2012 and February 2013].

91. BBC News. Anonymous hacktivists say WikiLeaks war to continue. http://www.bbc.com/news/technology-11935539; December 9, 2010 [last accessed between December 2012 and February 2013].

92. The Guardian. WikiLeaks releases first 200 of 5m Stratfor emails. http://www.guardian.co.uk/media/2012/feb/27/wikileaks-stratfor-emails-anonymous; February 27, 2012 [last accessed between December 2012 and February 2013].

93. IB Times. Anonymous reveals 'heavy crossover of personnel' with WikiLeaks. http://www.ibtimes.co.uk/articles/363328/20120716/anonymous-wikileaks-hackers-syria-files-antisec-paranoia.htm; July 16, 2012 [last accessed between December 2012 and February 2013].

94. InformationWeek. Anonymous hands WikiLeaks 2.4 million Syrian emails. http://www.informationweek.com/news/security/attacks/240003443; July 10, 2012 [last accessed between December 2012 and February 2013].

95. IB Times. Anonymous declares war on WikiLeaks after Syria files' row. http://www.ibtimes.co.uk/articles/362768/20120713/wikileaks-anonymous-war-anonymousirc-syria-files-stratfor.htm; July 13, 2012 [last accessed between December 2012 and February 2013].

96. Wired. Par:AnoIA: anonymous launches WikiLeaks-esque site for data dumps. http://www.wired.com/threatlevel/2012/07/paranoia-anonymous/all/; July 13, 2012 [last accessed between December 2012 and February 2013].

97. PCMag. With PasteBin 'compromised', anonymous launches anonpaste. http://www.pcmag.com/article2/0,2817,2403283,00.asp; April 19, 2012 [last accessed between December 2012 and February 2013].

98. Peoples Liberation Front. Internet Freedom Fighters. http://www.peoplesliberationfront.net/. [last accessed between December 2012 and February 2013].

99. Peoples Liberation Front. Internet Freedom Fighters. http://www.peoplesliberationfront.net/. [last accessed between December 2012 and February 2013].

100. Peoples Liberation Front. Peoples Liberation Front Manifesto. http://www.peoplesliberationfront.net/manifesto.html. [last accessed between December 2012 and February 2013].

101. Ibid.

102. Peoples Liberation Front. Allied Organizations. http://www.peoplesliberationfront.net/. [last accessed between December 2012 and February 2013].

103. Cyber War Zone. Christopher Doyon, one of the brains behind Anonymous. http://www.cyberwarzone.com/cyberwarfare/christopher-doyon-one-brains-behind-anonymous; May 13, 2012; Vancouver News. Christopher Doyon, one of the brains behind anonymous. http://vancouverne.ws/?p=80; May 13, 2012 [last accessed between December 2012 and February 2013].

104. TPM. Homeless Hacker' Christopher Doyon, aka 'Commander X', Joins up with occupy movement. http://idealab.talkingpointsmemo.com/2011/10/homeless-hacker-christopher-doyon-aka-commander-x-joins-up-with-occupy-movement.php; October 27, 2011 [last accessed between December 2012 and February 2013].

105. The Gazette. Christopher Doyon, one of the brains behind anonymous. http://www.montrealgazette.com/technology/Christopher+Doyon+brains+behind+Anonymous/6612381/story.html; May 12, 2012; National Post. Insider tells why anonymous might well be the most powerful organization on Earth. http://news.nationalpost.com/2012/05/12/insider-tells-why-anonymous-might-well-be-the-most-powerful-organization-on-earth/; May 12, 2012 [last accessed between December 2012 and February 2013].

106. CyberWarNews. Adult site digital play ground hacked, defaced and data leaked by @Th3Consortium. http://www.cyberwarnews.info/2012/03/05/adult-site-digital-play-ground-hacked-defaced-and-data-leaked-by-th3consortium/; March 5, 2012; CyberWarzone. Hackers Discover US government employees using work emails on porn websites. http://cyberwarzone.com/cyberwarfare/hackers-discover-us-government-employees-using-work-emails-porn-websites; March 13, 2012 [last accessed between December 2012 and February 2013].

107. Pastebin Entry by "A Guest." Untitled—#FuckSopa, #FuckActa, #FuckSec—TheConsortium—#Resistance, #AntiSec, #Riseup. http://pastebin.com/UYRcy3J9; March 7, 2012. [last accessed between December 2012 and February 2013].

108. The Independent. Team poison hackers claim to have recorded anti-terrorist hotline calls. http://www.independent.co.uk/news/uk/crime/team-poison-hackers-claim-to-have-recorded-antiterrorist-hotline-calls-7640090.html; April 12, 2012 [last accessed between December 2012 and February 2013].

109. CNet. RIM blog hacked in warning over London unrest. http://news.cnet.com/8301-1009_3-20090211-83/rim-blog-hacked-in-warning-over-london-unrest/; August 9, 2011; GeekTech. Team poison hits blackberry website. http://www.geektech.in/archives/2328; August 10, 2011 [last accessed between December 2012 and February 2013].

110. The Telegraph. Tony Blair's personal details 'hacked. http://www.telegraph.co.uk/news/politics/tony-blair/8598172/Tony-Blairs-personal-details-hacked.html; June 25, 2011 [last accessed between December 2012 and February 2013].

111. V3. TeaMp0isoN posts stolen United Nations credentials online. http://www.v3.co.uk/v3-uk/news/2128926/teampoison-post-stolen-credentials-online; November 30, 2011 [last accessed between December 2012 and February 2013].

112. MSNBC. Team poison hackers hit UN, Australian Government sites. http://www.msnbc.msn.com/id/47298755/ns/technology_and_science-security/t/team-poison-hackers-hit-un-australian-government-sites/#.UBNonrTY8Xs; May 4, 2012 [last accessed between December 2012 and February 2013].

113. CNet. RIM blog hacked in warning over London unrest, http://news.cnet.com/8301-1009_3-20090211-83/rim-blog-hacked-in-warning-over-london-unrest/; August 9, 2011 [last accessed between December 2012 and February 2013].

114. Ars Technica. Anonymous goes after Sony, makes it personal . . . very personal. http://arstechnica.com/tech-pol icy/2011/04/anonymous-goes-after-sony-makes-it-personal-very-personal/; April 7, 2011 [last accessed between December 2012 and February 2013].

115. Greenberg A. Anonymous and ex-anonymous hackers wage war of identification. *Forbes.* http://www. forbes.com/sites/andygreenberg/2011/03/22/anonymous-and-ex-anonymous-hackers-wage-a-war-of-identification/; March 22, 2011 [last accessed between December 2012 and February 2013].

116. Ars Technica. Anonymous goes after sony, makes it personal . . . very personal. http://arstechnica.com/tech-pol icy/2011/04/anonymous-goes-after-sony-makes-it-personal-very-personal/; April 7, 2011 [last accessed between December 2012 and February 2013].

117. Goodchild J. Social engineering: the basics. *CSO Data Protection.* http://www.csoonline.com/article/514063/ social-engineering-the-basics; not dated [accessed October 14, 2012].

118. Goodchild J. 15 Social media scams. *CSO Data Protection.* http://www.csoonline.com/slideshow/detail/52935/ 15-social-media-scams?source=csointcpt_ss#slide1; June 20, 2012 [last accessed between December 2012 and February 2013].

119. Bright P. Anonymous speaks: the inside story of the HBGary hack. *Ars Technica.* http://arstechnica.com/tech-pol icy/2011/02/anonymous-speaks-the-inside-story-of-the-hbgary-hack/; February 15, 2011 [last accessed between December 2012 and February 2013].

120. TriCk @ TeaMp0isoN. https://twitter.com/_TeaMp0isoN. [last accessed between December 2012 and February 2013].

121. The Telegraph. Two arrested after hackers attacked anti-terror hotline. http://www.telegraph.co.uk/news/ 9201621/Two-arrested-after-hackers-attacked-anti-terror-hotline.html; April 12, 2011 [last accessed between December 2012 and February 2013].

122. MSNBC. Team poison hacks MI6—then calls to boast. http://www.msnbc.msn.com/id/47032601/ns/technol ogy_and_science-security/t/team-poison-hacks-mi-then-calls-boast/#.UBN4M7TY8Xs; April 12, 2012 [last accessed between December 2012 and February 2013].

123. V3. Team poison hackers threaten authorities over leader's arrest. http://www.v3.co.uk/v3-uk/news/2167934/ team-poison-hackers-threaten-authorities-leaders-arrest; April 16, 2012 [last accessed between December 2012 and February 2013].

124. The Telegraph. Team poison' hacker who posted Tony Blair's details is jailed. http://www.telegraph.co.uk/ technology/internet-security/9432459/Team-Poison-hacker-who-posted-Tony-Blairs-details-is-jailed.html; July 27, 2012 [last accessed between December 2012 and February 2013].

125. FoxNews. Exclusive: rival hacker group racing police to expose LulzSec. http://www.foxnews.com/tech/2011/ 06/23/hacker-vs-hacker-group-races-police-to-expose-lulzsec/; June 23, 2011 [last accessed between December 2012 and February 2013].

126. PCMag. Hacker promises to leak personal details of Tony Blair, MPs. http://www.pcmag.com/article2/ 0,2817,2387563,00.asp; June 24, 2011 [last accessed between December 2012 and February 2013].

127. MSNBC. British Cops arrest third 'team poison' hacker. http://www.msnbc.msn.com/id/47388075/ns/ technology_and_science-security/t/british-cops-arrest-third-team-poison-hacker/#.UBNoi7TY8Xs; May 11, 2011 [last accessed between December 2012 and February 2013].

128. "iN^SaNe" quoted in PCMag. Hacker promises to leak personal details of Tony Blair, MPs. http://www.pcmag. com/article2/0,2817,2387563,00.asp; June 24, 2011 [last accessed between December 2012 and February 2013].

129. PCMag. Hacker promises to leak personal details of Tony Blair, MPs. http://www.pcmag.com/article2/ 0,2817,2387563,00.asp; June 24, 2011 [last accessed between December 2012 and February 2013].

130. FoxNews. Exclusive: rival hacker group racing police to expose LulzSec. http://www.foxnews.com/tech/2011/ 06/23/hacker-vs-hacker-group-races-police-to-expose-lulzsec/; June 23, 2011 [last accessed between December 2012 and February 2013].

131. FoxNews. Exclusive: rival hacker group racing police to expose LulzSec. http://www.foxnews.com/tech/2011/ 06/23/hacker-vs-hacker-group-races-police-to-expose-lulzsec/; June 23, 2011 [last accessed between December 2012 and February 2013].

132. FoxNews. Exclusive: rival hacker group racing police to expose LulzSec. http://www.foxnews.com/tech/2011/ 06/23/hacker-vs-hacker-group-races-police-to-expose-lulzsec/; June 23, 2011 [last accessed between December 2012 and February 2013].

133. Anonymous Central. OpRobinHood: TeaMp0isoN and anonymous. http://anoncentral.tumblr.com/post/ 13453268660/oprobinhood-teamp0ison-and-anonymous-hello-we; November 2011 [last accessed between December 2012 and February 2013].

134. V3. Anonymous and TeaMp0isoN launch Op Robin Hood to hack credit card details. http://www.v3.co.uk/v3-uk/news/2129032/anonymous-teamp0ison-launch-op-robin-hood-hack-card-details; November 30, 2011 [last accessed between December 2012 and February 2013].

135. V3. Team poison hackers threaten authorities over leader's arrest. http://www.v3.co.uk/v3-uk/news/2167934/team-poison-hackers-threaten-authorities-leaders-arrest; April 16, 2012 [last accessed between December 2012 and February 2013].

136. #FreeAnons. #Freeanons: solidarity with R3dH4ck—Redhack Ile Dayanisma. http://freeanons.org/freeanons-solidarity-with-r3dh4ck-redhack-ile-dayanisma/; April 23, 2012 [last accessed between December 2012 and February 2013].

137. Cyberguerilla. FreeAnons: solidarity with R3dH4ck—Redhack Ile Dayanisma. http://www.cyberguerrilla.info/?p=5492; April 27, 2012 [last accessed between December 2012 and February 2013].

138. http://twitter.com/r3dh4ck. [last accessed between December 2012 and February 2013].

139. #OpSupportRedHack. To all anons. http://www.dinkypage.com/152691/; undated. [last accessed between December 2012 and February 2013].

140. AnonymousNews. Anonymous takes down Turkish police, Intel Websites/#OpSupportRedHack. http://anonymousnews.blogs.ru/2012/07/19/anonymous-takes-down-turkish-police-intel-websites-opsupportredhack/; July 19, 2012 [last accessed between December 2012 and February 2013].

141. YouTube. MalSec—don't worry, we're from the internet. http://www.youtube.com/watch?v=Fu_8qD8BrWQ; April 11, 2011 [last accessed between December 2012 and February 2013].

142. The Inquirer. Malicious security joins the anonymous cause. http://www.theinquirer.net/inquirer/news/2167188/malicious-security-joins-anonymous-cause; April 11, 2012 [last accessed between December 2012 and February 2013].

143. YouTube. MalSec—don't worry, we're from the internet. http://www.youtube.com/watch?v=Fu_8qD8BrWQ; April 11, 2011 [last accessed between December 2012 and February 2013].

144. Security News Daily. New anonymous spinoff vows to be ethical, breaks vow. http://www.securitynewsdaily.com/1719-anonymous-malsec-ethical-hacking.html; April 11, 2012 [last accessed between December 2012 and February 2013].

145. Softpedia. MalSec leaks data from Arizona state legislature. http://news.softpedia.com/news/MalSec-Leaks-Data-from-Arizona-State-Legislature-269797.shtml; May 16, 2012 [last accessed between December 2012 and February 2013].

146. Ars Technica. Hackers politely deface security firm website, suggest fixes. http://arstechnica.com/business/2012/04/hackers-politely-deface-site-of-security-firm-suggest-fixes/; April 1, 2012 [last accessed between December 2012 and February 2013].

147. C4ss (Center for a Stateless Society). The anonymous hydra grows another head. http://c4ss.org/content/10179; April 25, 2012 [last accessed between December 2012 and February 2013].

148. C4ss (Center for a Stateless Society). The Anonymous Hydra Grows Another Head. http://c4ss.org/content/10179; April.25, 2012 [last accessed between December 2012 and February 2013].

149. LulzSec Facebook profile picture. https://www.facebook.com/TheLulzBoat?fref=ts [accessed October 14, 2012]. [last accessed between December 2012 and February 2013].

150. The Telegraph. LulzSec hacker group disbands. http://www.telegraph.co.uk/technology/news/8599700/LulzSec-hacker-group-disbands.html; June 26, 2011 [last accessed between December 2012 and February 2013].

151. The Telegraph. Lulz security: PROFILE. http://www.telegraph.co.uk/news/worldnews/northamerica/usa/8578707/Lulz-Security-profile.html; June 16, 2011 [last accessed between December 2012 and February 2013].

152. The Telegraph. Fear for patient's data after hackers hit NHS. http://www.telegraph.co.uk/technology/news/8567008/Fears-for-patients-data-after-hackers-hit-NHS.html; June 9, 2011 [last accessed between December 2012 and February 2013].

153. BBC News. LulzSec hackers claim CIA website shutdown. http://www.bbc.co.uk/news/technology-13787229; June 16, 2011 [last accessed between December 2012 and February 2013].

154. BBC News. Newsight online 'chat' with Lulz security hacking group. http://www.bbc.co.uk/news/technology-13912836; June 24, 2011 [last accessed between December 2012 and February 2013].

155. The Telegraph. Lulz security: profile. http://www.telegraph.co.uk/news/worldnews/northamerica/usa/8578707/Lulz-Security-profile.html; June 16, 2011 [last accessed between December 2012 and February 2013].

156. The Telegraph. Hackers place fake story on PBS website claiming Tupak Shakur is alive. http://www.telegraph.co.uk/news/8546912/Hackers-place-fake-story-on-PBS-website-claiming-Tupac-Shakur-is-alive.html; May 31, 2011 [last accessed between December 2012 and February 2013].

157. The Telegraph. Lulz security: profile. http://www.telegraph.co.uk/news/worldnews/northamerica/usa/8578707/Lulz-Security-profile.html; June 16, 2011 [last accessed between December 2012 and February 2013].

158. The Telegraph. CIA website hacked by Lulz security. http://www.telegraph.co.uk/news/worldnews/northamerica/usa/8578704/CIA-website-hacked-by-Lulz-Security.html; June 16, 2011 [last accessed between December 2012 and February 2013].

159. BBC News. LulzSec hackers claim CIA website shutdown. http://www.bbc.co.uk/news/technology-13787229; June 16, 2011 [last accessed between December 2012 and February 2013].

160. The Telegraph. FBI charges alleged anonymous hackers after supergrass claims. http://www.telegraph.co.uk/technology/news/9127004/FBI-charges-alleged-Anonymous-hackers-after-supergrass-claims.html; March 7, 2012 [last accessed between December 2012 and February 2013].

161. Pastebin entry by "A Guest." Operation anti-security. http://pastebin.com/9KyA0E5v; June 19, 2011 [last accessed between December 2012 and February 2013].

162. The Telegraph. Fear for patient's data after hackers hit NHS. http://www.telegraph.co.uk/technology/news/8567008/Fears-for-patients-data-after-hackers-hit-NHS.html; June 9, 2011 [last accessed between December 2012 and February 2013].

163. Huffington Post. LulzSec hacker group now taking requests. http://www.huffingtonpost.com/2011/06/15/lulzsec-hacker-group-now-_n_877309.html; June 15, 2011 [last accessed between December 2012 and February 2013].

164. KillerCube. LulsZec. http://pastebin.com/AC52iBuq; September 1, 2011 [last accessed between December 2012 and February 2013].

165. Pastebin entry "Sabu" by KillerCube. http://pastebin.com/76TsPHeU; June 22, 2011 [last accessed March 16, 2012].

166. Pastebin entry "Sabu" by KillerCube. http://pastebin.com/76TsPHeU; June 22, 2011 [last accessed March 16, 2012].

167. The Telegraph. Five 'Top LulzSec hackers' to face charges in New York. http://www.telegraph.co.uk/technology/news/9126410/Five-top-LulzSec-hackers-to-face-charges-in-New-York.html; March 6, 2012 [last accessed between December 2012 and February 2013].

168. Information Week. LulzSec Sabu arrest: don't relax yet, IT. http://www.informationweek.com/news/security/government/232602164; March 7, 2012 [last accessed between December 2012 and February 2013].

169. CNET. Will LulzSec arrests stop high-profile hacks? Don't bet on it. http://news.cnet.com/8301-27080_3-57391872-245/will-lulzsec-arrests-stop-high-profile-hacks-dont-bet-on-it/; March 6, 2012; The Register. The one tiny slip that put LulzSec chief Sabu in the FBI's pocket. http://www.theregister.co.uk/2012/03/07/lulzsec_takedown_analysis/page2.html; March 7, 2012 [last accessed between December 2012 and February 2013].

170. CNET. Will LulzSec arrests stop high-profile hacks? Don't bet on it.http://news.cnet.com/8301-27080_3-57391872-245/will-lulzsec-arrests-stop-high-profile-hacks-dont-bet-on-it/; March 6, 2012 [last accessed between December 2012 and February 2013].

171. CNET. UK police say they've arrested LulzSec's 'topiary'. http://news.cnet.com/8301-27080_3-20084255-245/u.k-police-say-theyve-arrested-lulzsecs-topiary/; July 27, 2011 [last accessed between December 2012 and February 2013].

172. The Daily Caller. Who is anonymous? A look at the hacktivists aiding revolution in the middle east. http://dailycaller.com/2011/02/26/who-is-anonymous-a-look-at-the-hacktivists-aiding-revolution-in-the-middle-east/2/; February 26, 2012 [last accessed between December 2012 and February 2013].

173. InformationWeek. LulzSec Sabu arrest: don't relax yet, IT. http://www.informationweek.com/news/security/government/232602164; March 7, 2012 [last accessed between December 2012 and February 2013].

174. The Telegraph. FBI charges alleged anonymous hackers after supergrass claims. http://www.telegraph.co.uk/technology/news/9127004/FBI-charges-alleged-Anonymous-hackers-after-supergrass-claims.html; March 7, 2012 [last accessed between December 2012 and February 2013].

175. InformationWeek. LulzSec Sabu arrest: don't relax yet, IT. http://www.informationweek.com/news/security/government/232602164; March 7, 2012 [last accessed between December 2012 and February 2013].

176. InformationWeek. LulzSec Sabu arrest: don't relax yet, IT. http://www.informationweek.com/news/security/government/232602164; March 7, 2012 [last accessed between December 2012 and February 2013].

177. The Telegraph. FBI charges alleged anonymous hackers after supergrass claims. http://www.telegraph.co.uk/technology/news/9127004/FBI-charges-alleged-Anonymous-hackers-after-supergrass-claims.html; March 7, 2012 [last accessed between December 2012 and February 2013].

178. CNET. UK police say they've arrested LulzSec's 'topiary'. http://news.cnet.com/8301-27080_3-20084255-245/u.k-police-say-theyve-arrested-lulzsecs-topiary/; July 27, 2011 [last accessed between December 2012 and February 2013].

179. The Guardian. Inside LulzSec: chatroom logs shine a light on the secretive hackers. http://www.guardian.co.uk/technology/2011/jun/24/inside-lulzsec-chatroom-logs-hackers; June 24, 2011 [last accessed between December 2012 and February 2013].

180. The Guardian. Inside LulzSec: chatroom logs shine a light on the secretive hackers. http://www.guardian.co.uk/technology/2011/jun/24/inside-lulzsec-chatroom-logs-hackers; June 24, 2011 [last accessed between December 2012 and February 2013].

181. The Telegraph. FBI charges alleged anonymous hackers after supergrass claims. http://www.telegraph.co.uk/technology/news/9127004/FBI-charges-alleged-Anonymous-hackers-after-supergrass-claims.html; March 7, 2012 [last accessed between December 2012 and February 2013].

182. Washington Post. LulzSec reborn' claims attack at military dating website. http://www.washingtonpost.com/business/technology/lulzsec-reborn-claims-attack-on-military-dating-site/2012/03/28/gIQA0UkJgS_story.html; March 28, 2012 [last accessed between December 2012 and February 2013].

183. The Inquirer. Anonymous offshoot 'CabinCr3w' member charged with hacking US police websites. http://www.theinquirer.net/inquirer/news/2168410/anonymous-offshoot-cabincr3w-charged-hacking-police-websites; April 17, 2012 [last accessed between December 2012 and February 2013].

184. MSNBC. FBI arrests cabin Cr3w hacker for Utah police attacks. http://www.msnbc.msn.com/id/47075277/ns/technology_and_science-security/t/fbi-arrests-cabin-crw-hacker-utah-police-attacks/#.UBN9e7TY8Xs; April 4, 2012 [last accessed between December 2012 and February 2013].

185. The Inquirer. Anonymous offshoot 'CabinCr3w' member charged with hacking US police websites. http://www.theinquirer.net/inquirer/news/2168410/anonymous-offshoot-cabincr3w-charged-hacking-police-websites; April 17, 2012 [last accessed between December 2012 and February 2013].

186. Softpedia. CabinCr3w hacker arrested, admits being FBI informant. http://news.softpedia.com/news/CabinCr3w-Hacker-Arrested-Admits-Being-FBI-Informant-262907.shtml; April 5, 2012 [last accessed between December 2012 and February 2013].

187. MSNBC. FBI arrests cabin Cr3w hacker for Utah police attacks. http://www.msnbc.msn.com/id/47075277/ns/technology_and_science-security/t/fbi-arrests-cabin-crw-hacker-utah-police-attacks/#.UBN9e7TY8Xs; April 4, 2012 [last accessed between December 2012 and February 2013].

188. NineMSN. The Internet Pranksters who started a war. http://news.ninemsn.com.au/article.aspx?id=459214; May 8, 2008 [last accessed between December 2012 and February 2013].

189. Baltimore City Paper. Serious business. http://www2.citypaper.com/columns/story.asp?id=15543; January 21, 2008 [last accessed between December 2012 and February 2013].

190. IT World. That new Facebook friend might just be a spy. http://www.itworld.com/internet/136830/that-new-facebook-friend-might-just-be-a-spy; February 13, 2011 [last accessed between December 2012 and February 2013].

191. Times of India. Anonymous hacks CIA website. http://articles.timesofindia.indiatimes.com/2012-02-11/security/31049746_1_cia-site-cia-website-anonymous; February 11, 2012 [last accessed between December 2012 and February 2013].

192. Crenshaw A. Crude, inconsistent threat: understanding anonymous. *Irongeek*. http://www.irongeek.com/i.php?page=security/understanding-anonymous; undated. [last accessed between December 2012 and February 2013].

193. Peoples Liberation Front. Public Campaigns. http://peoplesliberationfront.net/campaigns.html. [last accessed between December 2012 and February 2013].

194. RFE/RL. What is 'anonymous' and how does it operate. http://www.rferl.org/content/explainer_what_is_anonymous_and_how_does_it_operate/24500381.html; March 3, 2012 [last accessed between December 2012 and February 2013].

195. Crenshaw A. Crude, inconsistent threat: understanding anonymous. *Irongeek*. http://www.irongeek.com/i.php?page=security/understanding-anonymous; undated. [last accessed between December 2012 and February 2013].

196. Corman J, Martin B. Cognitive dissidents. Building a better anonymous' series, part ii: fact vs fiction. http://blog.cognitivedissidents.com/2011/12/29/building-a-better-anonymous-series-part-2/; December 29, 2011. [last accessed between December 2012 and February 2013].

197. ZDNet. Anonymous launches 'operation global blackout', aims to DDoS the root internet server. http://www.zdnet.com/blog/security/anonymous-launches-operation-global-blackout-aims-to-ddos-the-root-internet-servers/10387; February 17, 2012 [last accessed between December 2012 and February 2013].

198. The Hacker News. #RefRef—Denial of Service (DDoS) tool developed by anonymous. http://thehackernews. com/2011/07/refref-denial-of-service-ddos-tool.html; July 7, 2011 [last accessed February 21, 2012].

199. Information Week. WikiLeaks supporters download botnet tool 50,000 times. http://www.informationweek.com/ news/security/attacks/228800161; December 12, 2010 [last accessed between December 2012 and February 2013].

200. Crenshaw A. Crude, inconsistent threat: understanding anonymous. *Irongeek.* http://www.irongeek.com/i.php? page=security/understanding-anonymous; undated. [last accessed between December 2012 and February 2013].

201. Know Your Meme. Pool's closed. http://knowyourmeme.com/memes/pools-closed; April 2012 [last accessed between December 2012 and February 2013].

202. Know Your Meme. Pool's closed. http://knowyourmeme.com/memes/pools-closed; April 2012 [last accessed between December 2012 and February 2013].

203. Know Your Meme. Pool's Closed. http://knowyourmeme.com/memes/pools-closed; April 2012 [last accessed between December 2012 and February 2013].

204. Know Your Meme. Internet vigilantism. http://knowyourmeme.com/memes/subcultures/internet-vigilantism; May 2012 [last accessed between December 2012 and February 2013].

205. Cracked. Eight awesome cases of Internet vigilantism. http://www.cracked.com/article_17170_8-awesome- cases-internet-vigilantism_p2.html#ixzz1RZFPycz6; March 23, 2009 [last accessed between December 2012 and February 2013].

206. IB Times. Anonymous takes on child pornography sites. http://www.ibtimes.com/articles/236744/20111024/ anonymous-operation-darknet-child-pornography.htm; October 24, 2007 [last accessed between December 2012 and February 2013].

207. Mashable. Anonymous shuts down alleged twitter pedophile. http://mashable.com/2012/08/09/anonymous- twitter-pedophile/; August 9, 2012 [last accessed between December 2012 and February 2013].

208. Cracked. Eight awesome cases of internet vigilantism. http://www.cracked.com/article_17170_8-awesome- cases-internet-vigilantism_p2.html#ixzz1RZFPycz6; March 23, 2009 [last accessed between December 2012 and February 2013].

209. FoxNews. Hackers declare war on scientology. http://www.foxnews.com/story/0,2933,325586,00.html; January 25, 2008 [last accessed between December 2012 and February 2013].

210. WirtschaftsWoche (German language magazine). Wie anonymous scientology in die Knie Zwang. http:// www.wiwo.de/technologie/digitale-welt/hackernetzwerk-wie-anonymous-scientology-in-die-knie-zwang/ 6908658.html; July 23, 2012 (excerpt of Parmy Olson's 2012 book on Anonymous). [last accessed between December 2012 and February 2013].

211. The Guardian. Hackers declare war on scientologists amid claim of heavy-handed cruise control. http://www. guardian.co.uk/technology/2008/feb/04/news; February 3, 2008 [last accessed between December 2012 and February 2013].

212. LA Weekly. My date with anonymous: a rare interview with the elusive internet troublemakers. http:// www.laweekly.com/2009-02-05/columns/my-date-with-anonymous-a-rare-interview-with-the-illusive-internet- troublemakers/; February 4, 2009 [last accessed between December 2012 and February 2013].

213. Jacobson, J. We are legion: anonymous and the war on scientology. http://www.lisamcpherson.org/pc.htm; undated. [last accessed between December 2012 and February 2013].

214. WirtschaftsWoche (German language magazine). Wie anonymous scientology in die Knie Zwang. http:// www.wiwo.de/technologie/digitale-welt/hackernetzwerk-wie-anonymous-scientology-in-die-knie-zwang/ 6908658.html; July 23, 2012 (excerpt of Parmy Olson's 2012 book on Anonymous). [last accessed between December 2012 and February 2013].

215. Know Your Memes. Project chanology. http://knowyourmeme.com/memes/events/project-chanology; February 2012 [last accessed between December 2012 and February 2013].

216. Jacobson J. We are legion: anonymous and the war on scientology. http://www.lisamcpherson.org/pc.htm; undated. [last accessed between December 2012 and February 2013].

217. National Post. Online group declares war on scientology. http://web.archive.org/web/20080128145858/ http://www.nationalpost.com/news/canada/story.html?id=261308; January 26, 2008 [last accessed between December 2012 and February 2013].

218. Jacobson J. We are legion: anonymous and the war on scientology. http://www.lisamcpherson.org/pc.htm; undated. [last accessed between December 2012 and February 2013].

219. WirtschaftsWoche (German language magazine). Wie anonymous scientology in die Knie Zwang. http:// www.wiwo.de/technologie/digitale-welt/hackernetzwerk-wie-anonymous-scientology-in-die-knie-zwang/ 6908658.html; July 23, 2012(excerpt of Parmy Olson's 2012 book on Anonymous). [last accessed between December 2012 and February 2013].

220. WirtschaftsWoche (German language magazine). Wie anonymous scientology in die Knie Zwang. http://www.wiwo.de/technologie/digitale-welt/hackernetzwerk-wie-anonymous-scientology-in-die-knie-zwang/6908658.html; July 23, 2012 (excerpt of Parmy Olson's 2012 book on Anonymous). [last accessed between December 2012 and February 2013].

221. CNet. Technical aspects of the DDoS attacks upon the church of scientology. http://news.cnet.com/8301-10789_3-9858552-57.html; January 25, 2008 [last accessed between December 2012 and February 2013].

222. LAist. Church of scientology strikes back—anonymous responds. http://laist.com/2008/03/23/church_of_scien.php; March 23, 2008 [last accessed between December 2012 and February 2013].

223. LA Weekly. Anonymous' vs. scientology: group targets 'church' headquarters. http://www.laweekly.com/2008-03-20/news/8220-anonymous-8221-vs-scientology/2/; March 17, 2008 [last accessed between December 2012 and February 2013].

224. Mancunian Matters. Manchester anonymous to hold anti-scientology protest following cruise-holmes split. http://mancunianmatters.co.uk/content/13074409-manchester-anonymous-hold-anti-scientology-protest-following-cruise-holmes-split; July 13, 2012 [last accessed between December 2012 and February 2013].

225. NineMSN. The internet pranksters who started a war. http://news.ninemsn.com.au/article.aspx?id=459214; May 8, 2008 [last accessed between December 2012 and February 2013].

226. WirtschaftsWoche (German language magazine). Wie anonymous scientology in die Knie Zwang. http://www.wiwo.de/technologie/digitale-welt/hackernetzwerk-wie-anonymous-scientology-in-die-knie-zwang/6908658.html; July 23, 2012 (excerpt of Parmy Olson's 2012 book on Anonymous). [last accessed between December 2012 and February 2013].

227. Atlantic Wire. The Hacks that mattered in the year of the hack. http://www.theatlanticwire.com/technology/2011/12/hacks-mattered-year-hack/46731/; December 28, 2011 [last accessed between December 2012 and February 2013].

228. Peoples Liberation Front. Public Campaigns, Operation Syria. http://peoplesliberationfront.net/campaigns.html. [last accessed between December 2012 and February 2013].

229. IT World. A conversation with Commander X. http://www.itworld.com/internet/137590/conversation-commander-x?page=0%2C0; February 18, 2011 [last accessed between December 2012 and February 2013].

230. Al Arabiya. WikiLeaks might have triggered Tunis' revolution. http://www.alarabiya.net/articles/2011/01/15/133592.html; January 15, 2011 [last accessed between December 2012 and February 2013].

231. Al Jazeera. How Tunisia's revolution began. http://www.aljazeera.com/indepth/features/2011/01/2011126121815985483.html; January 26, 2011 [last accessed between December 2012 and February 2013].

232. BBC News. Tunisia suicide protester Mohamed Bouazizi dies. http://www.bbc.co.uk/news/world-africa-12120228; January 5, 2011 [last accessed between December 2012 and February 2013].

233. Al Jazeera. Tunisia's bitter cyberwar. http://www.aljazeera.com/indepth/features/2011/01/20111614145839362.html; January 6, 2011 [last accessed between December 2012 and February 2013].

234. Gawker. Anonymous attacks Tunisian Government over WikiLeaks censorship. http://gawker.com/5723104/anonymous-attacks-tunisian-government-over-WikiLeaks-censorship; January 3, 2011 [last accessed between December 2012 and February 2013].

235. Al Jazeera. Tunisia's bitter cyberwar. http://www.aljazeera.com/indepth/features/2011/01/20111614145839362.html; January 6, 2011 [last accessed between December 2012 and February 2013].

236. IT World. A conversation with commander X. http://www.itworld.com/internet/137590/conversation-commander-x?page=0%2C0; February 18, 2011 [last accessed between December 2012 and February 2013].

237. Al Jazeera. Tunisia's bitter cyberwar. http://www.aljazeera.com/indepth/features/2011/01/20111614145839362.html; January 6, 2011 [last accessed between December 2012 and February 2013].

238. Al Jazeera. Anonymous and the Arab Uprisings. http://www.aljazeera.com/news/middleeast/2011/05/201151917634659824.html; May 19, 2011 [last accessed between December 2012 and February 2013].

239. Al Jazeera. Tunisia's bitter cyberwar. http://www.aljazeera.com/indepth/features/2011/01/20111614145839362.html; January 6, 2011 [last accessed between December 2012 and February 2013].

240. Internetfeds. Remove Tunisian government phishing scripts. http://userscripts.org/scripts/show/94122; January 6, 2011 [last accessed between December 2012 and February 2013].

241. Al Jazeera. Anonymous and the Arab uprisings. http://www.aljazeera.com/news/middleeast/2011/05/201151917634659824.html; May 19, 2011 [last accessed between December 2012 and February 2013].

242. Agence France Press (AFP). Anonymous' group hacks Tunisian Islamist sites. http://www.google.com/hostednews/afp/article/ALeqM5hwgwVBJdpJa0Jm1LsoCpW0HnophQ?docId=CNG.a7aa7a5a7dd45ef26c7fad8a1c0a0dfe.401; March 17, 2012 [last accessed between December 2012 and February 2013].

243. Al Jazeera. Anonymous and the Arab uprisings. http://www.aljazeera.com/news/middleeast/2011/05/201151917634659824.html; May 19, 2011 [last accessed between December 2012 and February 2013].

244. Naked Security. Egypt versus the Internet—anonymous hackers launch DDoS-attack. http://nakedsecurity. sophos.com/2011/01/26/egypt-versus-the-internet-anonymous-hackers-launch-ddos-attack/; January 26, 2011 [last accessed between December 2012 and February 2013].

245. Naked Security. Egypt versus the Internet—anonymous hackers launch DDoS-attack. http://nakedsecurity.sophos. com/2011/01/26/egypt-versus-the-internet-anonymous-hackers-launch-ddos-attack/; January 26, 2011 [last accessed between December 2012 and February 2013].

246. Al Jazeera. Anonymous and the Arab uprisings. http://www.aljazeera.com/news/middleeast/2011/05/ 201151917634659824.html; May 19, 2011 [last accessed between December 2012 and February 2013].

247. Huffington Post. Syrian ministry of defense website hacked by anonymous. http://www.huffingtonpost.com/ 2011/08/08/syria-ministry-of-defense-hacked-anonymous_n_920733.html; August 8, 2011 [last accessed between December 2012 and February 2013].

248. Gawker. Anonymous hackers attack Yemeni government. http://gawker.com/5750513/ anonymous-hackers-already-taking-down-yemeni-websites; February 2, 2011 [last accessed between December 2012 and February 2013].

249. Softpedia. Anonymous hackers publish details of Yemen's Internet filtering systems. http://news.softpedia. com/news/Anonymous-Hackers-Publish-Details-of-Yemen-s-Internet-Filtering-Systems-281745.shtml; July 17, 2012 [last accessed between December 2012 and February 2013].

250. The Hacker News. Operation Algeria, part 2 by anonymous hackers released. http://thehackernews.com/2011/ 02/operation-algeria-part-2-by-anonymous.html; February 11, 2011 [last accessed between December 2012 and February 2013].

251. Naked Security. Pro-WikiLeaks hackers attack Zimbabwe government websites. http://nakedsecurity.sophos. com/2010/12/31/pro-wikileaks-hackers-attack-zimbabwe-government-websites/; December 31, 2010 [last accessed between December 2012 and February 2013].

252. The Hacker News. Operation Italy press release: anonymous hackers will soon strike again. http:// thehackernews.com/2011/02/operation-italy-press-release-anonymous.html; February 10, 2011 [last accessed between December 2012 and February 2013].

253. Daily Caller. Who is Anonymous? A look at the hacktivists aiding revolution in the middle east. http:// dailycaller.com/2011/02/26/who-is-anonymous-a-look-at-the-hacktivists-aiding-revolution-in-the-middle-east/2/; February 26, 2011 [last accessed between December 2012 and February 2013].

254. Al Jazeera. Anonymous and the Arab uprisings. http://www.aljazeera.com/news/middleeast/2011/05/ 201151917634659824.html; May 19, 2011 [last accessed between December 2012 and February 2013].

255. Ars Technica. Anonymous speaks: the inside story of the HBGary Hack. http://arstechnica.com/tech-policy/ 2011/02/anonymous-speaks-the-inside-story-of-the-hbgary-hack/; February 15, 2011 [last accessed between December 2012 and February 2013].

256. Olson P. We are anonymous—inside the hacker world of LulzSec, anonymous, and the global cyber insurgency. New York, Boston, London: Little, Brown and Company; 2012 p. 17.

257. eSecurity. Anonymous hackers target HB Gary. http://www.esecurityplanet.com/headlines/article.php/ 3923906/Anonymous-Hackers-Target-HBGary.htm; February 8, 2011 [last accessed between December 2012 and February 2013].

258. Ars Technica. Anonymous speaks: the inside story of the HBGary hack. http://arstechnica.com/tech-policy/ 2011/02/anonymous-speaks-the-inside-story-of-the-hbgary-hack/; February 15, 2011 [last accessed between December 2012 and February 2013].

259. Ars Technica. Anonymous speaks: the inside story of the HBGary hack. http://arstechnica.com/tech-policy/ 2011/02/anonymous-speaks-the-inside-story-of-the-hbgary-hack/; February 15, 2011 [last accessed between December 2012 and February 2013].

260. Olson P. We are anonymous—inside the hacker world of LulzSec, anonymous, and the global cyber insurgency. New York: Little Brown; 2012 p.20.

261. Ars Technica. Anonymous speaks: the inside story of the HBGary Hack. http://arstechnica.com/tech-policy/ 2011/02/anonymous-speaks-the-inside-story-of-the-hbgary-hack/; February 15, 2011 [last accessed between December 2012 and February 2013].

262. Ibid.

263. Ars Technica. Anonymous speaks: the inside story of the HBGary hack. http://arstechnica.com/tech-policy/ 2011/02/anonymous-speaks-the-inside-story-of-the-hbgary-hack/; February 15, 2011 [last accessed between December 2012 and February 2013].

264. eSecurity. Anonymous hackers target HB Gary. http://www.esecurityplanet.com/headlines/article.php/3923906/Anonymous-Hackers-Target-HBGary.htm; February 8, 2011 [last accessed between December 2012 and February 2013].

265. Ars Technica. Anonymous' attacks Sony to protest PS3 hacker law suit. http://arstechnica.com/tech-policy/2011/04/anonymous-attacks-sony-to-protest-ps3-hacker-lawsuit/; April 4, 2011 [last accessed between December 2012 and February 2013].

266. New Yorker. Machine politics—annals of technology. http://www.newyorker.com/reporting/2012/05/07/120507fa_fact_kushner; May 7, 2012 [last accessed between December 2012 and February 2013].

267. PS3News. PS3 is hacked by George Hotz—hello hypervisor, i'm GeoHot! http://www.ps3news.com/PS3-Hacks/ps3-is-hacked-by-george-hotz-hello-hypervisor-im-geohot/; undated. [last accessed between December 2012 and February 2013].

268. Technologizer. Sony and George Hotz settle PS3 hacking lawsuit. http://technologizer.com/2011/04/11/sony-george-hotz-settle-ps3-hacking-lawsuit/; April 11, 2011 [last accessed between December 2012 and February 2013].

269. BusinessInsider. Famous iPhone Hacker George Hotz has left Facebook. http://articles.businessinsider.com/2012-01-24/tech/30658124_1_george-hotz-location-data-iphone; January 24, 2012 [last accessed between December 2012 and February 2013].

270. Olson P. We are anonymous—inside the hacker world of LulzSec, anonymous, and the global cyber insurgency. New York, Boston, London: Little, Brown and Company; 2012 p. 423f.

271. Know Your Meme. Operation Antisec. http://knowyourmeme.com/memes/events/operation-antisec; March 1, 2012. [last accessed between December 2012 and February 2013].

272. PCMagazine. LulzSec, anonymous team up for 'operation anti-security'. http://www.pcmag.com/article2/0,2817,2387264,00.asp; June 20, 2011 [last accessed between December 2012 and February 2013].

273. PCMagazine. LulzSec, anonymous team up for 'operation anti-security'. http://www.pcmag.com/article2/0,2817,2387264,00.asp; June 20, 2011 [last accessed between December 2012 and February 2013].

274. Know Your Meme. Operation antisec. http://knowyourmeme.com/memes/events/operation-antisec; March 1, 2012 [last accessed between December 2012 and February 2013].

275. ITProPortal. Anonymous puts US counter terrorist program online. http://www.itproportal.com/2011/06/27/anonymous-puts-us-counter-terrorist-program-online/; June 27, 2011 [last accessed between December 2012 and February 2013].

276. Know Your Meme. Operation antisec. http://knowyourmeme.com/memes/events/operation-antisec; March 1, 2012 [last accessed between December 2012 and February 2013].

277. The Telegraph. FBI charges alleged anonymous hackers after supergrass claims. http://www.telegraph.co.uk/technology/news/9127004/FBI-charges-alleged-Anonymous-hackers-after-supergrass-claims.html; March 7, 2012 [last accessed between December 2012 and February 2013].

278. Peoples Liberation Front. Public campaigns, Operation Vendetta. http://www.peoplesliberationfront.net/campaignsArchive1.html; undated [last accessed August 12, 2012].

279. TPM. Occupy lawyer stuck with $35K bill after 'homeless hacker' jumps bail. http://idealab.talkingpointsmemo.com/2012/03/occupy-lawyer-stuck-with-35k-bill-after-homeless-hacker-jumps-bail.php; March 8, 2012 [last accessed between December 2012 and February 2013].

280. TPM. Homeless hacker' Christopher Doyon, AKA 'Commander X', joins up with occupy movement. http://idealab.talkingpointsmemo.com/2011/10/homeless-hacker-christopher-doyon-aka-commander-x-joins-up-with-occupy-movement.php; October 27, 2011 [last accessed between December 2012 and February 2013].

281. CBS News. Feds: homeless hacker 'Commander X' arrested. http://www.cbsnews.com/8301-31727_162-20110912-10391695.html; September 23, 2011 [last accessed between December 2012 and February 2013].

282. The Montreal Gazette. Christopher Doyon, one of the brains behind anonymous. http://www.montrealgazette.com/technology/Christopher+Doyon+brains+behind+Anonymous/6612381/story.html; May 12, 2012 [last accessed between December 2012 and February 2013].

283. Wired. Par:AnoIA: anonymous launches WikiLeaks-esque site for data dumps. http://www.wired.com/threatlevel/2012/07/paranoia-anonymous/all/; July 13, 2012 [last accessed between December 2012 and February 2013].

284. Wired. Anontune: the new social music platform from anonymous. http://www.wired.com/underwire/2012/04/anontune-anonymous/; April 19, 2012 [last accessed between December 2012 and February 2013].

285. RT.com. Anonymous unveils data-sharing websites amidst privacy concerns. http://rt.com/usa/news/anonymous-pastebin-new-internet-605/; April 23, 2012 [last accessed between December 2012 and February 2013].

286. RT.com. Anonymous unveils data-sharing websites amidst privacy concerns. http://rt.com/usa/news/anonymous-pastebin-new-internet-605/; April 23, 2012 [last accessed between December 2012 and February 2013].

287. RT.com. Anonymous unveils data-sharing websites amidst privacy concerns. http://rt.com/usa/news/anonymous-pastebin-new-internet-605/; April 23, 2012 [last accessed between December 2012 and February 2013].

288. Information Week. Anonymous builds New Haven for stolen data. http://www.informationweek.com/news/security/vulnerabilities/232900590; April 19, 2012 [last accessed between December 2012 and February 2013].

289. PC Magazine. With PasteBin 'compromised', anonymous launches AnonPaste. http://www.pcmag.com/article2/0,2817,2403283,00.asp; April 19, 2012 [last accessed between December 2012 and February 2013].

290. Wired. Par:AnoIA: anonymous launches WikiLeaks-esque site for data dumps. http://www.wired.com/threatlevel/2012/07/paranoia-anonymous/all/; July 13, 2012 [last accessed between December 2012 and February 2013].

291. Wired. Par:AnoIA: anonymous launches WikiLeaks-esque site for data dumps. http://www.wired.com/threatlevel/2012/07/paranoia-anonymous/all/; July 13, 2012 [last accessed between December 2012 and February 2013].

292. CNet. Anonymous OS: worth the risk? http://news.cnet.com/8301-13506_3-57397895-17/anonymous-os-worth-the-risk/; March 15, 2012 [last accessed between December 2012 and February 2013].

293. Mobiledia. Hackers' OS? Joke's on you. http://www.mobiledia.com/news/133380.html; March 16, 2012 [last accessed between December 2012 and February 2013].

294. The Next Web (TNW). Anonymous has just released its own operating system: anonymous OS. http://thenextweb.com/insider/2012/03/14/anonymous-has-just-released-its-own-operating-system-anonymous-os/; undated. [last accessed between December 2012 and February 2013].

295. The Hacker News. Anonymous-OS 0.1: Anonymous Hackers Released Their Own Operating System. http://thehackernews.com/2012/03/anonymous-os-01-anonymous-hackers.html; March 15, 2012 [last accessed between December 2012 and February 2013].

296. CNet. Anonymous OS: worth the risk? http://news.cnet.com/8301-13506_3-57397895-17/anonymous-os-worth-the-risk/; March 15, 2012 [last accessed between December 2012 and February 2013].

297. The Next Web (TNW). Anonymous has just released its own operating system: Anonymous OS. http://thenextweb.com/insider/2012/03/14/anonymous-has-just-released-its-own-operating-system-anonymous-os/; undated. [last accessed between December 2012 and February 2013].

298. Softpedia. SourceForge closes anonymous-OS live CD project. http://news.softpedia.com/newsImage/SourceForge-Closes-Anonymous-OS-Live-CD-Project-2.jpg/; March 16, 2012 [last accessed between December 2012 and February 2013].

299. The Next Web. Anonymous claims that the operating system, 'anonymous-OS' is fake. http://thenextweb.com/insider/2012/03/15/anonymous-claims-that-the-operating-system-anonymous-os-is-fake/; undated. [last accessed between December 2012 and February 2013].

300. Softpedia. SourceForge closes anonymous-OS live CD project. http://news.softpedia.com/news/SourceForge-Closes-Anonymous-OS-Live-CD-Project-258944.shtml; March 16, 2012 [last accessed between December 2012 and February 2013].

301. The Next Web. Anonymous claims that the operating system, 'anonymous-OS' is fake. http://thenextweb.com/insider/2012/03/15/anonymous-claims-that-the-operating-system-anonymous-os-is-fake/; undated. [last accessed between December 2012 and February 2013].

302. Mobiledia. Hackers' OS? Joke's on you. http://www.mobiledia.com/news/133380.html; March 16, 2012 [last accessed between December 2012 and February 2013].

303. The Next Web. Anonymous claims that the operating system, 'anonymous-OS' is fake. http://thenextweb.com/insider/2012/03/15/anonymous-claims-that-the-operating-system-anonymous-os-is-fake/; undated. [last accessed between December 2012 and February 2013].

304. ZDNet. Fluid structure, leadership keep anonymous' threat alive. http://www.zdnet.com/fluid-structure-leadership-keep-anonymous-threat-alive-7000000957/; July 16, 2012 [last accessed between December 2012 and February 2013].

305. Radio Free Europe. What is anonymous and how does it operate? http://www.rferl.org/content/explainer_what_is_anonymous_and_how_does_it_operate/24500381.html; March 3, 2012 [last accessed between December 2012 and February 2013].

306. Mobiledia. A rising war between hackers. http://www.mobiledia.com/news/139185.html; April 24, 2012 [last accessed between December 2012 and February 2013].

PART II

CYBER ESPIONAGE AND EXPLOITATION

In this part, we discuss *cyber espionage and exploitation*, which deals with the theft of information through and from computer systems. Throughout the last decade, there have been many such incidents which are believed to be politically motivated. In most of these cases, the data are stolen as part of intelligence collection, theft of intellectual property and/or to gain a technological knowledge of an adversary's weapons systems. Many such events were attributed to hackers from China. Hence, all of Chapter 7 is dedicated to cyber espionage attributed to China. This if followed by a discussion of the more recently discovered cyber-based intelligence gathering platforms such as *Duqu*, *Flame*, and *Gauss* in Chapter 8. Then we discuss of social network exploitation in Chapter 9—which is an emerging trend in social engineering and intelligence collection. Finally, in Chapter 10, we take a more tactical view of cyber exploitation in studying the interception of unencrypted video feed from the Predator drones during Operation Iraqi Freedom by Shi'ite militants.

7

Enter the Dragon: Why Cyber Espionage Against Militaries, Dissidents, and Nondefense Corporations Is a Key Component of Chinese Cyber Strategy

INFORMATION IN THIS CHAPTER

- Why cyber espionage is important to China
- Leveraging resources beyond the military: The cyber warriors of China
- Stealing information from the U.S. Industrial-Military Complex: Titan rain
- Cyber war against the corporate world: A case study of cyber intrusion attributed to China
- Monitoring dissidents: Gh0stNet
- Using legitimate Web sites for data exfiltration: The shadow network
- Cyber war through intellectual property theft: Operation Aurora
- An example of the current state of the art: Sykipot

INTRODUCTION

News reports in the first decade of the twenty-first century were seemingly littered with alleged Chinese cyber incidents. These activities have included instances of theft of guarded scientific data, monitoring of communication of the Dalai Lama, and theft of intellectual property from Google. In this chapter, we study these three incidents and others like them. What is more, cyber operations originating in China like these persevere to this day. Recently, in a testimony to the Congressional Armed Services Committee, General Keith Alexander, the commander of U.S. Cyber Command and head of the National Security Agency (NSA), stated that China is stealing a "great deal" of military-related intellectual property from the United States.[1] Clearly, cyber espionage, which includes the theft of intellectual property, is already a key component of Chinese cyber strategy.

The activities of exfiltration, monitoring, and theft of digital information described in this chapter can be easily labeled as incidents of cyber espionage. The apparent goal of this type of cyber operation is not to take the computers offline, as with the Russian cyber attacks against Georgia in 2008. Rather, the goal is to capture data of the opposing force. This being the case, such activities could not be labeled as cyber attacks because the targeted systems and their data must remain intact in order to obtain the desired information. Hence, we can define cyber espionage as the act of obtaining access to data from a computer system without the authorization of that system's owner for intelligence collection purposes.

Just like the incidents of computer network attacks described in earlier chapters, these incidents of cyber espionage too are notoriously difficult to attribute. What then leads us to believe Chinese involvement in the cyber espionage incidents discussed in this chapter? If attribution is so difficult, then why do these actions cause corporations like Google and Northrop Grumman, as well as high-level diplomats such as U.S. Secretary of State Hillary Clinton to issue strong statements against the Chinese government in the wake of such attacks? The issue lies in the origin of the incidents.[a] We shall see in this chapter that computers involved with the theft of digital information are often traced back to computer systems that are located on the Chinese mainland. Further, forensic analysis of malware from such incidents often indicates the use of Chinese language software development tools. Though it is virtually impossible to implicate the government of the People's Republic of China (PRC) in these cyber espionage actions, the fact that they can be consistently traced to the Chinese mainland raises serious policy questions. Is the Chinese government conducting active investigations against the hackers, and what legal actions are they taking once hackers are identified? Is the Chinese government transparently sharing information of these supposed investigations with the victims of the cyber espionage? Is Beijing taking any legal actions to prevent individual hackers from attacking organizations outside of China?

What would China have to gain by offering a permissive environment for hackers? It is unlikely that the Chinese government—hallmarked by state monitoring—would not have the resources to reduce such activity. It can further be expected that the fire drawn by the international community is diplomatically undesirable. These activities provide key benefits to the PRC. The nature of the stolen information—which ranges from details of American weaponry to trade secrets to the communications of the Dalai Lama—are all of highly particular interest to Beijing. Further, in the late 1990s and early 2000s, several Chinese military thinkers wrote on the topic cyber warfare. These writings indicate that obtaining unauthorized access to computer systems for the purpose of information exfiltration is an integral part of Chinese cyber strategy.

The information thefts throughout the first decade of the twenty-first century show a definite progression in sophistication. Initial forays into cyber espionage circa 2003-2005—such as what the American Federal Bureau of Investigation (FBI) terms "Titan Rain"—were certainly advanced for their time, these activities were often linked to hackers operating in real time—meaning that the hackers were working at the keyboard to exfiltrate data as opposed to using more automated means. Espionage directed against the Dalai Lama in 2008-2009 initiated by malware known as "Gh0stNet" was more sophisticated than "Titan Rain" in that it

---

[a] Origin cannot only refer to the source IP addressed (traced through intermediate proxies) but also the origin of the software as determined by technical analysis of the code (i.e., the origin based on the version of the compiler and the language of the operating system used to create the software in question).

relied on the use of botnets. However, locating the command and control (C&C) servers of these botnets—typically located in mainland China—was relatively easy for investigators. The successor to "Gh0stNet" became known as the "Shadow Network" and leveraged an innovative C&C structure that included the use of social media sites and obfuscated servers making it more difficult to pinpoint. Finally, in late 2009, "Operation Aurora," which involved the mass exfiltration of sensitive intellectual properties from major corporations, most notably Google, illustrates a high degree of sophistication, because it entailed multiple techniques including previously unheard of vulnerabilities[b] in Web browsers.

The chapter is organized as follows: first, we present a brief description of the writings of Chinese military thinkers on cyber espionage. After laying out the conceptual base of Chinese thinking on cyber war, we will attempt to identify some of the prominent Chinese cyber warriors. This is followed by a discussion of "Titan Rain" and a case study of an early cyber exfiltration incident described by Northrop Grumman in a presentation to the U.S.-China Economic Security Review Commission. Though Northrop Grumman does not disclose certain details of the attack (i.e., the company which was attacked or the exact date in which it occurred), it does provide good insight into some of the earlier Chinese cyber espionage operations. We then go on to discuss "Gh0stNet" and the "Shadow Network." This is followed by an example for intellectual property theft during "Operation Aurora." The chapter closes with a description of the more recent Chinese-attributed espionage operation using the "Sykipot" malware where cutting-edge techniques are used to steal information on the next generation of U.S. unmanned aerial vehicles (UAVs).

WHY CYBER ESPIONAGE IS IMPORTANT TO CHINA: A LOOK AT CHINESE CYBER DOCTRINE

Two Examples on Chinese Strategic Thought

Perhaps, the most striking aspect of Chinese cyber doctrine is how it seems radically different from Western thought. This section outlines two examples on how Chinese and Western thought on strategy contrast. These examples were originally presented by COL Edward Sobiesk, head of the Information Technology Program at West Point, in a 2003 SANS Institute paper.[2]

In the first example, we compare two classic board games—the Western game of chess and the game of Go, which originated in China more than 2500 years ago.[3] Over the course of a chess game, the players conduct a war of attrition by capturing the opponent's pieces with the ultimate goal of capturing or cornering the opponent's king. In Go, on the other hand, each player starts at an empty board and, at each turn, attempts to conquer parts of the game space with colored stones. Note that in chess the destruction of a player's opponent is required to win. Conversely, in Go, a player's opponent is more of an obstacle to victory. In many ways, the writings of Chinese military thinkers highlight these two ideas. With regard to the first idea, it may be preferable to focus on conquering parts of the cyber-playing field, rather than directly confronting the enemy. With respect to the second, it may be preferable to find ways

[b]Such vulnerabilities are known as "zero-day" exploits.

in which to neutralize certain capabilities of an opponent rather than seek his destruction. Perhaps, even such subtle methods can be conducted outside of a conflict. Clearly, cyber espionage offers an excellent set of tools to accomplish tasks within such a strategy.

The second example that illustrates the vast differences in Western and Chinese thought comes from a footnote in a 2002 Report to Congress on *The Military Power of the PRC* by the U.S. Secretary of Defense.[4] This report identifies one of China's strategic objectives as maximizing "strategic configuration of power" called "shi." In the report, a footnote for "shi" states "There is no Western equivalent to the concept of 'shi.' Chinese linguists explain it as 'the alignment of forces,' the 'propensity of things,' or 'potential born of disposition,' that only a skilled strategist can exploit to ensure victory over a superior force." Another interpretation of "shi" could focus on setting favorable conditions. If a nation-state attains a higher level of "shi" than a rival, the latter will be easily defeated when conflict does arise because any battle (if even necessary) will be conducted in conditions extremely favorable to the first nation—as the first nation has already set favorable conditions through the attainment of "shi." By attaining a high level of access to an adversary's active computer systems—the information stored on those systems has lost two critical aspects—confidentiality and integrity.[5] *Confidentiality* ensures that the information is not viewed by unauthorized individuals, while *integrity* ensures that the information, once retrieved, was not tampered with. Taking away these aspects of an adversary's information can contribute greatly to setting the conditions of the battlefield— perhaps even avoiding battle altogether. Considering "shi" cyber espionage appears to be a formidable strategic tool—by accessing the opponent's computer systems, the rival's information advantage is reduced while the same is gained on the initiating side.

From Active Defense to Active Offense

Traditionally, the People's Liberation Army (PLA) was focused on the traditional Chinese idea of "active defense" which refers to the idea of not initiating conflict, but being prepared to respond to aggression. In a 2008 Military Review article, Timothy Thomas points out that the late 1990s and early 2000s saw a shift from this mentality, particularly with regard to cyber warfare. The paradigm that seemed to emerge at this time was "active offense." Under this new rubric, the idea of setting the conditions of the battlefield (i.e., developing "shi") is still preeminent, but the manner in which it is pursued takes a different turn. In the cyber arena, this entails not only building one's defenses to deter attack but also utilizing cyber operations to obtain the upper hand in the case of a larger conflict (Figure 7.1).

This idea of "active offense" is introduced in the 1999 book *Information War* by Zhu Wenguan and Chen Taiyi. In this book, they include a section entitled "Conducting Camouflaged Attacks" where preemption and active offense are laid out.[6] A key component of active offense is network surveillance which includes obtaining an understanding of an opponent's command and control (C2), electronic warfare (EW), and key weapon systems. In 2002 and 2003, General Dai Qingmin echoes some of these ideas.[7] He stresses that it is necessary for information and cyber operations to be both "precursory" (i.e., done before operations take place) and "whole course" (performed throughout the operation). Where does cyber espionage fit into this schema? Preemption can take many forms. Earlier in this book, we saw how the Russians leveraged denial of service cyber attacks in the early phases of the

FIGURE 7.1 The Great Wall of China is the classic example of the Chinese principle of "active defense." However, within the world of cyber warfare, some authors see China shifting this policy toward "active offense." (For color version of this figure, the reader is referred to the online version of this chapter.) *CIA World Fact Book photo.*

Georgia campaign to hamper the opposing force's government, banking, and news media Web sites. However, preemption can take other more subtle forms as well. For example, having constant access to the Tibetan information systems would certainly be an advantage and would perhaps yield the possibility to avoid open conflict altogether. Theft of military secrets relating to new weapon systems may give the Chinese the technical intelligence (TECHINT) needed to find vulnerabilities, or even develop their own copies of said weapons. Stealing intellectual property from software vendors may give Chinese hackers a wealth of insight needed to identify new vulnerabilities for future cyber attack and cyber espionage operations.

The work *Information War* and the writings of General Dai illustrate the importance of the cyber aspect to Chinese military operations. However, many of the cyber espionage incidents that we will discuss in this chapter deal with theft of information from private companies during peacetime. How is this accounted for in the Chinese literature on cyber warfare? Answers to questions of this type seem to lay in the 1999 book *Unrestricted Warfare* by PLA Colonels Qiao Liang and Wang Xiangsui.[8] In this work, the authors assert that modern warfare extends beyond simply a military domain. Modern warfare includes political, scientific, and economic leaders in addition to military personnel. The notion of "unrestricted" warfare extends not only the domains of war but also the time at which such actions of war can take place. "Military" operations—that now include information, economic, and psychological aspects, can take place in peacetime in this perspective—further supporting the notion of "active offense." This may help explain why the early twenty-first century has been littered with stories of Chinese cyber espionage against corporations and scientific laboratories.

In this same vein, Colonel Wang Wei and Major Yang Zhen of the Nanjing Military Academy's Information Warfare and Command Department wrote in *China Military Science* that in a war against an information-centric society, a nation's political system, economic potential, and strategic objectives will be high-value targets.[9] They then go on to describe that the preferred method to attack such a society would be through the use of asymmetric warfare techniques. Asymmetric warfare refers to the ability of a combatant to defeat a superior force by using tactics that exploit a major weakness in their weapon systems, tactics, or information technology. In the America's war in Iraq from 2003 to 2011, insurgent often used asymmetric attacks such as road-side bombs as opposed to more traditional attacks that would otherwise expose them to the superior firepower of the Americans. Colonel Wei and Major Zhen espouse asymmetric attacks on a more strategic level—specifically calling for peacetime operations that have military and economic goals. To achieve such goals, under "informatized conditions," they state that both economic and trade warfare must be carried out.[10] Clearly, these authors were influenced by the earlier ideas of *Unrestricted Warfare*. It seems that the peacetime cyber espionage operations launched from the Chinese mainland against scientific, military, and commercial targets align well with this line of thinking.

The Three Warfares

The idea of "active offense" which espouses preemptive strikes, military in peacetime, and an extension of warfare beyond the military, while fitting nicely with the earlier Chinese intuitions of conquering territory in the game *Go* or establishing "shi" seem very bold. Even the book title *Unrestricted Warfare* has a very negative connotation to it. In an age where media perception during a conflict is often directly associated with the success or failure of a campaign, to appear as the aggressor seems a misinformed step. To avoid such negative perceptions, the Chinese have developed propaganda guidelines known as *Regulations on Political Work* which outline how to relate their side of the story to the media.[11] The key items in this regulation are the "three warfares."[c] These include (1) media which is used to support the righteous cause, (2) legal justification of the cause, and (3) psychological warfare which is used to aide friendly and attack the enemy's morale. Under this framework, Chinese propagandists have become adept in responding to accusations of cyber espionage operations. The usual response consists of a firm denial—which is performed with relative ease due to the difficulty of attribution in cyber warfare. The denial is normally followed by counterclaims of conspiracy, ulterior motives, etc. directed at those making the original claim. Later in this

[c]The "Three Warfares" was originally introduced to the western audience in Timothy Thomas's article "Google confronts China's three warfares" published in Parameters; Summer 2010. p. 101–5.

chapter, when we discuss Operation Aurora, directed against Google and other companies, we shall see what this framework looks like in action.

Another line of thought in Chinese writing to justify their seemingly bold moves in cyber space is that they believe these activities can be done with relative impunity. In a 2009 article in *China Military Science*, Senior Colonel Long Fangcheng and Senior Colonel Li Decai state that cyber operations directed against social, economic, and political targets can be done without fear of such activities leading to large-scale military engagements.[12] As such is the case, they generally regard cyber warfare as an element of soft power—albeit one with great effects. They then proceed to claim that the ultimate effect of this highly effective form of soft power is that the line between peacetime and wartime becomes blurred. This blurring may be a hallmark of cyber operations in general and might lead to the metaphorical endless war in the near future.

The Art of War

Perhaps, no discussion of Chinese military doctrine would be complete without a mention of how Sun Tzu's *The Art of War*—written about 2000 years ago—influences modern thought. Perhaps, the current Chinese cyber strategy can be best summed up by the following quotes from this famous work.[13]

> Therefore, to gain a hundred victories in a hundred battles is not the highest excellence; to subjugate the enemy's army without doing battle is the highest of excellence.
> Warfare is the Way of deception. Therefore, if able, appear unable, if active, appear not active, if near, appear far, if far, appear near *Sun Tzu, translation*[14]

Clearly, the Chinese are looking to set the conditions so that in the event of a looming conflict, an opposing force would seek negotiation and abandon direct conflict as futile—causing the Chinese to have won without fighting. Viewing the line between war and peacetime in the cyber arena aligns well with Sun Tzu's original idea. Likewise, the idea of deception also plays significantly into the plan of Chinese cyber strategy. Unlike the cyber attack events outlined in the earlier chapters of the book, cyber espionage is inherently more discrete—which may explain why it seems that the Chinese seem to prefer these types of operations. Further, the difficulty of attribution and the cleverly crafted public denials that utilize the "three warfares" also align well with Sun Tzu's ideas of deception.

Now, with a basic understanding of Chinese military thought, we will next discuss who is conducting cyber warfare operations in China.

LEVERAGING RESOURCES BEYOND THE MILITARY: THE CYBER WARRIORS OF CHINA

In the previous section, we have looked at the ways Chinese military thinkers and leaders view the role of cyber warfare for the PRC. Now, we shall look at who in China is actually carrying out the attacks. The cyber warriors of China have developed in two ways. First, they have developed top-down. Chinese military leaders who identified the need for cyber warfare in the late 1990s sought to adapt Chinese military organizations, doctrine, and training for this new form of warfare. Second, Chinese cyber warriors have developed bottom-up. Like many countries, China was home to several communities of hackers. Over the course of the first decade of the twenty-first century, leaders in the Chinese military identified some of the more talented groups. Since China also developed antihacking laws during this period, the general trend was that the members of these groups became integrated into legitimate entities—including computer security companies, consulting firms, and academia. These entities, in turn, forged close relationships with the Chinese government and military.

INEW and Cyber in the PLA

The general information warfare (IW) strategy in use by the PLA is known as Integrated Network Electronic Warfare (INEW).[15] This strategy was originally outlined in a book by General Dai Qingmin in 1999 known as *On Information Warfare*. This integration of cyber operations to traditional information warfare assets is a key component of the INEW strategy. INEW relies on simultaneous application of both electronic warfare and cyber operations to overwhelm an adversary's command, control, communication, computers, intelligence, surveillance, and reconnaissance (C4ISR). Hence, the mission of key pieces of cyber warfare (cyber attack, cyber espionage, and cyber defense)—are assigned to elements of the PLA General Staff traditionally given similar roles in electronic warfare.

According to a 2009 Northrop Grumman report to the US-China Economic and Security Review Commission, the General Staff of the PLA is divided into several departments. INEW generally assigns offensive tasks (cyber attack and more conventional electronic counter measures (ECM)) to the 4th Department—which has traditionally played a large role in offensive information warfare. Notably, General Dai Qingmin was promoted to the head of the 4th Department in 2000—perhaps an indication that the PLA intended to adopt his vision of INEW. Defensive and intelligence tasks—specifically cyber defense and cyber espionage are assigned to the 3rd Department—which traditionally focused on signal intelligence (SIGINT). It is thought that the 3rd Department is the headquarters for the Technical Reconnaissance Bureaus, whose normal mission is SIGINT collection. In the late 1990s, several of these Bureaus received awards relating to research in information warfare. Some analysts believe this indicates their role in cyber operations.[16]

To augment the information warfare specialists in the 3rd and 4th GSDs, the Chinese have also established information warfare militia units.[17] These militias can be thought of as a "cyber national guard" as they consist largely of personnel from the commercial information technology (IT) and academia. Open source reporting indicates that these units have been created from 2003 to 2008 in Guangzhou, Tianjin, Henan, and Ningxia provinces. There is even evidence that some of these militia received specific wartime tasks—most of which appear to be focused on cyber attack.

The Chinese Hacker Community: From Black Hat to White Hat

From 1999 to 2004, the Chinese hacker community, thought to consist of several thousand hackers, gained notoriety for several high-profile pro-PRC attacks. These included cyber attacks against Indonesia, Taiwan, and the United States in response to political incidents.

These attacks largely consisted of DoS and Web site defacement. Open source literature, such as the previously mentioned Northrop Grumman report, indicates that the government of the PRC was not involved with these attacks—hence, they can be considered as hacktivism—as discussed in previous chapters. Though not directly involved, the Chinese government's reaction to the attacks was initially encouraging—even publically lauding the efforts of the hackers. However, by 2002, this sentiment changed significantly—the PRC started to take a firm stance against freelance hacking of foreign systems. Perhaps, the watershed event was the PRC's reaction to large-scale DoS against the White House. The PRC responded to this attack according to the "Honker Union of China" by labeling the assault as "Web terrorism" and "unforgivable acts of violating the law" published in the official newspaper of the Communist Party.[18] With a few notable exceptions, such as an attempted DDoS against CNN, the activities of freelance Chinese hacker groups waned toward the later part of the first decade of the twenty-first century. The PRC further looked to cement their position on such activities with a national antihacking law in early 2009—which was followed by a series of high-profile arrests of prominent hackers (Figure 7.2).

Why did the PRC seem to shift their policy on hacking groups? Perhaps, as the power of cyber weaponry became more prevalent, the PRC sought to limit the proliferation of such capability. For instance, some military thinkers within the PLA expressed concern over members of cyber militias improperly using hacker tools.[19] Further, it also appears as though hacktivism, in general, is incompatible with INEW. There are three main aspects of this strategy that run counter to the notions of hacktivism: command and control (C2), precision

FIGURE 7.2   The front of the "Great Hall of People" in Tiananmen Square, Beijing. The Beijing government initially lauded the efforts of independent hacker groups in the late 1990s but in the early 2000s the government's attitude shifted, likely as such groups were operating outside of government control. This sentiment led to the enactment of antihacking laws starting in 2009. (For color version of this figure, the reader is referred to the online version of this chapter.) *CIA World Fact Book photo.*

targeting, and deception. Regarding C2, hacktivist operations can quickly grow into a self-sustaining operation, making such a movement easily uncontrollable by the PLA. INEW's focus on precision targeting and operational discipline (which we shall note in some of the case studies later in the chapter) is also difficult to foster in a hacktivist movement. Finally, as hacktivism is inherently public, operational security becomes extremely difficult, making deception and plausible deniability hard to implement.

With the PRC cracking down on hacking not condoned by the government and with hacktivism not fitting into the PLA strategy, what becomes of the Chinese hackers who were active in the early 2000s? It turns out that the PRC and PLA were able to leverage this pool of talent, but in a more controlled manner. This was accomplished by many key members of the hacker community making the transition from "black hat" (unsupervised, extragovernmental, or illegal hacking) to "white hat" ("ethical" hacking normal in the form of "security consulting"). There were two ways in which this occurred, one of which saw many hacker groups reinventing themselves as computer security firms—often seeking a relationship with the government. The chart below lists some hacker groups from the late 1990s/early 2000s that later became security firms that established a relationship with the Chinese government (Table 7.1).[20]

The second way in which the PRC encouraged members of the Chinese hacker community to turn "white hat" was through direct recruiting of skilled hackers. For example, according to Northrop Grumman's report in 2007 and 2008, a user known as "City_93" posted job announcements for the Ministry of Public Security's First Research Institute on two of the most well-established hacker forums.[d] Not only has the PRC attempted to recruit hacking talent but the PLA has succeeded in doing so as well. In 2005, they allegedly held a series of regional hacker competitions—most likely to identify and recruit hacker talent.[21]

In another example of the black hat-to-white hat transition, Peng Yinan, alleged cofounder of the Chinese hacking group Javaphile, is believed to be currently conducting research on behalf of the Chinese government. Based on the analysis by American security specialist Scott Henderson, Peng Yinan (under the screen name "CoolSwallow") is thought to have led the Javaphile hacking group to conduct a large-scale attack against the White House in response to the accidental bombing of the Chinese embassy in Serbia by the United States in 1999.[22] Yinan surfaced in 2008 when he published, under his own name, two academic articles on cyber espionage techniques. In the publications, he along with other former Javaphile members, was listed as researchers under the Shanghai Jiaotong University's Information Security

TABLE 7.1   Chinese Hacker Groups and Corresponding Security Firms

Hacker group	Security firm
Green Army Alliance	NSFocus
XCon	XFocus
Patriot Hackers-Black Eagle Base	Black Eagle Honker Base[a]

[a] The Black Eagle Honker Base is not a security firm, but rather an informal group that reformed 6 months after the Patriot Hackers—Black Eagle Base was shut down. The group then released a statement espousing that the group was now partaking in efforts to train individuals from the state and work to improve the PRC's network security industry.

[d] The hacker forums to where the job announcement were found were EvilOctal.com and XFocus.net.

Engineering Institute. This institute is led by Peng Dequan, a former director of the Science and Technology Commission under China's foreign intelligence service.[23]

Chinese Academia and Hacking

Peng Yinan's entry into the world of academia at Shanghai Jiaotong University is not the only example of Chinese academia being involved in cyber warfare. Later, in this chapter we discuss Operation Aurora, which was an incident of organized data theft directed against numerous American companies. According to open source reports, security experts traced the attacks to two Chinese schools—a vocational school and Shanghai Jiaotong University.[24] Incidents of Chinese involvement in cyber operations have appeared in the media. A 2009 academic paper entitled "Cascade-based attack vulnerability on the US power grid" by a graduate student at Dalian University of Technology caused uproar by the U.S. government[25]—particularly in the wake of Chinese cyber actions against U.S. infrastructure (further discussed later in this book). Later, in 2011, a propaganda film from a Chinese military school showed a student using a hacking tool—apparently being used to conduct a cyber attack against the University of Alabama.[26]

The main ideas of Chinese cyber operations grew out of the writings of PLA officers in the late 1990s and ultimately implemented in the INEW strategy, which aligns cyber attack and cyber espionage responsibilities with organizations conducting similar operations in the realm of EW. Though the Chinese hacker community came to prominence in the late 1990s and early 2000s with attacks that seemingly had goals congruent to the government, the PRC ultimately disapproved of these actions. As a result, many of the hackers turned "white hat" by either transforming their hacker groups into consulting firms or by obtaining employment with the government and/or academia. Chinese academia also appears to be highly involved with cyber warfare—not only in research but also potentially with operations.

STEALING INFORMATION FROM THE U.S. INDUSTRIAL-MILITARY COMPLEX: TITAN RAIN

The first major series of cyber espionage incidents largely attributed to China was known to American FBI investigators as "Titan Rain." It appears that the primary objective of this operation was the exfiltration of large amounts of data from numerous organizations in or related to the U.S. government. From 2003 to 2005, the hackers targeted a diverse list of organizations including the Defense Information Systems Agency (DISA), Sandia National Laboratories, the World Bank, Lockheed Martin, and NASA.[27] The hackers appeared to be well organized in that they conducted the operation in phases. It seemed that once they determined a given target set, they would first create and carry out a detailed cyber reconnaissance mission. Then, upon an evaluation of the results of that endeavor, they would carefully plan and execute the exfiltration of the desired data. In this section, we shall discuss cyber reconnaissance in general and then describe why the actions of the hackers in Titan Rain were considered sophisticated (at that time). Finally, we shall conclude the section by looking at indicators that point to Chinese involvement in this attack.

Cyber Reconnaissance: Footprinting, Scanning, and Enumeration

Cyber reconnaissance is often carried out through three basic steps: footprinting, scanning, and enumeration.[28] *Footprinting* is the process of examining the structure of an organization's computer network. The information the hacker wishes to determine at this stage pertains to the electronic traces users with the targeted organization leave, such as the range of IP addresses, the addresses of key network equipment such as routers, the availability of remote access to the network, and the presence of network-level security devices such as intrusion detection systems and firewalls. If we liken the targeting of information using cyber espionage with the targeting of a fugitive using conventional means, footprinting would be analogous to determining the neighborhood where the fugitive lives. This type of reconnaissance can be performed with varying levels of intensity. On the low end, reconnaissance can be in the form of simple lookups of system information—for example, using a domain name server (DNS) to identify the IP address associated with a URL. On the other end of the spectrum, specialized software can be used for this step as well.

Often, such footprinting can be accomplished without being detected at all. For instance, even on the low end, this task can be accomplished without queries made to the targets systems. In particular, queries to DNS servers and IP address registries can be made without the knowledge of the targeted organization. More intense footprinting reconnaissance could require accessing the target system (i.e., visiting Web pages maintained and written by the organization). However, information about the organization could also be found on Web pages not operated by the target institute, i.e., looking for employees talking about the company's network infrastructure on Web forums.

Scanning is examining a computer network at the next level of granularity. If we return to our analogy with the fugitive, we have identified the neighborhood where the fugitive lives and now wants information on potential hideouts. Likewise, with scanning, using the information about the computer network we gained in footprinting, the hacker now examines the individual systems of interest. Here, the intruder is interested in determining details of the systems such as what operating system is being used, what are the open ports on the system, and the configuration of the firewall. Earlier, less sophisticated and secure technology allowed the hacker to simply "ping" the targeted system—essentially sending a message to the system—to see if it was connected to the Internet. However, this rudimentary technique quickly became blocked. Further, hackers are able to obtain much more of the desired information using specialized pieces of software. This software tends to run in an automated fashion. The hacker normally enters a range of IP addresses and the software runs overnight. The next day, the hacker checks the results of the scan, which is presented to him in the form of an output file from the software. With the proper information of the specific systems identified, the hacker then proceeds to the next step of reconnaissance.

This next step is called *Enumeration* and involves the interrogation of specific systems. Returning to our fugitive example, we are now examining specific possible hideouts for certain vulnerabilities—i.e., determining the lock used on the door, determining if the fugitive has a guard dog, etc. With enumeration, the hacker often attempts to log into a system with the goal of finding specific data. The primary goal of this step is to determine the vulnerabilities of the system that may allow the intruder to obtain access. This process can be done manually, but again there are numerous pieces of specialized software that allow the hacker to accomplish this task. Examples of such software include *Crawl Web site*, *DumpSec*, *NetBIOS Auditing Tool*, *Network Scanner*, and others.

Titan Rain Dissected

To perform footprinting, scanning, and enumeration, the hackers involved in Titan Rain resorted to customized versions of software designed to automatically perform such tasks. Though much of the Titan Rain investigation remains confidential, the investigators disclosed the following time line of a typical day of cyber reconnaissance to *Time Magazine*[29] that started on November 1, 2004:

- 10:23 pm: Hackers identify vulnerabilities on systems at the U.S. Army Information System Engineering Command in Ft. Huachuca, AZ
- 1:19 am: Hackers identify the same vulnerabilities at the Defense Information Systems Agency in Arlington, VA
- 3:25 am: Hackers scan the Naval Oceanic Systems Center in San Diego, CA
- 4:46 am: Hackers scan U.S. Army Space and Strategic Defense installation in Huntsville, AL

Once the cyber reconnaissance phase of a mission was complete, the next step for the Titan Rain hackers was to infiltrate the systems of interest. Based on open source reports, we know that the first systems infiltrated in the Titan Rain operation were most likely done with a piece of software called a "Trojan Horse" (or simply a "Trojan"). These pieces of malicious software (or malware) appear to be innocuous (i.e., games, pirated commercial software, data files, etc.) but instead contain code that allows the hacker to access the system running the software. Often, after the user clicks on some ordinary appearing icon or link, a Trojan may start running on the system but remain completely unnoticeable—simply residing in the memory of a computer unknown to the user. In November 2003, a government alert described a wide-spread infection of U.S. Department of Defense (DoD) computer systems by such a Trojan.[30]

They Never Hit a Wrong Key

Shawn Carpenter, a veteran of the U.S. Navy, worked as a computer network security specialist for Sandia National Laboratories. He first became involved in the Titan Rain investigation in September of 2003 when he helped investigate a break-in of computer systems at Lockheed Martin. A similar event subsequently occurred at Sandia only a few months later. He noted that the hackers would move quickly to the archive and upload the desired information from a given system—spending a mere 10-30 min logged on to the target's system. Carpenter noted that unlike amateur hackers, whose mistakes become visible once they compromised a system, the Titan Rain hackers knew what their job was and what they wanted—they "never hit a wrong key."[31]

By regulation, military and government systems connected to the Internet do not contain classified data. So, what was the nature of the data stolen in Titan Rain? We return again to the Chinese ideas presented in the Chinese book *Unrestricted Warfare*. Although the compromised systems are, by nature, unclassified, they may still contain information concerning technology and innovation that is under export control. By obtaining such information, the hackers would be accomplishing the objectives of supporting economic warfare or of simply increasing their technological know-how for scientific or military purposes. For instance, data stolen by the Titan Rain hackers included U.S. Army's Falconview flight planning software, specifications for a U.S. Army aviation-planning system, and schematics of the propulsion system, solar panels, and fuel tanks for NASA's Mars Reconnaissance Orbiter.[32]

Additionally, information obtained from the target system, although typically unclassified, may provide the attackers other information for follow-on intelligence gathering operations—both through cyber warfare and conventional means. For instance, obtaining personal information such as documents and e-mails allows the penetrator to obtain "pattern of life" information on scientists and decision makers in key parts of the military and government. Information about personal relationships and political views expressed by employees, in private, monitored by emplaced Trojans, could be used for other purposes such as follow-on social engineering campaigns or more conventional espionage.

Indication of Chinese Involvement

Shawn Carpenter, the analyst from Sandia National Laboratories, worked to trace back the steps of the hackers, who exfiltrated data from Sandia. Ultimately, his search led him to three Chinese routers in the southern province of Guangdong.[33] Carpenter estimated that between six and ten workstations constantly working connected to these three routers. Files stolen from places like Sandia were first sent to other compromised systems, normally in an Asian country such as South Korea. Hailed by *Time Magazine* as a "stunning breakthrough" in cyber security, this finding, similar to the analysis done on Russian hacktivist servers described earlier in this book, provides only circumstantial evidence. Perhaps, the best use for this type of analysis would have been to use in a joint investigation with Chinese law enforcement personnel, but such an effort most likely did not occur. As expected in accordance with the media playbook of the "three warfares," the Chinese responded to the claims of data theft with a simple denial. However, albeit circumstantial, the patterns of this act of cyber espionage bears notable similarities to other operations initiated from the Chinese mainland discussed in this chapter.

Titan Rain illustrates some basic principles of a cyber espionage operation. Just as with the Russian cyber attacks described in the last chapter, these operations begin with a detailed reconnaissance phase. Upon completion of that task, the hacker then proceed to their mission of infiltrating target systems—which was likely accomplished through the use of Trojan software. Once the hackers had access to the systems, they worked quickly and efficiently to get the desired data off the targets and exfiltrated the data to an intermediary compromised system in an effort to cover their tracks. The nature of the data, though unclassified, was restricted under export control which may indicate that the attackers had strategic objectives related to obtaining technological know-how for economic and military purposes. Finally, the Chinese response to such intrusions was a firm denial, although there was no indication that they made an effort to investigate these operations that originated from their country. In the next section, we take a detailed view of another alleged cyber espionage operation against a large U.S. firm.

CYBER WAR AGAINST THE CORPORATE WORLD: A CASE STUDY OF CYBER INTRUSION ATTRIBUTED TO CHINA

This section presents a description of an alleged Chinese cyber intrusion into a U.S. firm occurring sometime in the middle of the first decade of the twenty-first century. This case study was originally presented in a report put together by Northrop Grumman for the U. S.-China Economic and Security Review Commission.[34] In this case study, certain details, such as the name of the U.S. firm and the precise year in which the intrusion occurred, are not revealed. However, the publication of the report (2009, the intrusion occurred "several years" earlier) indicates that this operation occurred either during or soon after Titan Rain. Throughout this section, we shall refer to this cyber intrusion incident as "Operation X" and the company that was broken into as "Company Y."

The theft of Company Y's data occurred in tandem with theft of data from several other large American firms. These operations ensued over a period of several weeks. The large scope of Operation X as well as the notion that hackers seem to work much more purposefully than amateurs suggests a certain level of professionalism. Rather than attempting to steal any bit of information they could find, the intruders appeared to desire only select data. Most likely, this indicates that the hackers were operating under a set of *information requirements* (IRs) and were executing a *collection plan*. Intelligence professionals refer to "information requirements" as pieces of information that, if known, could directly impact the effect of a military operation. A *collection plan* is literally a plan to gather such information. Traditionally, the means of collection could include human intelligence (HUMINT) or radio intercepts (signals intelligence or SIGINT). In this case, the information requirements were directly related to the files on Company Y's computer system. The hackers were professionals functioning in an efficient manner to obtain exactly what was needed. This self-discipline was directly related to an aspect of operational security (OPSEC) as they wanted to take every precaution to minimize the time that they were active on Company Y's computer network. By minimizing the time in which they were active, they also reduce the possibility that they were detected.

The hackers of Operation X likely worked in two teams. "Team 1" was the breach team, whose mission was to break into Company Y's servers. "Team 2" was the exfiltration team charged with actually stealing the data. Investigators determined the existence of the two teams by the types of tools employed and how these tools were used.[e] This division of labor is yet another example of the high degree of expertise employed in Operation X.

Reconnaissance and Initial Entry

The theft of Company Y's data was ultimately discovered midway during the exfiltration—and was halted (by Company Y). Hence, the details of this case study were assembled together after the fact. Prior to the data theft, the Company Y's information security specialists noted activity that was later attributed to hacker Team 1. This assessment was

---

[e]We note that, the Northrop Grumman report, from where this vignette is originally described, assesses that multiple teams were involved in the attack. However, notwithstanding additional indicators not included in that report, it possible that it could be one team using two different tool sets might also be responsible.

based on relatively low volumes of traffic through the network system. The security person-nel halted the traffic, but the attackers had apparently prepared to resort to other vulnerabil-ities to maintain access to Company Y's systems.

It is interesting to note that the hackers were savvy enough to minimize their traffic on Company Y's systems. This was most likely an effort to thwart any intrusion detection sys-tems (IDS) that Company Y may have had in place. An IDS is a piece of software designed to detect unauthorized traffic on computer networks. This type of software falls into two general categories. A *signature-based intrusion detection system* identifies attacks based on known attack patterns. On the other hand, *anomaly-based IDSs* look for certain irregularities in the network traffic. The hackers, by keeping the volume of traffic low, were making an effort to remain undetected by an anomaly-based system.

Although it does not seem as though Company Y had observed a great deal of the cyber reconnaissance that occurred on their systems (if so, they may have been able to preempt the theft), the ability of the hackers to adjust once discovered indicates that a very thorough re-connaissance had been conducted. Rather than relying on a single vulnerability to obtain ac-cess to Company Y's networks, the hackers allowed themselves in several ways to enter the network. We also note that network intrusion detection systems are able to find either com-promises or mere attempts of intrusion. Often, if network security people find an attempt at compromise, they consider this a useful metric to shut the intruder out. If the attackers make their way through a number of locations and are able to maintain access across the spectrum, the system remains compromised as long as there is a single pathway left unidentified by se-curity personnel. Once the reconnaissance phase was complete, it seems that the hackers were able to assemble a list of user accounts and credentials. The security personnel at Company Y identified almost 150 instances of this type of access leading up to the final movement of data.

Movement of Data on Company Y's Network

Where Team 1's mission ended (reconnaissance, identifying vulnerabilities, obtaining user credentials and NTLM hashes), Team 2's mission began (finding and preparing the desired data for exfiltration). It appears that Team 2 focused on a single compromised system in Com-pany Y's network to direct its activities. The Northrop Grumman report refers to this as the "Command and Control" or C2 node. Through the C2 node, the Team 2 hackers established multiple connections to compromised workstations in Company Y's network (see Figure 7.3). These connections were established through RDP—Remote Desktop Protocol—a Windows-based protocol to control other computers while not physically present at that system. Through these workstations, Company Y's file server was accessed and the targeted files were then copied to a "Staging Server" (systems internal to Company Y) in preparation of exfiltration. It is interesting to note that these staging servers were some of the most high-capacity servers on Company Y's network. The use of these high-performance machines indicates two things: (1) the comprehensiveness of the reconnaissance phase and (2) the time-conscious attitude of the hackers.

Team 2 purposefully and quickly copied data from the file servers to the staging servers. They had clearly done an analysis of the file structure ahead of time and had identified exactly what information they wished to target. For instance, they did not spend time opening files and examining their contents. Once the data were positioned on the staging servers, the hackers prepared it for exfiltration. First, they compressed the data into archive files and encrypted them. Compression has obvious benefits—reducing the file size to ensure that the transfer proceeds much faster. The encryption of the data was an interesting additional step that could serve multiple purposes. One reason for encryption (as with any data transfer) is that the hackers could be reasonably assured that a third eavesdropping party could not steal the data. A further aspect of encryption is its effect of covering up Team 2's tracks. Assuming Company Y would eventually analyze the traffic of the stolen data, it would have no way to know exactly what was stolen—making post-incident consequence management very difficult. It is also noteworthy that each of the compressed files was 650 MB in size—suggesting that the hackers were preparing to copy the stolen data to recordable CDs. Finally, Team 2 renamed the archived files to resemble innocuous Windows system files in an attempt to avoid detection through casual scans of network traffic and thus alerting system administrators.

Exfiltration of the Stolen Data

With the data prepared on the staging servers, the Team 2 hackers were ready to commence with the portion of Operation X where they assumed the most risk—exfiltration of the data. Due to the large amounts of data the attackers wished to steal, this part of the operation would require them to spend a relatively long time connected to the servers—potentially exposing their actions to security professionals. Forensic analysis of the operation indicates that Team 2 took numerous precautions to ensure that this part of the operation would go as smoothly as the previous parts. These precautions typically took the form of test runs, checks to ensure that they had adequate bandwidth, and connectivity checks to external machines. There is also some indication that Team 2 hackers also rehearsed a portion of the exfiltration task.

The Team 2 hackers' main goal was to upload the information from Company Y's networks to external Web servers—most likely under control of the hackers—located within the United States—at least one of which was associated with a U.S. university. There is some forensic evidence that suggests the hackers moved large amounts of the data from the staging servers to "exfiltration hosts" internal to the company—these would be used to forward the stolen data to the external Web servers.

The data were uploaded to the external Web servers using a common piece of software known as *file transfer protocol* or FTP. Initially, Team 2 used a custom-built piece of FTP software (which provided an additional layer of encryption), but this ultimately failed and they resorted to a standard piece of FTP software. It seemed that the large size of the files had caused too many failures, which is why the hackers had to forgo the custom software. It is somewhat ironic that a group skilled enough to penetrate into a large company's private network and remain undetected while exfiltrating large amounts of documents, is unable to write a secure FTP client. Perhaps, this reflects that the level of expertise of the hackers on Team 2 was not on par with the other team. Perhaps, if they were more highly skilled, the attack would have never been discovered by Company Y.

Multiple, redundant file upload sessions were utilized—sending redundant copies of a particular file of stolen data to multiple hosts. This was most likely done to maximize the

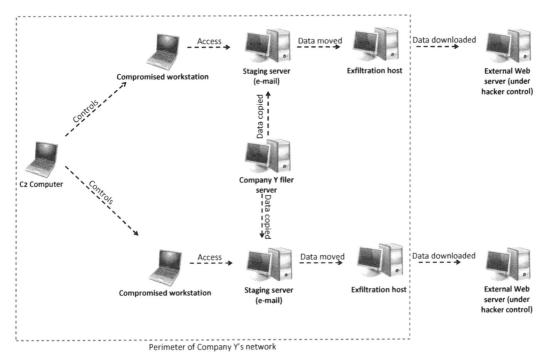

FIGURE 7.3 Diagram of the exfiltration route from the case study of Operation X on Company Y. (For color version of this figure, the reader is referred to the online version of this chapter.)

success of the operation. After several of the files were exfiltrated outside the perimeter of Company Y's network, security professionals detected the operation and stopped it midsession. For 5 h after the security personnel stopped the exfiltration, Company Y's network still received attempts from the hackers to return. Although it seems as if the hackers felt they had not met their objectives, the security professionals were unable to determine the intended scope of Operation X. Further, as previously discussed, there was no way to identify what data were actually stolen (Figure 7.3).

Evidence of Chinese Involvement

As with Titan Rain, the evidence of Chinese involvement is circumstantial at best—there are only indicators, but no direct proof. The main indicators of their involvement are some perceived slip ups of the cyber spies. For instance, due to the specific tools and techniques used, certain activities on Company Y's network attributed to the reconnaissance phase of Operation X originated from PRC IP addresses. During exfiltration, one of the external machines that compromised a workstation in Company Y used as a "C2" machine was located in Hong Kong.

In addition to these blunders, the techniques, tools, and operational profile of the attack were consistent with other attacks believed to originate from China during this time period (most likely attacks associated with Titan Rain). Further, the fact that the data were stolen from a U.S. company may also indicate Chinese involvement based on ideas such as those presented in *Unrestricted Warfare*.

The case study of Operation X where data were stolen from Company Y, presented by Northrop Grumman to the U.S.-China Economic and Security Review Commission, illustrates several important aspects of Chinese intrusions and cyber espionage in general. Perhaps, the most telling aspect of this case study is that the profile of the attackers substantially differs from amateur hackers. The scope of the mission, the division of labor among teams, the precautions taken to prevent detection, as well as contingency planning, and discipline of the hackers in this case are highly indicative of a professional organization. Such professionalism, in turn, increases the probability of an attack being associated with a nation-state. In general, this pattern of behavior can be viewed as a key differentiator between identifying an incident as cyber warfare as opposed to criminal hacking.

It appears that Operation X had a more strategic goal related to enhancing the economic and/or technological status of the perpetrators' sponsor. The overall strategy of the two hacker teams was to obtain access, consolidate the data, and exfiltrate over a relatively short duration. The actions of the intruders indicate that their mission ended once the stolen data were uploaded outside of Company Y's network. Based on their use of encryption of the stolen data, the perpetrators may have even expected to be detected. Suppose that the hackers in the case study were instead intending to monitor Company Y over a long period—perhaps focused on strategic communication of the executives. How would they change their tactics? This is the topic of the cyber espionage operation outlined in the next section—Gh0stNet—which deals with cyber espionage against the Dalai Lama.

MONITORING DISSIDENTS: GH0STNET

In the previous two sections, the operations discussed were primarily focused on events of data exfiltration. The hacker performs reconnaissance, obtains access to the systems, determines which data meets his information requirements, and then exfiltrates the data. The following case study deals with what is known as an advanced persistent threat (APT). With an APT, the hacker seeks not only to maintain access but also to maintain a foothold in the target system for a long period of time.[35] The cyber infiltrator may have multiple objectives on the target system, which can include long-term monitoring or even modification of data with the intent to disrupt the operations of the target. With the goal of staying on the target's system for a longer period of time, the hackers must adjust the way they operate and their goals.

For instance, in the case study of the previous section, it appears that the hackers attempted to upload several gigabytes of information outside of Company Y's network. Likely, they should have expected that the system administrators would, at some point, halt the ongoing exfiltration of such massive amounts of data. Hence, it appears that the movement of the data was likely understood to be the last part of that cyber operation.

The data movements of the case study in this section are more modest by comparison. The cyber spies in the present case study maintained a much longer presence on the target systems. The average duration a system was infected was 145 days, with many being infected for more than a year.

In this section, we shall describe a case study in which data were stolen from target systems belonging to the Office of His Holiness the Dali Lama (OHHDL, Tibetan Kuger Yigtsan), the Tibetan government in exile (TGIE), and systems of affiliated organizations (such as the pro-Tibetan non-government organization (NGO) Drewla) from May 2007 through March 2009.

At the request of the office of the Dalai Lama, researchers from the Canadian-based SecDev Group and the University of Toronto jointly investigated an outbreak of malware in the offices of the Tibetan authorities starting in September 2008. The project became known as the Information Warfare Monitor. Their inquiry led them to uncover a comprehensive APT that utilized command servers primarily located in the PRC. This cyber espionage operation took place during a 2-year period from 2007 to 2009 in which nearly 1300 computers belonging to the office of the Dalai Lama and the Tibetan government in exile were found to be infected. The computers were located in more than one hundred countries. The investigators refer to the cyber espionage operation as "Gh0stNet"—named after a piece of malware found on many of the machines. We describe this case study in the remainder of this section. First, we present a very basic model for cyber operations that applies very well to APT. Then, we discuss the initial malware infection and how social engineering was leveraged by the intruders. This is followed by a discussion of how the cyber operators used command servers to siphon information from the Buddhist networks over a long period of time. We conclude this section by examining some evidence that may suggest PRC involvement.

The Cycle of Cyber Operations Applied to APT

In reading the introduction to this section, one may wonder how the cyber operators were able to compromise such a large number of systems belonging to organizations affiliated with the Dalai Lama for such a long period of time. The answer lies in the use of *consolidation*—that is utilizing information obtained in a cyber espionage operation to target further systems. We can view this as the third step of a four-part cycle of operations (see Figure 7.4). The first step involves reconnaissance—the tasks of footprinting, scanning, and enumeration—which we laid out in the Titan Rain case study. The second step is *exploitation*—the actual theft or modification of data on target systems. The third step is to maintain persistence—that is to stay present on the target system while remaining undetected. In the third step, *consolidation*, some of the information garnered through exploitation is then used to identify and create new targets. Next, we shall discuss how hackers perform this last step.

Using Social Engineering and Malware to Perform Consolidation

Much like some of the compromised systems in Titan Rain, the cyber spies gained access to the Tibetan émigrés' systems using Trojans—seemingly innocuous pieces of software or data files that install malware onto the target system.[36] When the user clicks on a certain icon or link—normally received through e-mail or downloaded off the Internet—a series of events are commenced that allow an adversary access to that system. Often, this results in the Trojan constantly running on the affected system as either a piece of innocuous software or as an invisible process running on the system (hence maintaining persistence).

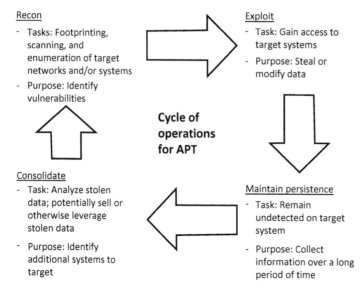

FIGURE 7.4 The cycle of operations for the Advanced Persistent Threats (APT).

In this case, the unsuspecting user received an e-mail with either an infected document or a link to a malicious Web site. When the user opens the document or clicks on the link, normally one of two things occurs: either the Trojan just simply executes on the target's computer system or it initiates contact with an outside server, which subsequently downloads and runs the actual Trojan to that machine.

In the first case, the user may be fooled into opening an executable file, say *report.doc.exe*, that instead of starting (for example) Microsoft Word, initiates the Trojan, thus compromising the system. In such a case, when security personnel identify the Trojan, they can easily identify the source (i.e., if the user received *report.doc.exe* in an e-mail).However, in the second case, the user opens a file inside a vulnerable program that initiates contact with an adversary's server. In this case, the user clicks on something like a malicious Adobe Acrobat file or a URL link. However, this malicious file or link, unlike *report.doc.exe*, is a real file or link (just containing malicious content). Hence, it is more difficult to detect. Further, this file or link is *not* the Trojan itself (instead, it is often simply called an "exploit" or "exploit kit"). Often, such an exploit kit will incorporate multiple software vulnerabilities (thereby allowing the adversary to get to the next step regardless of which version of the Web browser or other vulnerable software the user is running). The goal of the exploit is to initiate contact with the adversary's server. The exploit then ensures that the Trojan is downloaded to the target computer and starts working.

In this second scenario, investigations become more difficult. The discovery of the malicious software, in this case, does not necessarily tell a security professional of how it got to there. As the exploit must execute first, it is likely that by the time an investigation is conducted, the software (exploit) is long gone and all that remains is the Trojan running on the target computer. This makes it difficult to determine how the perpetrator initially gained access to the system—which means that it may happen again.

Using electronic communication, such as e-mail, for the purposes of obtaining unauthorized access to a computer system is often referred to as *phishing*. As phishing is an attempt to manipulate individuals to perform a certain action (i.e., activate a Trojan) or divulge information (i.e., disclose a password), it is considered a form of *social engineering*. In the case of the cyber espionage operations performed against the organizations affiliated with the Dalai Lama, the cyber operators used what is often referred to as *spear phishing*—extensive use of social engineering to craft an e-mail that has specific, personal information to entice a user to somehow activate a Trojan. As the attackers gained access to certain systems, they can start to understand relationships among employees based on things such as intra-office memorandums, e-mails, and other forms of communications. With this understanding, and access to certain computer systems, highly advanced spear phishing e-mails can be created. For instance, let us suppose the hacker obtains access to the computer of User A. In reviewing the user's e-mails, he finds that User A often works with User B. The hacker can then leverage his access to User A's computer to send an e-mail with an infected document to User B—perhaps asking User B to review the document. User B receives this seemingly normal message from his colleague and proceeds to activate the Trojan.

In the case of the intrusion into the Tibetan exiles' systems, the cyber spies initially used e-mails designed to interest a large number of the Tibetans in opening a malicious document. One such e-mail was sent from campaigns@freetibet.org and attached a Microsoft Word document entitled "Translation of Freedom Movement ID Book for Tibetans in Exile.doc."[37] Hence, by designing a legitimate-looking message, users were enticed to open the Microsoft Word file—which contained the Trojan. Later, e-mails were more highly targeted, using information harvested from those activating the initial Trojans.

One can also consider the spear phishing targeting the Buddhist organizations' computers in the context of the "security countermeasures" dimension of cyber security as discussed in the introduction of this book. Of the three components of security countermeasures—technology, policy/practices, and people, social engineering primarily relies on people being the weak link. Users in an organization not properly educated in the threat posed by malware-containing socially engineered e-mails are more likely to open such messages and their associated attachments. Hence, in any organization, education and training of the user population is a key factor in mitigating the effects of an adversary's cyber espionage campaign.

However, there is another aspect of security counter measures to be considered: technology. What tools do the system administrators have in place to detect and quarantine malicious documents? In addition to identifying such measures in the reconnaissance phase of the operation cycle, hackers also typically make an effort to use lesser known system vulnerabilities. The analysts at Information Warfare Monitor examined malicious files found on the Tibetan organizations' computers and found that of the 34 leading antivirus software packages in use at the time, only 11 were able to properly identify the files as containing Trojans.[38] Using lesser known vulnerabilities, or even discovering new vulnerabilities, are reliable methods for hackers to obtain access to systems and circumvent technological security countermeasure such as antivirus software.

Harvesting Data from the Compromised Systems

At least eight different families of Trojans were identified on the Tibetans expatriates' systems. Upon establishing connection with a command server, the malware allowed practically total access to the target systems. One of the first tasks performed by the malware installed by the Trojan is to communicate with a C&C server—much the same way as the botnets described earlier in this book do. About 70% of C&C servers identified by Information Warfare Monitor were in the PRC. Other locations of C&C servers included the U.S., Sweden, South Korea, and Taiwan. Further, the connections made to these C&C servers were employing HTTP—the standard protocol used for Web servers. By using this standard protocol, the network traffic to and from these servers appears less obvious—hence avoiding detection by intrusion detection systems (IDSs—see the previous section of this chapter for a brief discussion on these systems).

It turned out that several of the C&C servers identified by the Information Warfare Monitor researchers were still active during the time of the investigation. Based on the apparent configuration of these servers, members of this research team were able to deduce their file structure of the C&C server. Based on this logic, they were able to locate the software that allowed for remote administration of the machine and then obtained access to the administration interface for these servers. The administration interface is a software tool that allows the hackers to direct the actions of the compromised systems using easy-to-use Web-based screens. It turned out that the hypothesis of the researchers was correct. More bizarrely, they found administration interfaces on four of the C&C servers that were not secured. This allowed them to actually direct the actions of many of the compromised computers.[39]

The administrative interface of the C&C servers had three screens. These included a listing of infected machines in communication with the server, a tool to send commands to the infected computers, and a screen displaying the results of recently sent commands. The tool to send commands to the targets included several options. These commands included the acquisition of system information (such as listing of documents on the target machine), sending additional malware to the target (to add functionality), and a feature to make the malware on the target dormant. The ability to send additional malware to the target allows the hacker to perform such tasks as file management on the target, screen capture, key logging (which records all keystrokes taken on the target machine), audio capture (through the target's microphone), and webcam view. To disguise the traffic of the additional malware, the executable code is sent disguised as a digital image file.

One of the additional pieces of malware that can be uploaded to a target machine from the C&C server is a Chinese piece of software known as *gh0st RAT* (Remote Access Tool).[f] This provides many of the functionality (key logging, file management, etc.) described above by giving the hacker access to the target system in real time. We note that gh0st RAT can be configured to connect to a third-party command-and-control server (possibly different from the ones already described). Such use of an additional master server could be to obfuscate the lines of communication to the target or could resemble a division of labor (i.e., the breach and exploitation teams described in the Operation X case study earlier in the chapter).

The investigators at Information Warfare Monitor wanted more to fully understand the nature of the interaction between the version of gh0st RAT installed on the Buddhists' systems and their C&C servers. To do so, they set up what is known as a *honey pot*. A honey pot is a computer designed to appear vulnerable in order to lure hackers. Once the hackers

[f]Sometimes also referred to as "Remote Administration Tool."

gain access to the honey pot, their actions are then monitored by security professionals. However, instead of waiting for the honey pot to become infected, the researchers simply installed gh0st RAT on theirs. After installation, the researcher's honey pot attempted to established connection with master servers located in China. However, gh0st RAT can also use proxy servers—hence, the Chinese servers may have just been functioning as relays in the scheme.

Return to the issue of the administrative interface of the command-and-control server associated with the malware installed by the Trojan and consider the screen that shows the results of issued commands. Some of the results include information of the target system (amount of memory, disk space, computer name, operating system version, etc.), listing of files and folders, and even determining the geographic location of the target system. The listing of system information allows the cyber spy to be selective in what tool (i.e., gh0st RAT) he or she will use to further exploit the system. With this additional level of detail, the perpetrator can ensure that any additional malware sent to the target will not only function properly but also do so in the stealthiest manner possible. The listing of files and folders on the target's computer is also highly useful for exploitation. In this way, the attacker can preselect what information is to be exfiltrated from the target using gh0st RAT or similar tools. In this way, the hacker can often avoid searching through files on the target system in real time—which would increase the chances of detection (note that a similar technique was used by the hackers during Operation X in the previous section). Additionally, some of the newer versions of the administrative interface allowed the hackers to perform a geoIP lookup on the target—enabling them to determine which country an infected system was located. The geographic information aides not only in the exploitation but also in developing follow-on operations during the consolidation phase as precise country information of a system can enhance spear-phishing attacks.

Hints of PRC Involvement

As usual, we note that it is virtually impossible to state with certainty that the cyber espionage operations directed against the Tibetan émigrés truly originated from China—not to mention PRC sponsorship. However, there are some indicators that may point to PRC involvement. We have already discussed that many of the command-and-control servers involved in the operation were located in China—which is perhaps the most obvious hint at involvement of the Chinese government. Now we look at other factors that suggest an official hand in this operation.

In examining cyber espionage operations against any organization, the question arises who would benefit from the monitoring, theft, or modification of the target's data. As the office of the Dalai Lama and its affiliates are perhaps one of the best known dissident groups working against the Chinese occupation of Tibet, their activities are of much interest to the PRC. Given that the earliest observed communication to C&C servers took place in March 2007,[40] the operation commenced after the apparent shift in PRC policy against freelance hacking, although ahead of the enactment of stricter antihacking laws in 2009. This consideration makes it less likely that it was the work of freelance or patriotic Chinese hackers. Further, even though this operation took place before the passing of the new antihacking laws, the related attack of the Shadow Network (discussed in the next section) was actually launched afterward. If both operations were conducted by the same organization, the hackers behind Shadow Network were operating illegally—unless sanctioned by the PRC.

An alternative explanation is that the cyber espionage operation was conducted by a criminal organization. As we saw earlier in this book, several criminal organizations in Russia rent out botnets that could be capable of what is described in this section. It is feasible that a similar group or groups could exist in China, but what motive would they have collecting data on the Tibetans? The office of the Dalai Lama is responsible for much of the Dali Lama's strategic communication. Though the exact nature of the stolen documents is unknown (due to confidentiality issues), the researchers at Information Warfare Monitor note that some of the documents appeared significant to Sino-Tibetan negotiations. Additionally, of the nearly 1300 infected computers, the researchers labeled 397 of them as high-value targets due to their significant relationship between the PRC and Tibet, Taiwan, or India. Others were associated with embassies, diplomatic missions, government ministries, or international organizations. In order to obtain access to these systems, the hackers must have used social engineering via numerous phishing attempts. This level of effort seems unlikely for a criminal enterprise seeking to simply gain access to systems for activities such as fraud or large-scale phishing.

As Tibetans strive for autonomy, the targeted organizations essentially form Tibet's government in exile. Like in any other (international) conflict, negotiations may be accompanied by the show of military force[41] and as described earlier in this chapter, cyberspace is understood as a new addition to Chinese military strategy. In fall 2006, a deadly incident at the Nangpa La Pass propelled the plight of Tibetans once again into the focus of world attention. From the 75 Tibetans, who charged for neighboring Nepal, only 41 arrived safely in Kathmandu. Chinese border security opened fire on the unarmed refugees, who were mainly children and fatally shot a 17-year-old nun, a 13-year-old boy,[42] and a young man.[43] Around 9 to 14 children between the ages of 6 and 10 were arrested. The news of the tragedy was brought to the world stage only due to the reporting of Western eyewitnesses—mountaineers, some of who took photographs of or videotaped the event as it happened.[44,45] In spring of 2008, the 49th anniversary of the Tibetan Uprising Day and socio-economic grievances stirred considerable protest against Chinese repression, which spread quickly from Lhasa to other regions and monasteries of the Tibet Autonomous Region and beyond. In the year of the Beijing Olympics, it was in the government's interest to resolve the situation quickly. Diverging accounts of the total number of individuals on both sides who lost their lives eventually ranged between 20 (official Chinese reports) and more than 200 (according to Tibetan authorities).[46] Massive trials against arrested protestors sought to put a quick end to the riots themselves before the Olympic Games were to commence in August.[47]

The violence spawned subsequent negotiations with representatives of His Holiness the Dalai Lama, whom the Chinese government held responsible for instigating the unrest (Figure 7.5).[48] State media ran defamation campaigns against the Tibetan authority in exile.[49] Independent media is generally restricted especially in Tibet, but this time the Chinese government granted 26 foreign reporters access to Lhasa.[50] After the emanation of violence, Chinese officials apparently took every measure at hand to curb foreign publications on the situation in Tibet, ranging from the destruction of photographs and video footage to death threats against 10 journalists.[51] A German television station running an opinion poll on the cancellation of the Olympic torch relay experienced drastically increasing amounts of visitors to their Web site. Eventually, the television's correspondent in Beijing reported that the

FIGURE 7.5 The Dalai Lama, pictured here with President Barrack Obama, leads the Tibetan Government in exile. It is possible that the Chinese government leverages cyber espionage against Tibetans for critical information to obtain an advantage in their negotiations with this group. (For color version of this figure, the reader is referred to the online version of this chapter.) *Official White House photo by Pete Souza.*

information about the opinion poll had been posted on 7600 Chinese Web sites calling upon their visitors to "not cast the wrong vote."[52] Eventually, 600,000 users had voted against the premature end to the torch relay.[53] Although this incident was apparently the result of an aggregate effort of Chinese individuals, the BBC also reports on the government's sophisticated practice of keyword filtering and blocking foreign media and their Web sites.[54] As in October 2007, the Chinese government blocked access to social media Web sites.[55, 56] In addition to YouTube, the authorities apparently rendered the Web sites of online media, The Guardian, Yahoo, and L.A. Times unavailable to Chinese Internet users.[57] The Tibetan protests were neither the first nor the last occasion for the Chinese government to execute Internet censorship. In the wake and during the 2008 Olympic Games, Beijing blocked the Web sites of amnesty international and other human rights organizations as well as the online presence of Tibetan authorities in exile.[58] Other case studies of government filtering and use of the Internet against dissidents in Russia and Iran are described in greater detail in Chapter 5.

In the aftermath, Chinese academics and human rights activists called for press freedom and the independent investigation into the recent crisis in Tibet.[59] Chinese philosopher Zhang Boshu published an extensive treatise in which he points out that the Chinese problem with Tibet is first and foremost a human rights issue and that the arrogance of Han-dominated China prevents improvements in Sino-Tibetan relations. Although Boshu does not support Tibetan independence, he argues that violence and oppression cannot lead to peaceful coexistence and cooperation.[60]

Writings like this appear to voice the growing awareness among the Chinese public of not only the grievous situation of Tibetans in Tibet but also the drastic mishandling of the situation by their government. The latter now had to face increasing internal critique in addition to international accusations of human right abuses in Tibet.[61] To make matters worse, the envoys of the Dalai Lama presented the government officially with their "Memorandum on Genuine Autonomy for the Tibetan People" in the commencing round of negotiations in November 2008.[62] Chinese officials decried the advance as pretext for Tibetan independence and apparent violation of Chinese law.[63] After the long history of Sino-Tibetan negotiations, especially since the late 1980s, numerous revisions of the Memorandum and additional rounds of talks since 2008, the involved envoys of His Holiness the Dalai Lama, Lodi Gyari, and Kelsang Gyaltsen, resigned in summer 2012 in the face of the lack of positive Chinese reactions and a deteriorating situation in Tibet.[64]

Against this backdrop and the emerging Chinese cyber prowess described earlier in this chapter, the case of cyber espionage against the Tibetan institutions appears to have commenced as soon as the necessary infrastructure was in place and the necessary capabilities were achieved. Quite possibly, the information gathered in this case might have provided Beijing with great insight into the inner workings as well as external relations of this adversary and might have put Chinese negotiators, public relations specialists, and propagandists, as well as policy makers and military strategists at a significant advantage. Negotiators would be knowledgeable in the details of the Tibetans' agenda, effectively rendering their diplomatic strategy unworkable. Public relations specialists, who are aware of potentially upcoming buzz themes in the media war over public opinion, find themselves in the formidable position to prepare counter propaganda and take the punch out of the news from the Tibetan side. Almost needless to ponder is the plethora of actionable intelligence made available through cyber espionage to policy makers. The Chinese government's objective in regard to Tibet is to prevent its independence, because it views the territory as an intrinsic part of the motherland.[65] Knowing about every move Tibetan authorities make, would put the PRC in control and in the position to match and counter any forthcoming Tibetan policies and political advances. The Tibetans' foreign relations could be monitored and documented easily. Any rifts in internal or external relations could easily be exploited to further China's interests. If China is indeed using information stolen from Tibetan computers in order to obtain an edge at the negotiation table, then it would be a clear example of intelligence gathering (the cyber espionage) feeding into an operation (the negotiations). In this case, it would also be likely that information requirements identified by negotiators would be sent back to the cyber spies, which would cause them to target new systems in the hope of better supporting the negotiations.

In addition to the aforementioned described hints and hypotheses of PRC involvement, the researchers at Information Warfare Monitor present an anecdote that provides further insight into this issue. One of the organizations investigated by the researchers was a pro-Tibetan NGO known as Drewla. During the investigation, a young woman at a Drewla office in Dharamsala, India decided to visit her family in a village in Tibet after working for 2 years at the NGO. She claims that she was detained by the Chinese at the China-Nepal border for 2 months on suspicion of involvement in pro-Tibetan activities. When she denied such involvement during the interrogation, she was presented with transcripts of her Internet chat communications from her time at Drewla. Eventually, she was released to her village.[66]

This story, if true, highlights one way in which cyber espionage operations are used against dissident groups. In the past, authoritarian regimes leveraged signals intelligence (SIGINT, mainly phone taps) against potential rebels. In 2003, while Paulo Shakarian, one of the authors, was deployed to Iraq, many of the locals correctly identified antennas on top of a major hotel in Baghdad as one of Saddam Hussein's SIGINT stations. Upon inspection of the interior of the building, U.S. soldiers found aging pieces of equipment specializing in the collection of signal intelligence. Hussein was able to leverage this capability to answer some of his information requirements—particularly those internal to the country. There is some evidence that China has leveraged SIGINT in a similar manner. The anecdote above shows how intelligence gathered from a cyber espionage operation was used to support an interrogation. It is interesting to note that cyber espionage and SIGINT often can answer related information requirements and add redundancy and verification to an intelligence collection plan. Perhaps, this is why the People's Liberation Army tasked the 3rd General Staff Department (historically assigned a signals intelligence mission) with the cyber espionage tasks.

The story of Gh0stNet provides some good insight into the advanced persistent threat—where systems are monitored for months or even years—for the purpose of intelligence gathering. The challenges with this type of operation seem to differ somewhat from the more straightforward data exfiltrations of Titan Rain or the case of Operation X. Further, the use of social engineering allowed the hackers to perform the step of consolidation—completing a cyber operations cycle and allowing them to action follow-on targets.

While the operators behind Gh0stNet were largely successful, they still made several mistakes. Perhaps, the most glaring errors of the hackers dealt with the ease at which command-and-control servers could be found and the fact that they were not properly secured. About a year after Gh0stNet, the same investigators analyzed another cyber espionage ring—likely involving many of the operators from Gh0stNet. This is known as the Shadow Network and showed an increase in sophistication when compared to Gh0stNet, because it addressed some of the short comings. We shall explore the Shadow Network in the next section.

USING LEGITIMATE WEB SITES FOR DATA EXFILTRATION: THE SHADOW NETWORK

After the investigation of Gh0stNet, researchers from the Information Warfare Monitor noticed that the vast majority of domain names used for the Gh0stNet hackers' command-and-control servers went offline. But complaints about malware infections from the personal office of the Dalai Lama continued. Working with another group of researchers, known as the Shadowserver Foundation, the investigators found that one of the computers was compromised by two different types of malware. Upon examining the communication from the malware to its associated command-and-control servers, the investigators concluded that at least two different groups of spies were conducting cyber espionage operations against this particular machine in the office of the Dalai Lama.[67] The subsequent examination of the relationships among the command-and-control servers to identify potential espionage networks revealed that one of these networks, known as the *Shadow Network,* was found to be used for cyber espionage operations not only against the office of the Dalai Lama, but also targeting the Indian government and Indian military systems among others. The observed relationships among the involved command-and-control servers were found to be based on their respective domain names, which over time revolved to the same IP addresses, malware on one of the server being used to connect to another and similarities among file paths on these servers.

Leveraging Legitimate Web Sites for Data Exfiltration

The investigators assess that, as with Gh0stNet, the hackers behind the Shadow Network relied on spear phishing in order to gain access to targeted systems. They observed that the hackers used files such as Adobe Acrobat (PDF), Microsoft PowerPoint (PPT), and Microsoft Word (DOC) that contained Trojans that exploited one of several vulnerabilities. Although the vulnerabilities used by PPT and DOC files were older and hence better known, the PDF files used weaknesses that had been addressed by Adobe only several weeks prior to the infection. Hence, though a counter measure was available, it clearly was not in place in the Tibetan information systems due to its (then) very recent development.

When the researchers examined the actual malware installed by the Trojans, they noticed a significant departure from what they found in Gh0stNet. In several of the infected systems, the investigators found that the Shadow Network hackers were not relying on a simple command-and-control server or even a proxy thereto, but were rather using popular Web sites such as Yahoo! Mail and Twitter to add a layer of communication to the target system. For instance, several computers were found to connect to Yahoo! Mail. The hackers interfaced directly with a Yahoo!'s e-mail inbox using the associated application program interface (API)—the set of software libraries intended for the development of legitimate applications to access Yahoo! Mail. Using this communication with Yahoo! Mail, the infected computer periodically used a particular e-mail account to send and receive messages. In a scheme of direct communication, the hackers would send e-mails to the target machine, which contained executable code (computer code that is capable of actually running a piece of software) directing the computer to do further actions. These actions functioned similarly to the capabilities provided to the Gh0stNet hackers in the administrative interface of their command-and-control (C&C) servers. The investigators analyzed this executable code and found that it directs the target to download another piece of malware from a Web site publically hosted on a Google server. This malware, in turn, connected to another C&C server in order to download several files disguised as digital images, which allowed it to connect to the Tor anonymity network.[68] This network is used by individuals desiring anonymity such as journalists, law enforcement, and human rights activists. Tor is an anonymity system that uses a special protocol known as Onion Routing to hide the origin of the sender. A message sent on the Tor network relies on a series of servers to route the message to its destination. A given message travels from an "entrance node" to an "exit node." The sender's location is only known to the "entrance node" and the data are encrypted until they reach the "exit node" (full details of this protocol can be found in Goldschlag *et al.*[69]). Although the exit node has no memory of the original sender, it passes on the original, unencrypted message. The researchers from Information Warfare Monitor referred to a study by Dan Egerstad[70] where he examined network traffic leaving an exit node in the Tor network. He identified information, apparently from embassies belonging to countries such as Australia, Japan, Iran, and India. Based on his conversations with some embassy personnel, Egerstad suspected that someone hacked the accounts of the embassy personnel, sent data through Tor, and then eavesdropped on the exit nodes. In this way, he could capture the data in a stealthy manner, as the location of the eavesdropper would not be in the Tor network path. It is possible that members of the Shadow Network were using Tor in a similar manner to exfiltrate data from their targets.

Yahoo! Mail was not the only legitimate Web site being misused by members of the Shadow Network for data exfiltration. The Information Warfare Monitor investigators found

Shadow Network malware that used Baidu Blogs, Twitter, Google Groups, and other similar sites to control the compromised computers. These channels of communication were often used in conjunction with traditional HTTP-based C&C—similar to what was observed in Gh0stNet. However, unlike Gh0stNet, the hackers made better efforts to obfuscate the HTTP-based command-and-control servers as well. They relied on legitimate free Web-hosting services such as justfree.com and yourfreehosting.net and free domains provided by co.tv and net.ru. The IP addresses associated with C&C servers on the free domains were all traced back to locations in the U.S. and Germany. But when these free hosting accounts for whatever reason failed to function, the researchers observed that the hackers would send a message to the compromised systems via a blog post redirecting their HTTP traffic to what appeared to be the "core" C&C servers. This handful of servers, as it turned out, resided in the Peoples' Republic of China (Figure 7.6).

Targets of the Shadow Network

The researchers at Information Warfare Monitor and the Shadowserver Foundation used a novel technique known as *DNS Sinkholing* to investigate the Shadow Network. Often the command-and-control (C&C) server of a botnet or other network of compromised computers is either shutdown or becomes abandoned. In the aftermath of such abandonment, the compromised systems may still attempt to communicate with the server. With DNS Sinkholing, a security professional registers a machine using the name of the C&C server.

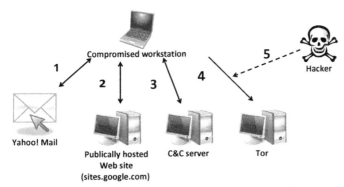

1 The target established a connection with a Yahoo! Mail account and receives an email with executable code that directs the target to download malware from a publically hosted web site.

2 The target downloads the malware from the publically hosted web site.

3 Directed by the new malware, the compromised system downloads files disguised as digital images from another C&C server.

4 The new files direct the target to upload unencrypted data files to Tor.

5 While uploading the files to Tor, the hacker monitors the unencrypted traffic, hence obtaining the desired data from the compromised system.

FIGURE 7.6 Use of Yahoo! Mail for command and control of a compromised workstation. The relationship to the Tor network is hypothesized based on a different investigation. (For color version of this figure, the reader is referred to the online version of this chapter.)

The compromised machines then connect to the server belonging to the security professional. The IP addresses of the compromised machines can then be identified in order to determine the extent of the spread of a given piece of malware.[8] The idea is similar to that of a "Honey Pot." A "Honey Pot" is a system set up by security professionals with the goal of enticing individuals to compromise it—hence, allowing the security pros to study the behavior of the hackers. A DNS Sinkhole is similar in that it is set up by security professionals to study the behavior of malicious software. However, it differs in that it is designed to capture traffic of compromised systems rather than lure attackers.

The investigators used this technique based on abandoned C&C servers to which the computers in the Office of His Holiness the Dalai Lama were attempting to connect. They found that a great many of systems were compromised—many completely unrelated to the Tibetan organizations whose infected computers initiated the analysis. Affected computers were located in academic institutions such as New York University, the University of Western Ontario, and Kaunas University of Technology (Lithuania); or pertained to media outlets such as the *Times of India*. Science and technology organizations such as the Commission for Science and Technology for Sustainable Development in Pakistan and the National Informatics Center in India as well as various Indian institutions, including the Chambers of Commerce and Industry and the New Delhi Railway station, had also been infected.

In addition to DNS Sinkholing, the investigators were able to recover stolen data from one of the C&C servers that was not properly secured. In addition to the documents captured from the Office of the Dalai Lama, the researchers found data relating to government diplomatic missions, national security, defense, academia, and the media. India was the predominant target of these exfiltrations. Several documents taken from Indian diplomatic computers were marked with "SECRET" (two documents), "RESTRICTED" (six documents), or "CONFIDENTIAL" (five documents) markings.[71] Many of these classified documents dealt with security assessments of certain Indian provinces as well as embassy information on India's relationship with Russia, West African nations, and the Middle East. Unlike the documents taken from diplomatic organizations, the data exfiltrated from defense systems appeared to be unclassified. However, it appears that the information taken was not generally known to the public. Documents were recovered relating to the Russian Pechora Missile System,[72] the Israeli Iron Dome air defense system, and an Indian artillery system known as Project Shakti.[73] The hackers also stole documents on several academics and journalists—focusing on those associated with writings either on the containment of the Peoples' Republic of China, Chinese military exports, the Chinese-Indian relationship, or armed groups within the PRC.

Much of the stolen data may seem to answer Chinese IRs, but there were other clues that pointed the researchers to suggest the involvement of the Chinese government.

Clues of Chinese Involvement in the Shadow Network

The investigators from Information Warfare Monitor captured several evidences that linked the operators to Chengdu, Sichuan. First, the IP addresses from which the e-mails were sent to the compromised machines via Yahoo! Mail (as described earlier) were traced back to Chengdu.

---

[8]For more on DNS Sinkholing, we suggest the SANS Institute paper "DNS Sinkhole" by Guy Bruneau available at http://www.sans.org/reading_room/whitepapers/dns/dns-sinkhole_33523.

Second, the investigators obtained a document describing how to use Yahoo! Mail to remote control-infected computers. This document also contained an e-mail address which when investigated by the researchers led to several advertisements for apartment rentals—also located in Chengdu. The Information Warfare Monitor researchers point out that a Technical Reconnaissance Brigade (TRB) of the Chinese government (traditionally tasked with SIGINT collection and believed to be involved in cyber espionage) is located in Chengdu. Unfortunately, there is not much more analysis that can link the attacks to the Chengdu TRB. However, it seems plausible that the Shadow Network, an international cyber espionage ring, is the type of operation that would fall within the TRB's traditional role—intelligence collection through SIGINT.

The stories of Gh0stNet and the Shadow Network illustrate how cyber espionage operators monitored target systems over a long period of time for intelligence collection purposes. The targets of these cyber espionage operations included Tibetan dissidents and governmental organizations from countries that China may have a substantial interest in. In the next section, we examine another attack largely attributed to the Peoples' Republic in China—Operation Aurora. The level of sophistication increases yet again in this cyber espionage operation, but this time the targets are mainly part of the industry sector.

CYBER WAR THROUGH INTELLECTUAL PROPERTY THEFT: OPERATION AURORA

On January 12, 2010, Google announced shocking news. The firm published on its official blog that it had been the victim of a cyber warfare originating from China. According to the blog, the purpose of the operation was to access the Gmail e-mail accounts of Chinese human rights activists.[74] As a result of this cyber espionage operation, Google announced that it would no longer censor results on its flagship search engine in China—google.cn—a move that caused consternation with the PRC. The company stated that if they could not run their search engine uncensored, they would be willing to close operations in China.

Literally, minutes after the announcement from Google, Adobe—another major software vendor—announced that their corporate systems had also been hacked.[75] It turns out that both Google and Adobe were targets of the same adversary—an adversary that conducted the very same operation against 32 more companies. These firms included Dow Chemical, Northrop Grumman, Symantec, and Yahoo.[76] It seems the purpose of the operation was to exfiltrate not only information about Chinese human rights activists but also intellectual property—namely, source code of commercially developed software.[77]

This operation—known as "Operation Aurora"—is the topic of this section. It leveraged social engineering along with an advanced Trojan known as Hydraq to steal intellectual property. Several analysts strongly suspect PRC involvement. Here, we review the attack, review the evidence of PRC involvement, and discuss the implications of intellectual property theft from corporations.

Trojan.Hydraq

The act of cyber espionage dubbed "Operation Aurora" employed an exploit in Microsoft Internet Explorer that was exploited by software referred to as *Trojan.Hydraq* by the security firm Symantec. As with several of the cyber espionage operations discussed in this chapter, Operation Aurora was initiated with spear phishing. In the case of the Google break-in, it is thought that this initial spear phishing was directed at an employee using the Microsoft Messenger instant chat software. The user supposedly received a link to a malicious Web site during one of his chat.[78] It is unknown if the operations against the other firms were also initiated with chat software. Based on similar operations (such as those discussed earlier in this chapter), it seems likely that e-mail may have also been used as a way to initiate the infiltration of the malicious software. Either way, the initial communication to these firms had three characteristics. First, they were sent to a select group of individuals, which suggests that this type of targeting (spear phishing) indicates that the hackers had some additional source of intelligence on their targets. Second, the communications were engineered in a way to appear as though they originated from a trusted source, which also shows that the perpetrators were operating with profiles of their targets. Third, they all contained a link to a Web site—clicking upon which initiated a certain series of events.

Once the user clicked on the link, their Web browser would visit a site based out of Taiwan. This Web site, in turn, executed malicious JavaScript code—this is source code that runs on a Web site normally used to provide interactive features to the user. The malicious JavaScript code exploited a weakness in the Microsoft Internet Explorer Web browser that was largely unknown at the time. Often, such a new vulnerability is termed a "zero-day exploit." The malevolent JavaScript code proceeds to download a second piece of malware from Taiwan—disguised as an image file. This secondary malicious software would proceed to run in Windows and set up a *back door* allowing a cyber-spy access to the targeted system.[79] A back door refers to a method of accessing a system that allows an intruder to circumvent the normal security mechanism.

The use of a zero-day exploit is significant because identifying such a vulnerability most likely required a skillful engineering effort. This, along with the highly targeted spear-phishing campaign (suggesting that the hackers had access to some additional intelligence on their targets), might hint at the backing of a larger organization—possibly a nation-state.

Theft of Intellectual Property

Several months after Google announced that it had been hacked, the *New York Times* reported that more than just e-mail accounts of Chinese human rights activists had been compromised. Citing an unnamed source with direct knowledge of the Google investigation, reporter John Markoff wrote that the source code to Google's state-of-the-art password system had likely been stolen during Operation Aurora.[80] The system, known as *Gaia*, was designed to allow users of Google's software to use a single username and password to access the myriad of Google services. This software is also known as "Single Sign-On." Markoff reported that Google addressed the problem by adding an additional layer of encryption to their password system.

The compromise of *Gaia* is significant for more than one reason. First, obtaining software source code of a commercial system is intellectual property theft and thus unlawful in the United States. As with the data stolen during Titan Rain, the stolen source code could allow certain developers to illicitly create software similar to *Gaia*. If we view Operation Aurora as the actions of a nation-state, theft of intellectual property can be thought of as a form of economic warfare—leveling the technological playing field in order to reduce the advantage of an adversary nation's industrial capability. Clearly, this is in line with the Chinese ideas of *Unrestricted Warfare*—where various forms of IW occur constantly (including during peacetime) and attack all aspects of a nation's power (including industry).

However, beyond the economic advantages gained by the theft of source code, major security implications are also imminent—particularly in the case of *Gaia*. Consider the cyber espionage operation cycle described earlier in this chapter (see the section on Gh0stNet). In the final phase of this cycle, the hackers consolidate their gains. Specifically, they used information obtained from their infiltration to help develop intelligence for follow-on operations. With Gh0stNet and the Shadow Network, the consolidation phase primarily relied on leveraging personal information obtained from computer systems to identify new targets and create socially engineered e-mails to entice those targets to allow access to their systems. The consolidation phase from these two operations can be thought of primarily as analysis and development of communications intelligence (COMINT). This type of intelligence deals with intercepted communications from people. Assuming the perpetrators of the Google hack follow the same *modus operandi*, the consolidation phase for *Gaia* would be different. Analysts working with the hackers would most likely determine technical vulnerabilities in the password system. The examination of a piece of technology in order to understand its inner workings and identify weaknesses is often referred to as technical intelligence (TECHINT).

Though it is clear that the theft of intellectual property is an important consideration for corporations, it also raises an important question. How were the attackers able to obtain source code for a system such as *Gaia* by leveraging a relatively small number of compromised computer systems? It turns out that many corporations work with specialized servers as storehouses for this type of data—often fittingly termed "intellectual property repositories." Centralized locations of this type of data make it easier for teams to work collaboratively on a project and share information with each other. These systems often take the form of Software Configuration Management (SCM) systems such as IBM Rationale© or content management systems such as Microsoft SharePoint©. Following Operation Aurora, McAfee examined Perforce© and found a few facets of that system that allowed unauthorized access.[81] We list a few below:

- By default, the passwords for the Perforce system are unencrypted. Hence, if intercepted during login, an adversary can easily read and reuse the password to obtain unauthorized access.
- An arbitrary user can list out all the workspaces on Perforce. Workspaces are areas on the server designed for a team to collaborate on a software project. Therefore, with a single compromise, an adversary can enumerate all workspaces—an important step in reconnaissance (see the section on "Titan Rain" in this chapter for more on reconnaissance).
- All communication between Perforce and the user is unencrypted. Hence, a third party somehow eavesdropping on their communication can steal intellectual property in transit.
- By default, user accounts created on Perforce have high privileges. If a system administrator does not change the default, a single compromised account on the system can potentially lead to theft of any intellectual property on the repository.

We illustrate these points about Perforce© as it is commonly used as an intellectual property repository and its particular vulnerabilities of that system are common to such repository systems in general.

Similar to the case of Stuxnet described later in this book, Operation Aurora invalidated a key assumption made by many system administrators and IP repository software vendors at the time. The professionals operating those networks assumed that the intellectual property would not be accessed due to security countermeasures taken to protect the network as a whole. The result of this perspective is a lesser focus on the security of an IP repository lying within the perimeter of a corporation's network. By utilizing a zero-day vulnerability for their mission, the perpetrators behind Operation Aurora were able to exploit this assumption.

Theft of intellectual property, as with the other types of data exfiltration, already discussed in this chapter also presents another key difficulty—determining what was actually stolen. In the wake of Operation Aurora, security researcher George Kurtz wrote an article entitled "Where's the body?"[82] As opposed to a physical theft where it is relatively easy to determine what was stolen, with cyber espionage and data exfiltration this is much more difficult to establish. Though systems administrators have a few tools at hand—such as the examination of server logs and the analysis of network traffic—in advanced cyber espionage operations hackers often take various steps to cover up their tracks and operate in a manner, which makes it difficult to ascertain what data were stolen. For instance, if we consider Operation X described earlier in this chapter, we see that the hackers encrypted the stolen information before exfiltration. In that case, even a reconstruction of the upload from the company's network would not reveal the stolen information. Though security vendors provide software solutions to help with this issue, determining "where's the body" in the wake of a cyber espionage operation is still often a difficult task.

Indicators of PRC Involvement

It is interesting that Google's announcement of the security breach seems to implicate Chinese involvement—or suggests at least complacency on the side of the government. Here are some indicators that Operation Aurora was executed with the full knowledge or even under the directive of the Chinese government.

The earliest signs of Chinese involvement were made public in January 2010—several weeks after Google's initial blog post. A report released by the security firm VeriSign stated that the "source IP's and drop server of the attack correspond to a single foreign entity consisting of either agents of the Chinese state or proxies thereof."[83] The researchers at VeriSign also found that the Aurora hackers used HomeLinux Dynamic DNS and "borrowed" IP addresses from the American firm Linode (a company specializing in Virtual Private Server Hosting). These are the same circumstances as in a July 2009 DDoS attacks against South Korea and Washington, D.C. Even more so the IP addresses for all these attacks were within the same subnet—in fact, only six addresses apart. These and other similarities between the two operations led the VeriSign researchers to conclude that Aurora and the attacks against Washington, DC and South Korea were possibly conducted by the same entity.

Just a few weeks later, *New York Times* reporters John Markoff and David Barboza published an article which stated that investigators had identified two Chinese schools of higher education involved in the attack[84]—Shanghai Jiaotong University and the Lanxiang Vocational School. The former's Information Security Engineering Institute is the workplace of Peng Yinan (alleged to be the Chinese hacker "CoolSwallow"). When *New York Times* reporters conducted an anonymous telephone interview with a professor from that institute, they were surprised with the candid response. He stated that students hacking into foreign computer networks were "quite normal."[85] However, as an alternate explanation, the professor stated that the university's IP address could also have been hijacked which he said "frequently happens."[86]

At the Lanxiang Vocational School, the investigators were able to identify a specific class taught by a Ukrainian professor suspected to be involved in Operation Aurora.[h] When confronted with the suspicion, the dean of the computer science department there (identified in the media only as Mr. Shao) stated that the students at the school simply would not have the ability to carry out such an attack. However, he did acknowledge that students from the school were often recruited into the military.[87]

The reports of Chinese involvement might have inspired U.S. Secretary of State Hillary Clinton's speech on Internet freedom given shortly after Google's announcement.[88] In this speech, she called upon China to perform a transparent investigation on the intrusions into Google. This was perhaps the strongest statement by a high-ranking U.S. government official made in response to a cyber warfare incident at the time. More recently, U.S. Secretary of Defense Leon Panetta also made statements in the wake of recent cyber warfare operations—this is discussed in the next chapter (Figure 7.7).

China responded to the accusations and Clinton's strong diplomatic statements by resorting to the "three warfares" as outlined earlier in this chapter.[89] First, in order to ensure that the media supported their righteous cause, the government imposed tight guidelines on all media outlets directing them to only use central government media when writing on the

FIGURE 7.7 U.S. Secretary of State, Hillary Clinton (pictured here in early 2010) spoke out on Internet freedom shortly after Operation Aurora was discovered. At the time, she was the highest ranking U.S. official to make a statement on a cyber operation. (For color version of this figure, the reader is referred to the online version of this chapter.) *State Department photo by Michael Gross.*

[h] As of the time of this writing, the extent of the involvement of the class and the name of the Ukrainian professor appear unavailable in open-source reporting.

incident and not investigate or analyze it further. With regard to the legal aspect of the "three warfares," the initial response from the Chinese Foreign Ministry spokesman focused not on Operation Aurora, but on Google's threat to not adhere to Chinese censorship laws. This move was designed to illustrate to the public that Google was the one breaking the law— not China. Finally, with regard to psychological warfare, Chinese media began publishing counterpoints to Google's claim—specifically accusing Google and the U.S. government of conspiring against China. Google and the U.S. government fabricated the claim in order to justify violation of Chinese censorship law, the Chinese government reasoned. In support of this argument, *China Daily* pointed out that four of Google's former executives were currently holding positions in the U.S. government.[90]

Operation Aurora illustrates the continued evolution of cyber espionage in the early twenty-first century. In this case of cyber espionage, the targeted information was deemed so important that the operators utilized a zero-day exploit and spear phishing to gain access to corporate systems, locate the target's intellectual property repositories, and steal company secrets. Originally reported by Google, this operation affected over 30 big-name companies. The stolen information was unlikely to only further economic gain, but is also feasibly beneficial for technical intelligence, such as the evaluation of vulnerabilities—possibly for use in further cyber attacks. Operation Aurora invalidated existing assumptions about the security of intellectual property repositories in corporations and again highlighted the difficulty of determining the specifics of the captured data. The news media accounts of potential involvement of China led to a diplomatic statement by the U.S. Secretary of State, which, in turn, elicited responses by the Chinese government which resolved to the "Three Warfares." Operation Aurora is not unique. In its aftermath, there have been other Chinese-attributed cyber maneuvers performed with the goal of stealing intellectual property. A series of events known as Nitro[91] (directed against the chemical industry) and Night Dragon[92] (against the energy sector) are but two examples. Finally, there are many potential second- and third-order effects of a major software vendor such as Google or Adobe being hacked. It is unknown what consequences the knowledge of potentially widely used software, such as Google's *Gaia* password system, will have in follow-on cyber operations. Though currently not connected to Aurora, it was recently revealed that Adobe's software certificate system was hacked— allowing malicious software to create seemingly safe add-ons to many of that firm's software.[93] In this case, a development server at Adobe was broken into. It is a clear example of how the cyber security of a major software vendor's own systems can have a direct impact on an extremely large population of users—hence, potentially providing ample opportunities to an adversary conducting follow-on cyber attacks.

AN EXAMPLE OF THE CURRENT STATE OF THE ART: SYKIPOT

In 2011, a class of malware known as "Sykipot" reemerged in cyber space. By this time, Sykipot had been around for a few years—with unconfirmed reports from as early as 2006.[94] This particular piece of malware is a Trojan—installing a back door onto the target machine for the purposes of exfiltrating information. In March 2010, Sykipot was loaded onto target computers using a zero-day vulnerability in Microsoft Internet Explorer. In late 2011, the malware was again being used in conjunction with a zero-day vulnerability—this time in

Adobe Acrobat and Acrobat Reader. The software was again distributed using spear phishing. The hackers sent e-mails to targeted individuals in federal agencies and contract organizations containing a malicious Adobe Acrobat PDF file that exploited the zero-day vulnerability, installing the back door that once initiated and created a secure connection with a command-and-control server. The *modus operandi* was very similar to the attacks described previously. The weakness in Adobe Acrobat was originally noticed by Lockheed Martin's security response team and the Defense Security Information Exchange (DSIE)—a group of major U.S. defense contractors that share knowledge on assurance information.

The e-mails and PDF files used in the spear-phishing campaign were particularly well crafted. One such message contained a PDF file that had the latest per-diem rates (daily allowances for U.S. government employees on travel to defray the costs of meals and other incidental expenses).[95] Another had a 2012 guide on the contract award process.[96] As with the previous attacks in this chapter, these messages illustrate the great care taken by the attackers to select their targets—this was not a mass e-mail campaign, but rather a highly precise operation.

The security firm AlienVault examined traffic to the C&C servers transmitted by Sykipot and noticed that some of the exfiltrated data dealt with American technology for unmanned aerial vehicles (UAVs) and space technology. Specifically, they found unclassified documents relating to Boeing's X-45 Unmanned Combat Air Vehicle (UCAV) and X-37 orbital vehicle.[97] The researchers at AlienVault also managed to trace the controlling server's traffic back to Chinese IP addresses. They noticed that the malware contained error messages in Chinese, a fact that was also confirmed by researchers at Symantec.[98] Based on the Chinese principles of information warfare, it would be feasible that the Chinese government had a vested interest in supporting these missions as information on experimental aircraft furthers both economic and military goals as espoused in *Unrestricted Warfare*. Further, considering the Sykipot campaigns since 2007, there were six total observed zero-day exploits—five of which were used in 2010 or later. These vulnerabilities could indicate that the operations were sponsored by a well-funded organization (i.e., a nation-state). The use of highly targeted spear-phishing e-mails may also point to a nation-state as they likely required a good source of intelligence to develop (Figure 7.8).

FIGURE 7.8 Documents relating to the X-45A Unmanned Combat Air Vehicle (shown here during a 2003 demonstration) were harvested by the Sykipot malware in 2011. (For color version of this figure, the reader is referred to the online version of this chapter.) *NASA photo by Lori Losey.*

After reading about Titan Rain, Operation X, Gh0stNet, the Shadow Network, and Operation Aurora, Sykipot may seem like a standard cyber espionage operation. However, the AlienVault researchers noticed that the latest Sykipot variants added a new twist. The U.S. Department of Defense employs smart cards to help protect sensitive-but-unclassified (SBU) information. The researchers found that Sykipot had the ability to steal the smart card credentials (security certificates stored on the user's machine) as well as the corresponding pin number that functions as the password.[99] Therefore, as long as the smart card is physically in the target's hardware, Sykipot hackers can access secure resources to which the user has permissions. Also noteworthy is that Sykipot specifically targeted ActivClient—the Smartcard software currently in use by the U.S. Department of Defense.

SUMMARY

This chapter has explored Chinese cyber espionage operations. We discussed several ideas espoused by China's military thinkers on information warfare—highlighting the ideas of *Unrestricted Warfare*—in which cyber operations are thought to extend into peacetime and involves military, political, economic, and scientific domains. We looked at how the Chinese structured their cyber warriors around the INEW strategy. In the PLA, cyber operations were put under the responsibility of organizations with similar missions in the realm of electronic warfare. Though the Chinese hacker community was initially lauded for their achievements in the early 2000s, the government shifted their stance as the decade progressed—likely due to their inability to control them. As a result, many Chinese hackers reemerged as members of legitimate security consulting firms or academia.

Throughout the early 2000s, there were many cyber espionage operations attributed to China. In 2004, the FBI investigated what became known as "Titan Rain"—a series of network penetrations into various government and defense contractor systems. The hackers took full advantage of cyber reconnaissance—footprinting, scanning, and enumeration—to learn about their targets and steal data. Years later, Northrop Grumman described what we termed "Operation X" where data were stolen from an unnamed U.S. company by Chinese-attributed operators. Those behind Operation X worked quickly to exfiltrate as much information from the target as possible. They focused on specific information on the systems and worked to minimize the time they spent on the network in order to avoid detection. Further, when they decided to exfiltrate data, they encrypted it first in order to make it difficult for the targeted company to determine which data were stolen. Based on the analysis of the events, evidence suggests that all these operations originated from China.

In the second half of the first decade of the 2000s, the Chinese also appeared to be heavily involved in using cyber espionage for the purposes of information gathering. In operations such as Gh0stNet (directed against the Dalai Lama) and the Shadow Network (directed against India and other nations), data were collected over long periods of time—likely as a source of intelligence. The systems in these incidents were often accessed once the target opened an attachment in an e-mail message. However, unlike phishing scams normally associated with cyber crime, these e-mails were skillfully crafted pieces of social engineering— often referred to as spear phishing. The nature of these messages had led analysts to conclude that the operators behind these missions had access to background information. Further, to exfiltrate data in a stealthy way, the personnel behind these missions leveraged legitimate Web sites—such as Yahoo! Mail—as a medium to communicate with the target machines. Based on the analysis of the command-and-control servers, investigators suspect that these operations too originated in China.

In Operation Aurora, a zero-day exploit allowed operators to steal intellectual property from repositories at Google, Adobe, and many other major companies in late 2009. The fallout of the incident led to strong statements from the U.S. Secretary of State directed against the Chinese government, which responded using the tactics of the "three warfares." *New York Times* journalists also reported that the attacks could be traced back to two Chinese schools of higher education. A more recent operation, also suspected to have originated from China, involves the "Sykipot" malware. This operation—taking place in late 2011—used spear phishing to target defense contractors in another effort to steal intellectual property—including information on the next generation of American UAVs. Sykipot also used techniques to obtain access to material requiring a smart card to authenticate the user.

SUGGESTED FURTHER READING

For further information on the origin of Chinese cyber military doctrine, we recommend the article "China's Electronic Long-Range Reconnaissance" by Timothy Thomas published in the November 2008 issue of *Military Review*. This article describes several different Chinese writings theorizing on the use of cyber operations for military means throughout the first decade of the 2000s. Another excellent article, from the SANS Reading Room by Edward Sobiesk entitled "Redefining the Role of Information Warfare in Chinese Strategy" provides good insight into how Chinese culture could influence their cyber operations. Written in 2003, Sobiesk's article was certainly a harbinger of things to come.

With respect to the hackers in China conducting cyber operations, we recommend the Northrop Grumman report entitled *Capability of the People's Republic of China to Conduct of Cyber Warfare and Computer Network Exploitation*, prepared for the U.S.-China Economic and Security Commission. This report also includes details of "Operation X" described in this chapter. We recommend that those interested in exploring the cyber warriors of China also consult *The Dark Visitor* by Scott Henderson, which provides a concise overview of the Chinese hacker community.

For more details on the case studies of "Gh0stNet" and the "Shadow Network," it is recommended to consult the reports by Information Warfare Monitor and the Shadowserver Foundation entitled T*racking Gh0stNet: Investigating a Cyber Espionage Network* (2009) and *Shadows in the Cloud: Investigating Cyber Espionage 2.0* (2010), respectively. At the time of this writing (October 2012), both reports are available on the online document repository Scribd (http://www.scribd.com).

In addition to the cited technical reports and blog posts—primarily by security firms Symantec and McAfee—we recommend the *Parameters* article "Google Confronts China's Three Warfares," also by Timothy Thomas (published in the summer 2010 issue). This article primarily focuses on how the Chinese government uses the techniques of the "three warfares" in the aftermath of a cyber operation. For more information on the 2011 Sykipot malware incidents, we recommend the analysis of the security firm AlienVault—http://labs.alienvault.com.

References

1. Nicholas Hoover J. NSA chief: China behind RSA attacks. *InformationWeek*. Retrieved from: http://www.informationweek.com/news/government/security/232700341?cid=RSSfeed_IWK_All; March 27, 2012 [retrieved 4 April 2013].
2. Sobiesk E. Redefining the role of information warfare in Chinese strategy. *SANS Institute InfoSec Reading Room*. http://www.sans.org/reading_room/whitepapers/warfare/redefining-role-information-warfare-chinese-strategy_896; March 2003 [accessed December 22, 2011].
3. McNeily M. Sun Tzu and the art of modern warfare. New York: Oxford Press; 2001, p. 22–3.
4. Office of the Secretary of Defense of the United States of America. Report to congress on *The military power of the People's Republic of China*; 12 July 2002. p. 5–6.
5. Maconachy WV, Schou CD, Ragsdale D, Welch D. A model for information assurance: an integrated approach. *Proceedings of the 2001 IEEE workshop on information assurance and security*. http://it210web.groups.et.byu.net/lectures/MSRW%20Paper.pdf; June 2001 [accessed 22 December, 2011].
6. Thomas T. China's electronic long-range reconnaissance. *Military Review*; November–December 2008. p. 47–54.
7. Ibid.
8. Sobiesk, 8.
9. Thomas T. Google confronts China's three warfares. *Parameters*; Summer 2010. p. 101–5.
10. Wei W, Zhen Y. Recent development in the study of the thought of people's war under informatized conditions. Chin Military Sci 2009;2d iss.
11. Thomas T. Google confronts China's three warfares. *Parameters*; Summer 2010. p. 101–5.
12. Fangcheng L, Decai L. On the relationship of military soft power to comprehensive national power and state soft power. Chin Military Sci 2009;(5):120–9.
13. Sobiesk, 5.
14. Tzu S. *The Art of War*, translated in 2000 by Sonshi.com [chapter 3].
15. DeWeese S, Krekel B, Bakos G, Barnett C. *Capability of the People's Republic of China to conduct of cyber warfare and computer network exploitation*. Northrop Grumman; October 2009.
16. Ibid.
17. Ibid.
18. Ibid.
19. Ibid.
20. Ibid.
21. Elegant S. Enemies at the firewall. *Time*. Available at: http://www.time.com/time/magazine/article/0,9171,1692063,00.html; December 6, 2007 [accessed December 30, 2011].
22. Henderson S. *The Dark Visitor*; 2007.
23. DeWeese S, Krekel B, Bakos G, Barnett C. *Capability of the People's Republic of China to conduct of cyber warfare and computer network exploitation*. Northrop Grumman; October 2009.
24. Markoff J, Barboza D. Two Chinese schools said to be tied to online attacks. *New York Times*; February 19, 2010.
25. Markoff J, Barboza D. Academic paper in China sets off alarms in U.S. *New York Times*; March 20, 2010.
26. Whittaker Z. Chinese documentary shows military university attacking U.S. targets. ZD Net. Available at: http://www.zdnet.com/blog/igeneration/chinese-documentary-shows-military-university-attacking-us-targets/12430; August 23, 2011 [accessed December 2011].
27. Thornburgh N. Inside the Chinese hack attack. *Time*; August, 25, 2005.
28. McClure S, Scambray J, Kurtz G. Hacking exposed. New York, NY: McGraw Hill; 2009.
29. Thornburgh N. Inside the Chinese hack attack. *Time*; August 25, 2005.
30. Thornburgh N. Invasion of the Chinese cyberspies. *Time*; August 29, 2005.
31. Ibid.
32. Ibid.
33. Ibid.
34. DeWeese S, Krekel B, Bakos G, Barnett C. Capability of the People's Republic of China to conduct of cyber warfare and computer network exploitation. Northrop Grumman; October 2009.
35. Daly M. The advanced persistent threat. In: 23rd large installation system administrator conference; 2009.
36. Information Warfare Monitor . Tracking Gh0stNet: Investigating a cyber espionage network. 2009.
37. Ibid.
38. Ibid.
39. Ibid.

40. Ibid.

41. Pillar Paul R. Negotiating peace—war termination as a bargaining process. Princeton, NJ: Princeton University Press; 1984, p. 144.

42. Doyle L. China tries to gag climbers who saw Tibet killings. *The Independent*. Retrieved from: http://www.independent.co.uk/news/world/asia/china-tries-to-gag-climbers-who-saw-tibet-killings-419528.html; October 11, 2006 [retrieved 4 April 2013].

43. Watts J. Death on Tibetans' long walk to freedom. *The Guardian*. Retrieved from: http://www.guardian.co.uk/world/2006/oct/30/china.worlddispatch; October 30, 2006.

44. Choephel T Nangpa La shooting—an eyewitness account. *Phayul*. Retrieved from: http://www.phayul.com/news/article.aspx?id=14211&article=Nangpa+La+Shooting+%E2%80%93+an+eye+witness+account&t=1&c=1; October 10, 2006 [retrieved 4 April 2013].

45. Watts J. Death on Tibetans' long walk to freedom. *The Guardian*. Retrieved from: http://www.guardian.co.uk/world/2006/oct/30/china.worlddispatch; October 30, 2006 [retrieved 4 April 2013].

46. Spiegel D. China gibt tödliche Schüsse auf Tibeter zu (China Admits Fatal Shooting of Tibetans). Retrieved from: http://www.spiegel.de/politik/ausland/proteste-china-gibt-toedliche-schuesse-auf-tibeter-zu-a-550658.html; April 30, 2008 4 [retrieved 4 April 2013].

47. Spiegel D. China stellt mehr als 1.000 Tibeter vor Gericht (China Tries More than 1,000 Tibetans). Retrieved from: http://www.spiegel.de/politik/ausland/massenprozesse-china-stellt-mehr-als-tausend-tibeter-vor-gericht-a-545175.html; April 3, 2008 [retrieved 4 April 2013].

48. Spiegel D. China legt angebliche Beweise über Dalai Lama als 'Drahtzieher' vor (China Claims Evidence that Dalai Lama Instigated Tibetan Crisis). Retrieved from: http://www.spiegel.de/politik/ausland/tibet-krise-china-legt-angebliche-beweise-ueber-dalai-lama-als-drahtzieher-vor-a-544450.html; March 30, 2008 [retrieved 4 April 2013].

49. Spiegel D. Chinas Staatsmedien beschimpfen Dalai Lama (Official Chinese Media Insult Dalai Lama). Retrieved from: http://www.spiegel.de/politik/ausland/tibet-konflikt-chinas-staatsmedien-beschimpfen-dalai-lama-a-551235.html; May 3, 2008 [retrieved 4 April 2013].

50. Spiegel D. Mutige Mönche stören chinesische Inszenierung (Courageous monks disturb Chinese representation). Retrieved from: http://www.spiegel.de/politik/ausland/reporter-in-tibet-mutige-moenche-stoeren-chinesische-inszenierung-a-543762.html; March 27, 2008 [retrieved 4 April 2013].

51. Spiegel D. Morddrohungen gegen Ausländische Berichterstatter (Death threats against foreign reporters). Retrieved from: http://www.spiegel.de/politik/ausland/pressefreiheit-in-china-morddrohungen-gegen-auslaendische-berichterstatter-a-550536.html; April 29, 2008 [retrieved 4 April 2013].

52. Faigle P. Meinungskampf im Netz (Battle of political opinions on the Internet). *Zeit Online*. Retrieved from: http://www.zeit.de/online/2008/17/china-tibet-reaktion-netz; April 18, 2008 [retrieved 4 April 2013].

53. Faigle P. Meinungskampf im Netz (Battle of political opinions on the Internet). *Zeit Online*. Retrieved from: http://www.zeit.de/online/2008/17/china-tibet-reaktion-netz; April 18, 2008 [retrieved 4 April 2013].

54. Davis M. China cracks down on protest news. *BBC News*. Retrieved from: http://news.bbc.co.uk/2/hi/asia-pacific/7302625.stm; March 18, 2008 [retrieved 4 April 2013].

55. Schwankert S. YouTube blocked in China; Flickr, Blogspot restored. *InfoWorld*. Retrieved from: http://www.infoworld.com/d/security-central/youtube-blocked-in-china-flickr-blogspot-restored-351; October 18, 2007 [retrieved 4 April 2013].

56. Heise Online. China blockiert nach Protesten in Tibet YouTube (China Blocks YouTube after Protests in Tibet). Retrieved from: http://www.heise.de/newsticker/meldung/China-blockiert-nach-den-Protesten-in-Tibet-YouTube-190792.html; March 17, 2008 [retrieved 4 April 2013]; Goldkorn J. Youtube Blocked in China. *Danwei*. Retrieved from: http://www.danwei.org/net_nanny_follies/youtube_blocked_in_china_1.php; March 15, 2008 [retrieved 4 April 2013]; and Global Voices. China: YouTube blocked yet again. Retrieved from: http://advocacy.globalvoicesonline.org/2008/03/16/china-youtube-blocked-yet-again/; March 16, 2008 [retrieved 4 April 2013].

57. Global Voices. China: YouTube blocked yet again. Retrieved from: http://advocacy.globalvoicesonline.org/2008/03/16/china-youtube-blocked-yet-again/; March 16, 2008 [retrieved 4 April 2013].

58. Kupfer K. Selektive Repression in China (Selective Repression in China). *Zeit Online*. Retrieved from: http://www.zeit.de/online/2008/32/china-internetzensur; October 10, 2008; *Zeit Online*. China lockert Internet Zensur (China Relax Internet Censorship). Retrieved from: http://www.zeit.de/online/2008/32/internet-zensur-lockerung; August 13, 2008 [retrieved 4 April 2013].

59. Spiegel D. Wir fordern unabhängige, glaubwürdige Ermittlungen in Tibet (We demand independent, credible investigations in Tibet). Retrieved from: http://www.spiegel.de/politik/ausland/menschenrechte-in-china-wir-fordern-unabhaengige-glaubwuerdige-ermittlungen-in-tibet-a-545700.html; April 6, 2008 [retrieved 4 April 2013].

60. Boshu Z. Zang Boshu: the way to resolve the Tibet issue (Original article was written April 22-28, 2008 in Beijing). *China Digital Times*. Retrieved from: http://chinadigitaltimes.net/2008/05/zhang-boshu-the-way-to-resolve-the-tibet-issue/; May 8, 2008 [retrieved 4 April 2013].

61. International Campaign for Tibet. The Sino-Tibetan dialogue. Retrieved from: http://www.savetibet.org/files/documents/SinoTibetan_Dialogue.pdf; 2008.

62. The Tibetan Government in Exile. Memorandum on genuine autonomy for the Tibetan people as presented by envoys of His Holiness the Dalai Lama. International Network of Parliamentarians on Tibet. Retrieved from: http://www.inpatnet.org/fileadmin/files/Resources_documents/Sino-Tibetan_Dialogue/MemorandumENG.pdf; 2008.

63. Xinhua News Agency. Dalai Lama's 'Genuine Autonomy' means 'Tibet independence'. Retrieved from: http://www.china.org.cn/china/tibet_democratic_reform/content_17489041.htm; March 23, 2009 [retrieved 4 April 2013].

64. Tibetan Political Review. The impact of the resignations of Gyari and Gyaltsen. *Phayul*. Retrieved from: http://www.phayul.com/news/article.aspx?id=31646&t=1; June, 26 2012 [retrieved 4 April 2013].

65. Xinhua News Agency. Dalai Lama's 'Genuine Autonomy' means 'Tibet independence'. Retrieved from: http://www.china.org.cn/china/tibet_democratic_reform/content_17489041.htm; March 23, 2009; Woodward D. Why Tibet must go it alone. *Herald Sun*. Retrieved from: http://www.heraldsun.com.au/opinion/why-tibet-must-go-it-alone/story-e6frfifo-1111115840903; March 20, 2008.

66. Ibid.

67. Information Warfare Monitor and Shadowserver Foundation. *Shadows in the cloud: investigating cyber espionage 2.0*; April, 2010.

68. Ibid.

69. Goldschlag D, Reed M, Syverson P. Onion routing for anonymous and private Internet connections. Commun ACM 1999;42(2):39–41.

70. Zetter K. Rogue nodes turn Tor Anonymizer into eavesdropper's paradise. *Wired*; September 2007.

71. Information Warfare Monitor and Shadowserver Foundation. *Shadows in the cloud: investigating cyber espionage 2.0*; April 2010.

72. Pechora-2M Surface-to-Air Anti-aircraft missile system. *Army Recognition*. Available at: http://www.armyrecognition.com/index.php?option=com_content&task=view&id=979 [accessed January 4, 2012].

73. Information Warfare Monitor and Shadowserver Foundation. *Shadows in the Cloud: Investigating Cyber Espionage 2.0*; April 2010.

74. Drummond D. A new approach to China. *The Official Google Blog*. Available at: http://googleblog.blogspot.com/2010/01/new-approach-to-china.html; January 12, 2010 [accessed January 8, 2012].

75. Prasad P. Adobe investigates corporate network security issue. *Adobe Featured Blogs*. Available at: http://blogs.adobe.com/conversations/2010/01/adobe_investigates_corporate_n.html; January 12, 2010 [accessed January 8, 2012].

76. Higgins KJ. More victims of Chinese hacking attacks come forward. *Dark Reading*. Available at: http://www.darkreading.com/security/attacks-breaches/222301032/index.html; January 14, 2010 [accessed January 8, 2012].

77. Zetter K. Google hackers targeted source code of more than 30 companies. *Wired Threat Level*. Available at: http://www.wired.com/threatlevel/2010/01/google-hack-attack/; January 13, 2010 [accessed January 8, 2012].

78. Markoff J. Cyber attack on Google said to hit password system. *New York Times*. Available from: http://www.nytimes.com/2010/04/20/technology/20google.html; April 19, 2010 [accessed January 15, 2012].

79. McAfee Labs and McAfee Foundation Professional Service. Protecting your critical assets: lessons learned from Operation Aurora. McAfee White Paper; 2010.

80. Markoff J. Cyberattack on Google said to hit password system. *New York Times*. Available from: http://www.nytimes.com/2010/04/20/technology/20google.html; April 19, 2010 [accessed January 15, 2012].

81. McAfee Labs and McAfee Foundation Professional Service. Protecting your critical assets: lessons learned from Operation Aurora. McAfee White Paper; 2010.

82. Kurtz G. Where's the body. McAfee Blog Central. Available from: http://siblog.mcafee.com/cto/where%E2%80%99s-the-body/; January 25, 2010 [accessed January 15, 2012].

83. VeriSign iDefense Security Lab report quoted by Ryan Paul. Researchers identify command servers behind Google attack. *ArsTechnica*. Available from: http://arstechnica.com/security/news/2010/01/researchers-identify-command-servers-behind-google-attack.ars; January 2010 [accessed January 15, 2012].

84. Markoff J, Barboza D. Two Chinese schools said to be tied to online attacks. *New York Times*; February 19, 2010.

85. Ibid.
86. Ibid.
87. Ibid.
88. Clinton HR. Remarks on Internet freedom. *U.S. Department of State*; January 21, 2010. Available at: http://www.state.gov/secretary/rm/2010/01/135519.htm [accessed January 15,2010].
89. Thomas T. Google confronts China's three warfares. *Parameters*; Summer 2010. p. 101–5.
90. Ibid.
91. Chien E, O'Gorman G. The nitro attacks, stealing secrets from the chemical industry. *Symantec Security Response*; 2011.
92. Global Energy Cyberattacks: 'Night Dragon.', McAffe White Paper; February 10, 2011.
93. Constantin L. Hackers compromise Adobe Server, use it to digitally sign malicious files. *CIO*. Available at: http://www.cio.com/article/717494/Hackers_Compromise_Adobe_Server_Use_it_to_Digitally_Sign_Malicious_Files; September 27, 2012 [accessed October 14, 2012].
94. Thakur V. The Sykipot attacks. *Symantec Official Blog*. Available at: http://www.symantec.com/connect/blogs/sykipot-attacks; December 14, 2011 [accessed January 21, 2012].
95. Another Sykipot sample likely targeting U.S. federal agencies. *Alien Vault Labs*. Available at: http://labs.alienvault.com/labs/index.php/2011/another-sykipot-sample-likely-targeting-us-federal-agencies/?utm_source=rss&utm_medium=rss&utm_campaign=another-sykipot-sample-likely-targeting-us-federal-agencies; December 12, 2011 [accessed January 21,2012].
96. Keizer G. Symantec confirms reader exploits targeted defense companies. *Computerworld*. Available at: http://www.computerworld.com/s/article/9222496/Symantec_confirms_Reader_exploits_targeted_defense_companies?taxonomyId=85&pageNumber=1; December 7, 2011 [accessed January 21,2012].
97. Are Sykipot's authors obsessed with next generation U.S. drones? *Alien Vault Labs*. Available at: http://labs.alienvault.com/labs/index.php/2011/are-the-sykipots-authors-obsessed-with-next-generation-us-drones/?utm_source=rss&utm_medium=rss&utm_campaign=are-the-sykipots-authors-obsessed-with-next-generation-us-drones; December 20, 2011 [accessed January 21,2012].
98. Thakur V. The Sykipot attacks. *Symantec Official Blog*. Available at: http://www.symantec.com/connect/blogs/sykipot-attacks; December 14, 2011 [accessed January 21, 2012].
99. Sykipot variant hijacks DoD and Windows smart cards. *Alien Vault Labs*. Available at: http://labs.alienvault.com/labs/index.php/2012/when-the-apt-owns-your-smart-cards-and-certs/; December 20, 2011 [accessed January 21, 2012].

Duqu, Flame, Gauss, the Next Generation of Cyber Exploitation

INFORMATION IN THIS CHAPTER

- Kernel mode rootkits
- Vulnerabilities in the Operating System
- Stolen keying material
- Commonalities between Stuxnet and Duqu
- Information-stealing Trojans

- The geography of Duqu
- TDL3 and other malware
- Object-oriented malware: Stuxnet, Duqu, Flame, and Gauss

INTRODUCTION

Though interesting, the cyber-espionage operations of Chapter 7 really represent an initial foray into the use of intelligence-gathering cyber platforms. In the past 3 years, several advanced pieces of malware have emerged: namely, Stuxnet, Duqu, Flame, and Gauss. Many believe that these four pieces of software represent the future of cyber warfare. In this chapter, we describe the Duqu intelligence-collecting platform in detail along with some preliminary information regarding Flame and Gauss—which also harvest information from the target system and are believed by some to be related to Duqu. Stuxnet, which many researchers believe to be related to the other three, was designed to primarily target industrial control systems, and is described in detail in Chapter 13. Here we discuss Stuxnet in the context of its technical similarities to the other pieces of software.

Stuxnet was the first of these advanced pieces of software that was discovered. In 2011, it took the world by surprise. Previously, the popular concept of a computer virus involved an unsophisticated piece of code that performed a few very basic steps to "infect" a computer, and then a few more steps to "propagate" to other computers. These viruses, such as the "Melissa" and "ILoveYou" viruses, were high-powered annoyances that caused indiscriminate mayhem. Stuxnet, as the media and open security community portrayed it, was not a virus but a complicated software system that was unique in its sophistication.[1] More than that, Stuxnet was a tool used by parties unknown to affect a direct change, allegedly to the nuclear program of Iran.[2]

Stuxnet was a system that needed very precise information to be effective. That malware concerned itself with the operation of high-precision motors used in industrial processes, and it made subtle modifications to the functional parameters of those motors. These modifications would be made to systems that were not connected to the Internet (a circumstance often referred to as "blind"); so, precise information was needed ahead of time. Additionally, future Stuxnet-type attacks would probably require similar information about their specific targets to be effective.[3]

The Duqu Trojan was detected in October 2011 and was identified as an information stealing Trojan. Some initial analysis revealed similarities between Duqu and Stuxnet, both in tactics and in the structure of the malicious programs. Both Duqu and Stuxnet, as pieces of software, were charged with executing on a computer system and remaining resident on the infected systems. Due to the similarities between the two pieces of malware and the fact that Stuxnet seems to have had a clear political motivation (curtailing the Iranian production on enriched Uranium), it is conceivable that Duqu was designed to steal information in preparation for a Stuxnet-like attack. Hence, we view Duqu as an intelligence-gathering/ cyber-espionage tool—although more advanced than other such tools (i.e., those discussed in Chapter 7). Further, it appears that advanced cyber-based intelligence-gathering campaigns are continuing. The more recent discoveries of related malware in the Middle East, specifically Gauss and Flame, indicate that malware such as Duqu is becoming the norm— displacing some of the more first-generation efforts discussed in Chapter 7.

Programs like these have long-term goals with infected computers and need to conceal their presence. Viruses such as "Melissa" and worms such as the "Slammer" worm did not have the goal of remaining undetected. So, similar to the efforts directed against the

Tibetan Government in Exile (see Chapter 7), Duqu (and later Flame and Gauss) was designed to harvest information for a long period of time undetected.

In this chapter, we take a detailed look at the Duqu platform and how it relates to the greater landscape of the related malware, specifically describing kernel-mode rootkits, operating system vulnerabilities that Duqu and others exploit, and the use of stolen keying material to add an element of stealth to the information harvesting. We also look at where Duqu was found, how it relates to other pieces of malware such as Stuxnet and TDL3. We further examine the more recent discoveries of Flame and Gauss and how they compare and relate to Duqu.

KERNEL MODE ROOTKITS

The operating system kernel represents the highest level of privilege in a modern general purpose computer. The kernel arbitrates access to protected hardware and controls how limited resources such as running time on the CPU and physical memory pages are used by processes on the system. When a process on the system wants to access files, the network, or view configuration data, the kernel is the piece of software with ultimate authority both for determining if it is appropriate for the process to take these actions, and also for carrying out those actions.

Since computers have been compromised, attackers have sought means to conceal their presence on compromised systems from the users and administrators of those systems. The term "root kit" refers to a collection of tools, or kit, which can be employed to retain access to the root (administrative) account of a system. Rootkits that modify system software can be detected with the cooperation of the operating system kernel, so the logical next step for rootkit developers and computer attackers is to compromise the operating system kernel. A compromised operating system kernel can deceive other programs, the users, and the administrators of that computer system in difficult to detect ways. A kernel-mode rootkit is extremely attractive as it allows complete access to all files and all processes on a computer.

Since the operating system kernel is the logical central unit of the operating system, it might be reasoned that kernel-mode rootkits represent a high degree of sophistication. While this might have been true at one point, there are many factors now that work against this hypothesis. "Cookbooks" for creating kernel-mode rootkits and understanding the concepts behind compromising an operating system kernel are available both freely on the Internet and for purchase from bookstores.

The creation of kernel-mode rootkits has become somewhat commercialized as many malicious actors on the Internet are willing to pay for a kernel-mode rootkit as a component of malicious software. Also, while the operating system kernel might seem complicated, the function and design of operating system kernels is well covered in many undergraduate curriculums and information about their function is freely available on the Internet.

Duqu included a kernel-mode component that was responsible for coordinating many of the actions of the malware as a whole. Typically, kernel-mode drivers can be used to take bodies of code that perform logical actions and inject those bodies of code into already-running processes. In the Windows operating system, processes are containers for units of execution known as "threads." Multiple threads can run within a single process, and it is possible that one thread executes the logic associated with this process, for example, a Web browser or Microsoft Word, while another thread executes code that is wholly unrelated to the actions of the process. In the case of Duqu and other frameworks, a kernel-mode driver takes code that is related to the functioning of the malware and injects it—along with a thread to run it—into processes that are already running on the system. Duqu would inject code and a thread into processes that matched a selection criterion, specifically the name of the process. The processes that Duqu preferred to insert code into were processes that were part of the core Windows operating system, such as services.exe or lsas.exe. Duqu would also inject components into firefox.exe, iexplore.exe, or svchost.exe, depending on its configuration, for communication with a command and control server.

Kernel-mode rootkits are usually separated from the actual functioning of a piece of malicious software. Kernel-mode rootkits' responsibility is usually to maintain a presence in an operating system and allow for the repeated execution of malware code, and also to position malware code to execute. However, once the malware's logic is executing, a kernel-mode rootkit stays in the background and provides services as needed to the malware logic.

VULNERABILITIES IN THE OPERATING SYSTEM

Duqu used a nonpublic exploit in a component of the Windows kernel. This component was the font specification parser in win32k.sys, which is a component of the Windows kernel that executes at the highest level of privilege in the operating system and is responsible for displaying graphical dialogs and rendering text. To support the rendering of text that is encoded in third party fonts, win32k.sys may load and process font specification files from external sources. The font specification format is extremely complicated and the data processed is entirely produced by a potentially untrusted individual. An error present in the processing of these font specification directives in win32k.sys could lead to the corruption of memory in the Windows kernel. This corruption could be leveraged into the execution of arbitrary code.[4]

Duqu was installed by a Microsoft Word or other Microsoft Office document that contained a font specification file that was specifically crafted to corrupt memory inside the operating system kernel so as to cause arbitrary code execution. In this way, simply by opening an Office document that had been appropriately prepared, the first stage of Duqu would begin executing on a victim's computer with the highest level of privilege.

The boundary between user-mode programs, such as Web browsers and Microsoft Word, and the operating system kernel is considered a trust boundary and is responsible for brokering all interactions between programs to enforce a security policy. An especially pernicious aspect of vulnerabilities that allow arbitrary code execution within the operating system kernel is that they entirely subvert any security mechanism that the operating system can implement. The use of these weaknesses allows a potential attacker to circumvent any security policy that is in place on a computer.

The boundary between user programs and the operating system is extremely broad and consists of every service or facility that the operating system provides to running programs. Every occasion in which a program presents data to the operating system to be inspected or parsed is an opportunity for the operating system to completely compromise the security of the system. Due to the incredibly broad nature of this attack surface, vulnerabilities in the operating system kernel have historically been plentiful and are generally described as "privilege escalation vulnerabilities."

STOLEN KEYING MATERIAL

Duqu and Stuxnet turned heads in the computer security community by making use of stolen code-signing keys. Starting with Windows Vista, Microsoft began requiring that any company or individual who wanted to create a device driver for Windows had to use the global Public Key Infrastructure (PKI) to "sign" device drivers. Such a signature would attest that the device driver was actually produced by the company that produced it.

Digitally signing a message, whether or not that message is human-readable text or the binary code of a device driver, allows for verification that the text has not been altered. With such a set of rules in place, the operating system can guarantee that only code that was signed by appropriate parties is executed.

Keys in the PKI are split into two halves, a public half and a private half. The public half is published and globally available, and the private half is kept secret and should be known only to the owner of that key. In the case of the code-signing PKI, the owners of code-signing keys would be companies that produce device drivers, and Microsoft, the operating system vendor. However, private keys are files that are stored on general purpose computers. Technology exists to protect private keys by storing them within high security modules whose only purpose is protecting cryptographic keys. However, the infrastructure that is used to produce signed device drivers is not compatible with the high security module infrastructure.

In such an environment, companies also have to work with their private keys practically. Microsoft provides a mechanism to place Windows into "test signing" mode, so that device drivers that are not signed with a globally recognized key may still be loaded. However, "test signing" mode is cumbersome and requires, effectively, the maintenance of a secondary PKI within the company writing device drivers. Additionally, the threat of theft of a code-signing private key, until recently, has been seen as both remote and abstract. The code-signing keys had little value and, apparently, no organization was attempting their mass compromise.[5]

It is not generally known how the Duqu and Stuxnet authors obtained the code-signing certificates to sign their device drivers. All that is known is that stolen certificates in Stuxnet were from Realtek Semiconductor Corp. and JMicron Technology Corp.,[6] while the Duqu certificates were stolen from C-Media Electronics, Inc.[7] It can be assumed that these companies were not complicit in the development of malicious software. Therefore, the best explanation for the use of the code-signing certificates is that they were stolen. It is notable that both Realtek and JMicron have offices in Hsinchu Science Park, Taiwan.[8] Hence, the geographic proximity may suggest physical theft in the case of Stuxnet. Further, C-Media is also a Taiwanese company.[9]

This is not wholly remarkable. The theft of private keys has always been a problem with deployments of PKI. For this reason, high-security modules were developed that could be trusted with holding private keys. These high-security modules have memory to store the private key and processors to interact with data and the private key, but they do not allow the transfer of the private key off of the high-security module. Using this technology, theft of a private key is only possible by the theft of the physical module.

However, on developer workstations, the private keys are loaded into the operating system. Hacking into one of those workstations would give the attacker the ability to sign device drivers as if they were the original owner of the key. The use of stolen private keys could continue until the theft was uncovered and the booty keys were added to a revocation infrastructure maintained by Microsoft. Once added to the revocation list, drivers signed with those keys would be blocked from executing.

Had the compromise of the keys been noticed before Stuxnet and Duqu were detected in the wild, the addition of those keys to revocation lists would have been quite inconvenient to the attackers.

COMMONALITIES BETWEEN STUXNET AND DUQU

Both Duqu and Stuxnet make use of a kernel-mode rootkit. Some analysts have attempted to draw parallels between the structure and functionality in the kernel-mode rootkits in both malwares. The overall functions of Stuxnet and Duqu differ significantly. Stuxnet is a worm that takes action independent of any human agent, while Duqu appears to be only responsive to command and control servers and is used largely for information theft. The assessment that Duqu is used largely for information theft is based on the presence of a keylogging component, as well as the recovery of some information from computers compromised with Duqu—such as info about computers on the local area network. Stuxnet did not, to the best of public knowledge, collect any information.[10] Perhaps Duqu, which did seem to collect such information, was more intended as an intelligence-gathering tool—used in preparation for future attacks.

However, Kaspersky Labs has identified several similarities between Duqu and Stuxnet that have led them to believe that they were projects created by the same team of developers.[11] In particular, they point out similarities in architecture—the overall scheme as to how the two pieces of software operate. Further, security experts from the US Air Force (conducting analysis outside of their official military duties) identified numerous source-code and binary similarities between Duqu and Stuxnet.[12]

Kaspersky also discovered two different device driver files, one of which was part of Stuxnet and the other of Duqu. They discovered that the same stolen digital signature was used to sign both of these files. This would mean that whoever prepared both files had access to the private key for that code-signing certificate. It could be that the same organization compromised this code-signing certificate and used it in both Stuxnet and Duqu, which would indicate that both were developed by the same team of developers. This aligns well with the theories of Kaspersky and the Air Force security experts. However, different organizations could have stolen the code-signing certificate independently because it was easy to compromise, due to its storage in an unsecured location. Or, a third group, compromised this code-signing certificate and sold or otherwise provided it to two different groups, one of which was responsible for Stuxnet and the other of which produced Duqu.[13]

INFORMATION-STEALING TROJANS

Information-stealing Trojans are directed by their controllers to search for and return different types of information. That information could be stored on the file system, or could be entered via keyboard by the compromised computer's operator. The type of information that the controller of the information-stealing Trojan will look for will generally vary, and the exact parameters of the search will certainly differ, so it is necessary for these Trojans to be in constant or near-constant contact with some central server that the controller of the Trojan has access to. The operation of these servers is generally perilous and is the weak link in any information-stealing malware campaign. These Trojans need to upload information to some server on the Internet that is generally not publically accessible. Most malware authors use either compromised servers, or servers that they rent or buy from "bulletproof hosting companies." These hosting companies advertise that they do not cooperate with international law enforcement and charge a premium to provide services to botnet operators.[14]

A danger of the server-centric model of malware command and control is its possible detection by an antivirus company or a law enforcement agency, which in their analysis of the malware code will likely discover the Internet address of the command and control servers. When this address is discovered, investigators can take steps to simultaneously neutralize the command and control servers and deny malware controllers access to them, as well as recover any information that was stored on those systems. This information could include both the information that the Trojan was able to access on compromised computers as well as information that could potentially identify and incriminate the controllers of the Trojan. We have previously described examples where security professionals have discovered and exploited command and control servers used by Iranian and Chinese hackers (in chapters 5 and 7 respectively).[15]

Kaspersky performed some forensic analysis of servers; themselves compromised systems that were used to control Duqu Trojans. Their forensic analysis revealed that much information was removed from these systems only days prior to Kaspersky gaining access to investigate these systems. However, some information that was left behind gave potential indicators as to the system administrators' habits of the controllers of the Duqu Trojans. Those indicators consisted of administrator commands as well as misspellings and incorrect commands to configure and operate the system. Also left behind by the controllers was a logfile maintained by the Linux operating system that detailed the remote addresses of administrators of the malware who accessed the compromised systems.[16]

THE GEOGRAPHY OF DUQU

During the response to Duqu, the antivirus community learned a lot about the geographic distribution of the Duqu command and control systems as well as computers that had been compromised. The owners and operators of the Duqu framework had complete and arbitrary choice regarding the geographic spread of their software, both in terms of the systems they used for command and control servers as well as the systems they targeted for the installation of the client software.

The choice of command and control servers was influenced by which servers were vulnerable. However, vulnerable servers exist globally; so an operator building, a network of compromised servers, could select servers that are as clustered or dispersed as desired. The controllers of Duqu opted to compromise servers that were dispersed around the world.

Additionally, the client software, which would be installed on desktop computers containing information that the controllers wished to extract, was focused in specific geographic areas. Where Duqu is deployed is also a choice wholly left up to its controllers, so where it is found is indicative of, to a least a broad degree, the type of information that its operators are looking to steal. Kaspersky reported finding Duqu only in Iran and in Sudan.[17]

Kaspersky, while researching the command and control structure for Duqu, discovered that at least 12 command and control servers had been used by the controllers of Duqu over the past 3 years. On every server that Kaspersky examined, large portions of information relevant to Duqu's activities had been erased days prior. This action does communicate a signal—the controllers of the operation were cognizant of their exposure and were willing and capable to take actions to mitigate the compromise.[18]

TDL3 AND OTHER MALWARE

There are other pieces of malicious software that are multistage and perform injection. The TDL3 rootkit (ca. 2009) included many of the features that Stuxnet and Duqu possess. TDL3 used a nonpublic exploit in Windows to elevate its privilege to kernel-mode in a way that bypassed antivirus software. TDL3 would also make changes to existing device drivers present on the operating system that would cause TDL3 to load and start every time the operating system loaded. TDL3 is a generic rootkit framework that allows customers who purchase the TDL3 software from its authors to assemble malware that can be installed onto compromised computers for a variety of reasons. Some pieces of malware that are built using TDL3 are information stealers, while others send spam or attempt to entice the user of the compromised computer to purchase fake antivirus software.

TDL3 evaded detection by exploiting a weakness in the algorithm that antirootkit technologies use. TDL3's successful evasion of detection was the result of studying antivirus software's responses to previous rootkits and exploiting weaknesses in those responses.[19]

The media has emphasized these and other advanced techniques that are employed by Duqu, but when viewed alongside other pieces of malware, the techniques used by Duqu do not seem particularly advanced, while many other successful pieces of malware incorporate similar effective techniques.

OBJECT-ORIENTED MALWARE: STUXNET, DUQU, FLAME, AND GAUSS

One aspect about Duqu and Stuxnet that has led some researchers to consider the two pieces of malware as "cousins" is that both pieces of software were written with the extensive use of a paradigm known as *object-oriented* programming (OOP). In more traditional methods of computer programming, software is designed to resemble a series of tasks that the computer must accomplish to achieve a desired outcome. In object-oriented programming, on the other hand, the programmer creates objects that manipulate data in various ways to reach a desired end state. One of the main advantages to using the object-oriented approach is that it is easier for a developer to create and maintain a large and complex piece of software. The use of OOP is less common in the design of malicious software where the desire to maintain a small footprint necessitates more traditional programming paradigms.

Flame: King-Sized Malware

There have been other pieces of malware recently discovered (in 2012) that were also created primarily using object-oriented code. The malware known as *Flame* is a large, complicated piece of software that was primarily identified in Iran and designed to aggressively harvest information from its target systems—for instance, it is known to be able to capture Skype calls as well as record audio, in addition to more conventional information theft (i.e., stealing email, password harvesting, etc.).[20] Due to the inclusion of a wide variety of information-gathering tools, as well as the wide variety of distribution mechanisms (including USB memory sticks, printer sharing, etc.[21]), Flame essentially is a general-purpose intelligence platform. This also results in an abnormally large footprint for malicious software. When all modules are considered, Flame is 20 MB in size.[22]

Flame was capable of infecting other computers on local area networks. The method it used to infect those computers has not been seen in any other malware. Traditionally, malware will attempt to copy itself to other computers on the local area network via a variety of means. Some use exploits in Windows server software to connect to remote computers, exploit them, and then infect. Others use techniques as simple as infecting executable files that are on remote computers and waiting for those computers to execute the infected files.

Flame would use network-level tricks to impersonate Microsoft's automatic update servers for Windows. This kind of attack, a local man-in-the-middle attack, is always possible and not sophisticated. The defensive countermeasure to this attack is the use of public key infrastructure (PKI) to verify the identity of the remote system. The authors of Flame implemented an attack against Microsoft's PKI infrastructure that allowed Flame to impersonate Windows Update. This attack allowed Flame to copy itself to other computers without using memory corruption exploits, password guessing, or any known form of attack.[23]

Gauss: Malware to Monitor Financial Transactions

Another highly advanced piece of malware that primarily uses object-oriented coding has also emerged in recent months (in 2012). Known as Gauss, this cyber-espionage platform is designed to steal as much information from the target system as possible.[24] Gauss steals system information—including data about the target's local area network, the processes running on the target, and hardware information. It also compromises information from the user's Web-browsing sessions by injecting its modules into various browsers. It is also capable of gathering information from social network, e-mail, and instant message accounts. Perhaps most significant, it includes routines to harvest data associated with specific Lebanese banks—including the Bank of Beirut, Byblos Bank, and Fransabank. It is also noteworthy that the majority of Gauss infections were discovered on Lebanese systems.

Like Stuxnet, Gauss also infects USB memory sticks. However, it uses the USB exploit differently. When a Gauss-infected USB drive is inserted into a computer, that system is not infected. Rather, information is harvested off that system and stored on the memory stick.

Astonishingly after being used a certain number of times,[a] Gauss removes itself from the USB stick. Like many of the modules in Gauss, the module that infects USB drives includes encrypted portions that—at the time of this writing—perform functions unknown to commercial and academic security researchers.[25]

Some security researchers predicted the use of encryption by malware. Nate Lawson authored an analysis of Stuxnet that described it as "embarrassing, not amazing." In this analysis, Lawson references the existence of a code protection system termed "secure triggers," first published by researchers at the University of Buenos Aires.[26] The "secure triggers" system defines a process by which a program can be bound to a specific computer system.[27]

Lawson argues that knowledge on how to construct such systems has existed in the public domain for many years (since 2003), and that it provides a high degree of security and protection. Lawson asserts that this system was not used in Stuxnet, but it was used in Gauss. Furthermore, he asserts that the use of this protection system in Gauss has protected it from analysis by Kaspersky.[28]

However, we should also note that some shortcoming of Stuxnet (such as its susceptibility to reverse-engineering) may be the result of the simple fact that this malware likely is the product of a large organization. It is likely that the different teams working on Stuxnet had varying levels of knowledge, skill, and ability. In such a scenario, we would expect the quality of different components of the malware to vary. The challenge for the management team designated to lead such a project would be to assign those with the better skill-sets to the more critical components of the project.

Relationships Among Object-Oriented Malware

As described earlier in this chapter, some security researchers, in particular those from Kaspersky Labs, believe that Stuxnet and Duqu were created by the same team of hackers. Due to the use of filenames starting with a "~d" in both Stuxnet and Duqu, Kaspersky labeled the source of these pieces of malware the "Tilded platform." [29] Though there is some similarity in structure and function of Duqu and Flame, most security researchers regard them as different platforms. Hence, Duqu is generally regarded as being less similar to Flame than it is to Stuxnet. For instance, Kaspersky's analysis of the Flame command and control server—performed using DNS sinkholing (see Chapter 7)—highlights significant differences between the command and control elements of Duqu and Flame.[30] While there is some evidence of collaboration between the creators of Flame and Stuxnet/Duqu, it appears that the current accepted hypothesis is that Stuxnet/Duqu constitutes one framework and Flame another.

At the time of this writing, the association of Gauss with Stuxnet, Duqu, or Flame is an issue of debate. Based on the modular design of Flame and Gauss, as well as the method in which they communicate to command and control servers, Kaspersky Labs has labeled Gauss as being based on the Flame platform.[31] However, the security firm ESET conducted a comparison of code in Gauss to Stuxnet and to Flame.[b] The researchers here found that Gauss was actually

---

[a] This has been observed to be 30 times in the current Gauss samples.

[b] The comparison was performed with the BinDiff plugin for the IDA Pro disassembler.

closer to Stuxnet based on the programming techniques and data structures used in the creation of these pieces of software.[32] These somewhat contrary findings highlight the challenges to analyzing and making accurate statements about pieces of malicious software found in the aftermath of a cyber operation.

SUMMARY

Duqu was an information-stealing Trojan operated by parties that remain unknown for purposes that remain unconfirmed. It was largely successful at evading detection by an antivirus software, operating for years before being publically revealed. Once revealed, it yielded insights into the priorities of and decisions made by its controllers. Duqu also continued the trend of using stolen code-signing material, and gives us to a small degree of insight into what a targeted information-stealing campaign looks like. The more recent discoveries of Flame and Gauss in the wild indicate that powerful intelligence-gathering platforms such as Duqu may become the standard for cyber-exploitation weaponry in the future.

SUGGESTED FURTHER READING

Duqu was first discovered and named by researchers from the Budapest University of Technology who subsequently wrote a report describing their findings as well as including some information on Flame and Guass in an article entitled "The Cousins of Stuxnet: Duqu, Flame, and Gauss" published in the journal *Future Internet*. Another excellent reference on Duqu is the "Duqu Faq" written be Kaspersky Lab researcher Ryan Naraine, posted on *SecureList*. Flame and Guass have also been extensively studied by Kaspersky Labs. Particularly interesting is their report *Gauss: Abnormal Distribution* and Alexander Gostev's "The Flame: Questions and Answers," available on *SecureList*. For information on how the Flame malware spreads in a network, we recommend Alex Sotirov's "Analyzing the MD5 collision in Flame" published by the firm Trail of Bits.

References

1. Matrosov A, Rodionov E, Harley D, Malcho J. *Stuxnet Under the Microscope*. Retrieved August 16, 2012, from ESET: http://go.eset.com/us/resources/white-papers/Stuxnet_Under_the_Microscope.pdf; October 20, 2010.
2. Gross M. *A Declaration of Cyber-War*. Retrieved August 16, 2012, from Vanity Fair: http://www.vanityfair.com/culture/features/2011/04/Stuxnet-201104; April 1, 2011.
3. Naraine R. *Duqu FAQ*. Retrieved August 16, 2012, from Securelist: http://www.securelist.com/en/blog/208193178/Duqu_FAQ; March 27, 2012.
4. Soumenkov I. *The Mystery of Duqu: Part Five*. Retrieved August 16, 2012, from SecureList: http://www.securelist.com/en/blog/606/The_Mystery_of_Duqu_Part_Five; November 15, 2011.
5. Khor S-M. *Digital Code Signing Step-by-Step Guide*. Retrieved August 16, 2012, from MSDN: http://msdn.microsoft.com/en-us/library/office/aa140234%28v=office.10%29.aspx; March 1, 2002.
6. Matrosov A, Rodionov E, Harley D, Malcho J. Stuxnet under the microscope revision 1.2. Bratislava, Slovakia: ESET; 2010.
7. Roberts Paul. *Virus Experts Warn of Stuxnet Variant 'Duqu'*. Retrieved February 4, 2012 from *ThreatPost*: http://threatpost.com/en_us/blogs/virus-experts-warn-stuxnet-variant-duqu-101811; October 18, 2011.

8. Matrosov A, Rodionov E, Harley D, Malcho J. Stuxnet under the microscope revision 1.2. Bratislava, Slovakia: ESET; 2010.

9. Roberts Paul. *Virus experts warn of Stuxnet Variant 'Duqu'*. Retrieved February 4, 2012 from ThreatPost: http://threatpost.com/en_us/blogs/virus-experts-warn-stuxnet-variant-duqu-101811; October 18, 2011.

10. Passeri P. *Stuxnet, Duqu, Stars And Galaxies. . . .* Retrieved August 16, 2012, from Hackmageddon.com: http://hackmageddon.com/2011/10/21/Stuxnet-Duqu-stars-and-galaxies/; October 21, 2011.

11. Gostev A, Soumenkov I. Stuxnet/Duqu: the evolution of drivers, SecureList December 28, 2011; https://www.securelist.com/en/analysis/204792208/Stuxnet_Duqu_The_Evolution_of_Drivers [accessed October 21, 2012].

12. Sparks J, Lee RM, Brandau P. Duqu: father, son, or unholy ghost of Stuxnet?, SC Magazine November 2, 2011; http://www.scmagazine.com/duqu-father-son-or-unholy-ghost-of-stuxnet/article/215851/.

13. Naraine R. *Duqu FAQ*. Retrieved August 16, 2012, from Securelist: http://www.securelist.com/en/blog/208193178/Duqu_FAQ; March 27, 2012.

14. Krebs B. *Body Armor for Bad Web Sites*. Retrieved August 16, 2012, from Krebs on Security: http://krebsonsecurity.com/tag/bulletproof-hosting/; November 9, 2010.

15. Shankland S. *The long arm of Microsoft tries taking down Zeus botnets*. Retrieved August 16, 2012, from CNet: http://news.cnet.com/8301-30685_3-57404275-264/the-long-arm-of-microsoft-tries-taking-down-zeus-botnets/; March 25, 2012.

16. Kamluk V. *The Mystery of Duqu: Part Six (The Command and Control servers)*. Retrieved August 16, 2012, from SecureList: http://www.securelist.com/en/blog/625/The_Mystery_of_Duqu_Part_Six_The_Command_and_Control_servers; November 30, 2011.

17. Gostev A. *The Mystery of Duqu: Part Two*. Retrieved August 16, 2012, from SecureList: http://www.securelist.com/en/blog/208193197/The_Mystery_of_Duqu_Part_Two; October 25, 2011.

18. Kamluk V. *The Mystery of Duqu: Part Six (The Command and Control servers)*. Retrieved August 16, 2012, from SecureList: http://www.securelist.com/en/blog/625/The_Mystery_of_Duqu_Part_Six_The_Command_and_Control_servers; November 30, 2011.

19. So'n NP. *TDL3: Part I "Why so serious? Let's put a smile . . .".* Retrieved August 16, 2012, from Open Malware: http://openmalware.org/?q=node/1442; November 25, 2009.

20. Morton KF, Grace D. A case study on Stuxnet and Flame Malware, viXa.org September 14, 2012; http://vixra.org/abs/1209.0040 [accessed October16, 2012].

21. Fiaidhi J, Gelogo YE. *SCADA cyber attacks and security vulnerabilities review*. Preprint from Department of Computer Science, Lakehead University, Canada. http://onlinepresent.org/proceedings/vol14_2012/37.pdf; 2012 [accessed October 21, 2012].

22. Gostev A. The Flame: questions and answers, SecureList May 28, 2012; http://www.securelist.com/en/blog/208193522/ [accessed October16, 2012].

23. Sotirov Alex. *Analyzing the MD5 collision in Flame*. Retrieved November 6, 2012, from . . . and You Will Know Us by the Trail of Bits: http://blog.trailofbits.com/2012/06/11/analyzing-the-md5-collision-in-flame/; June 11, 2012.

24. Kaspersky Lab Global Research and Analysis Team. *Gauss: abnormal distribution. Kaspersky Lab*. http://www.securelist.com/en/downloads/vlpdfs/kaspersky-lab-gauss.pdf; August 9, 2012 [accessed October 17, 2012].

25. Ibid.

26. Bendersky D, Futoransky A, Notarfrancesco L, Sarraute C, Waissbein A. Advanced software protection now. Buenos Aires: CORE Security; 2003.

27. Lawson N. Stuxnet is embarrassing, not amazing, Root Labs Rdist January 17, 2011; http://rdist.root.org/2011/01/17/stuxnet-is-embarrassing-not-amazing/ [accessed November 8, 2012].

28. Lawson N. Cyber-weapon authors catch up on blog reading, Root Labs Rdist August 14, 2012; http://rdist.root.org/2012/08/14/cyber-weapon-authors-catch-up-on-blog-reading/ [accessed November 8, 2012].

29. Gostev A, Soumenkov I. Stuxnet/Duqu: the evolution of drivers, SecureList December 28, 2011; https://www.securelist.com/en/analysis/204792208/Stuxnet_Duqu_The_Evolution_of_Drivers [accessed October 21, 2012].

30. Gostev A. The roof is on fire: tackling Flame's C&C servers, SecureList June 4, 2012; https://www.securelist.com/en/blog/208193540/The_Roof_Is_on_Fire_Tackling_Flames_C_C_Servers [accessed October 21, 2012].

31. Global Research and Analysis Team. *Gauss: abnormal distribution. Kaspersky Lab*. http://www.securelist.com/en/analysis/204792238/Gauss_Abnormal_Distribution; August 9, 2012 [accessed October 21, 2012].

32. Rodionov E. Interconnection of Gauss with Stuxnet, Duqu & Flame, ESET Security Blog August 19, 2012; http://blog.eset.com/2012/08/15/interconnection-of-gauss-with-stuxnet-duqu-flame [accessed October 21, 2012].

Losing Trust in Your Friends: Social Network Exploitation

INFORMATION IN THIS CHAPTER

- Do you really know all your LinkedIn connections? Imposters in social networks

- Duping corporations and military personnel: Robin Sage

- The dangers of transitive trust

- Getting your personal data compromised while trying to impress the boss: The case of the SACEUR imposter

- Designing common knowledge: Influencing a social network

- How the Syrian Electronic Army attacked rivals on Facebook

- The future of influencing social networks

INTRODUCTION

The early 2000s saw personal interaction and expression on the World Wide Web move beyond simple homepages and discussion forums to social media and networking sites such as Twitter, Facebook, and LiveJournal. These sites facilitate the spread of personal information by leveraging the inherent network structure of human interactions. The result has been millions of users maintaining these sites as a means to stay connected with family, friends, and coworkers. However, the security of such sites is often called into question. Individuals wanting to express themselves on these sites often do not adhere to the most robust security practices. As a result, services such as Facebook pose a significant operational security (OPSEC) issue to both the military and the corporate world alike.

In this chapter, we look beyond the simple security issues of social media which would allow an adversary to potentially harvest sensitive information in a passive manner. Instead, we focus on events in which cyber warriors exploit social media in a manner to either obtain information from or influence the social network. First, we look at how a social engineer can leverage the network to harvest information, particularly leveraging social media to exploit the propensity of individuals to easily share information with new "friends" on these sites. This point is illustrated by the experiment "Robin Sage" where an American security firm created fake Facebook accounts of a fictitious user in order to entice users to befriend her and inappropriately share information. A more recent incident involves the use of false Facebook accounts to gain information from users at the NATO headquarters. With regard to the second point, we study how cyber warriors influence social networks—specifically citing how pro-regime hackers in Syria designed a fake Facebook login page in an attempt to steal login credentials from pro-revolutionary Syrians in 2011. We then look to the future and discuss how attackers can more efficiently target social networks for a propaganda campaign by leveraging the network structure.

DO YOU REALLY KNOW ALL YOUR LINKEDIN CONNECTIONS? IMPOSTERS IN SOCIAL NETWORKS

Consider the following hypothetical situation. A businessman signs into his LinkedIn account. He sees a new friend request. He does not remember ever meeting the individual— the picture looks unfamiliar, and the name does not ring a bell. However, he clicks on the user's profile and sees that three of his friends are connected with this individual. They also attended the same MBA program only graduating in different years. "Ok," our businessman thinks, "this guy seems legit" and clicks "connect" granting the stranger access to his private profile.

If the previous vignette sounds familiar, or you suspect that people in *your* corporate or military organization act in this manner, please consider the following two case studies. In the first, a security firm creates a fake user persona on several major social networking Web sites (including LinkedIn) and successfully tricked literally hundreds of people from various corporations and military organizations into befriending her. The second case is a real-world example of an imposter infiltrating a social network using a Facebook account—this time "virtually disguised" as the NATO commander (the SACEUR).

Duping Corporations and Military Personnel: Robin Sage

In 2010, Thomas Ryan of the American security firm *Provide Security* conducted an experiment. He designed and subsequently operated fictitious user accounts on LinkedIn, Facebook, and Twitter under the name of "Robin Sage"[1]—the name is in reference to the culminating field exercise of the U.S. Army's Special Forces Qualification Course. Using the photo of a woman who posed for a pornographic Web site and creating an esteemed resume including education from MIT, an NSA internship, and a current position at the Naval Network Warfare Command, he created a seemingly convincing profile—albeit one that had some subtle hints that the accounts were fake.

Over the 28-day experiment, "Robin" was able to obtain 300 contacts on LinkedIn, over 100 connections on Facebook, and about 150 followers on Twitter. She managed to make connections with individuals on the Joint Chiefs of Staff, the Chief Information Officer (CIO) of the NSA, a Congressional chief of staff, and scores of other personnel of the Department of Defense (DoD) and DoD contractors. Ryan interacted through the guise of his faked Sage accounts, so convincingly that some firms (among them Lockheed Martin) even made "Sage" job offers. His expertise led "Sage" to foster discussions with military personnel. In the course of one discussion, an Army Ranger even uploaded geolocated photographs[a] to her wall. Ryan noted that individuals in the same command she claimed to work under befriended her on some of the sites—of course they had never met the fictitious "Sage." One cyber-security expert from NASA Ames Research Center asked her to review some technical papers.[2]

Ryan cites several factors that may have contributed to Robin Sage's success in making connections on the various social networks. One factor he cites is Robin's gender and attractiveness. He noted this with several anecdotal comments from male users who complimented her on the pictures in her online profile as well as the fact that the majority of her connections were male. Another aspect that may have drawn connections to Sage was her false credentials. While most users accepted them without verification, one user was able to call her bluff and reveal her identify as false.[3,4]

The Dangers of Transitive Trust

Perhaps the most interesting aspect of how Robin Sage's profile spread was through *transitive trust* relationships. Suppose user A trusts user B and user B trusts user C. Under transitive trust, user A will then also trust user C based simply on the fact that user B does. We show this graphically in Figure 9.1.

Transitive trust can be thought of as someone "vouching" for another person. In an online community, this can happen quickly by simply examining the friends of a new individual (i.e., user A in the figure would see user B listed as one of user C's friends). Further, research in social network analysis has indicated that relatively unconnected individuals with a mutual friend tend to form a relationship in order to reduce social pressure.[5] In the network, this forms a "triangle" (as depicted in the previous figure), also referred to as a "cluster."[6]

Ryan noted that transitive trust played a significant role in his fictitious profile adopting more friends.[7] This transitivity seemed to occur in three ways. First, transitivity would be

---

[a]Photographs included data specifying the geographic location of where there were taken.

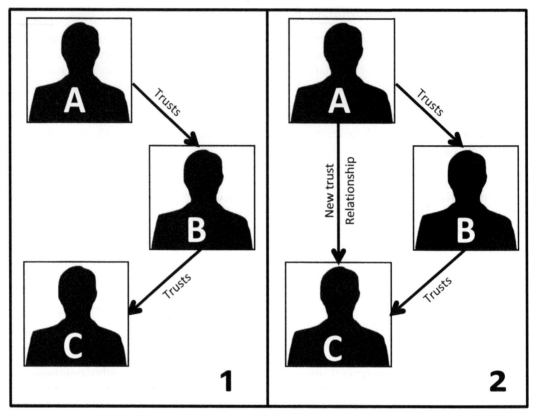

FIGURE 9.1   The trust relationships between A and B as well as the link between B and C can give rise to a transitive trust relationship between A and C.

based directly on personal relationships, as shown above. In the study, Ryan quoted one user messaging "Robin Sage" stating "I've never met you, but I saw you had Marty on your Facebook list, so that is good enough for me."[8] A second type of transitivity is based on a highly respected person befriending Sage. Other users see this occurring, and even though they do not have a direct relationship with the highly respected individual, they still view him as a trusted source—resulting in a new relationship directly with Sage. Ryan pointed out that once Sage established connections with some more respected individuals in the security community, the rate at which she gained friendship links increased. The third type of transitivity would simply be based on a similar tie to an institution. Clearly, this is even weaker than the previously mentioned types of transitivity as information about attending certain institutions can be faked easily. Ryan remarked that alumni of St. Paul's School and MIT (which was listed as her educational background) likely befriended her based on educational ties alone.[9]

We note that the Robin Sage "experiment" was not conducted under the highest academic standards. In many ways, it was more of a stunt than an experiment. However, it is notable that such an effort—even under very tight controls—would be difficult if not impossible to conduct in an academic setting or major noncommercial laboratory due to stringent ethical requirements those institutions have on studies dealing with human subjects. Hence, industry is normally where such efforts occur, and for obvious reasons, most firms would likely prefer not to disclose the results. This is why the Robin Sage experiment is important: it is perhaps the only publically available study that clearly demonstrates how such transitive trust relationships can propagate in a real-world online setting and thus shows how it could significantly aid an adversary in intelligence gathering.

On the other hand, though the "Robin Sage" experiment proved to be highly insightful, we have to consider an important aspect of this trial that somewhat divorces it from reality. Thomas Ryan himself is an information security professional who regularly interacts (legitimately) with many of the individuals who befriended Robin Sage. In fact, Ryan initially targeted certain individuals in the security community[10] and personally interacted with many of Sage's "connections" under the assumed persona.[11] Effectively, Ryan introduced a potentially confounding variable into the mix: himself. His personal and expert knowledge of the community that he was attempting to infiltrate through the Robin Sage identify made him a formidable opponent. In the real world, an adversary would likely have to go through significant initial intelligence collection in order to achieve knowledge close to Ryan's.

Another potentially confounding factor is the fact that Thomas Ryan would not allow those who discovered Robin Sage's true identity to divulge the information to the greater community. For instance, Omachonu Ogali researched Robin Sage, found her to be a fraud, and posted this information to her Facebook wall. He was subsequently contacted by Ryan and told to keep the true identify a secret.[12] This is an important aspect to consider the weakness of a social network exploited by Ryan—the ease at which individuals trust each other—may also be its strength—as an unknown party claiming that Robin Sage is untrustworthy (an "out-er") may also be readily trusted by those in the community. Unfortunately, the extent at which individuals believe an unknown "out-er" versus a potential imposter, and what factors affect this race condition were not studied in the Robin Sage case due to Ryan's experimental setup. However, this may be an interesting avenue for future work.

Getting Your Personal Data Compromised While Trying to Impress the Boss: The Case of the SACEUR Imposter

About 2 years after the Robin Sage experiment, a real-world Facebook imposter was able to collect a few high-level connections from NATO headquarters. In early 2012, several senior British military officers accepted friend requests on Facebook from an account belonging to American Admiral James Stavridis, the Supreme Allied Commander of European Forces (SACEUR) or NATO commander. However, it turned out that the account was a fake, and granting the friend request made their accounts susceptible to harvesting personal data by the imposter. Facebook quickly deactivated the bogus account. Representatives from the Supreme Headquarters of Allied Powers Europe (SHAPE) confirmed the incident but were quick to label it as mere "social engineering" and not "hacking" or "espionage."[13]

It is likely that those who set up the fake Facebook account of the SACEUR were not targeting Admiral Stavridis, but rather other higher-level individuals in the organization. If the goal was to quickly obtain some limited personal information about such individuals, the attack may have succeeded—as some of the friendship requests were granted. However, by impersonating such a prominent figure, the time to exploit the attack was likely limited[b]—as opposed to using a more innocuous account as done in the "Robin Sage" example. That being said, it should also be noted that by impersonating the SACEUR, it is more likely that other users would more immediately grant friendship requests—as opposed to Robin Sage who had to spend a few days or weeks building relationships in order to generate transitive trust. As the military is a hierarchical organization, it is likely that many senior officers would be quick to accept a friendship request from an Admiral.

We do not know the true purpose of why Admiral Stavridis was impersonated on Facebook. However, according to NATO officials, this imposter incident was not the first time that a fake Facebook account of the Admiral was identified.[14] While this type of social engineering likely has an intelligence-gathering purpose, it may also be used in preparation of future attacks. By harvesting information about a person—particularly one high ranking enough to comfortably befriend an Admiral on Facebook—an attacker gains some personal information from the privately viewable portion of that individual's account. This data can then be used to socially engineer emails to other personnel in the organization. As we saw in Chapter 7, such well-crafted social engineering messages offer an adversary a foothold into a given computer network. Interestingly, these techniques, pointed out in that chapter, were used in cyber operations attributed to China. Under the Chinese-attributed cyber campaign known as *Night Dragon*[15] (which occurred about a year prior to the Stavridis-Facebook incident), the hackers initially targeted high-ranking business executives in their social engineering efforts. We also note that the Stavridis-Facebook incident is also attributed to China (however, this is due to media sources, rather than technical analysis).[16] It is possible that modified version of the *Night Dragon* strategy used to gain corporate information was being leveraged against NATO (Figure 9.2).

The Robin Sage experiment illustrates how a fictitious user can gain trust of hundreds of individuals. A combination of seemingly valid credentials, attractive photographs, the

FIGURE 9.2 Navy Admiral James Stavridis, commander of U.S. European Command and NATO's Supreme Allied Commander-Europe speaking at a conference in Germany sponsored by U.S. European Command in 2011. In 2012, a false Facebook site for Admiral Stravidis sent out friend requests to several high-ranking officers in NATO. The fake Facebook page was likely used to gather intelligence. (For color version of this figure, the reader is referred to the online version of this chapter.) *EUCOM photo.*

---

[b]It is unknown how much data were harvested through the fake Facebook account of Admiral Stavridis. However, a NATO spokesperson is quoted as saying that such imposter accounts are normally deleted within 24-48 h (see Nick Hopkins' article in *The Guardian* cited in the endnotes of this chapter).

snowball effect of transitive trust, and the expertise of its operator allowed "Robin Sage" to infiltrate the American DoD (Department of Defense) information security community—allowing her access to unpublished technical papers and even some tactical information. Likewise, an alternative tactic of impersonating a high-ranking official may also lead to many friendship requests—particularly if the attacker knows whom he or she is targeting. However, the time window to harvest information using such a technique will likely be much shorter as opposed to using a "Robin Sage."

DESIGNING COMMON KNOWLEDGE: INFLUENCING A SOCIAL NETWORK

In early 2011, the "Arab Spring" spread to Syria. In particular, large portions of the Sunni Islam populace was rebelling against the Shiite-dominated government. As with many of the incidents during the "Arab Spring," social media was used extensively. With the effectiveness of social media is spreading a message and allowing international diasporas to provide moral and informational support, how can an entity (i.e., a state) influence the social network of a group of revolutionaries and perhaps reverse some of their progress on the propaganda front? This may have been the very question many supporters of the Syrian regime asked themselves.

In mid-2011, the *Syrian Electronic Army* (SEA) emerged—a pro-Syrian regime hacktivist group, which became prominent in public media for a series of various attacks against the revolutionaries. This group is believed to have a connection with the *Syrian Computer Society*, a group led by now current Syrian President Bashar al-Assad in the 1990s.[17] Noting the effective use of social media by the revolutionaries, the SEA set out to limit its value.

How the Syrian Electronic Army Attacked Rivals on Facebook

The SEA worked to target the social media site Facebook—which is the dominant general public social networking site at the time of this writing. One technique that the SEA used against Facebook was spamming. Often the focus was on popular or political Facebook pages. Once the target page was selected, in the course of 1 or 2 h, large numbers of comments were posted to these pages.[18] Hence, the volume of bogus messages would have the effect of making the targeted page unusable to the originally intended social group.

The SEA also used more technical means to attack the online social networks of the revolutionaries. Using various Twitter accounts, the SEA sent out links to a "fascinating video clip showing an attack on the Syrian Regime" which directed them to a fake Facebook login page. A follow-on Tweet informed the victim that he or she might be asked to log on to Facebook a second time as an "additional security measure."[19] If the victim clicked on the link, the first Facebook page would harvest the user name and password, sending this information to the SEA. The second page would actually log them into Facebook.

While this may seem like a transparent ploy, one must consider the real-world context of Internet usage in Syria. As of 2010, less than 18% of the population was online,[20] and the country of 22 million had only 420 hosts on the Internet—ranked 187 worldwide (a lower ranking

FIGURE 9.3   Syrian Electronic Army logo. (For color version of this figure, the reader is referred to the online version of this chapter.) *Source: http://victor.thepro.sy/.*

than the U.S. territory of Puerto Rico).[21] Hence, the lack of Internet prevalence in Syrian society may have increased the likelihood of individuals signing on to the false Facebook site (Figure 9.3).

Though it is unclear exactly which Facebook accounts were broken into, the SEA was clearly successful in breaking into several of them. Further, the attack may have been amplified by a well-known vulnerability in Facebook's password-reset system (circa mid-2011).[22] If a user attempts to login to Facebook and claims his password, it can be reset through a series of steps that include answering security questions. If these questions are answered incorrectly, Facebook then offers a password-reset feature based on codes sent to three of the users' friends selected by the person resetting the password. If the selected friends were previously compromised, then the codes are easily obtainable. The resulting dynamic is actually a case of the classic "tipping model" described later in this chapter.

The SEA was able to compromise at least 17 sites pertaining to regime opponents, which they defaced by pasting their logo prominently and thus co-opted the propaganda function of the accounts. The Facebook sites remained active after the break-ins and caused the number of (opposition) fans visiting them dropped significantly after SEA's actions.[23] We do not have any information on how long the Facebook accounts were rendered inaccessible to their rightful users or if access was ever returned.

The Future of Influencing Social Networks

Though somewhat effective in combating the revolutionaries' message on Facebook, the SEA really scratches only the surface of what may be possible with the influence of online social networks. One key aspect of the social networks formed out of the millions of connections in the site of Facebook is that information, trends, and behaviors can potentially spread through the network very quickly. Let us consider the "tipping" model introduced by Nobel Laureate Thomas Schelling[24] in which an individual adopts a new trend if a certain number (i.e., 50%) of his friends previously adopted it.[c] Depending on the characteristics of the original nodes, such tipping events could lead to a *social cascade* where the trend propagates through the network (see figure below for an example). More recently, Damon Centola of MIT has shown that the tipping model is viable based on real-world experiments (Figure 9.4).[25]

Can certain individuals in a network be targeted in order for us to ensure that such a cascade occurs? If a group can initiate a counter-information campaign on an adversary's online social network, they could potentially dominate it with their message (or rather misinformation). It turns out that our recent research indicates that it is possible to identify

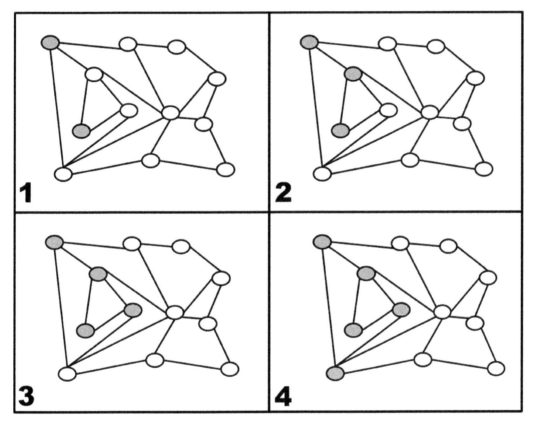

FIGURE 9.4   Example of the propagation of a trend under the tipping model when each individual adopts the trend after at least two of his friends do. The circles represent individuals and the lines between them relationships (i.e., "friendship" relationships in an online social network). Shaded circles represent individuals who have adopted some trend. In this example, in panel 1, only two individuals originally adopted the trend. Their presence leads to progressively more nodes becoming "tipped" as the cascade progresses in panels 2-4.

[c] If we consider the Facebook password-reset vulnerability, we can view the trend adopted as a "compromised account" and the number of friends previously "adopting" (becoming compromised) is three as that is the number of "trusted friends" that Facebook requires a user to have in order to reset a password without answering any security questions.

a "seed set" of individuals such that if they initially adopt a trend, then, following the tipping model, the trend will spread to the entire social network.[d] Further, it is relatively easy for a computer to find such a set, which is very small for most online social networks. For instance, our study found that a sample of the *Friendster* social network could be entirely influenced (assuming each user adopts if the majority of their friends do) with an initial seed set less than 1% of the population size.[26] So, a group such as the SEA could potentially break into a few Facebook accounts and map out the social network of the users. Then, using a technique such as the one we developed, they could target a select set of nodes for their message (or misinformation)—with the hopes of it "going viral" and spreading to the larger population.

Very recently, it seems that such research on influencing social networks for use in cyber and information warfare has taken a significant step toward operational use. In August 2012, *RT.com* reported that Russia's Foreign Intelligence Service has invested 1 million U.S. dollars in three pieces of software designed to monitor and influence online social networks.[27] The first system, called *Dispute*, is designed to monitor the spread of information in the blogosphere specifically identifying popular stories and authors. This is related to the second system, *Monitor-3*, which will be used to facilitate collection management (CM) for open-source intelligence (OSINT) collection. OSINT refers to the use of publically available information, such as news media Web sites, radio, and television broadcasts as intelligence. A collection management system allows intelligence leaders to efficiently assign tasks to individuals who are gathering the relevant information. The Russians likely see the creation of *Monitor-3* as a necessity to conduct proper gathering of publically available information often referred to as "Open Source Intelligence" or OSINT. This is because due to the staggering volume of information available on the Internet, which makes this type of intelligence gathering a particularly unwieldy effort. The third system is known as *Storm-12* and is designed to facilitate the spread of information through the blogosphere—likely using techniques to influence social networks similar to the ones discussed in this chapter. *Dispute* and *Monitor-3* are scheduled to be complete in 2012 while *Storm-12* is scheduled for completion in 2012. The projects are under work by a Russian firm known as *Kommersant*, which is headed by the former deputy head of the Russian Cryptology Institute, Igor Matskevich.

Urvan Parfentyev, head of Russia's *Center for Safe Internet*, stated that the software was the natural evolution of propaganda/counter-propaganda techniques. He is likely correct in this statement.[28] The current research and development efforts with respect to marketing in online social networks have a clear dual use in a conflict situation. Such techniques will likely become more prevalent as more is understood of how information flows in society's networks.

It is noteworthy that these Russian efforts are eerily similar to an American project started about a decade prior know at *Total Information Awareness* (TIA) that was funded under the Defense Advanced Research Projects Agency.[e] However, this program was ultimately cancelled over concerns over the privacy of American citizens.[29]

---

[d] One of the authors recently presented the research on this phenemon. A YouTube video of this lecture can be found at http://m.youtube.com/watch?v=cl_88YoY0PY.

[e] The Defense Advanced Research Projects Agency, or DARPA, is the DoD agency responsible for funding a variety of American technological advances, including the precursor to the Internet as well as military technology such as the Predator drone. We discuss DARPA more in the next chapter.

As we have seen in previous chapters, social media on the Internet can have a great impact in a civil conflict as it allows a group with limited resources to produce a message heard by the global community. As a result, an opposing group (i.e., an existing regime) shall seek to limit the effects of a social media-driven information operations campaign through a variety of means. Using social engineering techniques to exploit Facebook accounts, for example, is already being looked at by groups such as the SEA to limit the effects of social media. Further, the linkages among user accounts in such sites form a complex social network, which often is susceptible to the spread of ideas through cascades. This fact may indicate that in the near future techniques to influence large portions of an online user community in a propaganda campaign may appear in a conflict.

SUMMARY

Online social media has ushered in a new age of how information is managed in conflict situations. These information operations can both support or be supported by cyber warfare. We saw with the "Robin Sage" and the Facebook imposters that cyber warriors can leverage the trust relationships of such sites in order to obtain the sensitive information that can lead to cyber exploitation and espionage operations. On the other side, groups such as the SEA leverage cyber-warfare techniques to hack into user accounts of online social networks in an effort to destroy the credibility of an adversary. Finally, in the future, such techniques may be used with tools from the study of complex networks in an attempt to influence large portions of an online user community during a conflict.

SUGGESTED FURTHER READING

The Robin Sage experiment is outlined in Thomas Ryan's paper "Getting in Bed with Robin Sage" which was also presented at the *BlackHat* conference in 2010. *BlackHat* is one of the premier hacker conferences. The actions of the Syrian Electronic Army were described by the *Information Warfare Monitor* group in a paper entitled "The Emergence of Open and Organized Pro-Government Cyber Attacks in the Middle East: The Case of the Syrian Electronic Army" which is available on the Information Warfare Monitor Web site (http://www.infowar-monitor.net/2011/08/fake-facebook-page-targets-pro-revolution-syrian-users/).
Further information about common hacking techniques used to illicitly obtain access into a user's Facebook or Twitter account are described in the book *Hacking: The Next Generation* by Nitesh Dhanjani, Billy Rios, and Brett Hardin. This book also includes accounts of how many commercial Web-based email applications can be hacked—specifically noting how 2008 vice-presidential candidate's Sarah Palin's email account was compromised during her campaign. Incidentally, some of Palin's personal communications were posted on *4chan's b-board*, the significance of which is described in Chapter 6.
The study of complex social networks is a new and exciting emerging field of science combining techniques from computer science, sociology, physics, mathematics, economics, and biology. For an introduction to this exciting new field, we recommend *Networks, Crowds, and Markets: Reasoning About a Highly Connected World* by David Easley and Jon Kleinberg.

The "tipping model" was first introduced from an economic perspective by Thomas Schelling in his landmark book *Micromotives and Macrobehavior*. Around the same time in the late 1970s, sociologist Mark Ganovetter studied the same phenomenon in terms of social networks. Ganovetter's work can be found his doctoral dissertation as well as the paper "Threshold models of collective behavior" that appeared in the *American Journal of Sociology*. This model received popular attention due to the mainstream book *The Tipping Point* by Malcolm Gladwell. In that book, Gladwell describes several anecdotes in which the tipping phenomenon is demonstrated. In a more rigorous empirical study, Damon Centola showed that the probability of an individual adopting a new behavior is proportional to the number of his or her contacts that previously adopted the behavior. For his study, Centola created an isolated online social network in which he could be sure that the contagion he was studying could only be spread through the connections in the network. Recently, one of the authors of this book has also studied tipping. We designed a new algorithm that produces a set of nodes that, if initially infected, are mathematically guaranteed to cause a cascade that leads to the entire population adopting the contagion. This work, entitled "Large Social Networks Can Be Targeted for Viral Marketing with Small Seed Sets" was presented at the *IEEE/ ACM International Conference on Advances in Social Networks Analysis and Mining* in 2012.

References

1. Kelly Jackson Higgins. 'Robin Sage' Profile Duped Military Intelligence, IT Security Pros. *DarkReading*; 6 July, 2010.
2. Ryan Thomas. Getting in Bed with Robin Sage. *Provide Security*. Also presented at the BlackHat conference in 2010; 2010.
3. Ibid., Ryan.
4. Lisko Tim. The Robin Sage Experiment—Interview with Omachonu Ogali. Privacywonk blogspot. http://www. privacywonk.net/2010/09/the-robin-sage-experiment-interview-with-ogali-om.php; September 6, 2010.
5. Easley David, Kleinberg Jon. Networks, crowds, and markets: reasoning about a highly connected world. New York: Cambridge University Press; 2010.
6. Ibid.
7. Ibid., Ryan.
8. Ibid., Ryan.
9. Ibid., Ryan.
10. Ibid., Lisko.
11. Ibid., Ryan.
12. Ibid., Lisko.
13. Lewis Jason. How spies used Facebook to steal Nato chiefs' details. *The Telegraph*. http://www.telegraph.co.uk/ technology/9136029/How-spies-used-Facebook-to-steal-Nato-chiefs-details.html; March 2012 [accessed June 21, 2012].
14. Nick Hopkins. "China suspected of Facebook attack on Nato's supreme allied commander", The Guardian. http://www.guardian.co.uk/world/2012/mar/11/china-spies-facebook-attack-nato; March 10, 2012 [accessed October 7, 2012].
15. Global Energy Cyberattacks: 'Night Dragon'. *McAffe White Paper* February 10, 2011.
16. Ibid., Lewis, Hopkins.
17. Information Warfare Monitor.The Emergence of Open and Organized Pro-Government Cyber Attacks in the Middle East: The Case of the Syrian Electronic Army. http://www.infowar-monitor.net/2011/05/7349/; May 30, 2011 [accessed June 22, 2012].
18. Ibid, Information Warfare Monitor.

19. Information Warfare Monitor. Fake Facebook Page Targets Pro-Revolution Syrian Users. http://www.infowar-monitor.net/2011/08/fake-facebook-page-targets-pro-revolution-syrian-users/; August 29, 2011 [accessed June 22, 2012].

20. Syria Internet Usage and Marketing Report. *Internet World Stats*. http://www.internetworldstats.com/me/sy.htm; July 12, 2010 [accessed October 8, 2012].

21. *The World Fact Book*, U.S. Central Intelligence Agency. https://www.cia.gov/library/publications/the-world-factbook/geos/sy.html; [accessed October 7, 2012].

22. Shahapurkar Ashwin. Facebook's Security Question vulnerability—Bypassing Security Question! *hacker 9*. http://www.hacker9.com/facebooks-security-question-vulnerability-bypassing-security-question.html; May 24, 2011 [accessed October 7, 2012].

23. Information Warfare Monitor. Syrian Electronic Army: Disruptive Attacks and Hyped Targets. http://www.infowar-monitor.net/2011/06/syrian-electronic-army-disruptive-attacks-and-hyped-targets/; June 25, 2011 [accessed June 22, 2012].

24. Schelling Thomas C. Micromotives and macrobehavior. New York: W.W. Norton and Co.; 1978.

25. Centola Damon. The spread of behavior in an online social network experiment. Science 2010;329(5996):1194–7.

26. Shakrian Paulo, Paulo Damon. Large social networks can be targeted for viral marketing with small seed sets. *IEEE/ACM international conference on advances in social networks analysis and mining*, August 2012.

27. RT.com. Facespook: Russian spies order $1mln software to influence social networks. http://rt.com/politics/intelligence-orders-influencing-social-619/; August 27, 2012 [accessed August 27, 2010].

28. Ibid.

29. Lee Newton. Facebook Nation. New York: Springer; 2012.

How Iraqi Insurgents Watched U.S. Predator Video—Information Theft on the Tactical Battlefield

INFORMATION IN THIS CHAPTER

- The Predator UAV
- Hacking the Predator feed
- The Predator's vulnerability
- Attribution and the Kata'ib Hezbollah
- The history of the Predator vulnerability

INTRODUCTION

In Chapter 7, we discussed acts of cyber espionage that suggest Chinese involvement. These operations focused on either massive data exfiltration for the purposes of stealing intellectual property and industrial information and/or long-term monitoring of an adversary's information systems—most likely as a means of intelligence collection. In this chapter, we look at cyber-espionage operations that focus on exploitation of a different sort—the exploitation of data relating from ongoing tactical military operations. The exploitation incidents described in this chapter deal with the theft of information either transmitted or received from an unmanned aerial vehicle (UAV) system.[1] Hence, as opposed to what was discussed in Chapter 9, the incidents presented here are of much more immediate consequence. Further, unlike the cyber-espionage operations of Chapter 9, where the data stolen were normally in the "storage" state, the information pilfered in the operations of this chapter was normally in the "transmission" state. Here, the operators are more concerned about data traveling to or from a UAV system than static data on a hard drive. In this chapter, we briefly describe the Predator—flagship UAV of the U.S. military—and a 2009 incident where insurgent operating Iraq was found to intercept the video feeds of that system.

We note that although this chapter focuses on cyber operations against American UAVs, the cyber-espionage methods and techniques applied in such missions could most likely be used against UAVs from other nations too. We also note that American UAV programs are perhaps the most mature in the world. Hence, as other countries catch up in this military technology, they will most likely experience similar cyber-espionage operations against their systems as well.

THE PREDATOR UAV

The Defense Advanced Research Projects Agency (DARPA) is an organization within the Department of Defense tasked with maintaining technological superiority over America's adversaries. Unlike organizations that sponsor scientific research for the military services—such as Army Research Laboratories, the Office of Naval Research, and the Air Force Research Labs, DARPA does not conduct research in support of near-term needs of the military—but rather explore high-risk, high-payoff ideas that would allow the United States to obtain "strategic surprise" over its adversaries. Formed in 1958 in response to the Soviet launch of the Sputnik satellite, DARPA has been the organization responsible for military innovations such as stealth aircraft and the M16 rifle.[2] An even more notable technological contribution of this organization was known as ARPANET—which today is better known as the Internet.

In the late 1970s, a firm known as Leading Systems proposed a long-endurance unmanned aerial vehicles (UAV) design that DARPA funded in the early 1980s—resulting in an aerial platform known as the Gnat 750. Due to a shift in priorities pertaining to UAV-technology mandated by the U.S. Congress, the focus in the research community moved to systems designed for short-range missions. As a result, Leading Systems went out of business and the long-range UAV-technology they had developed was acquired by General Atomics. After a successful beyond line-of-sight test, the Gnat 750 was hailed as a "Revolution in Military

FIGURE 10.1 The Predator RQ-1 takes off at Balad Air Base, Iraq in September 2004 supporting Operation Iraqi Freedom. (For color version of this figure, the reader is referred to the online version of this chapter.) *Photograph from DARPA, www.darpa.mil.*

Affairs" and further development followed. The aircraft was modified with a longer fuselage and a greater wingspan and became the Predator—which first flew in July 1994 (Figure 10.1).[3]

The Predator was first employed for combat by the U.S. Air Force in support of Operation Nomad Vigil in late 1995 with flights over Albania. This was followed by the support combat operation in the Balkans for the remainder of the 1990s.[4] All the early missions of the Predator were reconnaissance; however, over time the UAV evolved into a targeting tool. After spotting an enemy target in the Balkans, the Predator could use its laser to mark the target in order for another aerial platform—such as an F-16 fighter—to launch munitions. Hence, weaponizing the Predator so it could attack targets appeared as a natural progression for the aircraft. By mid-2001, the U.S. Air Force began test-firing Hellfire missiles from the Predator. After the terrorist attacks on 9/11, the armed Predators were employed in Afghanistan to conduct kinetic operations. By 2008, the Predators were logging a total of 10,000 flight hours per month in Iraq and Afghanistan.[5]

HACKING THE PREDATOR FEED

In late 2008, U.S. military personnel operating in Iraq arrested a Shi'ite militant in whose possession a laptop was found that contained video footage of Predator feeds.[6] In July 2009, further finds of insurgent laptops with recorded Predator feeds followed. At the time, it was widely suspected that many of the Shi'ite militant groups operating in Iraq were being funded and trained in Iran—which led some officials to conclude that the ability to acquire such video feeds had become standard practice by then. One group in particular, the Kata'ib Hezbollah operating out of Sadr City, which was known to have been supported by Iran at the time, was also found to be in possession of feeds and the necessary equipment to obtain them.[7] Further, reports of Predator intercepts in Afghanistan also surfaced. The story was first reported in the news media by the *Wall Street Journal*, initiating a media fire-storm. In this section, we describe the vulnerability of the Predator and discuss potential reasons why the vulnerability may have gone unnoticed by the U.S. Air Force—ultimately leading to a significant breach of information confidentiality during military operations.

The Predator's Vulnerability

The Predator may include a variety of high-end reconnaissance tools, including synthetic aperture radar (SAR) with 1-foot resolution, laser designators and range finder, a moving target indicator (MTI), and the multi-spectral targeting system (MTS) which provides real-time imagery of the battlefield—complete with features such as zoom and a telescopic spotter.[8] These advanced tools can also be used for targeting—which is why the Predator became the UAV of choice for strike operations (using the Hellfire missile) (Figure 10.2).

Successful radio communication between two devices requires that they both utilize the same frequency. International standards have identified ranges of frequencies as "bands." The Predator is equipped to transmit information using a variety of different bands. Initial tests of the Predator relied on C-band line-of-sight communications (where the sender and receiver of the radio signal must be visible to one-another).[9] However, for real world beyond line-of-sight missions, K_u-band (K_u stands for Kurtz-under[a]) satellite communication (SATCOM) is normally utilized. Additionally, it is equipped with UHF and VHF radio relay links (these are bands often used for FM radio communication and noncable television).[10] It is important to note that K_u-band SATCOM is normally affiliated with commercial use. In fact, the Predator relies on commercial communication satellite infrastructure to transmit its data. The design decision to use commercial rather than military communication infrastructure is representative of

FIGURE 10.2   Airmen attach the radome to an MQ-1 Predator unmanned aerial vehicle at Balad Air Base, Iraq, in 2005. (For color version of this figure, the reader is referred to the online version of this chapter.) *Photograph from www. defense.gov, taken by Maj. Robert Couse-Baker.*

---

[a]This band is split into segments according to geographical regions as determined by the International Telecommunication Union (ITU).

a trend in the U.S. military at the turn of the century. In the late twentieth century, the U.S. military made a significant move toward using consumer off-the-shelf technology (COTS). The reason for this was twofold. First, it was a cost-saving technique as the prices of consumer information technology (IT) equipment plummeted in the 1990s. Second, it allowed the military to keep better pace with technology. Prior to the widespread use of COTS, the military would develop its own "hardened" systems, which normally leads to a second development cycle after the piece of technology would already have appeared in the marketplace. The result was that the military technology would often be a generation behind.

Wireless Networks

The use of K_u-band SATCOM in the Predator played a key role in the compromise of the intelligence data collected on the aerial platform. The data were particularly vulnerable as they were transmitted unencrypted on a widely understood medium. A key component to the vulnerability of the Predator was the unavoidable use of broadcast model, which is used in wireless networks (Figure 10.3).

In a wired computer network, devices such as switches and routers make decisions as to which computer to send a given piece of information. Alternatively, with a wireless network (that relies on radio signals) a broadcast model is used. All devices that are within the range of the transmitter and tuned to its frequency receive the transmitter's message. Normally (i.e., under most wireless protocols such as the 802.11 family), if the message is not addressed to the receiving device, it is discarded. However, if a system is set to accept any message (in what is known as "promiscuous mode") it keeps receiving all messages. In order to avoid an adversary computer in promiscuous mode intercepting communications, most administrators encrypt wireless traffic.

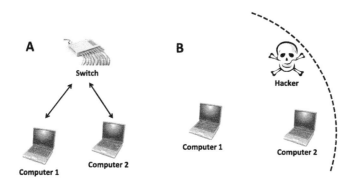

A On a wired network Computer 1 sends a message to Computer 2. A switch, connected to both computers, receives the message from Computer 1 and then sends it to the port to which Computer 2 is attached.

B In a wireless network, Computer 1 sends a message to Computer 2. Computer 1 has s transmission range indicated by the dashed line. Note that any computer within the transmission range can receive the message—even a hacker.

FIGURE 10.3   Wired vs. wireless networks. (For color version of this figure, the reader is referred to the online version of this chapter.)

The broadcast model offered by SATCOM communications allows multiple users to "tune in" to view the feeds. For example, during the Bosnia campaign, Predator feeds were viewed by the control station (the pilot), the Trojan Spirit communication terminal supporting the American forward-deployed headquarters conducting operations, and a communication station in Britain where the signal was then sent to Washington, DC and to the U.S. military's networks.[11] The Predator video feeds that were transmitted using the commercial K_u-band SATCOM were not encrypted, so that anyone capable of receiving the signal could potentially view it. Though the identification of the precise frequencies was not public knowledge, discovery was still possible. The practice of relying on little known, but discoverable pieces of information as a means of security is known as "security by obscurity." In such practice, there is no real access control—no software making decisions on whether to permit or deny access. Instead, an administrator relies on somehow hiding the access point to the system. However, once this access point is discovered, the system is essentially open to all users who can discover the access point. This is exactly what happened in the case of the Predator-system through the use of a piece of Russian hobbyist software known as "SkyGrabber." This type of eavesdropping is illustrated in Figure 10.4.

SkyGrabber is a piece of software designed to grant a computer admission to a wireless network using SATCOM switched to promiscuous mode—thus intercepting or "sniffing"

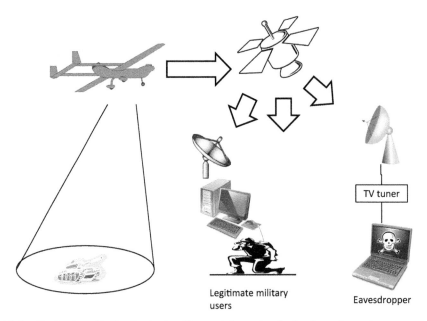

Legitimate military users

Eavesdropper

FIGURE 10.4 The Predator UAV collection intelligence information (in the above figure, its sensors detect an enemy tank). When using beyond-line-of-sight communication, the UAV broadcasts its data to a satellite. The satellite, in turn, broadcasts the data to the users. While normal military users can obtain the signal and decode it to view what the UAV sees, the information can potentially be viewed by a third-part eavesdropper. The use of the Skygrabber software, coupled with a television tuner card allowed a British hobbyist as well as KH insurgents in Iraq to intercept the feed of the Predator from commercial satellites in this manner. (For color version of this figure, the reader is referred to the online version of this chapter.)

the incoming network traffic. Normal SATCOM-based Internet relies—as its name suggests—on a satellite connection for receiving information and either on satellite or another connection for sending information. As most services on the Internet are interactive (i.e., requesting and receiving Web pages, online chat, and e-mail), information flows in both directions. However, some traffic, such as streaming video or Internet radio, the information flow is one-way. SkyGrabber is advertised as a tool to receive such one-way traffic for free. Hence, a user of SATCOM equipment trying to receive a signal, but who has no account for the respective service provider, could through SkyGrabber view the content downloaded by other users with accounts. Hence, SkyGrabber turned out to be a useful tool for intercepting unencrypted Predator videos. At the time the *Wall Street Journal* article broke in 2009, the software cost $26 only.[12] Perhaps as a result of the Predator incident, the cost of the software at the time of this writing is $91.[13]

Attribution and the Kata'ib Hezbollah

As with many incidents described in this book, attribution is an interesting issue to explore in regard to the case of the vulnerable Predator video feeds too. Due to the nature of the security flaw and the availability of the SkyGrabber software, it is certainly possible that an insurgent group in Iraq whose ranks included a few tech-savvy individuals could have, on their own, found the flaw and exploited it accordingly. However, there is some evidence that the compromise of the Predator feeds may have resulted from training classes offered by a nation state—specifically Iran. Kata'ib Hezbollah (KH, "Brigades of the Party of God"[14]) was found to have obtained Predator video feeds and the ensuing investigation of the group revealed its ties to the Iranian regime.[15]

Kata'ib Hezbollah was one of several "Special Groups" in Iraq that was active during Operation Iraqi Freedom. All of these groups were Shi'ite militias believed to be backed by the Iranian government.[16] The goal of this particular organization was to end the United States presence in Iraq and establish a Shi'ite Islamic government. Further, KH is thought to be sympathetic to the goal of the Lebanese Hezbollah of eradicating the state of Israel (Figures 10.5 and 10.6).[17] This group has been active in Iraq since 2007—predominantly in Sadr City and some of the southern provinces.[18] In June 2009, the U.S. Department of State designated them as a Foreign Terrorist Organization.[19]

Kata'ib Hezbollah's ties to Iran are more prominent than with other Special Groups and evidenced in open sources. Here are examples of some connections:

- Iraqi-born Jamal Ja'far Muhammad[b] a.k.a Abu[c] Mahdi al-Muhandis ("The Engineer"—he worked as an engineer in Kuwait City from the late 1970s to the early 1980s) is thought to be close to Qassem Suleimani, the head of Iran's Al-Quds force[20] and is believed to be involved in the militant group's leadership. Al-Muhandis' alleged involvement in the 1983

[b] Another source identifies his real name as Jamal al-Ibrahimi (CTC Sentinel [11/01/2010]). The Evolution of Iran's Special Groups in Iraq, available at: http://www.ctc.usma.edu/posts/the-evolution-of-iran%E2%80%99s-special-groups-in-iraq.

[c] "Abu" is a title (patronym) usually referencing the first born son of a man in many semitic languages can literally translated as "father of" and often functions as a nickname.

FIGURE 10.5 Logo of the Kata'ib Hezbollah. (For color version of this figure, the reader is referred to the online version of this chapter.)

FIGURE 10.6 Logo of the Lebanese Hezbollah. (For color version of this figure, the reader is referred to the online version of this chapter.)

bombing of the French and American embassies in Kuwait City as well as in the assassination attempt of the then Kuwaiti Emir in 1985 were probably meant to deter support for Iraq during the Iran-Iraq war. He fled subsequently to Iran where he fought as a senior leader of SCIRI's Badr Brigade against Saddam Hussain's forces during the Iran-Iraq war. He is a citizen of both Iran and Iraq and was a senior advisor to the Al-Quds force and served for the Shi'a United Iraqi Alliance in the Iraqi parliament in 2006. The Quds-force is an arm of the Islamic Revolutionary Guard Corps (IRGC) and handles Iranian-backed armed groups that operate outside of Iran. Lebanon's Hezbollah and Shi'a anti-Saddam militias are only the most popular examples of its work. KH is thought of Al-Quds' surrogate in Baghdad responsible for the extensive smuggle of weapons and explosives. From spring 2007 to summer 2008, the militant group targeted U.S. forces, which prominently featured on (Lebanon's) Hezbollah's media outlet Al-Manar, propelled KH into the ranks of the most popular Shi'a armed groups.[21] He also has been known to transport weapons between the two countries as well as to create militias such as KH and Jaysh al-Mahdi (JAM).[22,23]

- The U.S. Treasury Department named the Iranian Revolutionary Guard Corps (IRGC) as a supporter of KH in 2008.[24]
- In 2010, U.S. Army General Ray Odierno stated that KH fighters had recently returned from training in Iran to attack U.S. bases and that they were accompanied by IRGC advisors.[25]
- Iranian-supplied Improvised Rocket-Assisted Munitions, perhaps one of the most lethal improvised weapons used by insurgents in the Iraq war, have been used by KH.[26]

Though it is possible that the Predator flaw could have been found by KH independently of their Iranian backers, the level of cooperation between the two parties suggests that the system vulnerability was first found by the Iranians, who then trained their militant surrogates—either during attack preparations in Iran or an advising session in Iraq. It is also interesting to note that KH is perhaps one of the more technology-embracing militias—maintaining a high-quality, up-to-date interactive Web site featuring video downloads—which was uncommon for insurgent groups operating in Iraq.[27]

The History of the Predator Vulnerability

After the *Wall Street Journal* published their article, Wired Magazine followed up the story with a claim, that concerns over the Predator vulnerability were first raised in 1996 in an Air Combat Command presentation.[28] CBS News subsequently stated that a 1999 presentation by then Air Force Major Jeffrey Stephenson Air Force's School of Advanced Airpower Studies in Alabama had mentioned similar concerns. The media also noted that the Predator's successor high-altitude successor, DarkStar, operated with encrypted communication.[29] However, the DarkStar program was later canceled.[30]

CBS also aired a story in 2002 about a British hobbyist named John Locker who was able to intercept Predator feeds from NATO operations over Macedonia—in a manner similar to the insurgents' use of SkyGrabber. U.S. officials stated that the unencrypted communication was necessary to share information with NATO allies and did not pose a security risk since the feeds were reconnaissance-only.[31] However, in the wake of the KH intercepts in Iraq, the U.S. Air Force has resolved to encrypt all Predator feeds.[32]

The vulnerability of the Predator UAV illustrates a few interesting points. First, the *confidentiality* of the information was violated. The Predator was still sending accurate information to the ground control units, but the users of that information could no longer be certain that the information was guarded from an adversary. Second, the use of "security by obscurity" of the U.S. Air Force and associated contractors proved to be a poor idea. The exposure of the flaw in publically available material in the 1990s as well as the later by CBS news documented breach in the early 2000s may also have been recorded by an adversarial nation (such as Iran—and then provided to a proxy [such as Kata'ib Hezbollah]) for operational use. Third, the use of wireless networks—due to the use of the broadcast model—does provide a potential for eavesdroppers. Finally, the idea that operational surveillance video—even used for the more mundane operations of Macedonia—still pose a security risk as understanding the tactics, techniques, and procedures (TTPs) of Predator employment is likely important information to an adversary (not to mention that the technique was later used in a more heated conflict).

SUMMARY

In this chapter, we described the Predator system and how insurgents in Iraq managed to intercept its video feed. The downloading of Predator feeds by these insurgents violated the confidentiality of the information. However, it should be noted that during that incident the military reported that there was no evidence that the pilot's control of the UAV was ever compromised.[33] This follows directly from the fact that the intercepts were obtained by monitoring the SATCOM transmissions—the insurgents did not appear to make an effort at transmitting their own signals, which would require a much higher level of sophistication. In 2011, *Wired* magazine reported that Predator and Reaper Ground Control Stations (GCS)—computers used to pilot the UAV—were compromised at Creech Air Force Base in Nevada a key logger[34]—malware used to record keystrokes and report them to a third party. Later reports described the incident as the result of a much more mundane piece of malware, which was designed to simply steal user credentials.[35] Further, this malware did not actually affect the GCS, but rather separate systems that run lesser tasks such as backup power and environmental controls. Most likely this was malware simply transmitted from the Internet to the classified workstation by way of compact disc or memory stick by a careless user—not a sophisticated cyber-espionage payload designed to control the Predators or even steal video feeds. Additionally, as the malware was unintentionally operating on a classified system, it would not be able to communicate with its C&C server—as the U.S. military's classified networks are isolated from the Internet. To date, there is no evidence of an adversary using cyber-espionage to take control of an American UAV.

SUGGESTED FURTHER READING

The news story of the flaw in the Predator's communications system was first reported in the *Wall Street Journal* and was followed by later stories in other outlets such as *Wired* and *The Army Times*—specific references for these articles can be found at the end of the chapter.

For general information on the Predator, and more details on its history, we suggest Bill Yenne's *Birds of Prey: Predators, Reapers, and America's Newest UAVs in Combat* or *Smart Weapons* by Hugh McDaid and David Oliver. Information on Kata'ib Hezbollah (KH) is also well-documented by open-source information. In particular, http://www.understandingwar.org/ and the *Jamestown Foundation* (http://www.jamestown.org) are excellent resources for information on KH and other insurgent organizations.

References

1. Note that this differs from the Sykipot incident described in the last chapter where information about the UAV projects was stolen. This information had to do with U.S. DoD projects concerning the design and testing of the next generation of UAV's—not the theft of current operational UAV data.
2. Van Atta R. *Fifty years of innovation and discovery*. DARPA. Available from: http://www.darpa.mil/About/History/History.aspx; 2008 [accessed February 25, 2012].
3. Hirschberg M. *DARPA's legacy takes flight: contributions to aeronautics*. DARPA. Available from: http://www.darpa.mil/About/History/History.aspx; 2008 [accessed February 25, 2012].

4. Yenne B. Birds of prey: Predators, reapers, and America's newest UAVs in combat. North Branch, MN: Specialty Press; 2010, p. 39.
5. Hirschberg M. *DARPA's legacy takes flight: contributions to aeronautics*. DARPA. Available from: http://www.darpa.mil/About/History/History.aspx; 2008 [accessed February 25, 2012].
6. Gorman S, Dreazen YJ, Cole A. $26 software is used to breach key weapons in Iraq; Iranian backing suspected. Wall Street Journal December 17, 2009; Available from: http://online.wsj.com/article/SB126102247889095011.html [accessed March 11, 2012].
7. Hoffman M, Reed J, Gould J. Fixes on the way for nonsecure UAV links. Army Times December 18, 2009; Available at: http://www.armytimes.com/news/2009/12/airforce_uav_hack_121809w/ [accessed March 11, 2012].
8. Yenne B. Birds of prey: predators, reapers, and America's newest UAVs in combat. North Branch, MN: Specialty Press; 2010, p. 39.
9. McDaid H, Oliver D. Smart weapons. New York, NY: Welcome Rain; 1997 p. 113.
10. Yenne B. Birds of prey: predators, reapers, and America's newest UAVs in combat. North Branch, MN: Specialty Press; 2010, p. 39.
11. McDaid H, Oliver D. Smart weapons. New York, NY: Welcome Rain; 1997 p. 113.
12. Gorman S, Dreazen YJ, Cole A. $26 software is used to breach key weapons in Iraq; Iranian backing suspected. Wall Street Journal December 17, 2009; Available from: http://online.wsj.com/article/SB126102247889095011.html [accessed March 11, 2012].
13. *SkyGrabber: satellite Internet downloader*. Available at: http://www.skygrabber.com/en/skygrabber.php [accessed March 12, 2012].
14. Strouse T. Kata'ib Hezbollah and the intricate web of Iranian military involvement in Iraq. Jamestown Terrorism Monitor March 4, 2010;8(9). Available at: http://www.jamestown.org/single/?no_cache=1&tx_ttnews%5Btt_news%5D=36109.
15. Hoffman M, Reed J, Gould J. Fixes on the way for nonsecure UAV links. Army Times December 18, 2009; Available at: http://www.armytimes.com/news/2009/12/airforce_uav_hack_121809w/ [accessed March 11, 2012].
16. Cochrane M. Special groups regenerate. Institute for the Study of War; Iraq Report 11; August 29, 2008. Available at: http://www.understandingwar.org/sites/default/files/reports/IraqReport11.pdf [accessed March 12, 2012].
17. *Kata'ib Hezbollah*, International Center for Political Violence and Terrorism Research, S. Rajaratnam School of International Studies, Nanyang Technological University, Singapore. Available at: http://www.pvtr.org/pdf/GroupProfiles/Kata'ibHezbollah-05March10.pdf; March 5, 2010 [accessed March 12, 2012].
18. Harari M. Status update: Shi'a Militias in Iraq. Institute for the Study of War; August 16, 2010 Available at: http://www.understandingwar.org/sites/default/files/Backgrounder_ShiaMilitias.pdf [accessed March 12, 2012].
19. *Designation of Kata'ib Hezbollah as a Foreign Terrorist Organization*. U.S. Department of State. Available at: http://www.state.gov/r/pa/prs/ps/2009/july/125582.htm; July 2, 2009 [accessed March 12, 2012].
20. Strouse T. Kata'ib Hezbollah and the intricate web of Iranian military involvement in Iraq. Jamestown Terrorism Monitor March 4, 2010;8(9). Available at: http://www.jamestown.org/single/?no_cache=1&tx_ttnews%5Btt_news%5D=36109.
21. Strouse T. Kata'ib Hezbollah and the intricate web of Iranian military involvement in Iraq. Jamestown Terrorism Monitor March 4, 2010;8(9). Available at: http://www.jamestown.org/single/?no_cache=1&tx_ttnews%5Btt_news%5D=36109.
22. Designation of Kata'ib Hezbollah as a Foreign Terrorist Organization. U.S. Department of State, International Center for Political Violence and Terrorism Research. Available at: http://www.state.gov/r/pa/prs/ps/2009/july/125582.htm; July 2, 2009 [accessed March 12, 2012].
23. Ibid., Harari.
24. Ibid., International Center for Political Violence and Terrorism Research.
25. Ibid., Harari.
26. Ibid., Harari.
27. Ibid., Harari.
28. Shachtman N. Insurgents intercept drone videos in king-size security breach. Wired December 17, 2009; Available at: http://www.wired.com/dangerroom/2009/12/insurgents-intercept-drone-video-in-king-sized-security-breach/ [accessed March 12, 2012].
29. McCullagh D. U.S. was warned of Predator drone hacking. CBS News December 17, 2009; Available at: http://www.cbsnews.com/8301-504383_162-5988978-504383.html?tag=stack [accessed March 12, 2012].

30. Yenne B. Birds of prey: predators, reapers, and America's newest UAVs in combat. North Branch, MN: Specialty Press; 2010. p. 34.

31. Phillips M. Military surveillance hack warning. CBS News (posted) 17 December 2009; Available at: http://www.cbsnews.com/video/watch/?id=5990213n&tag=contentMain;contentBody [accessed March 12, 2012].

32. Hoffman M, Reed J, Gould J. Fixes on the way for nonsecure UAV links. Army Times December 18, 2009; Available at: http://www.armytimes.com/news/2009/12/airforce_uav_hack_121809w/ [accessed March 11, 2012].

33. Ibid.

34. Shachtman N. Exclusive: computer virus hits U.S. drone fleet. Wired October 7, 2011; Available at: http://www.wired.com/dangerroom/2011/10/virus-hits-drone-fleet/ [accessed March 13, 2012].

35. Hennigan WJ. Air Force says drone computer virus poses 'no threat'. Los Angeles Times October 13, 2011; Available at: http://latimesblogs.latimes.com/technology/2011/10/drone-computer-virus-air-force.html [accessed March 13, 2012].

CYBER OPERATIONS FOR INFRASTRUCTURE ATTACK

In this part, we discuss how cyber operations can be used to attack infrastructure. Unlike the cyber attacks presented in the first part of the book, which were focused on computer systems, the cyber operations described on the following pages were designed to cause damage in the physical world. We start out by introducing the class of systems affected by these operations—industrial control systems (ICS) in Chapter 11 featuring the case study of the Maroochy Water Breach—an incident where an Australian water treatment facility was attacked and manipulated using cyber means. This is followed by a discussion of the possibility of cyber attacks against power grids in Chapter 12. There, we describe how information technology is used on the American power grid and where the vulnerability of its components as well as its topology may present opportunities for cyber warriors. The Department of Energy's Aurora Test where a generator was destroyed will serve as real world example for the current danger posed by cyber attacks to essential civilian infrastructure, but also their limitations. We conclude this part with Chapter 13, where we describe the perhaps most significant cyber operation of the last decade—the Stuxnet—which was purportedly used to attack Uranium enrichment facilities in Iran.

Cyber Warfare Against Industry

INFORMATION IN THIS CHAPTER

- Industrial control systems: Critical infrastructure for modern nations
- Information technology vs. industrial control systems: Why traditional Infosec practices may not apply
- How real-world dependencies can magnify an attack: Infrastructure attacks and network topology
- How a cyber attack led to water contamination: The Maroochy Water Breach

INTRODUCTION

At the time we started writing this book, public fear of cyber attacks against infrastructure was heightened with supposed attacks on the Illinois water system[1] and the Northwest Rail[2]—both of which were later discovered *not* to be the targets of cyber attacks. However, cyber attacks on infrastructure *have* occurred in the past. For instance, in Australia, a cyber attack by a disgruntled contractor resulted in the release of one million liters of untreated sewage into local waterways in 2000.[3] A more recent example is Stuxnet, covered in a later chapter. Due to incidents like these, U.S. President Obama has recently issued an executive order to improve cyber security for critical infrastructure.[4] Headed by NIST (U.S. National Institute of Standards and Technology), this order is designed to streamline information sharing on cyber threats between the government and the private sector in addition to developing a Cybersecurity Framework to better thwart future attacks on critical infrastructure. This framework is also easily tailored to fit the cyber needs of interested private users (such as companies).[5] The Presidential Policy Directive (PPD) accompanying the Presidential order seeks to update the earlier Homeland Security Presidential Directive 7 (2003) recognizing new risks and technologies, implementing lessons learned regarding critical infrastructure protection against cyber threats.[6] The Presidential order stresses the importance of protecting privacy and civil liberties, for the lack of which earlier proposed legislation was harshly criticized.[7]

As infrastructure is often targeted in conventional military operations, cyber warfare directed against these installations should be expected. In this chapter, we introduce and discuss the specific concerns of critical infrastructure control systems with particular focus on how they differ from information technology. We also describe how their inbuilt structural interdependencies make them vulnerable to attacks that leverage network topology. We also briefly discuss the case study of the cyber attack against an Australian water treatment facility and its broader implications for infrastructure control systems.

INDUSTRIAL CONTROL SYSTEMS: CRITICAL INFRASTRUCTURE FOR MODERN NATIONS

Computer networks directly supporting the functioning of infrastructure systems such as water, sewage, electrical power, and public transportation fall under a category known as *industrial control systems* (ICS). This category includes various types of systems including supervisory control and data acquisition or SCADA, distributed control systems or DCS, and programmable logic controllers (PLCs)—all designed to manage the industrial equipment essential to the services rendered.[8]

In Figure 11.1, we illustrate the interactions among common components in an industrial control system. The components are configured in what is known as a *control loop*. For a given industrial process that is controlled by the system (i.e., water, electricity, sewage, etc.), sensors collect information—known as the "controlled variables." These are then sent to a controller that interprets them to produce "manipulated variables"—data relating to the controlled process that can be adjusted by actuators. If a process is disturbed or altered, the system reacts by adjusting the manipulated variables. A human operator interacts with the system through a *human-machine interface* (HMI) to set the parameters and/or algorithms involved in controlling

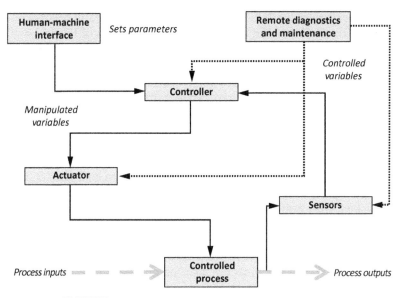

FIGURE 11.1   A generic diagram of an ICS control loop.

the system. Additionally, he also has a *remote diagnostics and maintenance* system that he uses for troubleshooting abnormal behavior.

INFORMATION TECHNOLOGY VS. INDUSTRIAL CONTROL SYSTEMS: WHY TRADITIONAL INFOSEC PRACTICES MAY NOT APPLY

On the surface, an industrial control system may appear to be just another type of information technology system—one that happens to contain additional specialty software to control a certain piece of industrial equipment. However, a report by the National Institute of Standards and Technology (NIST) points out some clear differences[9]:

- *Performance.* ICS systems typically have hard requirements for delay (how long it takes for information to be received) and jitter (the time or phase difference between the data signal and the ideal clock), but less stringent requirements on bandwidth (how much information is sent through the network). A typical IT system, on the other hand, typically has much softer requirements for delay and jitter and often calls for assurances relating to high bandwidth.
- *Availability.* ICS systems, particularly the power grid, are required to continuously deliver a service. Typical IT practices such as rebooting computers (which would, in turn, cause a temporary outage) often become unacceptable in an ICS setting.
- *Risk management requirements.* As stated in the "Introduction" section, the McCumber information security model states that the primary goals of IT security are to ensure availability, integrity, and confidentiality of data. A later extension to this model adds authentication and nonrepudiation as well. Though these are important aspects to

industrial control system, the NIST adds human safety and fault tolerance. These are important as the operation of ICS systems must prevent loss of life and avoid endangerment of public health or confidence. As a result, there is an important link between security and safety in the ICS world.

- *Architecture.* As we saw in the exploitation part of the book, many IT systems, particularly those dealing with intellectual property were set up to use a centralized "repository." Right or wrong, many IT professionals use this centralization to simplify requirements—they would just put more effort into the protection of the repository. In an industrial control system, centralized servers are still very important. However, periphery systems gain in significance: first, they often directly control industrial equipment (i.e., electrical substations are responsible for providing power directly to consumers), and second, outages in certain peripheral systems may lead to cascading failures.
- *Physical interaction.* Outages in typical IT systems may not have consequences outside the virtual world. However, outages in industrial control system often affect physical equipment—leading to real-world consequences.
- *Time-critical response.* In an IT system, often access control can be performed without regard to data flow. The NIST report points out that the question whether to compute an industrial control system with automated or software responses that require human interaction potentially become critical. For example, requiring an operator to enter a password at a certain juncture may delay an emergency operation that could result in loss of life or expensive damage to equipment.
- *System operations.* As industrial control systems are part of a larger, often complicated, structure of controlling equipment, their management would require an individual skilled as a control engineer who better understands the impact of implementing security features on the control of operations—in addition to mastering IT security.
- *Resource constraints.* Many legacy industrial control operating systems currently in use, particularly those used for power grids, may be devices that are extremely underpowered and resource-constrained by modern standards. These constraints may simply preclude common (and easy) IT solutions that would otherwise increase security. Further, license agreements in place for these often proprietary solutions may legally prevent the use of a third-party security solution.
- *Communication protocols.* As with industrial control operating systems, many ICS communication protocols may also be proprietary—again precluding a common/easy IT solution designed for more common network protocols such as IP. Further, in many structures, such as a power grid, a mix of different network protocols may be used as opposed to a single protocol such as IP.[10]
- *Change management.* In IT systems, upgrades and patches to system software can often happen swiftly and with relatively little difficulty once the vulnerability is found. Industrial control systems introduce several levels of complexity to the issue of patching/upgrading software. Due to the high-priority issues of avoiding loss of life or damage to equipment, software updates and patches go through a more rigorous certification process by vendors before being released. The end user (i.e., a local power company) will then also perform validation tests as an outage would be scheduled well in advance of the update. Further compounding difficulty here is the fact that some legacy ICS equipment will use

older versions of operating systems that are no longer supported by the vendor—resulting in unavailable patches for new vulnerabilities.

- *Managed support.* Due to industry-wide standards in the IT world, such as the Internet Protocol Suite with the Transmission Control Protocol and Internet Protocol (TCP/IP), HTTP, and others, multivendor interoperable solutions become possible. Often with industrial control systems, support is available only through a single vendor as the system in question may be proprietary.
- *Component lifetime.* IT system components have a lifetime of between 3 and 5 years. Many vulnerabilities may thus be resolved by the simple evolution of technology and the purchase of a new computer. With industrial control systems, components have a typical lifetime of 15-20 years or longer. This means that updates invariably rely on updates that are compatible with the aging hardware and the respective certification or brand.
- *Access to components.* IT systems are typically local and physically easy to access (i.e., a rack-mounted server in a computer room). Industrial control system components, by contrast, may be isolated, remote, and physically difficult to access due to their inherent linkage with certain industrial equipment. For example, consider a logic control card in a centrifuge (which we shall discuss later in this part of the book with our discussion of Stuxnet) or firmware in a protection relay (as we shall describe in the next chapter).

In the subsequent chapters, we describe several case studies highlighting the special concerns that are inherent in industrial control systems and which pose new challenges for security professionals.

HOW REAL-WORLD DEPENDENCIES CAN MAGNIFY AN ATTACK: INFRASTRUCTURE ATTACKS AND NETWORK TOPOLOGY

In the past decade, a new academic field known as "Network Science" emerged. In interdisciplinary cooperation physicists, sociologists, mathematicians, biologists, and computer scientists are studying complex systems for their representation as in network models. For example, a social network can be studied, if we draw a diagram where the individuals in the network are "nodes." An "edge" is drawn between each pair of nodes that has a friendship relationship.[a] Earlier in this book, we highlighted how certain aspects of social networks had implications for cyber war.

Many important pieces of critical infrastructure can be viewed as networks. For instance, we can represent a rail system as a network where the nodes are terminals and edges are between pairs of terminals for which a connection exists. We can even treat the Internet

---

[a] For example, one of the authors most recently modeled militant groups as social networks and concluded that decapitation does not necessarily impede the functioning of the organization. Together with his colleagues, Paulo found it more promising to disturb the relationship (edges) between certain strategically linked nodes in order to achieve longer term impairment in the functioning of militant organizations ("Shaping Operations to Attack Robust Terror Networks" by Devon Callahan, Paulo Shakarian, Jeffrey Nielsen, and Anthony Johnson. *ASE Hum J* 2013:**1**(1)).

(at coarse-grain resolution) as a network where the nodes are major service providers and edges represent their connections. In the next chapter, we look at how power grids can also be represented as a network.

The main concern with these types of networks is that when certain key nodes or edges are taken off-line, the effect of the failure can be compounded as other nodes may depend on it. For instance, the decommissioning of a certain rail line may have an effect on the whole rail system as other trains would then have to be rerouted. Further, if there was no alternative route for that single line, certain stations would become unreachable. Another real-world example of this is a 1990 incident, in which a phone switch in New York City conducted a self-reset once it hit its load limit for calls. When the switch returned back online, it attempted to handle signals that had collected while it was down. This dearth of signals, in turn, caused other switches to overload—leading to a cascading failure in the phone system. Over a 9-h period, approximately 50% of calls failed to go through and AT&T lost an estimated $60 million in unconnected calls (in addition to losses incurred by businesses dependent on the phone system at that time).[11]

The ideas of certain nodes becoming disconnected from the rest of the network (the unreachable stations) and that of missing nodes or edges causing signals to be transferred to other nodes are often referred to as network fragmenting and cascading failures, respectively. We will discuss cascading failures in more detail in the next chapter in connection with power grids. Here, we shall briefly introduce the idea of network fragmentation.

When describing a network, we say that there is a path between two nodes if there is a sequence of edges that ultimately connects them. For instance, in Figure 11.2A, there is a path

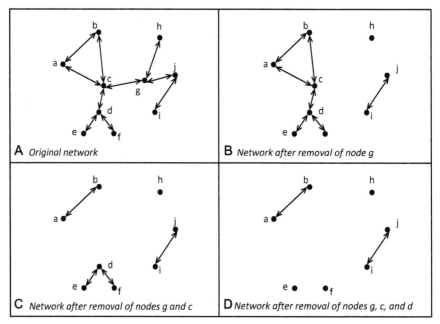

FIGURE 11.2   Example network and the fragmentation effect of removing select nodes.

from node "a" to node "h" that consists of nodes "c" and "g" along the way. However, in the network depicted in Figure 11.2B above the path between "a" and "h" is eliminated. In most infrastructure networks, particularly ones used for communication, transportation, and power generation, the presence of a path between most node pairs is often critical as it ensures the availability of any given node by way of any other. As a result, the concept of a "connected component" entails a set of nodes in a given network which are interconnected through paths between all pairs (within that set). Network scientists are often concerned with the "largest connected component" in a network—which can indicate the largest percentage of interconnected nodes.

Now, assume that an adversary attacks the network by removing nodes (this idea can be easily extended for edges as well) by simply deleting their representation (address) in the industrial control system. Perhaps she or he does so in a way to maximize fragmentation (and reduce the size of the "largest connected component"). For instance, if attacking a transportation network, the ability to function can be destroyed by targeting merely a small number of stations (due to the topology of the infrastructure grid). Perusing the above figure in order to visualize the example: panel A shows the complete network of 10 interconnected nodes; panel (B) depicts the same network after the removal of a single node (g). As a result three other nodes (h, i, and j) become isolated, effectively diminishing the original network as the largest connected component. If nodes h, i, and j were subway stations, they could no longer be serviced. At the same time, the remainder of the original network of subway infrastructure is prone to expect disruptions due to an overload of trains—caused by the trains that were meant to connect to the four lost stations (g-j). In (C) and (D), the fragmentation is compounded by the removal of two more nodes (c and d, respectively).

The number of edges each node is connected to is often referred to as "node degree." Consequently, an obvious attack strategy would be to target a few of the nodes with many connections, i.e., high-degree nodes in order to maximize the resulting disconnections most effectively. However, a more advanced strategy would be to select target nodes based on the degree they achieve after an (initial) attack has struck the network. For instance, in Figure 11.2, node "d" initially has a degree of 3 (in A and B), but after "c" is removed (see panel C), its connections are reduced to two (node degree of 2). Schneider and his colleagues show in a paper published in Proceedings of the National Academy of Science[12] that this strategy can lead to harmful results. The researchers studied the effects of node removal in a European power network and a network of major European Internet service providers (known as the "Point of Presence" or PoP network). In the power network, using the above-mentioned advanced attack strategy, the removal of a mere 10% of the nodes resulted in a dramatic 90% loss of network integrity. The loss of 12% of the nodes in the PoP network yielded similar results in that study.

From this discussion on fragmentation, a natural question arises: how can such an attack be stopped? One way to minimize the harm to the network is to make it more resilient by adding redundancy. This is done mainly by adding edges and/or nodes. Clearly, building new train stations, laying train tracks, erecting power lines make this a difficult and expensive operation. Schneider *et al.* propose a simple strategy to improve the strength of a network without the high costs in time and resources. They leverage a robustness metric of the network and iteratively select pairs of edges, adding additional edges where needed for further fortification. In their paper, they show that this algorithm substantially increases the robustness of the network to these node-removing attacks—thus, better informing the design and upgrade of such infrastructure networks.

Robustness strategies such as Schneider's are vitally important as many industrial control systems are not only susceptible to individual attacks, but the interactions between groups of these systems (such as among regional power grids which we will discuss in the next chapter) are also important as well. Research is important not only for creating a strategy to strengthen the network (which may not always be realizable) but also for the identification and monitoring of critical or "at risk" nodes and edges that could lead to catastrophic and/or cascading failures when exploited. Though cascading and fragmenting failures among interdependent systems is an area that we are just now beginning to understand, their importance cannot be understated.

HOW A CYBER ATTACK LED TO WATER CONTAMINATION: THE MAROOCHY WATER BREACH

We close the chapter with a brief case study on how a cyber attack against an industrial control system caused significant damage in the real world. The attack was directed against Maroochy Water Services on Queensland's Sunshine Coast in Australia.[13] The Maroochy SCADA system consisted of two monitoring stations utilizing three radio frequencies to control 142 sewage pumping stations. Several faults raised the concern of employees at the facility, which included unexplained alarms, increased radio traffic, unexplained modifications to SCADA software, lack of alarms for certain events (such as pump shutdowns), and pumps running continuously. Robert Stringfellow, the civil engineer in charge of operations at Maroochy first suspected the faults were due to installation errors. This was a sensible explanation as the system had undergone recent upgrades. However, after a thorough examination that included reinstallation of some of the SCADA software, he noticed that the system parameters continued to change in unexpected ways. This led him to conclude that the liabilities were the result of malicious activity and not a normal malfunctioning.

Using monitoring equipment, Stringfellow discovered that a hacker was using wireless communication technology to connect to the SCADA system. Security experts Jill Slay and Michael Miller describe him as at one point "dueling" with the hacker as he attempted to gain access. Ultimately, the hacker was found to be a man named Vitek Boden, a former contractor who conducted the attack as revenge against the Maroochy Shire Council for not hiring him. Boden was able to take control of the 142 pumping stations with just a laptop and a radio transmitter for 3 months. During this time, he released over 1 million liters of untreated sewage into a stormwater drain that flowed into local waterways. He was ultimately arrested and jailed for his crime.

This incident highlights some difficulties in the security of an industrial control system. First, identifying an attack as such may be difficult. This is a result of the sheer complexity of an ICS system. An abnormal fault could be the result of mechanical failure, improper parameters, and inexperienced operators are just a few of the many possible sources of problems. Second, ICS systems are particularly vulnerable to an insider threat. As described earlier in the chapter, they often feature many vulnerabilities (i.e., due to the inability to patch or update a system as often as a normal IT system). As a result, it is more likely that an insider would have knowledge of the system's vulnerabilities—as Boden clearly had of the Maroochy plant. Finally, the damage caused by such a system more directly affects human lives than the compromise of an IT system. The water contamination resulting from the release of the sewage into the stormwater drain very likely affected many people in the Sunshine Coast.

SUMMARY

In this chapter, we introduced industrial control systems, described aspects in which they differ from standard IT systems, and discussed how their complex interactions—in the form of network(s)—led to special concerns. We also provided a brief case study of the attack on Maroochy Water Services in 2000 which illustrates some of the difficulties in safeguarding an industrial control system as well as the real-world consequences of a cyber attack against such a system.

SUGGESTED FURTHER READING

For further reading, we highly recommend NIST Special Publication 800-82: "Guide to Industrial Control System Security" as it provides an in-depth discussion on ICS security that is applicable in a variety of settings as well as strategies for minimizing ICS vulnerabilities.

We also recommend the *Proceedings of the National Academy of Science (PNAS)* paper "Mitigation of malicious attacks on networks" (Vol. 108, No. 10, March 2011) which offers a great discussion on a novel mitigation strategy against fragmentation attacks on complex interaction networks—with a focus on ICS systems.

References

1. Schwartz MJ. DHS, FBI Dispute Illinois Water Hack. *InformationWeek*. Available at: http://www.informationweek.com/news/security/attacks/232200199; November 23, 2011 [accessed May 6, 2012].
2. Sternstein A. Hackers manipulated railway computers, TSA memo says. *NextGov*. Available at: http://www.nextgov.com/cybersecurity/2012/01/hackers-manipulated-railway-computers-tsa-memo-says/50498/; January 23, 2012 [accessed May 6, 2012].
3. Slay Jill, Miller Michael. Lessons learned from the Maroochy Water Breach. In: Goetz E, Shenoi S, editors. Crit Infrastruct Prot. New York, Heidelberg, Dordrecht, London: Springer; 2007.
4. Obama B. Executive order—improving critical infrastructure cybersecurity. *Office of the Press Secretary, The White House*. Available at: http://www.whitehouse.gov/the-press-office/2013/02/12/executive-order-improving-critical-infrastructure-cybersecurity; February 12, 2013.
5. Office of the Press Secretary. Executive order on improving critical infrastructure cybersecurity. *The White House*. Available at: http://www.whitehouse.gov/the-press-office/2013/02/12/executive-order-improving-critical-infrastructure-cybersecurity-0; February 12, 2013.
6. Office of the Press Secretary. Fact sheet: presidential policy directive on critical infrastructure security and resilience. *The White House*. Available at: http://www.whitehouse.gov/the-press-office/2013/02/12/fact-sheet-presidential-policy-directive-critical-infrastructure-securit; February 12, 2013.
7. Andy G. President Obama's cybersecurity executive order scores much better than CISPA on privacy. *Forbes*. Available at: http://www.forbes.com/sites/andygreenberg/2013/02/12/president-obamas-cybersecurity-executive-order-scores-much-better-than-cispa-on-privacy/; February 12, 2013.

8. Stouffer Keith, Falco Joe, Scarfone Karen. Guide to Industrial Control System Security. Washington, DC: National Institute of Standards and Technology; 2011.

9. Stouffer Keith, Falco Joe, Scarfone Karen. Guide to Industrial Control System Security. Washington, DC: National Institute of Standards and Technology; 2011.

10. Wei Dong, Lu Yan, Jafari Moshen, Skare Paul M, Rohde Kenneth. Protecting smart grid automation systems against cyber attacks. IEEE Trans Smart Grid 2011;2(4):782–95. http://ieeexplore.ieee.org/xpl/login.jsp?tp=& arnumber=6003813&url=http%3A%2F%2Fieeexplore.ieee.org%2Fxpls%2Fabs_all.jsp%3Farnumber% 3D6003813 [accessed April 6, 2012].

11. Burke D. All circuits are busy now: the 1990 AT&T long distance network collapse. *California Polytechnic State University technical report CSC440-01.* Available at: http://users.csc.calpoly.edu/jdalbey/SWE/Papers/ att_collapse.html; November 1995.

12. Schneider Christian M, Moreira André A, Andrade Jr. José S, Havlin Shlomo, Herrmann Hans J. Mitigation of malicious attacks on networks. Proc Natl Acad Sci USA 2011;108(10):3838–3841.

13. Ibid., Slay and Miller.

Can Cyber Warfare Leave a Nation in the Dark? Cyber Attacks Against Electrical Infrastructure

INFORMATION IN THIS CHAPTER

- Cyber attacks directed against power grids
- Destroying a generator with a cyber attack: The Aurora Test
- Taking the power grid offline with minimal effort: Attacks leveraging network topology
- Targeting key transmission substations
- Causing cascading failure
- Dependencies on computer networks can lead to cascading failure

INTRODUCTION

In April, 2009, the *Wall Street Journal* ran an article entitled "Electricity Grid in U.S. Penetrated by Spies" where several unnamed government sources claimed that Chinese and Russian hackers had broken into power-grid systems, leaving open back doors that would allow them to destroy certain components of the power grid.[1] The following year, after "Operation Aurora" where intellectual property from Google and other U.S. firms was stolen by Chinese hackers (see Chapter 7),[2] in a testimony before congress, the commissioner of the U.S.-China Economic and Security Review Commission identified an academic paper where Chinese researchers explored cascade-based attacks on the U.S. power grid.[3] Though we have little information on actual attacks against the power grid, there is much literature that describes how such an attack might occur. In this chapter, we explore the vulnerabilities of a power grid with both legacy and the "smart grid" technologies becoming more prevalent in the United States. We then look at the "Aurora Test" (different from "Operation Aurora") in which the U.S. Idaho National Labs conducted an experiment to see if a cyber attack could lead to damaged power generation equipment. Finally, we also describe how an adversary could leverage power-grid network topology to magnify the effects of his attack—which would cause more overall damage by precise targeting of a limited number of power-grid components.

CYBER ATTACKS DIRECTED AGAINST POWER GRIDS

Simply put, a power grid is the infrastructure that connects electricity consumers with a source of electrical power generation. Various requirements of the grid, such as metering and identifying points of failure, require information to be transmitted between certain points of the grid—necessitating the need for various forms of information technology (IT). Currently, the IT equipment used for communication in the power grid ranges from state-of-the-art to decades-old telephony. Current initiative referred to as "smart grid" refers to a range of efforts to upgrade this communication equipment for improved monitoring, protection, and efficiency.[4] However, regardless of whether the power grid in question is using legacy or modern equipment, as with any system involving computer networks, cyber security should be a major concern. Further, due to modern society's dependence on electrical power, attacking the power grid may be viewed as a military option by many nations—hence our inclusion of this topic in our discourse on cyber warfare. This section summarizes the work of Wei *et al.*[5] in order to give an overview of how a power-grid functions, its major components, and possible cyber attacks against them.

As stated earlier, a power grid is designed to connect electrical power consumers to electrical power producers. There are two basic components of the grid: transmission and distribution. Transmission entails the delivery of power from the generation source to substations located closer to the consumers. This portion of delivery typically operates at high voltage (100 kV or greater). The second component is distribution where power is delivered from the substations to the consumers and carries a voltage typically less than 100 kV. Transformers at the substation step the power down from high voltage to medium or low voltage in order for it to be distributed.

Wei *et al.* divide the major functions of the power grid into three different levels: corporate, control center, and substation. Business management and operations management functions are performed at the corporate level. Monitoring, forecasting, and other real-time operations are performed at the control center level. At the substation level, primarily real-time monitoring associated with normal operations is performed. IT systems are used in various capacities at these three levels. At the corporate level, IT systems are relied on in planning the amount of electricity that must be generated the next day as well as performing *asset management*—predicting when certain substations may experience maintenance—which would lead to a decision to reroute power from that substation. At the control level, automation systems such as energy management systems (EMS), human-machine interfaces (HMIs), and a Front End Processor (FEP) are primarily used for the purposes of regulating and monitoring the power transmitted to the substations. Finally, at the substation level, IT is primarily used for monitoring the power distributed to consumers. Devices such as remote terminal units (RTUs) and programmable logic controllers (PLCs) can be found at this level.

Cyber attacks against power grids can be broadly categorized into three categories: component wise, protocol wise, and topology wise. *Component-wise* attacks focus on a specific part of the power-grid IT infrastructure. An example for a component-wise attack described in this chapter is the Aurora Test—where a breaker switch was opened and closed in a manner to put a power generator out of synchronization with the rest of the power grid—causing damage. We describe this attack later in the chapter. Other examples of component-wise attacks include (but are not limited to) the following and their combinations:

- Attacks designed to mislead the data presented to an operator (i.e., a violation of nonrepudiation)
- Attacks designed to damage power-grid equipment (i.e., the Aurora Test which we shall describe later in this chapter)
- Attacks designed to shut-down a piece of power-grid equipment

In *protocol-wise* attacks, the perpetrator targets the protocol used to transmit information about the power grid. As stated earlier, power-grid control centers and substations often use protocols not typical to normal IT equipment such as Inter Control Center Protocol (ICCP) and DNP (Distributed Network Protocol). However, these protocols are somewhat common among electrical power automation equipment. For example, Wei *et al.* point out that the DNP specification can be obtained for a nominal fee. The main type of attack accomplished protocol-wise is a Man-In-the-Middle attack where the attacker is able to manipulate communications between two parties. Some potential results of this type of attack could include

- Financial loss to power generation companies due to excessive power output
- Safety issues (i.e., energizing a line when electrical personnel are attempting to repair it)
- Equipment damage resulting from power overloads

One example of a very rudimentary protocol-wise attack was discussed in the previous chapter—the attack on Maroochy Water Services. In this incident, the attacker was able to leverage a vulnerability common to virtually every unsecured wireless communication scheme to take control of the sewage pumping stations.

The third type of attack deals with the topology of the power-grid network. This type of attack could have multiple goals. For instance, a denial-of-service (DoS) attack against a system at a substation level would then lead to an incorrect decision at the control level, etc. Another example of a topology attack would be to create a *cascading* power failure—which we shall discuss in detail later in this chapter.

The last part of the paper of Wei *et al.* that we will summarize is the typical methodology for a cyber attack against a power grid. They view it as a three-step process: access, discovery, and control. They also note that a sophisticated attacker will add a fourth step—concealing of the action (i.e., deleting entries on log files, etc.) in order to make it difficult for the system administrator to determine the intruder's presence on the system (this is similar to the actions of the hackers in Operation X of Chapter 6). We discuss each of the three components in turn.

Access

The hacker must first gain access to a SCADA system used to monitor or control an element of the power grid. Wei *et al.* describe three common methods for obtaining unauthorized access to such a system: corporate network to SCADA communication, virtual private network (VPN) links, and remote site communication to the SCADA system. We briefly discuss each in turn here. Users at the corporate level regularly require information from the various SCADA systems. Often the SCADA systems interface with a SQL (or sometimes a customized) database—which, in turn, corporate users query for business purposes. This juncture—where data is passed from the SCADA system to the database server—may provide a hacker the opportunity to attack. Virtual Private Network (VPN) connections to SCADA systems are another common method for obtaining unauthorized access. Normally used for vendor support or users requiring access to SCADA systems from an office, these connections can be hacked if a client system running VPN software is compromised. A third method of obtaining access is through remote site communication. This is due to implicit trust relationships among certain power-grid components that may be physically separated. If the communication link between two such systems is compromised, access may be obtained. Examples of such remote sites include backup facilities, quality systems, and substations.

Discovery

Once the hacker has obtained access to the system, he or she needs to understand how it functions in order to properly conduct the attack intended. Unless the hacker has access to an additional source of intelligence (as suspected in the case of the Stuxnet worm, described in a later chapter), he or she must scour the power-grid automation systems for information to decipher the inner workings of the targeted SCADA system. As Wei *et al.* point out: "the complexity of SCADA systems is one of the best defenses against attack" which results in the attacker investing a good deal of time to decipher. The attacker's methods for doing so may also include passive monitoring of traffic to and from a SCADA system to identify the communications protocol in use (and, in turn, possibly the vendor) as well as active scanning—which may be of high risk to the attacker as scanning activities may be noticed by a security administrator.

Control

Upon gaining an understanding of the SCADA system, the hacker will then attempt the actual attack—which involves controlling the system. At this point, the hacker will likely seek high-payoff targets (HPTs)—systems whose compromise would greatly enhance the intruder's ability to gain control. Wei *et al.* point out two such systems: the Front End Processor (FEP) and Human Machine Interface (HMI). The Front End Processor (or in some cases, multiple FEPs) sends commands from the SCADA system to the different process controllers. Though the protocols to these controllers may vary, the FEP will have the ability to communicate with all of them. Hence, if the attacker obtains access to the FEP, the problem of deciphering the protocols to each of the process controllers is avoided. In many cases, the FEP does not require authentication or verification of the commands sent to it. Further, in most cases, the FEP does not log commands. Attacking the FEP is done at the protocol level as the hacker has to send it commands. The second high-payoff target we will discuss is the Human Machine Interface. The HMI resides on a computer workstation and is used by operators to interface with the SCADA system. Hence, if an attacker compromises it, it would be easier to understand and manipulate. Unlike the FEP attack, which is a protocol-level attack, the HMI is a component-level attack. Further, as it resides on a workstation, the hacker may be able to leverage known IT-style vulnerabilities on the machine. However, the HMIs often attempt to protect against operator error—so it may be more difficult to cause damage here. As an alternative, an intruder may instead attempt to access the Engineering Work Station (EWS) which is designed for development. It may have similar screens to an HMI, but less security features.

Next, we look at how such an attack could work in practice by examining Idaho National Labs' "Aurora Test" in which researchers managed to destroy a power generator through cyber attacks.

DESTROYING A GENERATOR WITH A CYBER ATTACK: THE AURORA TEST

A test conducted in 2007 by the U.S. Department of Energy (DoE) known as the "Aurora Test" (note this is different than "Operation Aurora"—the cyber attack designed to steal intellectual property from Google and other major corporations) was meant to determine the feasibility of a cyber attack against an actual generator. In the 2007 test, held by DoE's Idaho National Laboratory, a power generator was subjected to cyber attacks.[6] The generator was diesel powered, operating at 3.8 MV and working at 60% of its rated power.[7] The result was presented in a video that the U.S. Department of Homeland Security (DHS) declassified and distributed to Associated Press. In the video, the generator starts to shake. After several seconds, smoke starts to appear, which begins to fill the screen indicating a catastrophic failure (see the figure for frames from the video; Figure 12.1).

When a generator is connected to a power grid, the frequencies, voltage, and phase rotation must match within a certain preset tolerance. If not, protective relays will not allow it to connect. However, in order to ensure a consistent power supply, some variation to the tolerances for these parameters is allowed for short periods of time—in this way, premature

FIGURE 12.1   The generator from the Aurora Test as the repeated high-electrical torque causes stress on the shaft of the rotating equipment—quickly shortening its lifespan (frames from Department of Homeland Security video footage). (For color version of this figure, the reader is referred to the online version of this chapter.)

disconnection of generators can be avoided. It is these short time periods that were exploited during the Aurora Test. To cause the generator to fail, the "Aurora attack" seeks to place the generator out of synch with the power grid during one of these short time intervals—hence avoiding disconnection and causing damage.[8]

The Aurora vulnerability opens and closes a breaker in a time interval less than the maximum allowed by the protective relays. During the time the generator is operating out of sync with the power grid, it undergoes much stress—particularly on the shaft. The sequence of events is as follows: the breaker opens, the generator undergoes stress for a short period of time while being out of sync with the grid, and then the breaker closes again—just in time to avoid disconnection by the protective relay (Figure 12.2). If this is repeated over multiple

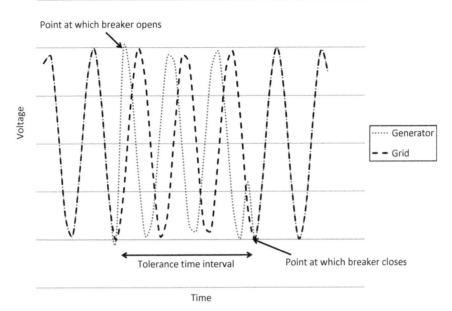

Point at which breaker opens

Voltage

Generator

Grid

Tolerance time interval

Point at which breaker closes

Time

FIGURE 12.2   Notional graph displaying voltage as a function of time for a generator and the power grid based on the results of Wei *et al.* Note that the generator and grid must be matched with respect to frequency, voltage, and phase rotation. The opening of the breaker—followed by a closing—moves the generator out of sync with the power grid. However, this occurs within a certain permissible time tolerance (designed to prevent premature separation of the generator from the grid). Repeated opening and closing of the breaker result in severe stress on the shaft of the rotator in the generator—drastically shortening its lifespan. (For color version of this figure, the reader is referred to the online version of this chapter.)

iterations, the cumulative stress on the shaft leads to failure. In the Aurora Test, after 13 iterations, the generator began to vibrate abnormally. After 22 iterations, smoke emerged[9].

Implementing an Aurora-Style Attack

The Idaho National Labs test is revealing, but may lead to wonder if an attack of this type is possible in the real world. While it is true that the test—particularly the demonstration video released to the Associated Press—did not include certain security measures relatively common to this type of generator (i.e., vibration monitoring limit switches, over-speed limitation on the diesel engine, synchronization check on the tie breaker were all disabled during the test and synchronization check on the protective relay was disabled during the video demonstration).[10] However, with knowledge of the computer network and power generator, the attack is still possible. Mark Zeller, an engineer with Schweitzer Engineering Laboratories described several strategies an attacker would consider at the IEEE Conference for Protective Relay Engineers[11]:

1. *Physical attack*: The adversary manually sabotages the power generator by opening and closing the breaker. Although such a method would be less than sophisticated if repeated and/or done at random intervals, it could result in serious harm to the machine.

2. *Compromising the communication channel:* In this scenario, the attacker is able to send commands through whichever medium is used to communicate with the breaker. The breaker receives commands to open and close as per the attacker's instructions.

3. *Direct hack into the protection relay:* The hacker connects directly to a port on the protection relay, thus bypassing any network security measures that would prevent him from compromising the communications channel. The protection algorithm which ensures that the voltage, frequency, and phase rotation parameters match before connecting the generator to the grid could be outright eliminated in this scenario. The attacker could also control the breaker using the same method.

4. *Embedded program in the protection relay:* In what appears to be the most advanced type of attacks, the hacker uploads new software or firmware into the relay (note that here the attacker would also likely have to leverage attack strategy 2 or 3 above). By directly embedding code in the logic or operating system of the relay, the intruder can directly manipulate time or power levels—possibly in coordination with other attacks. If the hacker is successful in planting such a program, bypassing most security measures is easy, providing the opportunity to render false reports (violating nonrepudiation) stating that the relay is functioning normally.

In addition to the above four attack schemes, several other factors should be considered when planning countermeasures for an Aurora-style attack. For instance, some generators may include a "synchronization check" that only allows breakers to be opened or closed when the voltage and frequency of the generator and grid match. In the Aurora Test, this feature was disabled on the generator.[12] However, there are also some breakers that are not directly attached to the generator. If an Aurora-style attack is initiated on a breaker at a tie-in point separately from the generator, the synchronization check would not take place[13] (provided, of course, that there is no synchronization check on the tie-in breaker).

Salmon *et al.* review the security measures that an attacker must overcome in order to conduct an Aurora-style attack.[14] They identify three categories of such obstacles to the attacker, all of which address the cyber security of the system. In regard to general cyber security, the attacker must have an understanding of the computer network on which the generator operates and has to overcome normal cyber issues such as authentication, encrypted communications, etc. Protecting the breakers of power generators is crucial (as is evident from the Aurora Test) as an aggressor might attempt to disrupt the synchronization of the power generator and the grid—either by opening and closing the relay or by accessing the protective dispatch. If the breaker is to be opened and closed, the intruder must be able to manipulate the device in such a way as to avoid the protective relay to disconnect the power generator (either by precise timing or by sabotaging the protective relay). Finally, the attacker must have accurate knowledge of the target system. For instance, if manipulating the breaker in order to cause system failure, the assailant needs to be aware of the fact that the breaker must be capable of multiple recloses and/or sequences of open/close events before actual damage is implemented.

Preventing an Aurora-Style Attack. Several methods to prevent an Aurora-style attack have been proposed.[15] Here, we discuss a few such measures that can be taken:

- **Time Delay on Breaker Closing**: This technique enforces an extra time interval before the breaker is closed. The idea is to eliminate the time window an attacker has for conducting an Aurora-style attack. This can be implemented in hardware to avoid a manual attack. Clearly, it would be preferable to also implement time delays for commands sent through a computer network as well.

- **Command monitoring on the protective relay**: With this technique, the administrator is notified of certain patterns of open/close commands and can even set policies to provide warnings, prevent breaker closures, enforce time delays, etc.
- **Implement a second relay**: This countermeasure adds a redundant relay to the setup, providing defense in-depth to the generator. The second relay could be operating on a different network, utilize different authentication, etc., than the first.
- **Local generator island detection logic**: Here, the rate of change of the frequency is monitored. When this rate falls outside acceptable ranges (an "island condition"), the generator is disconnected.

In practice, it will take a combination of measures such as the ones listed above—in addition to solid security practices as described earlier. There are also trade-offs, as an Aurora-style attack is a high-impact, low-frequency event, any mitigation device must not interfere with normal power operations. For instance, relay-based Hardware Mitigation Devices (HMDs)—which employ protection similar to the methods listed above—are thought to have exasperated the massive European power failure in November 2006.[16]

Albeit an experimental test, the Aurora Test successfully demonstrated to the world that a cyber attack could have severe repercussions in the physical world. Further, this test led to important research on how to better mitigate cyber attacks against the power grid. Like other attack methods described in earlier chapters of this part of the book, the Aurora Test is a cyber attack directed at a specific piece of industrial equipment. In the next section, we discuss how attacks on key systems in a power grid can lead to more serious failures. These attacks rely on leveraging the topology of the power-grid network to magnify their effects.

TAKING THE POWER GRID OFFLINE WITH MINIMAL EFFORT: ATTACKS LEVERAGING NETWORK TOPOLOGY

In the introduction to this chapter, we mentioned how a 2009 paper by Chinese researchers Jian-Wei Wang and Li-Li Rong led to comments by the chairman of the U.S.-China Economic Security and Review Commission in 2010 where he stated that the researchers "published a paper on how to attack a small power grid sub-network in a way that would cause cascading failure to the entire U.S. west-coast power grid."[17] A later report in the New York Times discussed the comments and downplayed the significance of the research.[18] Upon a close read of the paper, it becomes apparent that the work of these Chinese researchers is simply a new addition to an up-and-coming area of academic research where academic researchers study where infrastructure topologies are vulnerable to attacks and explore potential mitigation strategies. It is likely that Chinese researchers studied the power grid of the western United States because the data was available rather than for purposes of ill will.

However this is not to say that attacks leveraging power-grid network topology are unimportant—or not possible. For example, in the summer of 2003, much of the eastern United States experienced blackouts resulting from a cascading failure that originated in

Ohio. Later that same year, much of Italy also experienced cascading failure of power infrastructure.[19] While we have not seen any confirmed reports of cyber attacks resulting in such failures, numerous academic papers have demonstrated that it is possible to do so. In this section, we explore three scenarios in which network topology is leveraged. First, we look at how the targeting of key transmission substations can magnify the effects of an attack. Then we look at how targeting certain power lines can lead to cascading failure in a power grid. Finally, we describe how a codependency between a power grid and Internet infrastructure can lead to cascading failure.

Targeting Key Transmission Substations

Perhaps the most notable work on vulnerabilities of power-grid topology was a paper by Albert *et al.* published in 2004.[20] Using a network science approach, the authors model the North American power grid as a series of nodes and edges. The edges represented transmission lines, while the nodes were classified in one of three categories: generators, transmission substations (substations that step down high-voltage input from generators in order to distribute the power to distribution substations), and the distribution substations (which are designed to deliver lower-voltage power to consumers). Power is transmitted from a generator node to a distribution substation node. Along the path of the power transmission, between the generator and distribution substation nodes are one or more transmission substations. Albert *et al.* define the load of a transmission node (also called betweenness) as the number of paths that pass through it. In Figure 12.3, the transmission node has a load of four: it lies on the path from generator A to distribution substation X, from generator A to distribution substation Y, from generator B to distribution substation X, and from generator B to distribution substation Y.

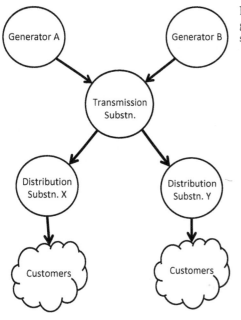

FIGURE 12.3 Example power grid network consisting of generators, transmission substations, and distribution substations.

Albert *et al.* viewed the substations with high load as key components of the power grid, which is important from a topological standpoint as substations allow for multiple paths between generators and distribution. From a power generation standpoint, these nodes are important because load is thought to be analogous to the power passed through a certain substation. Computer simulations show that an attack strategy focusing on the high-load substations cause the network to fragment. The fragmentation results in isolated distribution substations, rendering it unable to receive any power from a generator, leaving the customers associated with that substation in a blackout condition. We illustrate this type of attack in Figure 12.4.

In the simulation performed by Albert *et al.*, after targeting only 2% of the nodes, the power network experiences a connection loss of 60%. After taking out 8% of the nodes, the majority of the power network becomes effectively powerless. Targeting high-load nodes leads to significantly more fragmenting of a network than pursuing random nodes or targeting nodes of a high degree (nodes connected to a large number of power lines).

Causing Cascading Failure

Iterative targeting of transmission nodes has not only the effect of isolating substations but can also lead to *cascading failure*. In a cascading failure, the failure of certain components leads to the failure of others, which in turn causes even more parts to stop working and so on.

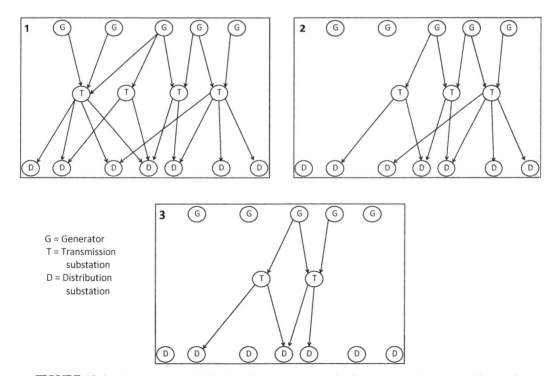

FIGURE 12.4   Iterative removal of high-load transmission nodes from an example power grid network.

In a power-grid network, this would mean that when a transmission substation fails, the load it normally carries is redistributed to other substations. This may cause the capacity of some of these other substations to be exceeded—causing them to collapse as well. An important paper by researchers from Arizona State University used a mathematical model to illustrate how this could happen.[21] The researchers investigated several attack strategies—in particular, they examined targeting of randomly selected, high-degree, and high-load nodes in a network representing the power grid of the western United States. Interestingly, they found that targeting only a single high-load node tended to cause cascading failures (in addition to causing network fragmentation as described earlier), which theoretically could result in the connected component of that power-grid network to be reduced by over half of its original size.

Dependencies on Computer Networks Can Lead to Cascading Failure

In a seminal paper published in *Nature*,[22] a team of physicists introduced a new model (that we shall refer to as the "Buldyrev model") for cascading failure in power grids. In this particular model, two infrastructure networks are considered, that of the power grid and that of the Internet. An outage in a substation will lead to an outage in certain routers on the Internet, which could potentially leave a transmission or control station unable to communicate and thus cause more substation outages. We illustrate this type of cascade in Figure 12.5.

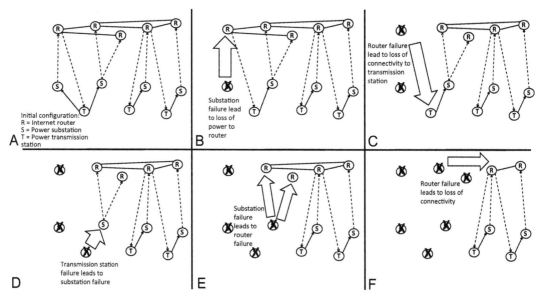

FIGURE 12.5   (A) Initial power grid and Internet router network (S, power substation; T, power transmission station; R, Internet router). (B) A single power substation is targeted by a cyber attack. (C) The substation outage causes a corresponding outage to the Internet router. (D) The outage of the Internet router causes a power transmission node to fail. (E) The failure of the transmission node leads to another substation outage. (F) The second substation outage leads to more Internet routers failing.

Prior to this chapter, it was well documented that many real-world infrastructure networks are unlikely to fragment in the face of random failures. In the case of power networks, this is due to the fact that the number of power lines connected to a given power station varies widely in the network. However, if we consider the potential for cascading failure resulting from dependence on another network (i.e., the network of Internet routers), then the network becomes much more susceptible to random failure. To an adversary, this means that power-grid networks highly dependent on communication infrastructure may be much easier to target.

The Buldyrev model is of great value beyond theoretical interest as in September 2003 the Italian power grid—in its communication highly dependent on the Internet—experienced this type of failure, resulting in power outages for large portions of the country.

SUMMARY

In this chapter, we explored the potential for cyber attacks against a power grid. These attacks can be classified as component wise, protocol wise, or topology based. A basic attack methodology for operations of this type could consist of three steps: access, discovery, and control. The "Aurora Test" conducted by Idaho National Labs where a power generator was destroyed by way of a cyber attack is a real-world example of a component-wise attack. We also described how the topology of a power-grid network can be leveraged to enhance an attack—either by fragmenting the network or causing a cascading failure.

SUGGESTED FURTHER READING

The classification of attacks against power grids and attack methodology where introduced by Dong Wei, Yan Lu, Moshen Jafari, Paul M. Skare, and Kenneth Rohde in a paper entitled "Protecting Smart Grid Automation Systems Against Cyberattacks" published in *IEEE Transactions on Smart Grid*.

For further information on the Aurora Test and possible counter measures, we recommend the conference paper "Myth or Reality – Does the Aurora Vulnerability Pose a Risk to My Generator?" written by Mark Zeller of Schweitzer Engineering Laboratories and presented at the IEEE 64th Annual Conference for Protective Relay Engineers in 2011.

For further reading on cascading power-grid failures based on topology, we recommend "Structural vulnerability of the North American power grid" by R. Albert, I. Albert, and G. L. Nakarado published in *Physical Review E*.

References

1. Gorman S. Electricity grid in U.S. penetrated by spies, Wall Street Journal April 9, 2009; http://online.wsj.com/article/SB123914805204099085.html [accessed March 26, 2012].
2. See Chapter 6.
3. Wortzel LM. *China's approach to cyber operations: implications for the United States, Testimony before the Committee on Foreign Affairs. House of Representatives, Hearing on* "The Google Predicament: Transforming U.S. Cyberspace

Policy to Advance Democracy, Security, and Trade." Available at: http://www.internationalrelations.house.gov/111/wor031010.pdf; March 10, 2010 [accessed March 26, 2012]. See also: Markoff J, Barboza D. Academic Paper in China Sets Off Alarms in U.S. *New York Times*; March 20, 2010.

4. Joskow PL. Creating a smarter U.S. electricity grid. J Econ Perspect 2012;26(1):29–48.

5. Wei D, Yan L, Jafari M, Skare PM, Rohde K. Protecting smart grid automation systems against cyberattacks, IEEE Trans Smart Grid 2011;2(4):782–95. http://ieeexplore.ieee.org/xpl/login.jsp?tp=&arnumber=6003813&url=http%3A%2F%2Fieeexplore.ieee.org%2Fxpls%2Fabs_all.jsp%3Farnumber%3D6003813 [accessed April 6, 2012].

6. Meserve J. Sources: staged cyber attack reveals vulnerability in power grid, CNN September 26, 2007; http://articles.cnn.com/2007-09-26/us/power.at.risk_1_generator-cyber-attack-electric-infrastructure?_s=PM:US [accessed March 15, 2012].

7. Bernabeu EE, Katiraei F. Aurora vulnerability issues & solutions hardware mitigation devices (HMDs), In: IEEE 2011 power and engineering society general meeting; 2011. http://www.ieee-pes.org/images/pdf/pesgm2011/supersessions/mon/Aurora_Vulnerability-Issues_Solutions_PES-GM-V2.pdf [accessed March 15, 2012].

8. Zeller M. Myth or reality—does the Aurora vulnerability pose a risk to my generator?, In: IEEE 64th annual conference for protective relay engineers; 2011. http://ieeexplore.ieee.org/xpl/freeabs_all.jsp?arnumber=6035612 [accessed March 15, 2012].

9. Emanuel E, Katiraei F. Aurora vulnerability issues & solutions hardware mitigation devices (HMDs), In: IEEE 2011 power and engineering society general meeting; 2011. http://www.ieee-pes.org/images/pdf/pesgm2011/supersessions/mon/Aurora_Vulnerability-Issues_Solutions_PES-GM-V2.pdf [accessed March 15, 2012].

10. Zeller M. Common questions and answers addressing the aurora vulnerability. *Schweitzer Engineering Laboratories Technical Report*. http://www.selinc.com/WorkArea/DownloadAsset.aspx?id=9487; 2010 [accessed March 15, 2012].

11. Ibid., Zeller 2011.

12. Ibid., Bernbeau and Katiraei 2011.

13. Ibid., Zeller 2011.

14. Salmon D, Zeller M, Guzman A, Mynam V, Donolo M. Mitigating the aurora vulnerability with existing technology. *Schweitzer Engineering Laboratories Technical Report*. http://www.selinc.com/WorkArea/DownloadAsset.aspx?id=6379; 2009 [accessed March 15, 2012].

15. See Zeller 2011, Bernbeau and Katiraei 2011, Salmon et al. 2009 or Zeller 2010.

16. Ibid., Bernbeau and Katiraei 2011.

17. Wortzel LM. China's approach to cyber operations: implications for the United States, testimony before the committee on foreign affairs. House of representatives, hearing on "The Google Predicament: Transforming U.S. Cyberspace Policy to Advance Democracy, Security, and Trade", March 10, 2010. http://www.internationalrelations.house.gov/111/wor031010.pdf [accessed March 26, 2012].

18. Markoff J, Barboza D. Academic paper in china sets off alarms in U.S. NY Times 2010.

19. Buldyrev SV, Parshani R, Paul G, Stanley HE, Havlin S. Catastrophic cascade of failures in interdependent networks. Nature 2010;464:1025–8.

20. Albert R, Albert I, Nakarado GL. Structural vulnerability of the North American power grid. Phys Rev E 2004;69:025103.

21. Motter AE, Lai Y-C. Cascade-based attacks on complex networks. Phys Rev E 2002;66:065102R.

22. Ibid., Buldyrev.

INFORMATION IN THIS CHAPTER

- How Stuxnet targets industrial control systems
- Stuxnet successfully targeted the Natanz FEP
- Stuxnet is a significant advancement in malware
- Stuxnet invalidates several security assumptions

INTRODUCTION

In the previous two chapters, we discussed cyber-warfare considerations of industrial control systems (ICS) and the power grid. While incidents described in those chapters illustrated that cyber warfare against ICS was possible, none of them are actual incidents of cyber war. For instance, the Maroochy water breach was a crime motivated by revenge, the Aurora Test was an experiment, and the cascading power outage in Italy resulted from equipment failure rather than from malicious attack. In this chapter, we describe Stuxnet, which successfully targeted the Iranian Natanz Uranium Fuel Enrichment Plant (FEP). Unlike the previously mentioned incidents dealing with ICS, Stuxnet appears to have been politically motivated, which is why we consider it an act of cyber war.

Interestingly, before the discovery of Stuxnet many believed a cyber-war operation against an industrial control system would be impossible—or at least unlikely. For instance, in 2004, Marcus Ranum asserted that the sheer complexity of the power grid would make it an unlikely target of attack.[1] However, in July 2010, the discovery of a new piece of malware by a small Belarusian firm known as VirusBlockAda[2] changed these perceptions. The malware discovered would later become known as Stuxnet.

In the months that followed VirusBlockAda's discovery, there was a flurry of activity in the computer security community—revealing that this malware was a "worm" in other words "self-propagating" and designed to target industrial control systems (ICS). Once it was revealed that the majority of infections were discovered in Iran,[3] along with an unexplained decommissioning of centrifuges at the Iranian fuel enrichment plant (FEP) at Natanz,[4] many in the media speculated that the ultimate goal of Stuxnet was to target Iranian nuclear facilities. In November of 2010, some of these suspicions were validated when Iranian President Mahmoud Ahmadinejad publically acknowledged that a computer worm created problems for a "limited number of our [nuclear] centrifuges."[5]

Reputable experts in the computer security community have labeled Stuxnet as "unprecedented,"[6] an "evolutionary leap,"[7] and "the type of threat we hope to never see again."[8] In this chapter, we study how this malicious software represents a fundamental advance in cyber warfare—an advance that is often called a revolution of military affairs (RMA).[9] We first describe the Iranian Natanz fuel enrichment facility—which is widely thought to be the primary target of Stuxnet. Then, we describe how Stuxnet works, why it represents an advance in the state of the art of malware design, and how it invalidated several common assumptions about cyber security.

THE ALLEGED TARGET: THE NATANZ FUEL ENRICHMENT FACILITY

Natanz was Iran's main fuel enrichment facility at the time of Stuxnet's supposed deployment. Its existence was brought to the world's attention in summer 2002, while it was under construction, which by then was underway for 2 years, and the IAEA monitored the further development of the site. Apparently designed to withstand airstrikes, two cascade halls with the capacity to hold an estimated 50,000 centrifuges each, are basically thick-walled cement boxes with 8 m of soil covering the roofs (Figure 13.1).[10]

FIGURE 13.1   GoogleEarth image of Natanz' Fuel Enrichment Plant (FEP) and the Pilot Fuel Enrichment Plant (PFEP). (For color version of this figure, the reader is referred to the online version of this chapter.) *Image copyright 2012, Google.*

In late April 2007, IR-1 centrifuges at Natanz started enriching uranium.[72] It was not until the IAEA reported in February 2009 that six cascades of 164 centrifuges each were actually enriching uranium in one of the underground facilities (as opposed to working under vacuum, which precedes the actual enrichment process).[73]

In late 2009, Natanz reached what was so far its peak with 9000 installed IR-1 centrifuges.[74] The number of gas centrifuges estimated to be actually enriching uranium at the Natanz FEP was 5000 in spring 2009. Possibly an effect of Stuxnet,[a] this number diminished by about a thousand within the following year, but in spring 2011, 6000 centrifuges were fed with uranium hexafluoride (UF_6).[75]

The discovery of the Natanz site initiated an international dispute about its function. American officials fear that Iran intends to build nuclear weapons, while Iranian officials strongly reject this idea referring to future electricity needs in the country. In late summer 2009, the construction of another fuel enrichment plant near the city of Quom was publically revealed by three western powers causing further apprehension over Iran's nuclear ambitions. The underground Fordow fuel enrichment plant is designed to house 3000 gas centrifuges.[76] Over the following years, the uranium enrichment to contain 19.95% U-235 was shifted to this facility.[77]

Uranium hexafluoride that is enriched to contain 20% U-235 offers multiple uses. In Iran, its sole civilian reason to exist is its use in the Tehran's Research Reactor (TRR), although the

---

[a]The virus is also thought to have introduced a greater inefficiency in the production of enriched uranium as the product to feed ratio appeared to have suffered substantially.

experts at ISIS deem that much more of the 20% low-enriched uranium (LEU) already exists than immediately needed. Further, Iran lacks the capability to transform this stockpile into the fuel to power the research reactor.[78]

In 2009, R. Scott Kemp and Alexander Glaser of Princeton University estimated that it will take Iran between 8 months and 3 years to produce weapon-grade highly enriched uranium.[79] Later (2011) ISIS-experts concluded that Natanz will not be able to produce the material needed to fuel Iran's only nuclear power plant near the city of Bushehr in the foreseeable future.[80,81] They furthermore suggest that the fuel enrichment in Natanz will resort to enriching uranium hexafluoride (UF_6) to contain 3.5% U-235 to be further enriched in Fordow.[82] There, cascades of 174 interconnected IR-1 centrifuges enrich uranium in 17 stages as opposed to the 15 stages of enrichment in Natanz.[83]

In November 2012, Iran had produced 7611 kg of enriched (5%) uranium hexafluoride (UF_6), 1029 kg of which have been fed into the more advanced gas centrifuges at Fordow for the enrichment to contain 19.95% U-235. Together, the preexisting 232.8 kg of 19.75% LEU and the ongoing further enrichment to this higher percentage of U-235 are causing immense tremors in concerned western countries as 200 kg of this nearly 20% enriched uranium hexafluoride is deemed sufficient to produce weapon-grade uranium (WGU) for one first-generation nuclear weapon.[84]

In a report published in fall of 2008, David Albright and two of his colleagues analyzed the possibility to weaken Iran's ability to produce weapon-grade nuclear material using conventional military means and concluded that vulnerability of Natanz site (impossibility to destroy via airstrike or other physical military means) makes cyber weapons like Stuxnet tools of choice.

HOW STUXNET TARGETS INDUSTRIAL CONTROL SYSTEMS

Several major computer security firms have thoroughly examined Stuxnet,[85] and all conclude that the primary goal of this piece of software was to cause subtle failures to industrial equipment. Additionally, it appears that the targeting of ICS was most likely the sole goal of the software. For instance, other malware include standard code for a variety of criminal activities—including identity and password theft, launching denial-of-service attacks, and sending spam emails.[86] Despite its high degree of technical sophistication, Stuxnet was not designed to perform any of these activities.[87] Rather, the software attempts to propagate itself with the goal of infecting a Microsoft Windows-based computer which communicates with the industrial equipment. This is in stark contrast to the myriad of malicious software on the Internet that is used for a variety of criminal purposes. Stuxnet was designed solely for sabotage, not a sophisticated tool for identity-theft.

The type of ICS that Stuxnet infects is known as SCADA (Supervisory Control and Data Acquisition) systems. These systems are designed for real-time data collection, control, and monitoring of critical infrastructure, including power plants, oil or gas pipelines, refineries, water systems, or other applications requiring computer-controlled equipment.[11] SCADA systems often use PLCs (Programmable Logic Controllers)—computer hardware to control a physical component. To program this device, the administrator connects it to a standard Windows computer and usually subsequently unplugged when it is ready for use. So, for example, if the velocity of centrifuges were to be increased, the PLC needs to be attached to a Windows machine, which runs a piece of software that communicates with it and uploads new instructions. Once *Stuxnet* has infected the computer attached to the PLC, it essentially runs a "man-in-the-middle" attack against the system: Stuxnet intercepts the originally intended commands to the PLC and instead sends its own instructions (Figure 13.2). However, the software then falsely reports back to the Windows computer that the original instructions were uploaded. By rendering the false report, Stuxnet hides itself and thus ensures repeat future operations. The rendering of a false success note is how Stuxnet violates the security guarantee of *nonrepudiation* (discussed in Chapter 1). This guarantee assures that the sender of the data is provided with proof of delivery and the receiver is provided with proof of the sender's identity. Stuxnet falsifies the proof of delivery.

Stuxnet was designed to attack PLCs controlled by Siemens' *Step 7* software[12]—more exactly it only infects two models of PLCs—the Siemens S7-315 and S7-417. The former is a general purpose controller which operates a single array of devices. Such an array or group of devices controlled by the S7-315 may, for example, operate different phases of a manufacturing process. The latter is a top-of-the line model, operating multiple arrays and thereby being able to control more equipment than the S7-315.[13] Security experts have determined that Stuxnet only launches attacks if the PLC is attached to devices configured in a very specific manner. For example, when the worm detects the S7-315, it only attacks if the PLC is attached to 33 or more frequency converter drives—devices used to control the speed of certain equipment (i.e., the rpms of a motor).[14] Likewise, when attacking the S7-417 PLC, it

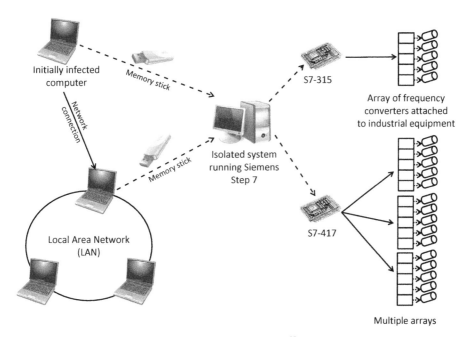

FIGURE 13.2 The sophisticated propagation of the Stuxnet worm.[18] (For color version of this figure, the reader is referred to the online version of this chapter.)

expects to find six cascades of 164 frequency converter drives.[15] The malware also ensured that the frequency converter drives were manufactured by either the Iranian company *Fararo Paya* or the Finish company *Vacon*.[16]

Once Stuxnet has ascertained the preprogrammed correct number of the configuration of frequency converters to be targeted, it launches the attack. Based on analysis of the software, experts have found that it expects the drives to be running between 807 and 1210 Hz. It then periodically alters this setting to values between 2 and 1410 Hz.[17] In this way, the device being controlled by the frequency converter is operating in an unexpected manner. As Stuxnet reports that the PLC was programmed correctly, the operator would assume that the devices are functioning in the normal range. The fact that Stuxnet adjusts these settings illustrates an important point—the worm was intended to actually damage the industrial equipment. If Stuxnet were simply a proof-of-concept, or a stunt, the adjustment of the frequencies would probably be unnecessary.[19]

There has been some debate whether the Stuxnet code designed to attack the S7-417 PLC was functional. According to the security firm Symantec, the S7-417 attack code was incomplete and hence not functioning—referring to a missing data block (numbered 8061), code errors, and portions of the code that are never called.[20] However, Ralph Langner, a German industrial control system expert, who also played a major part in the analysis of Stuxnet due to his proficiency with Siemens software,[b] believes that the Symantec analysis may be incomplete.[21] First, he points out that analysis by Siemens found Stuxnet leverages the "missing" block—hence not having to create it.[22] Langner then notes that the coding errors in the S7-417 attack code would not prevent it from executing and remarks that such errors are common for a software project of such a scale (about 12,000 lines of code). Finally, he remarks that the portions of the S7-417 attack routine that are not called appear to be the result of software development tools.

STUXNET SUCCESSFULLY TARGETS THE NATANZ FUEL ENRICHMENT PLANT

Not only was Stuxnet designed to target very specific ICS but there is also evidence that it was successful in doing so. The indicators for success arise from the following line of reasoning. First, it appears that the initial infections of the worm occurred in Iran. Second, the data structures in the Stuxnet code resemble the exact configuration of centrifuges at the Iranian Fuel Enrichment Plant (FEP) at Natanz. Last, Iranian government officials admitted that their centrifuge operations were affected by the worm.

Stuxnet Was Predominantly Found in Iran

It appears that Iran was the epicenter of the Stuxnet attacks. This is indicated by the volume of infections as well as analysis of malware samples. The security firm Symantec tracked

---

[b]Langner's Web site with more information on Stuxnet and the computer science behind it can be found here: http://www.langner.com/en/news/.

100,000 infected machines as of September 29, 2010—approximately 60,000 of which were located in Iran; Indonesia followed with about 15,000 infections.[23] We note that Indonesia, a predominantly Muslim country, has many economic and political ties to Iran.[24] Hence, the spread from Iran to Indonesia seems probable.

Symantec, in cooperation with other security firms, gathered 3,280 unique samples of the Stuxnet software and its variants.[25] These samples represent 12,000 total infections since the malware maintains a list of previous systems it infected. For each given sample, researchers were able to determine the path the worm propagated in order to arrive at that computer and in each case traced the infection history to one of five different organizations—all of which have a presence in Iran.[26]

Stuxnet Source Code Resembles the Cascade Configuration at Natanz

From what is known of the Natanz FEP, there seems to be a striking resemblance between their centrifuge configuration and the Stuxnet code. According to the IAEA, the IR-1 centrifuges at the Natanz FEP operate in six cascades of 164.[27] This precisely aligns with the configuration Stuxnet searches for when attacking the S7-417 controller. Another potential indicator is the maximum speed of an IR1 centrifuge: 1400–1432 Hz[28]—a frequency range very close to the maximum speed the malware sets during the attack (1410 Hz).[29] An IR-1 centrifuge set to such a high frequency would likely incur damage.

The process of Uranium enrichment can be optimized if it is divided into a series of phases with multiple centrifuges operating at each phase.[30] It was revealed in a 2006 interview that the Iranians were conducting their Uranium enrichment with a method using 15 phases.[31] At each phase, a certain number of centrifuges are allocated for optimal production. Alexander Glaser, a professor at Princeton's Nuclear Futures lab, studied the optimal arrangement of centrifuges in a 164-sized centrifuge cascade. SCADA specialist Ralph Langner compared Glaser's analysis to the data structures in Stuxnet. He found that the data structures in the malware reflect Glaser's analysis.[32]

Other evidence pointing to the targeting of Natanz comes again from Ralph Langner who closely examined photographs of Iranian President Mahmoud Ahmadinejad visiting Natanz in early 2008.[33] Albeit out of focus and perched on the bottom, one picture features parts of two computer screens—apparently SCADA controllers, from which Langner was able to glean the structural organization of the centrifuges. Langner noted that the arrangement of the cascades depicted in the photograph align *precisely* with the data structures uncovered in his firm's analysis of the malware. The depiction provided strong evidence that Stuxnet was designed to target this exact arrangement of individual centrifuges into cascades only present at Natanz (Figure 13.3).[34]

The Effectiveness of Stuxnet Against the Natanz Facility

If Stuxnet successfully targeted Natanz, it would be reasonable to expect seeing an increase in the decommissioning of centrifuges and a decrease in LEU production. In late 2009 or early 2010, Iran decommissioned and replaced about a thousand IR-1 centrifuges at the Natanz FEP (6 cascades of 164 centrifuges each).[35] The timing of the decommissioning, along with the

FIGURE 13.3   Posted in mid-April 2008 on the official Web site of the Iranian President a snapshot from his visit to Natanz revealing what was meant to be kept secret, below a crop with enhanced contrast. (For color version of this figure, the reader is referred to the online version of this chapter.)

number of centrifuges taken offline is consistent with the timing and data structures of Stuxnet. IAEA reports show an increase in the amount of enriched uranium during the first quarter of 2008.[36] It is also notable that in the summer of 2009—the approximate time of Stuxnet's deployment to Natanz—Iranian officials estimated that in the then past half year, 5723 kg of uranium hexafluoride had produced 500 kg of LEU, which an Institute for Science and International Security (ISIS) report estimates is a 20% increase in the daily production of LEU.[37] However, this is considered to be an underperformance as at the time more centrifuges were assembled into cascades and the rate of LEU production was increasing as well.[38] Again, the timing of this stagnation in LEU production is also consistent with the accepted timeline of the Stuxnet deployment.

The obvious alternative explanation for the failure is a manufacturing defect. The IR-1 gas centrifuge is commonly held to be rather unreliable with design problems and a short lifespan. For instance, in 2011, the noticeably low output of 3.5% low-enriched uranium (LEU) was attributed to the breakage of these old model centrifuges. The poor condition of the IR-1s might have been furthered by Stuxnet, which caused the centrifuges to spin at different speeds.[39] However, the problems with the IR-1s could also hint at the inability on the part of the Iranians to maintain and repair, let alone manufacture these centrifuges facing shortages of key material due to import sanctions.[40] At the time of Stuxnet's deployment in at least one of the underground cascade halls at Natanz, the enrichment process employed exclusively the apparently targeted IR-1 centrifuges. However, as of November 2012, more advanced centrifuges are employed in the above-ground Pilot Fuel Enrichment Plant (PFEP) in the same military compound.

Another aspect to consider is the intent of Stuxnet. There were two theories: the first being that the malware intended to immediately destroy centrifuges, while the second is that it is more subtlety sabotaged centrifuges causing their output to be suboptimal over a relatively long period of time. The first theory is largely based on the findings of Symantec[41] and ISIS,[42] while the second is derived from the findings of Langner Communications.[43]

According to the first theory, were Stuxnet was designed to destroy centrifuges, the thousand decommissioned IR-1s was the malware's main success.[44] By this theory, only the portion of Stuxnet attacking the S7-315 PLC was active which causes the centrifuges to operate at near maximum frequency (the S7-417 attack code, which is more subtle, is assumed to be incomplete, hence in-line with Symantec's analysis and not Langner's). By this theory, Stuxnet had only limited success due to the relatively small number of centrifuges destroyed (approximately 10%). However, ISIS notes that the loss of these 1000 centrifuges likely directly contributed to Iran delaying the expansion of its enrichment operations.[45]

The second theory, purported mainly by Langner, suggests that destruction of centrifuges would run contrary to the overall "spirit" of Stuxnet. In short, a piece of malware that obviously took a great deal of time, effort, and money to develop was not designed to simply destroy centrifuges as such an action would likely lead to discovery—an aspect which the malware's creators went through great lengths to delay. Along these lines, Langner points out that the centrifuges operating at high frequencies would not necessarily destroy them instantly, but cause mechanical damage that would be realized over time. Additionally, by this theory, the code attacking the S7-417 controller is thought to be active—hence opening the door to a more discrete attack. If this theory is correct, then the decommissioning of the 1000 centrifuges would appear to be well aligned with the intent of Stuxnet's creators. Further, the stagnation of LEU production would also be viewed as evidence of this theory. This more subtle approach would be more difficult to detect, as the IR-1s are more prone to mechanical failure. This would make it difficult to determine if a problem was caused by the worm or some other part of the enrichment process.

However, there has been a recent discovery by Symantec that seems to shed further light on the issue. An older version of the worm known as "Stuxnet 0.5" was discovered by Symantec in early 2013.[46] This version of the code contained routines used to fingerprint the target S7-417 controller and build the (previously thought) missing portion of the software for use in the attack.[47] In fact, Stuxnet 0.5 was designed *only* to conduct the more subtle attack against the S7-417 controller and not the S7-315. In viewing the source code, Symantec analysts concluded that this attack was designed to disrupt the valves controlling the flow of uranium hexafluoride gas (UF6) to the centrifuges—a more subtle approach than the method used to increase the speed of centrifuges in the S7-315 code found in the later versions of Stuxnet.[48] Symantec personnel hypothesized that the creators of Stuxnet may have been unsatisfied with this restrained approach and moved toward the more forceful S7-315 attacks.[49]

Reactions on Stuxnet from the Iranian Regime

In addition to the aforementioned indicators, there is also some evidence of the software's potential effectiveness in the statements of Iranian leaders. President Ahmadinejad confirmed the presence of malicious software affecting the centrifuges in November 2010—although he did not explicitly describe the presence of Stuxnet.[50] In an interview with SPIEGEL ONLINE, the general secretary of Iran's Supreme National Security Council, Saeed Jalili, was asked specifically about Stuxnet being used to attack Natanz. Jalili did not go into details on the damage done by the worm (again downplaying the effect it had), but did admit that an incident had occurred by stating that "our experts already warded off this attack a long time ago."[51]

In regard to the physical deployment of Stuxnet, there is the possibility that Stuxnet was installed at Natanz by a saboteur using a memory stick.[52] In such an event, the designers of the worm would greatly increase their probability of success, as opposed to passively waiting for the software to propagate to the facility. In October 2010, Iran's intelligence minister, Heydar Moslehi, announced that an unspecified number of "nuclear spies" were arrested in connection with Stuxnet.[53] While the details and nature of the arrests are unknown, this illustrates at the very least that Iran recognizes the various methods by which the worm could have spread—as well as the seriousness of its impact on their operations.

Despite the Iranian claims in late 2010 that the Stuxnet worm had minimal impact on their nuclear operations, security expert Ralph Langner asserts that the malware set Iran's nuclear program back two years.[54] The reasons for this are bifold. First, as stated earlier, damage caused by Stuxnet is more subtle—although most likely effective. Hence, equipment failure caused by the software is difficult to attribute. Second, due to the prolific nature of Stuxnet, it is very difficult to clean the malware of all computing devices involved in the enrichment process. These concerns may explain why Iran temporarily halted all enrichment operations at Natanz in November 2010 (for unstated reasons).[55]

Was Natanz the Sole Target of Stuxnet?

A naturally arising question is "what other countries were affected by Stuxnet?" Although there were reports of the worm on SCADA equipment in Germany,[56] Finland,[57] and China,[58] none of these infections resulted in damage to industrial systems. This could be due to the specific configuration of the PLC, as Stuxnet only launches the attacks on certain setups. Siemens states that users of only 15 systems running their software reported infections. Of these 15 systems, none of them incurred any damage.[59] Iran most likely did not report infections to Siemens. Although they acquired S7-315 and S7-417 controller cards between 2002 and 2003, the IAEA established that Iran most likely diverted such hardware to its nuclear program—which caused Siemens to halt sales.[60] However, after this time, they did obtain the Siemens-manufactured S7-417 through a Russian firm known as Power Machines Corp., who installed it as part of their Teleperm system at the Bushehr facility.[61] It may be possible that Bushehr was also a Stuxnet target. However, there is less evidence indicating this to be the case as opposed to Natanz. The data structures present in Stuxnet are indicative of the latter and not the former.

The specific targeting of the Natanz Fuel Enrichment Plant, as evidenced by Stuxnet's specific targeting of the hardware and configuration of the centrifuges present at that facility, indicate that the authors of the malware had significant intelligence on their target gathered *a priori*. Though it is possible that the intelligence was gathered using more conventional means—such as human or signals intelligence—some believe that this intelligence was collected through a cyber operation as well. One theory is that the Duqu malware (described in Chapter 8) was designed for this purpose.

STUXNET IS A SIGNIFICANT ADVANCEMENT IN MALWARE

As with other pieces of malicious software, Stuxnet takes advantage of previously unidentified security holes in system software known as "zero-day" vulnerabilities. It is the nature of this type of exploit that it has been previously undetected, they are also unidentified by existing antivirus software. As a point of reference, "Operation Aurora" (Chapter 6) relies on one zero-day vulnerability. The use of two zero-day vulnerabilities would be unprecedented.[62] Stuxnet contains four zero-day vulnerabilities for the Microsoft Windows operating system and an additional one for the Siemens software. Two of the Windows vulnerabilities used in Stuxnet deal with privilege escalation. These allow the worm illegitimate root or administrator-level access to the infected system. Further, by using this root kit methodology to obtain this level of access, the worm avoids detection by most antivirus software.[63] The other two deal with the propagation of the worm either through a memory stick or through a local network. At the time of this writing, self-propagation is less common in malware as it is often difficult to control. For example, consider a "botnet"—a large number of computers infected with malware and controlled by a "command and control" server which is not legitimately affiliated with the infected machines.[64] With a botnet, propagation occurs primarily through spam emails and malicious Web sites—self-propagation methods are very limited.[65] By contrast, it seems as though Stuxnet primarily relies on self-propagation rather than the other methods typically affiliated with botnets.

STUXNET INVALIDATES SEVERAL SECURITY ASSUMPTIONS

Our final aspect of the Stuxnet as revolution of military affairs (RMA) is that it invalidates several security assumptions. The first such assumption is that isolated systems are more secure than interconnected setups. As SCADA systems, by definition, control mission critical machinery, many administrators do not connect these computers to a network—attempting to achieve security by isolation. As a result, file transfer to such machines is conducted by removable media. This is often referred to as an "air-gap" system or "sneakernet." The designers of Stuxnet exploited this assumption by enabling the worm to spread through memory sticks. Once the stick is infected, the Stuxnet software runs itself on the as target-identified computers, which subsequently use the infected drive. The infection commences when the user simply clicks on the icon for the memory stick in Windows. This is a direct application of one of the zero-day vulnerabilities that Stuxnet leverages.

Another key security assumption Stuxnet invalidates is the trust relationship set in place by digitally signed certificates. In order to provide more stability, modern operating systems, including Microsoft Windows, limit a computer program's access to system components. A normal program requests systems calls to hardware via driver software. As such is the case, the driver software has more access to lower-level system components than other programs. To avoid the easy creation of malicious driver software, Microsoft Windows relies on digitally signed certificates. In order to prevent detection by antivirus software, Stuxnet uses legitimate digitally signed certificates. This is another aspect of the malware that has not been previously observed. Early versions of Stuxnet used certificates by Realtek Semiconductor Systems—later versions used certificates from JMicron Technology Corp. The use of these certificates gives the worm the appearance of legitimate software to Microsoft Windows. Security experts at ESET note that both companies were based out of Taiwan and suspect that the certificates were stolen. Further, they believe it was most likely physical theft (perhaps even an inside job) as digital certificates for driver software are not commonly found in black markets on the Internet.[66]

IMPLICATIONS FOR THE FUTURE

Stuxnet is highly significant—it is a next-generation piece of malware that poked flaws in existing security assumptions and was able to inflict damage on industrial systems that were not connected to the Internet. Let us consider two other attacks as a comparison. First, the Russian cyber attacks against Georgia in 2008 (described in Chapter 3) relied primarily on botnets and activist hackers to conduct denial-of-service attacks against the Georgian Internet infrastructure. These attacks resulted in Georgia temporarily losing its connection to the Internet, primarily during Russian conventional operations. While the methods of attack were well known in the security community at the time, they were still significant due to its scale and the fact that they occurred in tandem with conventional operations. However, the attacks against Georgia were targeting computer infrastructure—not SCADA. In many ways, those attacks were a classic example of a cyber attack with the aim to degrade a computer network.

Another operation contemporary to Stuxnet was "Operation Aurora" (Chapter 6) in which hackers managed to penetrate the corporate networks of Google in December 2009 to steal information, including email accounts and possibly computer source code. Aurora used a zero-day vulnerability in Microsoft Internet Explorer—taking advantage of a common application many use on a daily basis.[67] This particular cyber attack is a good example of cyber espionage—the attackers sought to steal information from the target.

Stuxnet differs from these two cases in several ways. Both the attacks on Georgia and Google were targeting computer networks directly or indirectly attached to the Internet. In either of these instances, a system disconnected from the network would have been unharmed. Not so with Stuxnet. This advanced worm had the capability to bridge the "air-gap." Network administrators charged with the security of isolated systems face an interesting dilemma. In order to ensure that such systems are protected from the latest malware, they must periodically perform updates. However, in doing so, they run the risk of spreading an infection (i.e., by memory stick or through a local area network—both of which Stuxnet could propagate through).

Another key difference is that the targets in both Aurora and the attacks against Georgia were other computers. Stuxnet, on the other hand, inflicts minimal damage to information systems. Rather, its goal is to damage a piece of equipment in the physical world. The admission of the Iranians tells us that Stuxnet successfully affected a nonvirtual entity. This is a significant advance in weaponry, a piece of software that only exists when a computer is turned on was able to successfully conduct sabotage in the real world. Stuxnet clearly demonstrates that cyber weapons can cause significant real-world damage—as opposed to the previous idea that such software can only amount to "weapons of mass annoyance" (see Chapter 1).

What are the implications of malicious software that can affect real-world equipment? There are numerous questions that must now be addressed. Senate hearings in the wake of Stuxnet explore how the United States can better protect its critical infrastructure from like attacks.[68] However, prevention is only part of the puzzle. There are many policy questions—some associated with cyber warfare, in general—now taking on increased importance.[69] How do we attribute such an attack? How do we respond to cyber attacks on SCADA infrastructure by extragovernmental groups? How does the law of land warfare apply to cyber weapons that cause real-world damage?

There are several operational and technical questions that must be answered as well. In the realm of cyber warfare, technical and operational concerns often blend together. For example, how do we best identify zero-day vulnerabilities (which by definition are unknown)? How can we locate malicious software, such as Stuxnet, which was designed to go undetected? What security assumptions are we making that can be invalidated? How do we template an unknown cyber threat?

Will cyber weapons such as Stuxnet proliferate? Several security experts have predicted Stuxnet-like variants to become more common.[70] There have already been reports of non-Stuxnet cyber attacks on industrial equipment in China.[71] Freely available analysis by Symantec, Kaspersky Labs, ESET, and Langner Communications GmbH, while useful from a defensive standpoint, can also be turned on its head and used as inspiration for Stuxnet-like worms.

By its nature, cyber warfare changes quickly. Motivated individuals and teams from government, corporate, academic, and black-hat (hacker) communities are constantly scrutinizing systems for the latest vulnerabilities. However, Stuxnet represents a clear advance in state-of-the art—both as a piece of software and in what it accomplishes. It has revealed flawed assumptions of security that need to be revisited on multiple levels, but perhaps most important, it showed that software can also be used as a decisive weapon system.

SUMMARY

In this chapter, we saw how Stuxnet was designed to target ICS and successfully targeted the Natanz FEP. It exploited not only five zero-day exploits but also many of the implicit trust relationships common in ICS. This highly-specific piece of malware was designed with a certain target in mind and seemed to be designed to limit collateral damage. Perhaps Stuxnet may be an indicator of cyber weapons to come.

SUGGESTED FURTHER READING

This chapter is based on the article "Stuxnet: Cyberwar Revolution in Military Affairs" by Paulo Shakarian that originally appeared in the April 2011 edition of *Small Wars Journal*—published online at smallwarsjournal.com. A Spanish-language translation of the article is also available from *Air and Space Power Journal*.[c]

Perhaps the best-known technical description of Stuxnet was written by Nicolas Falliere, Liam O Murchu, and Eric Chien of the Symantec Corporation entitled "W32.Stuxnet Dossier." Another good technical description entitled "Stuxnet under the Microscope" was written by Aleksandr Matrosov, Eugene Rodionov, David Harley, and Juraj Malcho of ESET.

[c]http://www.airpower.au.af.mil/apjinternational/apj-s/2012/2012-3/2012_3_06_shakarian_s.pdf.

The Symantec and ESET documents tell the technical story of Stuxnet from an information assurance perspective. However, Ralph Langner of Langner Communications GmbH has written much on Stuxnet from an industrial control system (ICS) perspective. It is interesting to note that some of Langner's findings differ somewhat from that of Symantec. Langner's writing can be found on his blog at http://www.langner.com.

References

1. Ranum MJ. CyberWar: reality or hype? In: Vanguard security conference, 2004, Reno Nevada; 2004. http://www.ranum.com/security/computer_security/archives/myth-of-cyberwar.pdf [accessed April 17, 2013].
2. Oleg K, Sergey U. Trojan-Spy.0485 and Malware-Cryptor.Win32.Inject.gen.2 Review; July 2010 VirusBlockAda.
3. Falliere N, Murchu LO, Chien E. W32.Stuxnet Dossier Version 1.4. Symantec Corporation; February 7, 2011.
4. Albright D, Brannan P, Walrond C. Did Stuxnet take out 1,000 centrifuges at the Natanz Enrichment Plant? Institute for Science and International Security (ISIS). Washington, DC; 2010.
5. Erdbrink T. Ahmadinejad: Iran's nuclear program hit by sabotage, Washington, DC: Washington Post; November 29, 2010. http://www.washingtonpost.com/wp-dyn/content/article/2010/11/29/AR2010112903468.html [accessed February 16, 2011].
6. Quote from Roel Schouwenberg, Senior Anti-Virus Researcher at Kaspersky Labs in an interview at the Virus Bulletin conference. http://www.youtube.com/watch?v=C9H3MrtLgUc; October 2010 [accessed February 16, 2011].
7. Brunner M, Hofinger H, Krauss C, Roblee C, Schoo P, Todt S. Infiltrating critical infrastructures with next-generation attacks W32.Stuxnet as a showcase threat. Fraunhofer SIT; December 2010. Version 1.4. p. 23.
8. Falliere et al. 55.
9. Murray W. Thinking about revolutions in military affairs. Joint Forces Q 1997;(Summer).
10. Brannan P, Albright D. SIS imagery brief: new activities at the Esfahan and Natanz nuclear sites in Iran. The Institute for Science and International Security; 2006. http://isis-online.org/uploads/isis-reports/documents/newactivities.pdf [accessed April 17, 2013].
11. Fernandez JD, Fernandez AE. SCADA systems: vulnerabilities and remediation. J Comput Sci Coll 2005;20 (4):160–8.
12. Brandstetter T. Stuxnet Malware. CIP Seminar, Siemens; November 2010.
13. Langer Ralph. How to hijack a controller—why stuxnet isn't just about Siemens PLCs, Control Mag January 13, 2011; http://www.controlglobal.com/articles/2011/IndustrialControllers1101.html [accessed February 16, 2011].
14. Falliere et al. 39.
15. Langer R. 417 Data structures=cascade structure=reported damage. Langer Communications GmbH Blog; December 29, 2010. http://www.langner.com/en/2010/12/29/417-data-structures-cascade-structure-reported-damage/[accessed February 16, 2011].
16. Falliere et al. 39.
17. Ibid., 41.
18. Shakarian P. Stuxnet: cyberwar revolution in military affairs, Small Wars J 2011; http://smallwarsjournal.com/jrnl/art/stuxnet-cyberwar-revolution-in-military-affairs [accessed February 26, 2013].
19. Langer. Control Magazine.
20. Falliere et al. 45.
21. Langner R. Matching Langner's Stuxnet analysis and Symantic's dossier update, Langner Communications GmbH; February 2011. http://www.langner.com/en/2011/02/21/matching-langner%E2%80%99s-stuxnet-analysis-and-symantec%E2%80%99s-dossier-update/[accessed December 29, 2012].
22. SIMATIC WinCC/SIMATIC PCS 7: information about Malware/Viruses/Trojan horses. Siemens. http://support.automation.siemens.com/WW/llisapi.dll?func=cslib.csinfo&lang=en&objid=43876783&caller=view; November 2011 [accessed December 29, 2012].
23. Falliere et al. 5.
24. Farrar-Wellman A, Frasco R. Indonesia-Iran foreign relations, AEI Iran Tracker June 2010; http://www.irantracker.org/foreign-relations/indonesia-iran-foreign-relations [accessed December 29, 2012].

25. The designers of Stuxnet launched attacks in three phases, each phase using an updated version of the software. The technical details can be found in Falliere *et al.*

26. Ibid., 7.

27. Albright *et al.* 2.

28. Ibid., 4.

29. Falliere *et al.* 41.

30. Glaser A. Characteristics of the gas centrifuge for uranium enrichment and their relevance for nuclear weapon proliferation (corrected). Sci Global Secur June 2008; vol. 16, 1–25, 14.

31. Ibid.

32. See Ralph Langner's January 2012 talk at the S4 conference. http://www.digitalbond.com/blog/2012/01/31/langners-stuxnet-deep-dive-s4-video/ [accessed 29.12.12].

33. Langner R. The Prez shows his cascade shape. Langner Communications GmbH. Hamburg: Germany; December 2011. http://www.langner.com/en/2011/12/07/the-prez-shows-his-cascade-shape/ [accessed December 29, 2012].

34. Pauli D. Stuxnet a 'perfect match' to Iran nuclear facility, photo reveals, SC Magazine December 9, 2011; http://www.scmagazine.com.au/News/282735,stuxnet-a-perfect-match-to-iran-nuclear-facility-photo-reveals.aspx [accessed April 17, 2013].

35. Albright *et al.* 2.

36. Kerr PK. Iran's nuclear program: status, Congressional Research Service, Washington, DC.; August 11, 2009. http://isis-online.org/uploads/conferences/documents/CRS_Iran_August2009_1.pdf [accessed April 17, 2013].

37. Kerr PK. Iran's nuclear program: status, Congressional Research Service, Washington, DC.; August 11, 2009. http://isis-online.org/uploads/conferences/documents/CRS_Iran_August2009_1.pdf [accessed April 17, 2013].

38. IAEA Report by the Director General . Implementation of the NPT Safeguards Agreement and Relevant Provisions of Security Council Resolutions 1737 (2006), 1747 (2007), 1803 (2008), and 1835 (2008) in the Islamic Republic of Iran, http://www.iranwatch.org/international/IAEA/iaea-iranreport-060509.pdf [accessed April 17, 2013].

39. Albright D, Walrond C. Performance of the IR-1 Centrifuge at Natanz, Institute for Science and International Security, Washington, DC.; October 18, 2011. http://isis-online.org/uploads/isis-reports/documents/IR1_Centrifuge_Performance_18October2011.pdf [accessed April 17, 2013].

40. Albright D, Walrond C. Performance of the IR-1 Centrifuge at Natanz, Institute for Science and International Security. Washington, DC.; October 18, 2011. http://isis-online.org/uploads/isis-reports/documents/IR1_Centrifuge_Performance_18October2011.pdf [accessed April 17, 2013].

41. Falliere *et al.*

42. Albright D, Brannan P, Walrond, C. Stuxnet Malware and Natanz: update of ISIS December 22, 2010 Report. *ISIS Reports.* http://isis-online.org/isis-reports/detail/stuxnet-malware-and-natanz-update-of-isis-december-22-2010-reportsupa-href1/8; February 15, 2011 [accessed December 29, 2012].

43. See Ralph Langner's January 2012 talk at the S4 conference. http://www.digitalbond.com/blog/2012/01/31/langners-stuxnet-deep-dive-s4-video/; 2012 [accessed December 29, 2012].

44. Albright, Brannan, and Walrond.

45. Albright, Brannan, and Walrond.

46. McDonald G, Murchu LO, Doherty S, Chien E, *Stuxnet 0.5: The Missing Link,* Symantec Corporation; February 2013.

47. Stuxnet 0.5: disrupting uranium processing at Natanz. Symantec Connect (blog). http://www.symantec.com/connect/blogs/stuxnet-05-disrupting-uranium-processing-natanz; February 26, 2013 [accessed February 26, 2013].

48. Ibid.

49. McDonald *et al.*, ibid.

50. Erdbrink.

51. Bednarz D, Follath E. Iran's chief nuclear negotiator: we have to be constantly on guard. SPIEGEL ONLINE January 18, 2011; http://www.spiegel.de/international/world/0,1518,739945-2,00.html [accessed February 16, 2011].

52. Falliere *et al.* 3.

53. Leyden J. Iran boasts of Stuxnet 'nuclear spies' arrests. *The Register.* http://www.theregister.co.uk/2010/10/04/stuxnet_conspiracy_theories/; October 4, 2010 [accessed February 16, 2011].

54. From an interview with Ralph Langer by Yaakov Katz in "Stuxnet Virus Set Back Iran's Nuclear Program by 2 Years." Jerusalem Post. http://www.studentnewsdaily.com/daily-news-article/stuxnet-virus-set-back-irans-nuclear-program-by-2-years/; December 15, 2010 [accessed February 16, 2011].

55. Albright *et al.* 6.
56. Stuxnet also found at industrial plants in Germany. The H Security. http://www.h-online.com/security/news/item/Stuxnet-also-found-at-industrial-plants-in-Germany-1081469.html; September 17, 2010 [accessed February 16, 2011].
57. Stuxnet Spreads to Finland. *The New Internet.* http://www.thenewnewinternet.com/2010/10/14/stuxnet-spreads-to-scandinavia/; October 2010 [accessed February 16, 2011].
58. Leyden J.Stuxnet worm slithers into China. *The Register* http://www.theregister.co.uk/2010/10/01/stuxnet_china_analysis/; October 2010 [accessed February 16, 2011].
59. Brandstetter.
60. Albright *et al.* 5.
61. Langer R. 417 Installed in Bushehr NPP. *Langer Communications GmbH Blog.* http://www.langner.com/en/2010/12/14/417-installed-in-bushehr-npp/; December 14, 2010 [accessed February 16, 2011].
62. Interview with Roel Schouwenberg at Virus Bulletin (see note 2).
63. Davis M. Stuxnet reality check, Inf Week analytics 2013; http://www.savidtech.com/wp-content/themes/sti/images/stories/PDF/S2840511_DR_stuxnet.pdf [accessed February 26, 2013].
64. Barford and Yegneswaran, 2.
65. Ibid., 3.
66. Matrosov *et al.* 13. Also see the related ESET technical blog post at http://blog.eset.com/2010/07/22/why-steal-digital-certificates; [accessed February 16, 2011].
67. Matrosov *et al.* 5.
68. For details on the November 2010 U.S. Senate hearing in the aftermath of Stuxnet, see http://hsgac.senate.gov/public/index.cfm?FuseAction=Hearings.Hearing&Hearing_id=954c3149-042e-4028-ae23-754868902c44 [accessed February 16, 2011].
69. See Jeffrey Carr, Inside Cyber Warfare for a detailed analysis of these issues.
70. Stuxnet-like attacks have been predicted by several computer security professionals, including Symantec Corporation (see MessageLabs Intelligence: 2010 Annual Security Report). Several experts also make such predictions in eWeek (http://www.eweek.com/c/a/Security/Stuxnet-Variants-Will-Wreak-Havoc-on-More-Information-Systems-in-2011-373179/) ComputerWeekly (http://www.computerweekly.com/Articles/2010/12/22/244626/StuxNet-prepare-for-worse-in-2011.htm) [accessed April 17, 2013].
71. Rashid F. Stuxnet-Like Trojans Can Exploit Critical Flaw in Chinese Industrial Software. *eWeek.* http://www.eweek.com/c/a/Security/StuxnetLike-Trojans-Can-Exploit-Critical-Flaw-in-Chinese-Industrial-Software-296674/; January 12, 2011 [accessed February 16, 2011].
72. Kerr PK. Iran's nuclear program: status, Congressional Research Service. Pdf-file available at; http://isis-online.org/uploads/conferences/documents/CRS_Iran_August2009_1.pdf; August 11, 2009 [accessed April 17, 2013].
73. IAEA. *Implementation of the NPT Safeguards agreement and relevant provisions of Security Council Resolution 1737 (2006), 1747 (2007), 1803 (2008) and 1835 (2008) in the Islamic Republic of Iran,* Pdf-file available at: http://www.iaea.org/Publications/Documents/Board/2009/gov2009-8.pdf; February 19, 2009 [accessed April 17, 2013].
74. Albright ,WalrondC. *Performance of the IR-1Centrifuge at Natanz.* Institute for Science and International Security: Pdf-file available at; http://isis-online.org/uploads/isis-reports/documents/IR1_Centrifuge_Performance_18October2011.pdf; October 18, 2011 [accessed April 17, 2013].
75. Albright D,Walrond C. *Performance of the IR-1 Centrifuge at Natanz.* Institute for Science and International Security: Pdf-file available at; http://isis-online.org/uploads/isis-reports/documents/IR1_Centrifuge_Performance_18October2011.pdf; October 18, 2011 [accessed April 17, 2013].
76. ISIS Report. *Satellite imagery of two possible sites of the Qom enrichment facility in Iran.* Available at: http://isis-online.org/isis-reports/detail/satellite-imagery-of-two-possible-sites-of-the-qom-enrichment-facility-in-i/8#images; September 25, 2009 [accessed April 17, 2013].
77. Albright D, Brannan P, Stricker A, Walrond C. *Natanz Enrichment Site: Boondoggle or Part of an Atomic Bomb Production Complex?* ISIS Reports. Available at: http://isis-online.org/isis-reports/detail/natanz-enrichment-site-boondoggle-or-part-of-an-atomic-bomb-production-comp/; September 21, 2011 [accessed April 17, 2013].
78. Albright D, Brannan B, Stricker A, Walrond C. *Natanz enrichment site: Boondoggle or part of an atomic bomb production complex?* ISIS Reports. Available at: http://isis-online.org/isis-reports/detail/natanz-enrichment-site-boondoggle-or-part-of-an-atomic-bomb-production-comp/; September 21, 2011 [accessed April 17, 2013].

79. Kemp SR, Glaser A. *Statement on Iran's ability to make a nuclear weapon and the significance of the 19 February 2008 IAEA Report on Iran's Uranium-Enrichment Program.* Pdf available at: http://www.princeton.edu/~aglaser/2009aglaser_iran.pdf; March 2, 2009 [accessed April 17, 2013].

80. Albright D, Walrond C. *Performance of the IR-1 centrifuge at Natanz.* Institute for Science and International Security. Pdf-file available at: http://isis-online.org/uploads/isis-reports/documents/IR1_Centrifuge_Performance_18October2011.pdf; October 18, 2011 [accessed April 17, 2013].

81. Albright D, Brannan P, Stricker A, Walrond C. *Natanz enrichment site: Boondoggle or part of an atomic bomb production complex?* ISIS Reports. Available at: http://isis-online.org/isis-reports/detail/natanz-enrichment-site-boondoggle-or-part-of-an-atomic-bomb-production-comp/; September 21, 2011 [accessed April 17, 2013].

82. Albright D, Brannan P, Stricker A, Walrond C. *Natanz enrichment site: Boondoggle or part of an atomic bomb production complex?* ISIS Reports. Available at: http://isis-online.org/isis-reports/detail/natanz-enrichment-site-boondoggle-or-part-of-an-atomic-bomb-production-comp/; September 21, 2011 [accessed April 17, 2013].

83. Albright D, Walrond C. *Iranian production of 19.75 percent enriched uranium: beyond its realistic needs.* ISIS Report. Pdf available at: http://isis-online.org/uploads/isis-reports/documents/Twenty_percent_production_15June2012.pdf; June 15, 2012. p. 3 [accessed April 17, 2013].

84. Albright D, Walrond C. *Iranian production of 19.75 percent enriched uranium: beyond its realistic needs.* ISIS Report. Pdf available at: http://isis-online.org/uploads/isis-reports/documents/Twenty_percent_production_15June2012.pdf; June 15, 2012. p. 9 [accessed April 17, 2013].

85. These include Symantec, Kaspersky Labs, ESET, and Langer Communications GmbH.

86. Barford P, Yegneswaran V. An inside look at Botnets. In: Christodorescu M, Jha S, Maughan D, Song D, Wang C, editors. *Malware detection.* New York: Springer; 2007.

87. Matrosov A, Rodionov E, Harley D, Malcho J. *Stuxnet under the Microscope Revision* 1.2. ESET; November, 2010. p. 5.

Conclusion and the Future
of Cyber Warfare

This book explored many of the major incidents of cyber warfare over the past decade. Prior to the year 2000, cyber warfare was theorized about, but there was little indication (at least in the public discourse) that it actually occurred. During the late 1990s and early 2000s, detractors even claimed cyber warfare would never amount to a serious threat. Since then, incidents such as the Russia-Georgia war of 2008, the theft of UAV video feeds publicized in 2009, the accounts of Stuxnet in 2010, and Anonymous' support of the Arab Spring in 2011 seem to have shifted the debate on cyber warfare from "Is cyber war important?" to "What should we do about cyber war?" One thing we learned while writing this book is that many attacks that were theorized about in the 1990s were realized just over a decade later. We have examined how the Internet plays a part in real-world conflicts from governments' use of the Internet as propaganda tool (Chapter 4) or to curb internal discord (Chapters 5 and 7) to the support of physical operations on the ground (Chapters 3 and 10). Nevertheless, the employment of the Internet as means to political ends is not limited to nation states and their official institutions. Most notably, the Internet crusades of the Anonymous collective and various affiliates come to mind. In Chapter 6, the reader caught a glimpse of the consequences of emerging global, border-transgressing online social networks. Albeit highly prominent in the past 2 years, it is merely the amplification of the global citizen, who now is more able than ever to voice his/her discontent over matters far removed from his/her actual home base. The inherent dangers of the global interconnectedness, which is unfortunately only slowly entering the body of common knowledge, are highlighted in mostly criminal and to a lesser extent politically motivated social network exploitations. We outline the most prominent mechanism that makes such an endeavor likely to be highly successful in Chapter 9 with the outline of the Robin Sage experiment. In 2012, 34% of the world population finds itself in the favorable position to have Internet access—a growth of more than 500% since December 2000. In this book, we were able to touch only marginally how the use of social media by ordinary citizens of this world is quickly gaining in its potential to change the world (Chapters 2 and 5). Moreover, it can be alleged that we focused on the organized, concerted efforts that significantly stood out in the successfulness of their operation—alas, reports about most of them can be found in popular media outlets. Thus, later chapters (Chapter 8, and all the chapters in Part 3) describe imminent and possible future threats to industrial control systems and other industrial infrastructure. Here we dedicate an entire chapter (Chapter 13) to the highly sophisticated worm Stuxnet, which apparently was meant to curb the enrichment of Uranium at Iran's primary production site—a large high-security site with underground structures that house the cascade halls.

Several parts of this book not only describe historical case studies but also highlight possibilities the future of cyberspace might bring. Extending the latest in scientific research and technology, the authors attempt to forecast realistic scenarios of future cyber warfare tactics. There are other issues that we should consider that could perhaps make the next decade of cyber warfare even more interesting than the last, specifically:

- Nearly every major encryption technique in use today relies on the difficulty of finding the prime factorization of large numbers. A major advance in theoretical computer science came in the late 1990s when Peter Shor created an algorithm that could factor prime numbers quickly.[1] However, this algorithm would require a new type of computer system that relies on *quantum mechanics*—the physics that governs the extremely small subatomic particles of nature. Such a computer is often referred to as a "quantum computer" and a practical quantum computer does not exist as of the time of this writing. Recently, some of the technical difficulties involved in creating such a system have been solved as advances have been made in quantum computing by IBM,[2] UC Santa Barbara,[3] and Yale.[4] It turns out that the research team at UC Santa Barbara actually developed a quantum processor that is capable of factoring the number fifteen[5]—a modest but important step toward finding the prime factors of larger numbers. Once researchers can scale this approach, much of the world's current encryption techniques could become obsolete.
- Will the emerging market for exploits on which hackers sell the latest zero-day vulnerabilities for six-digit figures[6,7] to intelligence organizations lead to a cyber arms race?
- How will the much-theorized "mobile botnet,"[8] massive armies of compromised, Internet-capable, high-bandwidth mobile phones, change the cyber battleground with respect to conducting DDoS attacks? Some preliminary evidence of such a botnet has already been observed.[9]
- Highly successful cyber espionage against American companies and institutions conducted in recent years is strongly suggested to have been condoned by the Chinese government. After considering hallmark Chinese literature on the philosophy of warfare, is it feasible to assume that China is already conducting cyber warfare by extension to nonmilitary operations in order to either secure a higher hand in future actual conflicts or gain advantages while preventing all-out military ground operations?
- Is Iran attempting to create a "Cyber Shi'ite Crescent" by becoming the dominant cyber power in the Middle East? As we are writing this book, we noticed not only a focus on cyber warfare within Iran (see Chapter 5) but also that Iranian allies and proxies have operated with increased cyber savvy. Consider Lebanese Hezbollah (Chapter 3), the Syrian Electronic Army (Chapter 9), and Kata'ib Hezbollah in Iraq (Chapter 10). All these groups are associated with organizations supported by the Shi'ite Islamic state and all have been successful in various cyber operations. Perhaps analogous to the "Shi'ite Crescent"[10] that Iran was often thought to be creating through proxies in Iraq, Lebanon, and Syria, a "Cyber Shi'ite Crescent" is being created using cyber warriors in those same countries as well.

In short, the battlefields of cyber warfare will continue to evolve along many dimensions. We are only at the beginning of a new era of information security that will likely change many times before reaching some sort of steady state—if such a steady state is even possible.

References

1. Shor PW. Polynomial-time algorithms for prime factorization and discrete logarithms on a quantum computer. Proceedings of the 35th annual symposium on foundations of computer science, Santa Fe, NM, November 20–22, 1994.
2. IBM Research Advances Device Performance for Quantum Computing. *IBM*. http://www-03.ibm.com/press/us/en/pressrelease/36901.wss; February 28, 2012.
3. Physicists Make Breakthrough in Quantum Computing. *UC Newsroom*. http://www.universityofcalifornia.edu/news/article/26209; September 1, 2011.
4. Gershon E. At Yale, quantum computing is a (qu)bit closer to reality. *Yale News*. http://news.yale.edu/2012/02/14/yale-quantum-computing-qubit-closer-reality; February 14, 2012.
5. Researchers Make Quantum Processor Capable of Factoring a Composite Number into Prime Factors. *Science Daily*. http://www.sciencedaily.com/releases/2012/08/120819153743.htm; August 19, 2012.
6. Greenberg A. Meet the Hackers Who Sell Spies the Tools to Crack Your PC (and Get Paid Six-Figure Fees). *Forbes*. http://www.forbes.com/sites/andygreenberg/2012/03/21/meet-the-hackers-who-sell-spies-the-tools-to-crack-your-pc-and-get-paid-six-figure-fees/; April 9, 2012.
   Greenberg A. Shopping for Zero-Days: A Price List for Hackers' Secret Software Exploits. *Forbes*. http://www.forbes.com/sites/andygreenberg/2012/03/23/shopping-for-zero-days-an-price-list-for-hackers-secret-software-exploits/; March 23, 2012.
7. The Digital Arms Trade. *The Economist*. http://www.economist.com/news/business/21574478-market-software-helps-hackers-penetrate-computer-systems-digital-arms-trade; March 30, 2013 [accessed April 23, 2013].
8. Traynor P, et al. On cellular botnets: measuring the impact of malicious devices on a cellular network core. ACM conference on computer and communication security, November 2009; 2009.
9. Zink T. Spam from an Android botnet. *Terry Zink's Cyber Security Blog*. http://blogs.msdn.com/b/tzink/archive/2012/07/03/spam-from-an-android-botnet.aspx; July 3, 2012.
10. For further discussion on Iranian influence in the Middle East and the Shi'ite crescent, we recommend Vali Nasr's *The Shia Revival: How Conflicts Within Islam Will Shape the Future*. W.W. Norton; 2006.

I

Chapter 6: LulzSec Hacktivities

Following is a list of hacktivities blamed on and/or claimed by the original or first crew of the "LulzBoat"/LulzSec hacker group (not LulzSec Reborn or other spin-offs and successors). Due to the nature of the activity, it is not feasible to present a complete account of hacks associated with the group. Although they were highly vociferous about their hacks and gained considerable media attention from its very beginnings, the account of LulzSec's hacktivities is likely to reflect what the group intended to reach public attention. In media control, LulzSec was able to hide likely failures and only hone successful attacks. For the compilation of the list below, we only used open source media and included details such as motivation where available to add more depth to the identity of this hacker group. Although LulzSec repeatedly proclaims fun as the motivation for its breaches on some occasions, political opinions certainly played a role:

Approximate date	Target, hacktivity, and modus operandi (where available)	Details
May 5, 2011	Personal information of at least 73,000 X-factor contestant hopefuls by hacking into Fox.com[1,2]	Lulz[3]
May 10, 2011	Fox.com sales database and personal information on users released[4]	
May 13, 2011	Intrusion and publication of names and e-mails (passwords and user names) of more than 400 Fox Broadcasting employees, encourages sympathizers to use the published information for harassment[5,6]	@FOXUPTV, dislike of Fox News channel,[7] Lulz[8]
May 15, 2011	LulzSec steals and releases of the transaction logs of 3100 ATMs in the UK[9,10]	
May 23, 2011	Sony's Japanese Web site (sonymusic.co.jp) sees database pilfered and published (redacted)[11–13]	#Sownage[14]; SQL injection, to embarrass Sony[15–17]
May 30, 2011	Defacement of the official Web site of the American Public Broadcasting Service (PBS); the exploitation of vulnerabilities in PBS' system also allowed the gleaning and subsequent publication of more than 2000 PBS passwords and login details[18,19]	Frontline documentation about WikiLeaks which was perceived to be partial[20]

Continued

Approximate date	Target, hacktivity, and modus operandi (where available)	Details
June 2, 2011	Sony BMG Belgium (sonybmg.be) database intruded and exposed[21]	#Sownage[22]
June 2, 2011	Sony Pictures may have seen private information of more than 1 million[23,24] of its customers compromised, at least 50,000 of which are published[25–28]	#Sownage,[29] SQL injection, no password encryption,[30] published on MediaFire, in order to expose Sony's vulnerability/inability to keep user data safe[31,32]
June 2, 2011	Sony BMG Netherlands (sonybmg.nl) database breached and exposed[33]	#Sownage[34]
June 3, 2011	Breach of Nintendo and posting of the vulnerabilities that allowed the intrusion and the timely response to the breach on part of Nintendo,[35] apology states "we like the N64 too much—we sincerely hope Nintendo plugs the gap"[36]	Exposing of vulnerabilities in the company's IT-security[37]
June 3, 2011	The Atlanta Infragard chapter experiences Web site defacement as well as the theft and subsequent publication of personal data pertaining to 180 members affiliated with the FBI; among the data gleaned are also the passwords of the CEO of Unveillance, a network security company who later releases screenshots of alleged chats with LulzSec members trying to extort money and sensitive information, while LulzSec retorted Unveillance had offered money for attacking competitors' Web sites[38,39]	In response to Pentagon considering schemata according to which acts of computer sabotage emanating from other countries can be considered acts of war and would be responded to accordingly[40,41]
June 4, 2011	Hacking magazine 2600 hacked[42]	Due to its affiliation with Dutch hacker whom the LulzSec crew opposes[43]
June 6, 2011	Release of about 54 MB source code for Sony Computer Entertainment's Developer Network site and network maps from Sony BMG's New York offices[44,45]	#Sownage[46]; the source code allows to reverse engineer the network and possibly create new versions of the software[47]
June 7, 2011	28-year-old Hector Xavier Monsegur aka (The Real) Sabu arrested (10.15 pm) in New York City's Lower East Side (Jacon Riis public housing development), Monsegur was member to Anonymous, LulzSec, and Internet Feds[48–52]	"rooter", i.e., detection of vulnerabilities in targeted computer systems[53]
June 8, 2011	Defacement of Black & Berg Cybersecurity Consulting Web site after challenge, turns down prize[54]	
June 9, 2011	LulzSec hacks into the British National Health Service (NHS)[55–57]	Informing the administrators of the Web site of the vulnerabilities via Twitter[58–60]

Continued

Approximate date	Target, hacktivity, and modus operandi (where available)	Details
June 11, 2011	Information gleaned from pornography Web site, www.pron.com, published around 26,000 user e-mail addresses and passwords[61]	
June 13, 2011	Intrusion, theft, and release of e-mail addresses and passwords of users of the Web site www.senate.gov (Web site of the U.S. Senate)[62]	In their claim of responsibility, LulzSec stated a dislike of the U.S. government and claimed its hack was helping to fix vulnerabilities[63]
June 13, 2011	Intrusion and theft, but without release of user data of the Bethesda Game Studios network[64,65]	
June 14, 2011	Web sites of Minecraft, Eve Online, League of Legends, The Escapist,[66] and FinFisher[67] (IT security company) experience downtime due to DDoS attacks[68]	"Titanic Take-down Tuesday," disruption of service in order to raise awareness[69]; by request[70–72]
June 15, 2011	LulzSec launches DDoS-attack on www.cia.gov (Web site of the U.S. Central Intelligence Agency), rendering it inaccessible between 5.48 and 8 pm EST[73,74]	Lulz[75]
June 16, 2011	LulzSec publishes 62,000 e-mails and passwords to MediaFire (free file and image sharing Web site) challenging readers to find out to which Web sites they will be granted access to by trial and error[76]	
June 19, 2011	InfraGard Connecticut intrusion and exposure of personal information on more than 1000 FBI-affiliated members[77]	SQL infection[78]
June 20, 2011	LulzSec declares its merger with Anonymous launching Operation Anti-Security (#OpAntiSec)[79,80]	#AntiSec[81,82]
June 20, 2011	Web site of the British Serious Organized Crime Agency (SOCA, soca.gov.uk) is hit with DDoS attacks[83,84]	#AntiSec[85]
June 21, 2011	Scotland Yard arrests 19-year-old Ryan Cleary of Wickford, Essex, UK; Anonymous outlet denies any affiliation while LulzSec tweets that he merely hosted one of their public forums; charges pertain to the Computer Misuse Act and Fraud Act[86]	Cleary admits to compromising and/or DDoS-ing the Web sites of the following institutions: National Health Service (UK), British Serious Organized Crime Agency (SOCA), CIA, News International, Sony, Nintendo, Arizona State Police, twentieth century Fox among others[87]
June 22 and 25, 2011	Web sites affiliated with the Brazilian government and Brazilian energy giant Petrobras experience downtime due to DDoS-attack; 2 days later compromised Petrobras employee data, which the company denies[88,89]	Brazilian chapter,[90] political reasons[91]

Continued

Approximate date	Target, hacktivity, and modus operandi (where available)	Details
June 23, 2011	Documents, e-mail addresses, and passwords from the Web site of the Arizona Department of Public Safety gleaned and published, "chinga la migra"[92]	OpAntiSec[93]; in protest of Arizona's controversial immigration law[94]
June 25, 2011	LulzSec declares an end to its "50-day voyage,"[95,96] releases cache of gleaned data including documents from NATO, AOL,[97] FBI,[98] hackforums.net, and AT&T, e-mail addresses and passwords from Priority Investigations, lists of public facing routers with default authentication settings,[99] usernames and passwords of various online game environments, including Battlefield Heroes Beta as well as IP block information, including IP address ranges for Sony, Disney, ViaCom, Liquid Web, EMI, Saga, QWEST, and others[100,101]	Boredom, giving AntiSec and its cause priority[102,103]
July 4, 2011	Apple server targeted,[104] user names and passwords gleaned and published[105]	#AntiSec[106]
July 18, 2011	LulzSec hijacks the Web site of British newspaper *The Sun* and redirects it to the hacked *The Times*, which was defaced and presenting an article on the death of Rupert Murdoch. Later the Web site linked to LulzSec's Twitter account, but was taken offline shortly thereafter[107]	
July 19, 2011	Authorities arrest 16 in association with Anonymous and LulzSec,[108] among whom is alleged LulzSec member Tflow in London—a 16-year-old male[109]; Christopher Wayne Cooper, 23, aka "Anthrophobic"; Joshua John Covelli, 26, aka "Absolem," and "Toxic"; Keith Wilson Downey, 26; Mercedes Renee Haefer, 20, aka "No," and "MMMM"; Donald Husband, 29, aka "Ananon"; Vincent Charles Kershaw, 27, aka "Trivette," "Triv," and "Reaper"; Ethan Miles, 33; James C. Murphy, 36; Drew Alan Phillips, 26, aka "Drew010"; Jeffrey Puglisi, 28, aka "Jeffer," "Jefferp" and "Ji"; Daniel Sullivan, 22; Tracy Ann Valenzuela, 42; and Christopher Quang Vo, 22, Scott Matthew Arciszewski, 21 (LulzSec, Infragard Tampa), Lance Moore, 21[110,111]	
July 19, 2011	Web sites of News International experience downtime due to DDoS attacks, Web site of the British tabloid, *The Sun*, defaced with fake story reporting Rupert Murdoch's death and subsequently redirected to LulzSec's Twitter feed[112]	

Continued

Approximate date	Target, hacktivity, and modus operandi (where available)	Details
July 27, 2011	19-year-old Jake Davis aka Topiary arrested in Lerwick, Shetland, UK,[113] later pleads guilty to two counts of conspiracy[114]	Allegedly responsible for the hacks into Web sites of the British NHS, News International, Sony, Nintendo, Arizona State Police, Twentieth Century Fox, Westboro Baptist Church, Bethesda Games, Eve Online, HBGary and HBGary Federal, PBS Inc., Infragard (with Ryan Cleary)[115]
August 15, 2011	Hector Xavier Monsegur pleads guilty to 12 criminal charges including 3 counts of conspiracy to engage in computer hacking, computer hacking in furtherance of fraud, conspiracies to commit access device as well as bank fraud, and aggravated identity theft—harges that add up to 124 years prison[116–118]	
August 18, 2011	1 GB of personal information gleaned from e-mail account of Richard Garcia (senior vice president at Vanguard Defense Industries), subsequently published on Pastebin[119,120]	#AntiSec; Garcia is affiliated with InfraGard and former Assistant Director to the FBI's Los Angeles office[121]
September 22, 2011	23-year-old Cody Andrew Kretsinger (a.k.a. "recursion") arrested in Phoenix, AZ[122,123]	Allegedly responsible for Sony Pictures Entertainment breach[124,125]
September 22, 2011	48-year-old Christopher Doyon (a.k.a "Commander X" (PLF)) arrested on conspiracy charges in Santa Cruz, CA, subsequently released on bail,[126] later evades authorities by emigrating to Canada[127,128]	DDoS-attack on Santa Cruz County servers (December 16, 2010)[129–131]
November 18, 2011	IACIS' internal e-mail archives and personal data (including 38,000 e-mails, voicemails, SMS text message logs) pertaining to white hat computer crime investigator[132,133]	#AntiSec, #FFF; against white hat hackers who work to protect the status quo Anonymous and affiliates are seeking to destroy[134]
December 3, 2011	LulzSec Portugal launches DDoS attacks on Web sites associated with the Portuguese government in response to police's violent reaction to protests on November, 24[135]	
December 11, 2011	Coalition of Law Enforcement and Retail (CLEAR) sees member details, personal information and more than 2400 hashed passwords exposed[136]	Exphin1ty, AntiSec- and Anonymous-affiliated hacker; in protest of law enforcement violent treatment of Occupy Wall Street protestors[137]
December 6-24, 2011	Web site of private intelligence company, Stratfor (Strategic Forecasting Inc.), defaced; nearly 3 million e-mails gleaned, personal information of 860,000 subscribers exposed some of which (60,000) also see their banking information used to make donations to charitable organizations ($700,000)[138,139]	#AntiSec,[140] #Lulzmas,[141] in pursuance of research on state-corporate alliance in its attempts to curb information freedom,[142] internal e-mails later leaked via WikiLeaks, Jeremy Hammond alleged ring leader[143,144]

Continued

Approximate date	Target, hacktivity, and modus operandi (where available)	Details
February 3, 2012	@AnonymousIRC tweets about the eavesdropping and recording (including link to YouTube) of a conference call between the American FBI and U.K. law enforcement over investigations into Anonymous collective[145]	Donncha O'Cearrbhail allegedly responsible[146]
March 6, 2012	In a wave of arrests spanning two continents and the authorities of three countries get hold of further five alleged LulzSec, Internet Feds, and Anonymous members: Ryan Ackroyd (a.k.a. "kayla," "lol," "lolspoon"), Jake Davis (a.k.a. "topiary," "atopiary"), Darren Martyn (a.k.a. "pwnsauce," "raepsauce," "networkkitten"), Donncha O'Cearrbhail (a.k.a. "palladium"), as well as Jeremy Hammond (a.k.a. "Anarchaos," "sup_g," "burn," "yohoho," "POW," "tylerknowsthis," "crediblethreat"; declared #AntiSec member)[147,148]	
March 26, 2012	Military dating Web site, militarysingles.com, compromised, e-mail addresses and other personal information of 170,937 users are published on Pastebin[149–151]	LulzSec Reborn, "Laughing at your security since 2011!"[152–154]
November 6, 2012	Web sites affiliated with the Ecuadorian government and military experience defaced[155]	LulzSec Ecuador[156]

References

1. Landesman M. LulzSec: X-factor, Fox, and the FBI. Available at: http://antivirus.about.com/b/2011/05/13/lulzsec-x-factor-fox-and-the-fbi.htm; May 13, 2011.
2. Mack E. Lulzsec: A Short History of Hacking. *PC World*. Available at: http://www.pcworld.com/article/231215/lulzsec_a_short_history_of_hacking.html; June 27, 2011.
3. Landesman M. LulzSec: X-factor, Fox, and the FBI. Available at: http://antivirus.about.com/b/2011/05/13/lulzsec-x-factor-fox-and-the-fbi.htm; May 13, 2011.
4. Don. LulzSec Hacks. *KnowYourMeme*. Available at: http://knowyourmeme.com/memes/events/lulzsec-hacks; May 2011.
5. Liebowitz M. Hackers leak Fox.com employee info. NBC News Security. Available at: http://www.nbcnews.com/id/43027482/ns/technology_and_science-security/#.URWNwqX7JjY; May 13, 2011.
6. Mack E. Lulzsec: a short history of hacking. *PC World*. Available at: http://www.pcworld.com/article/231215/lulzsec_a_short_history_of_hacking.html; June 27, 2011.
7. Liebowitz M. Hackers leak Fox.com employee info. *NBC News Security*. Available at: http://www.nbcnews.com/id/43027482/ns/technology_and_science-security/#.URWNwqX7JjY; May 13, 2011.
8. Landesman M. LulzSec: X-factor, Fox, and the FBI. Available at: http://antivirus.about.com/b/2011/05/13/lulzsec-x-factor-fox-and-the-fbi.htm; May 13, 2011.
9. Farrah K. Hacker Group LulzSec Signals Break Up. *Silicon Angle*. Available at: http://siliconangle.com/blog/2011/06/27/hacker-group-lulzsec-signals-break-up/; June 27, 2011.
10. Cramer D. The rise of LulzSec: a hacking chronology. *mybroadband*. Available at: http://mybroadband.co.za/news/security/29706-the-rise-of-lulzsec-a-hacking-chronology.html; July 21, 2011.
11. Attrition.org. Absolute Sownage—a concise history of recent Sony hacks. Available at: http://attrition.org/security/rants/sony_aka_sownage.html; June 4, 2011.

12. Kumar M. LulzSec Leak Sony's Japanese website database. *The Hacker News*. Available at: http://thehackernews.com/2011/05/lulzsec-leak-sonys-japanese-websites.html; May 23, 2011.
13. Wisniewski C. Sony Music Japan hacked through SQL injection flaw. *Naked Security*. Available at: http://nakedsecurity.sophos.com/2011/05/24/sony-music-japan-hacked-through-sql-injection-flaw/; May 24, 2011.
14. Stuart K. Why are LulzSec and Anonymous hacking games companies? *The Guardian*. Available at: http://www.guardian.co.uk/technology/2011/jun/16/lulzsec-anonymous-hacking-games-companies; June 16, 2011.
15. Attrition.org. Absolute Sownage—a concise history of recent Sony hacks. Available at: http://attrition.org/security/rants/sony_aka_sownage.html; June 4, 2011.
16. Kumar M. LulzSec Leak Sony's Japanese website database. *The Hacker News*. Available at: http://thehackernews.com/2011/05/lulzsec-leak-sonys-japanese-websites.html; May 23, 2011.
17. Wisniewski C. Sony Music Japan hacked through SQL injection flaw. *Naked Security*. Available at: http://nakedsecurity.sophos.com/2011/05/24/sony-music-japan-hacked-through-sql-injection-flaw/; May 24, 2011.
18. Mack E. Lulzsec: a short history of hacking. *PC World*. Available at: http://www.pcworld.com/article/231215/lulzsec_a_short_history_of_hacking.html; June 27, 2011.
19. Paul I. Hackers Deface PBS Site, Promise More Lulz. *PC World*. Available at: http://www.pcworld.com/article/228983/hackers_deface_pbs_site_promise_more_lulz.html?tk=rel_news; May 30, 2011.
20. Paul I. Hackers Deface PBS Site, Promise More Lulz. *PC World*. Available at: http://www.pcworld.com/article/228983/hackers_deface_pbs_site_promise_more_lulz.html?tk=rel_news; May 30, 2011.
21. Attrition.org. Absolute Sownage—a concise history of recent Sony hacks. Available at: http://attrition.org/security/rants/sony_aka_sownage.html; June 4, 2011.
22. Stuart K. Why are LulzSec and Anonymous hacking games companies? *The Guardian*. Available at: http://www.guardian.co.uk/technology/2011/jun/16/lulzsec-anonymous-hacking-games-companies; June 16, 2011.
23. Attrition.org. Absolute Sownage—a concise history of recent Sony hacks. Available at: http://attrition.org/security/rants/sony_aka_sownage.html; June 4, 2011.
24. Wisniewski C. Sony Pictures hacked again, 4.5 million records exposed. *Naked Security*. Available at: http://nakedsecurity.sophos.com/2011/06/02/sony-pictures-attacked-again-4-5-million-records-exposed/; June 2, 2011.
25. Mack E. Lulzsec: a short history of hacking. *PC World*. Available at: http://www.pcworld.com/article/231215/lulzsec_a_short_history_of_hacking.html; June 27, 2011.
26. Mediati N. LulzSec Hacks SonyPictures.com; 1 million accounts exposed. *PC World*. Available at: http://www.pcworld.com/article/229308/lulzsec_sacks_sonypictures.html; June 2, 2011.
27. Biddle S. Hackers spill over 1,000,000 Sony pictures online accounts. *Gizmodo*. Available at: http://gizmodo.com/5807996/hackers-spill-over-1000000-sony-online-accounts; June 2, 2011.
28. Mills E. Alleged LulzSec, Anonymous hackers arrested in Ariz., Calif. *CNet*. Available at: http://news.cnet.com/8301-27080_3-20110264-245/alleged-lulzsec-anonymous-hackers-arrested-in-ariz-calif/; September 22, 2011.
29. Stuart K. Why are LulzSec and Anonymous hacking games companies? *The Guardian*. Available at: http://www.guardian.co.uk/technology/2011/jun/16/lulzsec-anonymous-hacking-games-companies; June 16, 2011.
30. Mediati N. LulzSec hacks SonyPictures.com; 1 million accounts exposed. *PC World*. Available at: http://www.pcworld.com/article/229308/lulzsec_sacks_sonypictures.html; June 2, 2011.
31. Biddle S. Hackers spill over 1,000,000 Sony pictures online accounts. *Gizmodo*. Available at: http://gizmodo.com/5807996/hackers-spill-over-1000000-sony-online-accounts; June 2, 2011.
32. Ars Technica. Lulz? Sony hackers deny responsibility for misuse of leaked data. Available at: http://arstechnica.com/tech-policy/2011/06/lulz-sony-hackers-deny-responsibility-for-misuse-of-leaked-data/; June 3, 2011.
33. Attrition.org. Absolute Sownage—a concise history of recent Sony hacks. Available at: http://attrition.org/security/rants/sony_aka_sownage.html; June 4, 2011.
34. Stuart K. Why are LulzSec and Anonymous hacking games companies? *The Guardian*. Available at: http://www.guardian.co.uk/technology/2011/jun/16/lulzsec-anonymous-hacking-games-companies; June 16, 2011.
35. Dotson K. LulzSec Hacks Nintendo with gentle pat on the head and candy. *Silicon Angle*. Available at: http://siliconangle.com/blog/2011/06/06/lulzsec-hacks-nintendo-with-gentle-pat-on-the-head-and-candy/; June 6, 2011.
36. The Lulz Boat. Twitter "tweet". Available at: https://twitter.com/LulzSec/status/76783069939511296; June 3, 2011.
37. Dotson K. LulzSec Hacks Nintendo with gentle pat on the head and candy. *Silicon Angle*. Available at: http://siliconangle.com/blog/2011/06/06/lulzsec-hacks-nintendo-with-gentle-pat-on-the-head-and-candy/; June 6, 2011.

38. Wisniewski C. Infraguard Atlanta, an FBI affiliate, hacked by LulzSec. *Naked Security*. Available at: http://nakedsecurity.sophos.com/2011/06/04/infragard-atlanta-an-fbi-affiliate-hacked-by-lulzsec/; June 4, 2011.

39. Ribeiro J. LulzSec claims it hacked FBI linked organization. *PC World*. Available at: http://www.pcworld.com/article/229430/article.html; June 5, 2011.

40. Gorman S, Julian EB. Cyber Combat: Act of War. *Wall Street Journal*. Available at: http://online.wsj.com/article/SB10001424052702304563104576355623135782718.html; May 30, 2011.

41. Bartz D, David M. Hackers might face stiffer sentences in U.S. *Reuters* Available at: http://www.reuters.com/article/2011/06/18/us-usa-cybersecurity-sentences-idUSTRE75H0ZM20110618; June 18, 2011.

42. Mick, J. Updated: LulzSec's strikes latest victim—Hacker Mag. 2600, FBI affiliate *Daily Tech*. Available at: http://www.dailytech.com/Updated+LulzSecs+Strikes+Latest+Victims++Hacker+Mag+2600+FBI+Affiliate/article21818.htm; June 4, 2011.

43. Mick J. Updated: LulzSec's strikes latest victim—Hacker Mag. 2600, FBI affiliate. *Daily Tech*. Available at: http://www.dailytech.com/Updated+LulzSecs+Strikes+Latest+Victims++Hacker+Mag+2600+FBI+Affiliate/article21818.htm; June 4, 2011.

44. Oswald E. Sony gets hacked again and again, pilfered data released. *PC World*. Available at: http://www.pcworld.com/article/229520/sony_gets_hacked_again_and_again_pilfered_data_released.html?tk=rel_news; June 6, 2011.

45. Olson P. LulzSec hackers post Sony Dev. Source Code, Ge $7K Donation. *Forbes*. Available at: http://www.forbes.com/sites/parmyolson/2011/06/06/lulzsec-hackers-posts-sony-dev-source-code-get-7k-donation/; June 4, 2011.

46. Stuart K. Why are LulzSec and Anonymous hacking games companies? *The Guardian*. Available at: http://www.guardian.co.uk/technology/2011/jun/16/lulzsec-anonymous-hacking-games-companies; June 16, 2011.

47. Shan R. LulzSec hacker arrested, group leaks Sony database. *The Epoch Times*. Available at: http://www.theepochtimes.com/n2/technology/lulzsec-member-arrested-group-leaks-sony-database-57296.html; July 2, 2011.

48. Bray, C. FBI's Sabu' hacker was a model informant. *Wall Street Journal*. Available at: http://online.wsj.com/article/SB10001424052970204603004577269844134620160.html; March 9, 2012.

49. Bright P. Doxed: how Sabu was outed by former Anons long before his arrest. *Ars Technica*. Available at: http://arstechnica.com/tech-policy/2012/03/doxed-how-sabu-was-outed-by-former-anons-long-before-his-arrest/; March 2, 2012.

50. Uncovered. The Sabu Connection. Available at: http://ceaxx.wordpress.com/uncovered/; Aug. 17, 2011.

51. Chen A. I m Not Scared of Jail: My Phone Call With Sabu, the FBI's Anonymous Informant. *Gawker* Available at: http://gawker.com/hector-monsegur/; March 6, 2012.

52. FBI New York Field Office. Six hackers in the United States and Abroad charged for crimes affecting over one million victims. Available at: http://www.fbi.gov/newyork/press-releases/2012/six-hackers-in-the-united-states-and-abroad-charged-for-crimes-affecting-over-one-million-victims; March 6, 2012.

53. Mills E. Will LulzSec arrests stop high-profile hacks? Don't bet on it. *CNet*. Available at: http://news.cnet.com/8301-27080_3-57391872-245/will-lulzsec-arrests-stop-high-profile-hacks-dont-bet-on-it/; March 6, 2012.

54. Podolak E. LulzSec hacks security firm Black & Berg, Turns Down $10,000 Prize. *GeekoSystem*. Available at: http://www.geekosystem.com/lulzsec-black-berg-hack/; June 8, 2011.

55. Mills E. Will LulzSec arrests stop high-profile hacks? Don't bet on it. *CNet*. Available at: http://news.cnet.com/8301-27080_3-57391872-245/will-lulzsec-arrests-stop-high-profile-hacks-dont-bet-on-it/; March 6, 2012.

56. Solomon K. LulzSec reveals NHS web security holes. *TechRadar*. Available at: http://www.techradar.com/us/news/internet/lulzsec-reveals-nhs-web-security-holes-964323; June 10, 2011.

57. BBC News Technology. Hackers warn NHS over security. Available at: http://www.bbc.co.uk/news/technology-13712377; June 9, 2011.

58. Mills E. Will LulzSec arrests stop high-profile hacks? Don't bet on it. *CNet*. Available at: http://news.cnet.com/8301-27080_3-57391872-245/will-lulzsec-arrests-stop-high-profile-hacks-dont-bet-on-it/; March 6, 2012.

59. Solomon K. LulzSec reveals NHS web security holes. *TechRadar*. Available at: http://www.techradar.com/us/news/internet/lulzsec-reveals-nhs-web-security-holes-964323; June 10, 2011.

60. BBC News Technology. Hackers warn NHS over security. Available at: http://www.bbc.co.uk/news/technology-13712377; June 9, 2011.

61. Cluley G. 26,000 sex website passwords exposed by LulzSec. *Naked Security*. Available at: http://nakedsecurity.sophos.com/2011/06/12/26000-sex-website-usernames-and-passwords-exposed-by-lulzsec/; June 12, 2011.

62. Mack E. Lulzsec: a short history of hacking. *PC World*. Available at: http://www.pcworld.com/article/231215/lulzsec_a_short_history_of_hacking.html; June 27, 2011.

63. Mack E. Lulzsec: a short history of hacking. *PC World*. Available at: http://www.pcworld.com/article/231215/lulzsec_a_short_history_of_hacking.html; June 27, 2011.

64. Mack E. Lulzsec: a short history of hacking. *PC World*. Available at: http://www.pcworld.com/article/231215/lulzsec_a_short_history_of_hacking.html; June 27, 2011.

65. McMillan R. Lulzsec sets sights on U.S. Senate and Game-maker Bethesda. *PC World*. Available at: http://www.pcworld.com/article/230235/article.html; June 13, 2011.

66. Stuart K. Why are LulzSec and Anonymous hacking games companies? *The Guardian*. Available at: http://www.guardian.co.uk/technology/2011/jun/16/lulzsec-anonymous-hacking-games-companies; June 16, 2011.

67. Administrator. Eve Online, Minecraft, Finfisher, & Escaptist Magazine—all hacked by LulzSec. *InfoSecWreck*. Available at: http://www.infosecwreck.com/eve-online-minecraft-finfisher-escaptist-magazine-all-hacked-by-lulzsec; June 14, 2011.

68. Gilbert D. LulzSec takes down CIA website—calls for requests. *Trusted Review*. Available at: http://www.trustedreviews.com/news/lulzsec-take-down-cia-website-call-for-requests; June 16, 2011.

69. Stuart K. Why are LulzSec and Anonymous hacking games companies? *The Guardian*. Available at: http://www.guardian.co.uk/technology/2011/jun/16/lulzsec-anonymous-hacking-games-companies; June 16, 2011.

70. Administrator. Eve Online, Minecraft, Finfisher, & Escaptist Magazine—all hacked by LulzSec, *InfoSecWreck*. Available at: http://www.infosecwreck.com/eve-online-minecraft-finfisher-escaptist-magazine-all-hacked-by-lulzsec; June 14, 2011.

71. Gilbert D. LulzSec takes down CIA website—calls for requests. *Trusted Review*. Available at: http://www.trustedreviews.com/news/lulzsec-take-down-cia-website-call-for-requests; June 16, 2011.

72. BBC News Technology. LulzSec opens hack request line. Available at: http://www.bbc.co.uk/news/technology-13777129; June 15, 2011.

73. Newman J. LulzSec hacks Arizona State Police, Posts Officer Info. *PC World*. Available at: http://www.pcworld.com/article/231156/lulzsec_hacks_arizona_state_police.html; June 24, 2011.

74. Gilbert D. LulzSec takes down CIA website—calls for requests. *Trusted Review*. Available at: http://www.trustedreviews.com/news/lulzsec-take-down-cia-website-call-for-requests; June 16, 2011.

75. Batty D. LulzSec hackers claim breach of CIA website. *The Guardian*. Available at: http://www.guardian.co.uk/technology/2011/jun/16/cia-website-lulzsec-hackers; June 15, 2011.

76. Newman J. LulzSec hacks Arizona State Police, Posts Officer Info. *PC World*. Available at: http://www.pcworld.com/article/231156/lulzsec_hacks_arizona_state_police.html; June 24, 2011.

77. Levinson M. Anonymous, LulzSec, AntiSec, etc.: a brief history of hacktivism. *CIO*. Available at: http://www.cio.com/slideshow/detail/24995#slide13; Jan. 6, 2012.

78. Levinson M. Anonymous, LulzSec, AntiSec, etc.: a brief history of hacktivism. *CIO*. Available at: http://www.cio.com/slideshow/detail/24995#slide13; Jan. 6, 2012.

79. Mills E. LulzSec, Anonymous announce hacking campaign. *CNet*. Available at: http://news.cnet.com/8301-27080_3-20072675-245/lulzsec-anonymous-announce-hacking-campaign/; June 20, 2011.

80. Kumar M. 50 days of Lulz—LulzSec says goodbye & operation AntiSec will continue. *The Hacker News*. Available at: http://thehackernews.com/2011/06/50-days-of-lulz-lulzsec-says-goodbye.html; June 25, 2011.

81. Mills E. LulzSec, Anonymous announce hacking campaign. *CNet*. Available at: http://news.cnet.com/8301-27080_3-20072675-245/lulzsec-anonymous-announce-hacking-campaign/; June 20, 2011.

82. Kumar M. 50 days of Lulz—LulzSec says goodbye & operation AntiSec will continue. *The Hacker News*. Available at: http://thehackernews.com/2011/06/50-days-of-lulz-lulzsec-says-goodbye.html; June 25, 2011.

83. Keizer G. LulzSec launches anti-government crusade, takes down U.K. Police Site,. *PC World*. Available at: http://www.pcworld.com/article/230760/LulzSec_launches_anti_government_crusade_takes_down_UK_police_site.html; June 20, 2011.

84. BBC News Technology. Soca website taken down after LulzSec 'DDoS attack'. Available at: http://www.bbc.co.uk/news/technology-13848510; June 20, 2011.

85. Keizer G. LulzSec launches anti-government crusade, takes down U.K. Police Site. *PC World*. Available at: http://www.pcworld.com/article/230760/LulzSec_launches_anti_government_crusade_takes_down_UK_police_site.html; June 20, 2011.

86. BBC News Technology. Teenager arrested on suspicion of hacking. Available at: http://www.bbc.co.uk/news/technology-13859868; June 21, 2011.

87. The Telegraph. LulzSec's Ryan Cleary admits to hacking into CIA and the Pentagon. Available at: http://www.telegraph.co.uk/technology/news/9354188/LulzSecs-Ryan-Cleary-admits-hacking-into-CIA-and-the-Pentagon.html; June 25, 2012.

88. Rapoza K. LulzSec strikes Brazil again; Petrobras denies being hacked. *Forbes*. Available at: http://www.forbes.com/sites/kenrapoza/2011/06/25/lulzsec-strikes-brazil-again-petrobras-denies-being-hacked/; June 25, 2011.

89. McMillan R. Brazilian government, energy company latest LulzSec victim. *Network World*. Available at: http://www.networkworld.com/news/2011/062211-brazilian-government-energy-company-latest.html; June 22, 2011.

90. Rapoza K. LulzSec strikes Brazil again; Petrobras denies being hacked. *Forbes*. Available at: http://www.forbes.com/sites/kenrapoza/2011/06/25/lulzsec-strikes-brazil-again-petrobras-denies-being-hacked/; June 25, 2011.

91. McMillan R. Brazilian government, energy company latest LulzSec victim. *Network World*. Available at: http://www.networkworld.com/news/2011/062211-brazilian-government-energy-company-latest.html; June 22, 2011.

92. Newman J. LulzSec hacks Arizona State Police, Posts Officer Info. *PC World*. Available at: http://www.pcworld.com/article/231156/lulzsec_hacks_arizona_state_police.html; June 24, 2011.

93. Newman J. LulzSec hacks Arizona State Police, Posts Officer Info. *PC World*. Available at: http://www.pcworld.com/article/231156/lulzsec_hacks_arizona_state_police.html; June 24, 2011.

94. Mack E. Lulzsec: a short history of hacking. *PC World*. Available at: http://www.pcworld.com/article/231215/lulzsec_a_short_history_of_hacking.html; June 27, 2011.

95. Kumar M. 50 days of Lulz—LulzSec says goodbye & operation AntiSec will continue. *The Hacker News*. Available at: http://thehackernews.com/2011/06/50-days-of-lulz-lulzsec-says-goodbye.html; June 25, 2011.

96. A Guest. 50 days of Lulz. *Pastebin*. Available at: http://pastebin.com/1znEGmHa; June 25, 2011.

97. A Guest. AOL internal data, *Pastebin*. Available at: http://pastebin.com/08zJHQeA; June 25, 2011.

98. A Guest. FBI Being Silly. *Pastebin*. Available at: http://pastebin.com/hCnvTy0z; June 25, 2011.

99. A Guest. Silly routers. *Pastebin*. Available at: http://pastebin.com/ennsYDM5; June 25, 2011.

100. Ragan S. As LulzSec sails into Anonymous seas—AntiSec lives on. *The Tech Herald*. Available at: http://www.thetechherald.com/articles/As-LulzSec-sails-into-Anonymous-seas-AntiSec-lives-on/13903/; June 27, 2011.

101. Kumar M. 50 days of Lulz—LulzSec says goodbye & operation AntiSec will continue. *The Hacker News*. Available at: http://thehackernews.com/2011/06/50-days-of-lulz-lulzsec-says-goodbye.html; June 25, 2011.

102. A Guest. 50 days of Lulz. *Pastebin*. Available at: http://pastebin.com/1znEGmHa; June 25, 2011.

103. Ragan S. As LulzSec sails into Anonymous seas—AntiSec lives on. *The Tech Herald*. Available at: http://www.thetechherald.com/articles/As-LulzSec-sails-into-Anonymous-seas-AntiSec-lives-on/13903/; June 27, 2011.

104. Mills E. Will LulzSec arrests stop high-profile hacks? Don't bet on it. *CNet*. Available at: http://news.cnet.com/8301-27080_3-57391872-245/will-lulzsec-arrests-stop-high-profile-hacks-dont-bet-on-it/; March 6, 2012.

105. Dignan L. Hackers target Apple server. *CNet*. Available at: http://news.cnet.com/8301-1009_3-20076688-83/hackers-target-apple-server/; July 4, 2011.

106. Dignan L. Hackers target Apple server. *CNet*. Available at: http://news.cnet.com/8301-1009_3-20076688-83/hackers-target-apple-server/; July 4, 2011.

107. Levinson M. Anonymous, LulzSec, AntiSec, etc.: a brief history of hacktivism. *CIO*. Available at: http://www.cio.com/slideshow/detail/24995#slide15; Jan. 6, 2012.

108. Mills E. Will LulzSec arrests stop high-profile hacks? Don't bet on it. *CNet*. Available at: http://news.cnet.com/8301-27080_3-57391872-245/will-lulzsec-arrests-stop-high-profile-hacks-dont-bet-on-it/; March 6, 2012.

109. Zetter K. Feds arrest 14 'Anonymous' suspects over PayPal attack, raid dozens more. *Wired*. Available at: http://www.wired.com/threatlevel/2011/07/paypal-hack-arrests/; July 19, 2011.

110. Zetter K. Feds arrest 14 'Anonymous' suspects over PayPal attack, raid dozens more. *Wired*. Available at: http://www.wired.com/threatlevel/2011/07/paypal-hack-arrests/; July 19, 2011.

111. Mills E. FBI arrests 16 in Anonymous hacking investigation. *CNeT*. Available at: http://news.cnet.com/8301-27080_3-20080746-245/fbi-arrests-16-in-anonymous-hacking-investigation/; July 19, 2011.

112. Meyer D. News International sites taken down in LulzSec attack. *ZDNet.* Available at: http://www.zdnet.com/news-international-sites-taken-down-in-lulzsec-attack-3040093444/; July 19, 2011.

113. Mills E. Will LulzSec arrests stop high-profile hacks? Don't bet on it. *CNet.* Available at: http://news.cnet.com/8301-27080_3-57391872-245/will-lulzsec-arrests-stop-high-profile-hacks-dont-bet-on-it/; March 6, 2012.

114. The Telegraph. LulzSec's Ryan Cleary admits hacking into CIA and the Pentagon. Available at: http://www.telegraph.co.uk/technology/news/9354188/LulzSecs-Ryan-Cleary-admits-hacking-into-CIA-and-the-Pentagon.html; June 25, 2012.

115. The Telegraph. LulzSec's Ryan Cleary admits hacking into CIA and the Pentagon. Available at: http://www.telegraph.co.uk/technology/news/9354188/LulzSecs-Ryan-Cleary-admits-hacking-into-CIA-and-the-Pentagon.html; June 25, 2012.

116. Bright P. Doxed: how Sabu was outed by former Anons long before his arrest. *Ars Technica.* Available at: http://arstechnica.com/tech-policy/2012/03/doxed-how-sabu-was-outed-by-former-anons-long-before-his-arrest/; March 2, 2012.

117. Uncovered. The Sabu Connection. Available at: http://ceaxx.wordpress.com/uncovered/; August 17, 2011.

118. Chen A. 'I'm Not Scared of Jail': my phone call with Sabu, the FBI's Anonymous Informant. *Gawker.* Available at: http://gawker.com/hector-monsegur/; March 6, 2012.

119. Voice. #FFF IV: Vanguard Defense. *Pastebin.* Available at: http://pastebin.com/PjiXmwNk; August 18, 2011.

120. Skillings J. AntiSec hackers target Vanguard Defense exec. *CNet.* Available at: http://news.cnet.com/8301-1009_3-20094621-83/antisec-hackers-target-vanguard-defense-exec/; August 19, 2011.

121. Skillings J. AntiSec hackers target Vanguard Defense exec. *CNet.* Available at: http://news.cnet.com/8301-1009_3-20094621-83/antisec-hackers-target-vanguard-defense-exec/; August 19, 2011.

122. Mills E. Alleged LulzSec, Anonymous hackers arrested in Ariz., Calif. *CNet.* Available at: http://news.cnet.com/8301-27080_3-20110264-245/alleged-lulzsec-anonymous-hackers-arrested-in-ariz-calif/; September 22, 2011.

123. Zetter K. FBI arrests U.S. suspects in LulzSec Sony Hack; Anonymous also targeted. *Wired.* Available at: http://www.wired.com/threatlevel/2011/09/sony-hack-arrest/; Sept. 22, 2011.

124. Mills E. Alleged LulzSec, Anonymous hackers arrested in Ariz., Calif. *CNet.* Available at: http://news.cnet.com/8301-27080_3-20110264-245/alleged-lulzsec-anonymous-hackers-arrested-in-ariz-calif/; September 22, 2011.

125. Zetter K. FBI arrests U.S. suspects in LulzSec Sony Hack; Anonymous also targeted. *Wired.* Available at: http://www.wired.com/threatlevel/2011/09/sony-hack-arrest/; September 22, 2011.

126. Mills E. Alleged LulzSec, Anonymous hackers arrested in Ariz., Calif. *CNet.* Available at: http://news.cnet.com/8301-27080_3-20110264-245/alleged-lulzsec-anonymous-hackers-arrested-in-ariz-calif/; September 22, 2011.

127. Anderson N. Anon on the run: how Commander X jumped bail and fled to Canada. *Ars Technica.* Available at: http://arstechnica.com/tech-policy/2012/12/anon-on-the-run-how-commander-x-jumped-bai/; December 11, 2012.

128. Solyom C. Insider tells why Anonymous 'might well be the most powerful organization on Earth. *National Post.* Available at: http://news.nationalpost.com/2012/05/12/insider-tells-why-anonymous-might-well-be-the-most-powerful-organization-on-earth/; May 13, 2012.

129. Mills E. Alleged LulzSec, Anonymous hackers arrested in Ariz., Calif. *CNet.* Available at: http://news.cnet.com/8301-27080_3-20110264-245/alleged-lulzsec-anonymous-hackers-arrested-in-ariz-calif/; September 22, 2011.

130. Anderson N. Anon on the run: how Commander X jumped bail and fled to Canada. *Ars Technica.* Available at: http://arstechnica.com/tech-policy/2012/12/anon-on-the-run-how-commander-x-jumped-bai/; December 11, 2012.

131. Solyom C. Insider tells why Anonymous 'might well be the most powerful organization on Earth. *National Post.* Available at: http://news.nationalpost.com/2012/05/12/insider-tells-why-anonymous-might-well-be-the-most-powerful-organization-on-earth/; May 13, 2012.

132. A Guest. #FuckFBIFriday official #antisec release text. *Pastebin.* Available at: http://pastebin.com/NwN8ehFW; November 18, 2011.

133. Levinson M. Anonymous, LulzSec, AntiSec, etc.: a brief history of hacktivism. *CIO.* Available at: http://www.cio.com/slideshow/detail/24995#slide19; January 6, 2012.

134. A Guest. #FuckFBIFriday official #antisec release text. *Pastebin.* Available at: http://pastebin.com/NwN8ehFW; November 18, 2011.

135. Michael S. LulzSec: Anonymous hacktivists strike Portugal after police brutality. *Examiner.* Available at: http://www.examiner.com/article/lulzsec-anonymous-hacktivists-strike-portugal-after-police-brutality; December 3, 2011.

136. Levinson M. Anonymous, LulzSec, AntiSec, etc.: a brief history of hacktivism. *CIO*. Available at: http://www.cio.com/slideshow/detail/24995#slide21; January 6, 2012.

137. Exphin1ty. Exphin1ty—CLEARUSA.org Leak. *Pastebin*. Available at: http://pastebin.com/HkP55NWC; December 11, 2011.

138. Levinson M. Anonymous, LulzSec, AntiSec, etc.: a brief history of hacktivism. *CIO*. Available at: http://www.cio.com/slideshow/detail/24995#slide23; January 6, 2012.

139. Perlroth N. Inside the Stratfor attack. *The New York Times Bits*. Available at: http://bits.blogs.nytimes.com/2012/03/12/inside-the-stratfor-attack/; March 12, 2012.

140. Levinson M. Anonymous, LulzSec, AntiSec, etc.: a brief history of hacktivism. *CIO*. Available at: http://www.cio.com/slideshow/detail/24995#slide23; January 6, 2012.

141. Durden T. Stratfor Hacked, 200 GB of emails, credit cards stolen, client list released, includes MF Global, Rockefeller Foundation. *fwe*. Available at: http://www.zerohedge.com/news/stratfor-hacked-200gb-emails-credit-cards-stolen-client-list-released-includes-mf-global-rockef; December 24, 2011.

142. BarrettBrown. On Stratfor. *Pastebin*. Available at: http://pastebin.com/WPE73rhy; December 26, 2011.

143. Perlroth N. Inside the Stratfor Attack. *The New York Times Bits*. Available at: http://bits.blogs.nytimes.com/2012/03/12/inside-the-stratfor-attack/; March 12, 2012.

144. Sengupta S. Arrests sow mistrust inside a clan of hackers. *New York Times*. Available at: http://www.nytimes.com/2012/03/07/technology/lulzsec-hacking-suspects-are-arrested.html?_r=2&hp&; March 6, 2012.

145. LaMonica M. Anonymous: we snooped an FBI cybercrime call. *CNet*. Available at: http://news.cnet.com/8301-1009_3-57371146-83/anonymous-we-snooped-an-fbi-cybercrime-call/; February 3, 2012.

146. Sengupta S. Arrests sow mistrust inside a clan of hackers. *New York Times*. Available at: http://www.nytimes.com/2012/03/07/technology/lulzsec-hacking-suspects-are-arrested.html?_r=2&hp&; March 6, 2012.

147. FBI New York Field Office. Six hackers in the United States and abroad charged for crimes affecting over one million victims. Available at: http://www.fbi.gov/newyork/press-releases/2012/six-hackers-in-the-united-states-and-abroad-charged-for-crimes-affecting-over-one-million-victims; March 6, 2012.

148. Mills E. U.K. police say they've arrested LulzSec's 'Topiary'. *CNet*. Available at: http://news.cnet.com/8301-27080_3-20084255-245/u.k-police-say-theyve-arrested-lulzsecs-topiary/; July 27, 2012.

149. A Guest. *#LulzSecReborn*. *Pastebin*. Available at: http://pastebin.com/JRY3cA5T; March 25, 2012.

150. Liebowitz M. 'LulzSec Reborn' hacks military dating site. *Tech News Daily*. Available at: http://www.technewsdaily.com/7636-lulzsec-reborn-military-singles.html; March 27, 2012.

151. Sottek TC. LulzSec claims hack of Military Singles dating website, dumps over 170,000 account details. *The Verge*. Available at: http://www.theverge.com/2012/3/26/2904641/lulzsec-reborn-with-military-singles-hack; March 26, 2012.

152. A Guest. #LulzSecReborn. *Pastebin*. Available at: http://pastebin.com/JRY3cA5T; March 25, 2012.

153. Liebowitz M. 'LulzSec Reborn' hacks military dating site. *Tech News Daily*. Available at: http://www.technewsdaily.com/7636-lulzsec-reborn-military-singles.html; March 27, 2012.

154. Sottek TC. LulzSec claims hack of Military Singles dating website, dumps over 170,000 account details. *The Verge*. Available at: http://www.theverge.com/2012/3/26/2904641/lulzsec-reborn-with-military-singles-hack; March 26, 2012.

155. Kovacs E. LulzSec Ecuador hacks military and government websites. *softpedia*. Available at: http://news.softpedia.com/news/LulzSec-Ecuador-Hacks-Military-and-Government-Websites-304823.shtml; November 6, 2012.

156. Kovacs E. LulzSec Ecuador hacks military and government websites. *softpedia*. Available at: http://news.softpedia.com/news/LulzSec-Ecuador-Hacks-Military-and-Government-Websites-304823.shtml; November 6, 2012.

II

Chapter 6: Anonymous Timeline

Following are examples of hacktivities blamed on and/or claimed and by respected Anonymous' publicity outlets and/or spokespersons and/or at least one of its different affiliates. Due to the nature of the pursued activity, it is not feasible to present a complete timeline of hacks executed by Anonymous. Understandably in the beginning when Anonymous was not yet as popular, accounts of their activities were comparatively sparse, increasingly gaining media attention with extremely high coverage even of failed hacks, and may at some point in the future fall out of the news' "fashion" will likely return to the occasional media coverage (if at all). The list of hacks as shown below was compiled using open source media only and therefore of course reflects individual stages of this cycle. In addition, the kind of activity pursued by many individuals in the name of Anonymous allows a multitude of hacks in a 24-hour period, especially considering the global scope and spread of the movement. In order to provide further insight into the movement when available, we provided information on the ideological motivation as stated by one or more of the cited outlets for the respective hack. If nothing else a glance at the list will reveal the collective's evolution from the trolling horde of image boards, whose main interest lies in annoying other Internet users or interfering with peoples' offline lives—apparently without any moral restraint and guidance to a congregation of political activists. Anonymous has nothing but a likening in the name in common with its roots. Trolls (e.g., 4chan/b-tards or fags) decry the online, meanwhile globally spread collective "Moralfags" because under the banner of Anonymous hackers agree and adhere to moral standards. It appears that the protest against the Church of Scientology, Project Chanology, forms a turning point. The huge turnout of real-world protesters and of prank callers might have been a wake-up call for those participants, who associated a moral duty with the campaign. Increasingly the motives became more political in nature. Increasingly the hacks were picked up and reported about in the media. After two years of insurmountable numbers of hacks in the name of political activism, Anonymous has become an institution—a house, in which anybody disgruntled or idealist enough to take action can reside (Internet-access-world-wide):

Approximate date	Target, hacktivity, and modus operandi (where available)	Motivation as stated (where available)
2006	*Habbo* Hotel Raid—online game (repeatedly) invaded by uniform avatars blocking the entrance to the hotel's pool with undertones pertaining or addressing racism (*Habbo* did not provide African-American avatars, banned users with that avatar, avatars formed swastika like patterns)[1]	Bored Anons seeking to annoy other Internet users[2]
2006-2007	4chan/b/-tards/fags pick up news about the suicide of a seventh-grader and mock that his motivation was the loss of his iPod (a message he had posted on his MySpace page), b-tards deface his MySpace page, post images of the dead with iPod as well as a YouTube clip of a re-enactment of his suicide, but also call the parents pretending to be the ghost of their son for over a year[3]	Lulz[4]
2006-2007	4chan/b/-tards/fags and Anonymous disrupt white supremacist online radio show by making prank phone calls blocking out calls of its constituency; Web site experiences DDoS attacks from b-tards, publication of personal data after encouraging his fans to retaliate as well as publishing personal details of prank callers[5]	Lulz/in protest of racist nature of radio show[6]
July 2007	A Fox News channel airs its investigation into "Anonymous"[7]	No statement of motivation found
Decmber 7, 2007	Chris Forcand is arrested on accounts of after Anons lure him on the Internet and alarm the police[8]	No statement of motivation found
January 21, 2008	Project Chanology is launched inspired by a YouTube video, in which actor Tom Cruise promotes Scientology; attacks included harassing phone calls, prank pizza deliveries, and black faxes as well as in-person protests in front of Scientology branches[9]	In protest of Scientology's retraction of the video, which are viewed as Internet censorship[10]
June 2008	Support Online Hip Hop (SOHH) experiences multiple DDoS-caused take-downs and defacement (cross-site scripting)[11]	Anons claimed responsibility justifying the attacks as reaction to insults made by members of SOHH's "Just Bugging Out" forum[12]
January 2009	Anons target administrator of the Web site, No Cussing Club, and use the personal information found to make harassing phone calls and play practical "jokes"[13]	No Cussing Sucks—Campaign[14]
January 26, 2009	Video release declares growing public awareness and new technology that will put an end to conservative forces that depend on the exploitation and misinformation of the American public[15]	No statement of motivation found

Continued

Approximate date	Target, hacktivity, and modus operandi (where available)	Motivation as stated (where available)
June 2009	Anons team up with The Pirate Bay to support the Green Movement in Iran after suspicions arise that the recent Iranian election was rigged; the Web site launched informs about privacy maintenance on the Internet and how to launch cyber attacks (DDoS) on government Web sites, and the uploading of files despite government censorship as well as connects with other activists over Twitter[16]	Antigovernment protests flare up throughout the country in reaction to Mahmoud Ahmedinejad being declared the winner of the recent election; Iranian government filters the Internet and disrupt social networking sites, Twitter and Facebook due their role in the organization of the protests[17]
June 2009	Project Skynet launched to protect the Internet from censorship worldwide[18]	Project Skynet (quite possibly in reference to the fictional self-aware computer system featured in the movie series "Terminator")
September 9, 2009	#OpDidgeridie is launched in response to Australian government's plans to censor the Internet at ISP level[19]	#OpDidgeridie[20]
September 10, 2009	Web site of Australian Prime Minister, www.pm.gov.au, is briefly taken offline via DDoS attack[21,22]	#OpDidgeridie[23]
February 10, 2010	DDoS attacks compromise Web sites affiliated with the Australian government, e.g., the office of the Attorney General, the Department of Broadband, Communications, and the Digital Economy; the cyber attack was planned to be followed up by harassing phone calls, black faxes, and e-mails feat. The specific kinds of pornography (hence the name "OpTitstorm") the Australian government is censoring[24,25]	#OpTitstorm—in protest of the Australian government's initiative to filter the Internet[26]
From September 17, 2010	#OpPayback targets antipiracy groups, supporting lawyers and lobbyists; using the Anonymous-moniker hacktivists target ACS:Law, RIAA, Aiplex Software, the American MPAA, Sony,[27] IFPI as well as the British Phonographic Industry and others; across the globe denial-of-service attacks associated with OpPayback caused 550 h of downtime and 742 service interruptions in its first month[28–30]	Initially reaction to Sony's suing a hacker[31] and DDoS attacks on file-sharing Web sites turned protest against pro-copyright and antipiracy organizations, dubbed OpPayback[32,33]
October 6, 2010	Spanish Copyright Protection Society (SGAE), Spanish Culture Ministry, and Promusicae Web sites experience denial-of-service attacks causing 119 service interruptions and more than 68 h of downtime altogether[34,35]	OpPayback—perpetrating cyber activists seek to defend free P2P file sharing[36,37]
October 18, 2010	Two Web sites of Gene Simmons, bassist with rock band KISS, are target of distributed denial attacks[38]	OpPayback[39]
October 19, 2010	The Web site of ACAPOR, Associação do Comércio Audiovisual de Portugal, is hacked, and 640 MB of e-mail data is stolen and later published on The Pirate Bay[40]	OpPayback—the Association intended to block The Pirate Bay-Web site in Portugal[41]

Continued

Approximate date	Target, hacktivity, and modus operandi (where available)	Motivation as stated (where available)
From December 2, 2010 on	PayPal, SwissBank, Visa, and Mastercard Web sites are repeatedly taken offline with denial-of-service attacks[42,43]	OpPayback—companies ended their business relations with WikiLeaks after its publishing of U.S. diplomatic cables[44]
December 2, 2010	Attempt to collapse amazon.com failed[45,46]	OpPayback—amazon stops hosting WikiLeaks Web site[47,48]
Early December 2010	Facebook removes "Operation Payback" page[49,50]	Facebook states its policy to take action against unlawful activities and what it declares as sensitive content[51]
December 2010	Web sites of Joe Lieberman and Sarah Palin are targeted due to anti-WikiLeaks statements by the politicians[52]	OpPayback—Criticizism or impediment of WikiLeaks or Julian Assange is perceived as being contrary to freedom of information and speech[53]
December 2010	According to PandaLabs Anonymous' online headquarters for OpPayback suffers downtimes, albeit mostly of brief duration[54]	Perpetrators are thought to be anti-WikiLeaks hacktivists[55]
December 6, 2010	Operation Avenge Assange is launched and aims to aide WikiLeaks in publishing U.S. government cables[56]	#OpAvenge Assange[57]
December 8, 2010	Twitter and Facebook suspend Anonymous-affiliated accounts (@Anon_Operation) used to organize and report on #OpPayback[58,59]	#OpPayback[60]
December 9, 2010	Twitter suspends Anonymous account, Anon-Operation, which was used to organize cyber-operations; OpPayback and AnonOpsNet accounts opened[61]	No comment from Twitter[62]
December 9, 2010	Swedish government Web site targeted with DDOS attack[63]	#OpPayback[64]/#OpAvenge Assange
December 13, 2010	#OpLeakspin is launched with the call on every Internet user to help spread the secret U.S. cables Bradley Manning leaked to WikiLeaks[65,66]	#OpLeakspin, freedom of information[67,68]
December 28, 2010	4Chan becomes a victim of DDoS attacks and remains unavailable for more than 24 h,[69] and 4chan had experienced similar attacks in January and July 2010	Although the perpetrator(s) remain unknown, it is assumed that 4chan was targeted by anti-Anonymous/anti-WikiLeaks hacktivists[70]
December 30, 2010	Zimbabwean government Web sites targeted[71]	Zimbabwean's President's wife, Grace Mugabe, sues newspaper over WikiLeaks article, in which she was linked with illicit diamond trading (OpPayback), Government censorship (#AntiSec)[72,73]

Continued

Approximate date	Target, hacktivity, and modus operandi (where available)	Motivation as stated (where available)
January 2, 2011	DDoS attacks on Tunisian government affiliated Web sites (Tunisian stock exchange, Tunisian Ministry of Industry)[74]	#OpTunisia, in protest of Internet censorship as executed by Tunisian government of president Zine al-Abidine Ben Ali[75]
January 10, 2011	Irish party Fine Gael's Web site defaced[76]	Posted message criticized the party over its policies[77]
January 27, 2011	5 Britons (all between 15 and 26 years of age) arrested as alleged Anonymous hacktivists targeting Web sites of companies associated with anti-WikiLeaks actions[78]	#OpPayback[79]
January 27, 2011	Internet anonymizer Tor is used to circumvent the blockage of the Internet by the Egyptian government,[80] the French Data Network is also offering free dial-up connections for Egyptians[81]	No statement of motivation found
February 2, 2011	Egyptian government Web sites experience DDoS attacks[82]	Earlier in the day the Egyptian government reinstated Internet-connection to the country, which it had cut off earlier in an attempt to take the momentum out of the public protest[83] the organization of which made heavy use of social media[84]; the Internet blackout followed the momentary blocking of social media sites, Twitter, Google, and Facebook as well as Blackberry and SMS services[85]
February 6, 2011	HBGary computer security firm suffers intrusion, data theft, and publication,[86] as well as Web site defacement; another of Greg Hoglund's (owner HB Gary) Web sites, rootkit.com, DDoS-ed as well as data stolen and published[87]	Aaron Barr, CEO of HB Gary Federal, had claimed that he had identified core Anonymous leaders after infiltrating the movement[88]
February 6, 2011	Italian government's Web site (governo.it) is briefly taken offline by Anonymous Italy[89]	In protest of recent policies seen to curb media freedom[90]
February 17, 2011	OpBahrain is launched in sympathy with Bahrainian protesters against an non-transparent governance, the curbing of free speech and the right to protest, the censorship of the Internet[91]	#OpBahrain[92]
February 28, 2011	OpWisconsin targets billionaire Koch brothers, calls for boycott of Koch-produced items (Georgia-Pacific brand),[93,94] and takes down two Koch-supported Web sites (Americans for Prosperity, Northern Quilt)[95]	#OpWisconsin; Koch brothers are targeted for their anti-union sponsoring[96,97]
March 4, 2011	Operation Bradley is launched with Barrett Brown publically threatening to expose those involved in the Bradley Manning case[98]	Operation Bradley/Bradical[99]; news about Manning's treatment at Quantico Brig cause outrage[100]

Continued

Approximate date	Target, hacktivity, and modus operandi (where available)	Motivation as stated (where available)
April 2, 2011 and throughout April	Sony's PlayStation Network and various Sony Web sites experience repeated DDoS attacks and downtime[101]	In protest of Sony banning (and later suing) PS-user GeoHot for modifying his equipment and posting this know-how from the PlayStation Network[102]
April 20, 2011	Formula One Web site (Formula1.com) and F1-racers.net experience downtime due to DDoS attack[103]	#OpBahrain criticizes the organizers of Formula 1's Grnad Prix to ignore (and thus support) the human rights abuses of the Al Khalifa government; Anonymous demands release of political prisoners[104]
May 1, 2011	#OpIran launched[105]	#OpIran in protest of a repressive Iranian government[106]
May 2, 2011	#OpBlitzkrieg launched,[107] sets up information Web site, nazi-leaks.net (defunct), to reveal interconnections between various white supremacist organizations in many western countries, a year later mainly DDoS attacks against white supremacist and affiliates Web sites remain	#OpBlitzkrieg, in opposition to white supremacist-ideology[108]
May 3, 2011	Several Web sites pertaining to white supremacist organizations and affiliated Web host experience downtime[109]	#OpBlitzkrieg[110]
May 6, 2011	#OpIndia launched[111]	#OpIndia, in protest of the Indian government blocking The Pirate Bay, vimeo, DailyMotion Web sites,[112] later the government's general Internet censorship and corruption is added to the agenda[113]
May 18, 2011	Several Web sites affiliated with the Indian government (Supreme Court, two political parties (BJP, INC), Indian telecommunications department, Indian electronics, and IT ministry), the Web site of antipiracy company Copyrightlabs experience downtime due to DDoS attacks[114]	#OpIndia[115]
June 2011	#OpTurkey is launched to protest against controversial plans by the Turkish government to further Internet filtering[116]	#OpTurkey[117]
June 9, 2011	Real-world protest criticizing Indian law to enable the government to rightfully censor the Internet in New Delhi, Anonymous is urging Indians to file Right to Information (RTI) applications to seek insights into the governments filtering of information disseminated through the Internet[118]	#OpIndia, OpRTIEngaged[119]
June 11, 2011	10,365 e-mails are gleaned from servers of the Iranian Ministry of Foreign Affairs and subsequently published on MediaFire; the associated Web site experiences downtime[120]	#OpIran[121]

Continued

Approximate date	Target, hacktivity, and modus operandi (where available)	Motivation as stated (where available)
June 11, 2011	Web sites affiliated with the Malaysian government experience downtime due to DDoS attacks and/or are intruded for the purpose of data extraction and subsequent publication[122]: www.malaysia.gov.my—down www.sabahtourism.com—intruded, released www.cidb.gov.my/—intruded Land Public transport Commission (www.spad.gov.my)—suspected target of intrusion Malaysian Meteorological Service (www.kjc.gov.my)—suspected target of intrusion (www.aseanconnect.gov.my)—suspected target of intrusion Ministry of Education (www.moe.gov.my)—down Firefighters (Bomba), www.bomba.gov.my—down Election Commission (Suruhanjaya Pilihanraya Malaysia), www.daftarj.spr.gov.my—down Malaysian primary communication service (TMNet), www.tm.com.my—down Ministry of Works, www.kkr.gov.my—down Ministry of Finance, www.treasury.gov.my—down Malaysian Parliament, www.parlimen.gov.my—down Ministry of Information, Communications and Culture, www.kpkk.gov.my—down www.jobsmalaysia.gov.my—down[123]	#OpMalaysia in protest against Internet censorship as executed by the Malaysian government[124]
June 11, 2011	#OpEmpire State Rebellion launched aims to put an end to what it has declared to be the corruption and fraud committed by the Federal Reserve as well as to government lobbying and the power and extortion of global, "too-big-to-fail" banks[125,126]	#OpEmpire State Rebellion (ESR) to destroy organized, governmental structures enabling profiteering by large corporations and banks to the detriment of 99.9% of the American population[127,128]
June 20, 2011	#Operation Anti-Security (AntiSec) unifies part of LulzSecurity and Anons to expose corruption in governments, banks, and other high ranking institutions around the world; stated objectives are the gleaning and leaking of classified government information.[129] Among the first sites targeted belong to the FBI (not the first time (see LulzSec); repeatedly) and affiliated Web sites (Infraguards)[130,131]	#OpAntiSec[132]
June 23, 2011	#OpOrlando is launched and vows to take down one Orlando-related Web site each day, starting out with a tourism Web site (www.orlandofloridaguide.com), the Web site of the city of Orlando, as well as the Web site of Orlando's Chamber of Commerce[133,134]	#OpOrlando in support of the homeless people of Orlando who received food donations from the nonprofit organization, Food not Bombs, until police arrested members of the group giving out the food[135]

Continued

Approximate date	Target, hacktivity, and modus operandi (where available)	Motivation as stated (where available)
June 28, 2011	#OpIntifada launched and targets Israeli parliament (Knesset) Web site[136]	#OpIntifada in protest of Stuxnet, which is thought to be created and deployed by Israel in cooperation with America, targeting the Iranian nuclear program in Natanz[137]
June 29, 2011	Mayor of Orlando, running a re-election campaign, sees his Web site getting attacked repeatedly; Anons claim that they seek to keep it down for the entire duration of the campaign; they minimize resources spent on this task by exhausting the Web sites' newsletter subscription feature and a script that enters new fake e-mail addresses for newsletter requests and the site hangs itself up processing these repeated requests[138]	#OpOrlando[139]
June 29, 2011	Web site for Lodge 25, Fraternal Order of Police in Orlando, experiences repeated downtime due to DDoS attack[140]	#OpOrlando[141]
July 6, 2011	Orlando court Web sites experience downtime due to DDoS attack[142]	#OpOrlando[143]
July 11, 2011	Military Meltdown Monday—intrusion, gaining unauthorized access to Booz Allen Hamilton contacts within the U.S. military[144]	"Audit" of security systems (#AntiSec)[145]
July 12, 2011	Project Tarmageddon seeks to uncover what is behind the media blackouts concerning the Canadian company, Alberta Tar Sands, and stands behind the locals in Idaho who protest the widening of U.S. Highway 12 and the associated destruction of national forest for the sole purpose of shipping refinery equipment to Alberta Tar Sands[146,147]	#OpGreenRights[148]
July 13, 2011	Operation Green Rights—new campaign against companies perceived as polluting the environment; Monsanto experiences DDoS attack on their corporate Web site, further personal information on 2500 employees and associates is gleaned from the Monsanto server and published[149]	#OpGreenRights against environmental pollution citing mainly these companies: Exxon Mobil, ConocoPhillips, Canadian Oil Sands Ltd., Imperial Oil, Royal Bank of Scotland, Monsanto[150]
July 13, 2011	Adbusters blog, "#OCCUPYWALLSTREET," calls for 20,000 protestors to demonstrate in Manhattan on September 17[151]	Wall Street stockmarket is perceived as "the greatest corrupter of our democracy: Wall Street, the financial Gomorrah of America"[152]
July 14, 2011	Agricultural biotech company Monsanto—intrusion, data heist, and publication of personal information on circa 2500 associated with Monsanto[153]	Monsanto was sueing organic farmers who (negative) advertised their produce as not containing Monsanto products[154]

Continued

Approximate date	Target, hacktivity, and modus operandi (where available)	Motivation as stated (where available)
July 18, 2011	(Part of) Anonymous launches AnonPlus[155]	Social networking site Google+ bans accounts of Anonymous members[156]
July 19, 2011	FBI arrests 14 suspected Anonymous members throughout the United States[157]	#OpPayback[158]
July 21, 2011	Anonymous claims to have intruded an NATO Web site and to have garnered "about one Gigabyte of data from NATO now, most of which we cannot publish as it would be irresponsible"[159]	No statement of motivation found
July 22, 2011	AnonPlus, a social networking site launched by Anons, is defaced by the Turkish hacker group Akincilar ("Ottoman Raiders"[160])[161]	AnonPlus hacked[162]
July 30, 2011	U.S. government security contractor, ManTech International Corporation, sees about 400 MB of data pilfered from their servers and subsequently published on The Pirate Bay[163]	#OpAntiSec, FFF; ManTech is hired by among others government agencies and NATO for providing cyber security; hence although no sensitive data were leaked, the intrusion and theft of company data appear to be embarrassing[164]
August 5, 2011	Shooting Sheriffs Saturday: Intrusion, data heist (10 GB), and publication in more than 70 Sheriffs and law enforcement-related sites, most of which were hosted by Brooks-Jeffrey Marketing Servers and were launched in the past 24 h[165,166]	#OpAntiSec; in retaliation of July arrests[167]
August 6, 2011	Web site of white supremacist organization, Blood & Honour, suffers intrusion, theft and publication of personal data (nazi-leaks.net)[168]	#OpBlitzkrieg[169]
August 11, 2011	#OpPharisee seeks to disrupt the World Youth Day in Madrid and slow down the associated Web sites through DDoS attack[170]	#OpPharisee; seeks to bring attention to cases of sexual abuse of children by representatives of the Catholic church[171]
August 14, 2011	#OpBART is launched and targets the Web site of San Francisco's Bay Area Rapid Transit (BART); for the following day, protest in front of the Civic Center (the place where Charles Hill was shot and killed by two BART officers on July 3) is planned; in the following weeks, personal information on BART employees was leaked and Web sites were defaced[172,173]	#OpBART is in response to the shutting down of cell phone service[174] in order to curb an ongoing protest about the violent deaths of Charles Hill and Oscar Grant III and four others since the force's inception in 1972, three of the shootings occurred in 3 years between 2009 and 2011[175]
August 15, 2011	Vanguard Defense Hack (Vanguard Defense Industries (VDI)), U.S. Defense Contractor—intrusion and data heist (4713 e-mails, thousands of documents) with subsequent publication[176]	#OpAntiSec; VDI's affiliation with law enforcement agencies (FBI, Infraguard)[177]
August 23, 2011	Anonymous endorses the Occupy Wall Street Movement in a video post on YouTube[178]	Shared goals and objectives[179]

Continued

Approximate date	Target, hacktivity, and modus operandi (where available)	Motivation as stated (where available)
September 1, 2011	Defacement of Web site of Texas Police Chiefs Association, intrusion, and data heist with subsequent publication[180]	#OpAntiSec, #FreeAnon, in retaliation of arrests[181]
September 13, 2011	German Anonymous launches OpSummerstorm by taking down Web site of far right-wing political party, NPD[182]	#OpSummerstorm[183]
September 17, 2011	Magazine Adbuster's campaign against corporate corruption on Wall Street takes to the street after months of planning; the movement spreads around the world (Chicago, Toronto, London, Tokyo, Milan, Madrid, Stockholm) in the following months, often protesters hide their faces behind Guy Fawkes masks[184]	Occupy Wall Street Movement[185]
October 14, 2011	Child pornography site, Lolita City, is ousted (via DDoS) and information on 1589 registered users is published (via SQL-injection)[186]	#OpDarknet[187]
October 15, 2011	#OpDarknet is launched and warns Web host Freedom Hosting, which is believed to host child pornography[188]	The support of child pornography plays into the hands of pedophiles and endangers children[189]
October 24, 2011	Boston Police department Web site intruded; personal information is gleaned and published[190]	In protest of massive arrests and perceived police brutality against Occupy Wall Street protesters on October 11, 2011[191]
November 7, 2011	#OpBrotherhood Takedown launched targets the Muslim Brotherhood and repeatedly causes downtime for their Web site (ikhwanonline)[192]	#OpBrotherhood Takedown warns the Muslim Brotherhood, which is seen as threat to the Egyptian Revolution[193]
November 15, 2011	4Chan experiences downtime after DDoS attack similar to the ones it had experienced in April and July[194]	No statement of motivation found
November 22, 2011	#OpPigRoast launched targeting the Police Executive Research Forum (PERF) and police and security officers who are reported to have employed extraneous measures; spearheaded by Cabin Cr3w hackers[195]	#OpPigRoast; in protest of police brutality exercised against protestors of the Occupy Movement[196]
November 23, 2011	Release of videotape featuring personal information on a security guard at UC Davis who is seen spraying peaceful and unarmed Occupy protestors with pepper spray[197]	In protest of extraneously harsh treatment of protestors at UC Davis[198]
November 29, 2011	United Nations Development Program Web site is pilfered for 1000 e-mail addresses, usernames, and passwords, which are subsequently released on Pastebin by a team of TeaMp0isoN, Anonymous (p0isaNoN), and others[199]	In protest of the UN's role in western imperialism and its failure to act in the face of the atrocities committed in Rwanda, Darfour, Yugoslavia, Israel/OPT[200]

Continued

Approximate date	Target, hacktivity, and modus operandi (where available)	Motivation as stated (where available)
December 7, 2011	Web site of Monsanto's public relation partner, Bivings Group, suffers extended downtime and defacement, and hundreds of e-mails were gleaned and published; the Bivings Group, since October 2011 "The Brick Factory", has its seat in Washington, DC[201–203]	#OpEndMonsanto[204,205]
December 25, 2011	The Web site of Stratfor Global Intelligence Service suffers downtime and suffers leakage of its customer list including credit card details, which was announced to be used for donating $1 million to charities[206]; WikiLeaks subsequently begins to publish Stratfor e-mails gleaned during the attack[207]	(see LulzSec) Apparently in protest of the arrest of Pfc Bradley Manning[208] or possibly to mock Stratfor which specializes in security and intelligence[209]
January 1, 2012	Launch of #OpMegaUpload; 10 Web sites affiliated with the U.S. government (U.S. Justice Department, FBI, U.S. Copyright Office) and American music industry (Redord Industry Association of America (RIAA), Motion Picture Association of America (MPAA)) suffered outages due to DDoS attacks[210]	#OpMegaUpload, in support of file-sharing Web site/Kim Dotcom[211]; in protest of the seizure of file-hosting service by U.S. Justice Department (on January 19, 2012); @Anonops declared the operation successful with 5635 participants using LOIC[212]
January 1, 2012	#OpNigeria II commences 2 months of supporting the Nigerian Occupy movement[213]	#OpNigeria II (Occupy movement)[214]
January 4, 2012	PasteBin experiences DDoS attacks[215]	Unknown perpetrators[216]
January 5, 2012	Occupy Nigeria and local Anonymous-arm publicly demand an end to government corruption[217]	Government corruption and mismanagement in Nigeria[218,219]
January 9, 2012	Finnish government Web sites experience cyber attacks[220]	In protest of largest Finnish Internet Provider, Elisa, being ordered to block access to PirateBay ("Elisagate")[221]
January 10, 2012	Finnish Copyright Information and Anti-Piracy Center (CIAPC) Web sites experience downtime[222]	#OpPayback; October 2011 saw the Helsinki District court decide in CIAPC's and IFPI's favor and order Finnish Internet provider Elisa to block The Pirate Bay or face fines[223]
January 12, 2012	Dutch antipiracy group, BREIN's Web site experiences downtime[224]	#OpPayback; the Court of The Hague decided in favor of BREIN and ordered major Dutch Internet providers, Ziggo and XS4ALL, to block The Pirate Bay[225]
January 20, 2012	As published by "Guest" (presumably on behalf of the collective) an estimated 10,000 participants DDoS-ed, disabled or defaced the following Web sites[226]: http://pastebin.com/cujqqtcn http://www.paulafernandes.com.br (defaced)	#OpPayback[227]

Continued

Approximate date	Target, hacktivity, and modus operandi (where available)	Motivation as stated (where available)
	http://universalmusic.com.br (defaced) http://www.selenagomezweb.com (defaced) http://www.justinbieberweb.com (defaced) http://www.allsupergames.com http://www.newalbumreleases.net http://www.emimusicbrasil.com http://www.copyright.gov http://www.vivendi.com http://www.UniversalStudios.com http://www.justice.gov http://www.ifpi.se http://store.warnerbrosshop.com http://ofcanz.govt.nz http://www.siae.it http://www.usdoj.gov http://police.govt.nz http://justice.govt.nz http://shop.mgm.com	
January 21, 2012	As published by "Guest" (presumably on behalf of the collective), an estimated 15,000 participants DDoS-ed, disabled, or defaced the following Web sites[228]: http://wando.com.br http://www.somlivre.com http://www.universalmusic.com http://www.iamfiss.com (defaced) http://sony.co.uk http://www.monsanto.com http://ecad.org.br http://bit.ly/AdewTp (dumped) http://premier.gov.pl http://visa.com.br http://www.aflcio.org http://sejm.gov.pl http://pm.go.gov.br http://www.netlinx.net (defaced)	#OpPayback[229]
January 21, 2012	"Polish Revolution" targets Polish government and affiliated Web sites[230]; political opposition to the signing of the ACTA agreement don Guy Fawkes masks, Donald Tusk, suspends ratification later[231]	In protest of the intention of the Polish government to sign ACTA agreement[232]
January 22, 2012	As published by a "Guest" (presumably on behalf of the collective), an estimated 15,000 participants DDoS-ed, disabled, or defaced the following Web sites[233]: http://pastebin.com/GpEd0ssP (DDoS) http://sefanet.pr.gov.br (DDoS) http://tjm.rs.gov.br (disabled)	#OpPayback[234]

Continued

Approximate date	Target, hacktivity, and modus operandi (where available)	Motivation as stated (where available)
	http://sjc.sp.gov.br (DDoS) http://paranoa.df.gov.br (DDoS) http://parkway.df.gov.br (DDoS) http://abw.gov.pl (DDoS) http://guara.df.gov.br (disabled) http://aguasclaras.df.gov.br (disabled) http://www.rihannaonline.net (defaced) http://sobradinho.df.gov.br (defaced) http://sudoeste.df.gov.br (defaced) http://www.vivendi.com (DDoS) http://www.giannifava.org (DDoS) http://dof.ca.gov (DDoS) http://www.vivendi.fr (defaced) http://brasilia.df.gov.br (defaced) http://www.prezydent.pl (DDoS) http://ms.gov.pl (DDoS) http://www.vagla.pl (defaced) http://bor.gov.pl (DDoS) http://policiamilitar.rj.gov.br (DDoS) http://pm.go.gov.br (DDoS) http://www.cbs.com (disabled)	
January 23, 2012	As published by a "Guest" (presumably on behalf of the collective), an estimated 5000 participants DDoS-ed, disabled, or defaced the following Web sites[235]: http://www.usipr.gov (disabled) http://www.boavista.rr.gov.br (disabled) http://www.senado.gov.br (disabled) http://boavista.rr.gov.br (disabled) http://fssul.pr.gov.br (disabled) http://bomdepesca.com.br (defaced) http://acertai.com.br (defaced) http://emailsender.com.br (defaced) http://mikrocenter.psi.br (defaced) http://diretorepocanegocios.com.br (defaced) http://tabapua.sp.gov.br (defaced) http://mikrocenter.net.br (defaced) http://goo.gl/O8A2n (dumped) http://goo.gl/crINx (dumped) http://www.load.to/e6arTZSBjt/onguard2.sql.gz (dumped) http://goo.gl/akUCH (dumped) http://guapiacu.sp.gov.br (defaced) http://newsletter.editoraglobo.com.br (defaced) http://www.onguardonline.gov (defaced) http://sja.go.gov.br (defaced) http://canalford.com.br (defaced) http://alexandria.rn.gov.br (defaced) http://tjm.rs.gov.br http://tjmrs.jus.br	#OpPayback[236]

Continued

Approximate date	Target, hacktivity, and modus operandi (where available)	Motivation as stated (where available)
	http://biuro-gov.cba.pl (defaced) www.itau.com.br www.bundeskanzler.at http://esporte.gov.br http://apcm.org.br http://justiz.gv.at http://caixa.gov.br http://kprm.gov.pl http://kprm.gov.pl http://justica.sp.gov.br http://kaspersky.com.br	
January 24, 2012	Federal online security Web site of the U.S. Federal Trade Commission (onguardonline.gov) is taken down and pilfered; data including personal information of FTC officials are published[237,238]	In protest of the shutdown of MegaUpload and proposed antipiracy laws, SOPA (Stop Online Privacy Act), PIPA (Protect IP Act), and ACTA (Anti-Counterfeiting Trade Agreement)[239,240]
January 26, 2012	Web site of the European Parliament suffers downtime due to DDoS attack[241]	In protest of ACTA ratification[242]
January 28, 2012	OpEthiopia is launched in protest of human rights abuses, mismanagement of resources, and illicit financial transactions/corruption within the Ethiopian government[243]	#OpEthiopia[244]
January 30, 2012	Intrusion and theft of personal details concerning Dana White, the President of Ultimate Fighting Championship (UFC), additionally to defacement of official UFC Web site[245]	#OpUFC, in response to Dana White Twitter feed accusing Anonymous of being cowards[246]
February 2012	Intrusion and theft of millions of Syrian government e-mails, later handed over to WikiLeaks[247]	#OpSyria (FreedomOps)[248]
February 1, 2012	Anonymous Brazil targets banks (including Banco Bradesco, Banco do Brasil) with DDoS attacks[249]	#OpWeeksPayment[250]
February 1, 2012	Salt Lake City police Web site hijacked and defaced; confidential information on informants leaked[251]	In protest against proposed bill that criminalizes the possession of graffiti paraphernalia[252]
February 2, 2012	Intrusion of U.S. white supremacist (American Third Position, A3P) Web site and theft of and publication of forum messages, e-mails indicating links between British white supremacists, the chairman of the British National Party, Nick Griffin[253]	#OpBlitzkrieg; in opposition to A3P's disguised racism[254]
February 3, 2012	Virtual community Web site of the Boston police department (bpdnews.com) experiences defacement and 6 days of downtime due to DDoS attack[255]	#OpAntiSec; in response to perceived brutality against Occupy Wall Street protestors[256]

Continued

Approximate date	Target, hacktivity, and modus operandi (where available)	Motivation as stated (where available)
February 3, 2012	Intrusion and release of conference call between FBI and Scotland Yard recorded on January 17, 2012 concerning the investigation of Anonymous[257]	The phone call had the international hacker collective as subject
February 3, 2012	Intrusion and theft of 2.6 GB of e-mail data from the American law firm that represented the commander of troops who are responsible for killing 24 unarmed civilians in Haditha, Iraq in 2005[258]	No statement of motivation found
February 3, 2012	Boston Police Department Web site (BPDnews.com) defacement[259]	In protest of police brutality against Occupy Wall Street protesters[260]
February 4, 2012	DDoS attack on Swedish government Web site (CyberForce)[261]	Coincided with real-world protests in Stockholm and Goeteborg against Anti-Counterfeiting Treaty Agreement (ACTA)[262]
February 4, 2012	DDoS attack against the Web site of the Department of Homeland Security (www.dhs.gov)[263]	Op#FuckFBIFriday[264]
February 5, 2012	Defacement of the Web site of Bulgarian music industry group, Prophon[265]	In protest against the support of Anti-Counterfeiting Treaty Agreement (ACTA)[266]
February 8, 2012	Intrusion into Web sites of the West Virginia Chiefs of Police Association and leakage of personal data on more than 150 police officers (CabinCr3W)[267]	Alleged monitoring of police brutality[268]
February 9, 2012	DDoS attacks on regional offices of Russia's leading party, United Russia, in Moscow and Kaluga[269]	No statement of motivation found[270]
February 9, 2012	Intrusion into and theft of classified data from the Web site of the German Parliament, the classified data contained details of Germany's war in Afghanistan[271]	No statement of motivation found[272]
February 9, 2012	DDoS attack against the Web site of the Croation presidency[273]	In protest of Josipovic's support of the Anti-Counterfeiting Treaty Agreement (ACTA)[274]
February 9, 2012	"Cmd. X" crosses the U.S.-Canadian border to evade U.S. trial; his flight was made possible by "Operation Xport," in which resources of Anonymous collective and Occupy movement are used to enable an "underground railroad" for persecuted hackers[275]	Operation Xport[276]
February 10, 2012	Blanket DDoS attack on Mexican on 136 Mexican Web sites (including Mexican Senate and Interior Ministry), list of affected sites published on Pastebin (Anonymous Mexico (Twitter: @AnonnymousMexi))[277,278]	#OpMexico In protest against the adoption of SOPA law[279,280]

Continued

Approximate date	Target, hacktivity, and modus operandi (where available)	Motivation as stated (where available)
February 10, 2012	Intrusion and theft of 400 MB of e-mails from the Mexican National Chamber of Mines ("Camimex")[281]	In protest of the working conditions for miners[282]
February 10, 2012	Intrusion and theft of personal data on more than 40,000 Alabama state and law enforcement employees, published on PasteBin[283]	Alabama is criticized to exhibit "racist" immigration laws and/or to the police department's ignominy in its inability to secure personal data[284]
February 10, 2012	Anonymous announces crusade against Israel in a YouTube video[285]	Israel becomes a target due to its "crimes against humanity" in its treatment of Palestinians[286]
February 10, 2012	cia.gov experiences downtime due to DDoS attack[287]	(Law Enforcement Friday)[288]
February 11, 2012	Interpol Web site experiences DDoS attack[289]	Interpol aided in the arrest of Saudi journalist Hamza Kashgari[290]
February 11, 2012	Panama government Web site, www.presidencia.gob.pa; others suffer downtime due to DDoS attack[291]	In solidarity with protesting Ngäbe Bugle Indians who seek to avert mining and hydroelectric projects in their region[292]
February 14, 2012	Intrusion into and theft of personal data from Turkish satellite provider Digiturk, published on Pastebin[293]	In protest of censorship: Digiturk blocks Web sites such as Pastebin, blogger.com, and inci.sozlukspot.com (#OpDigiturk)[294]
February 14, 2012	Release of 400 MB data of U.S. Army Intelligence Knowledge Network, published on Rapidshare[295]	No statement of motivation found[296]
February 14, 2012	DDoS attack against the Web site of Combined Systems, a company supplying tear gas used by Egyptian law enforcement against protesters[297]	In honor of the first "Arab Spring" uprisings in Bahrain on February 14, 2011[298]
February 16, 2012	L0NGwave99 affiliated with Anonymous takes down the public Web sites of NASDAQ, NYSE, Miami Stock Exchange, BATS stock exchange, and the Chicago Board Options Exchange (CBOE) with a DDoS attack[299,300]	"Operation Digital Tornado," in solidarity with the "99%" and the Occupy Movement[301,302]
February 17, 2012	The following Web sites experience defacements and downtime: business.ftc.gov, consumer.gov, ncpw.gov, ftcstaging.mt.fhdbeta.com, ncpw.gov, consumer.ftc.gov, ftcdev.mt.fhdbeta.com[303,304]	AntiSec; In protest against ACTA (Anti-Counterfeiting Trade Agreement)[305,306]
February 20, 2012	Defacement of online presence and intrusion, data theft, and publication (Pastebin) of details pertaining to 1100 customers of streetwear clothing vendor, Streetfightversand.de[307]	#OpBlitzkrieg[308]
February 23, 2012	German branch, Anonymous Kollektiv, initiates a "comment flash mob" on the facebook pages of the Wall Street Journal[309]	In response to an article equating Anonymous with Al Qaeda[310]

Continued

Approximate date	Target, hacktivity, and modus operandi (where available)	Motivation as stated (where available)
February 23, 2012	Spanish police arrests six alleged Anons[311]	No statement of motivation found
February 24, 2012	Infraguard chapter Dayton, OH Web site hijacked and defaced[312]	#OpAntiSec[313]
February 24, 2012	Web site defacement against GEO Group (www.geogroup.com), the second-largest proprietor of private prisons in the United States[314]	#OpAntiSec[315]
February 24, 2012	Spanish National Police, DDoS attack against Web site[316]	In retaliation to the arrest of six alleged Anons the day before[317]
February 28, 2012	25 Anons arrested in Spain, Argentina, Chile, and Colombia[318,319]	No statement of motivation found
February 28, 2012	Interpol Web site experiences short downtime due to DDoS attack[320,321]	Downtime happens shortly after Interpol's announcement of the arrest of 25 suspected Anonymous members[322,323]
February and March 2012	Multiple attempted and successful attacks on the official Web site of the Vatican (www.vatican.va) starting out with intrusion and seeking to exploit Web application vulnerabilities (unsuccessful) to concluding with DDoS attacks[324,325]	Attack not against Christians, but against the Catholic church,[326] its handling of sexual abuse cases,[327] as well as historic policies, e.g., the Inquisition[328]
March 1, 2012	E-mails and contact information are pilfered from a database of the Bivings Group, PR partner to Monsanto[329]	#OpEndMonsanto[330]
March 4, 2012	#OpOccupyAIPAC[331]/#OpPalestine[332] launched, AIPAC Web site experiences DDoS attack	Op Occupy AIPAC for its lobbyism and sponsoring system, which endangers and denigrates America's democracy and its image in the Muslim world, undermines support for democratic movements in SW Asia, its unconditional support of Israeli govt. contrary to international law, diversion of tax money to Israel[333]
March 6, 2012	Five LulzSec members arrested in Ireland, UK, and USA [Jeremy Hammond of Chicago, IL (aka Anarchaos aka tylerknowsthis aka crediblethreat; most notably Stratfor hack), Ryan Ackroyd (aka Kayla aka lol aka lolsoon), Jake Davis (aka Topiary aka atopiary), Darren Martyn (aka pwnsauce aka raepsauce aka networkkitten), Donncha O'Cearrbhail (aka Paladium)][334]	No statement of motivation found
March 7, 2012	Vatican's official Web site (www.vatican.va) experiences downtime due to DDoS attack[335]	In protest of the inquisition and the most recent scandals of sexual child abuse involving Catholic priests[336]

Continued

Approximate date	Target, hacktivity, and modus operandi (where available)	Motivation as stated (where available)
March 7, 2012	PandaLabs Web site defacement[337]	PandaLabs is criticized of aiding law enforcement apprehend alleged Anonymous members[338]
March 8, 2012	Critique on Invisible Children's "Kony 2012" and the nonprofit organization itself[339,340]	The nonprofit organization's activity is seen as not being productive in the capture of Kony and only spends little over 30% for their charitable programs[341,342]
March 9, 2012	Panda Security: Intrusion, DDoS attack and defacement, release of personal information on 114 employees[343]	Panda Security had long taken public stance against LulzSec, and the attack is part of the revenge in the aftermath of the LulzSec arrests[344]
March 9, 2012	Release of Symantec's 2006 antivirus source code[345]	In protest of the arrest of five LulzSec members[346,347]
March 9, 2012	New York Ironworks police equipment supplier: Web site defacement[348]	AntiSec, #FFF[349]
March 12, 2012	Online store of the German extreme right-wing party, NPD sees customer data pilfered and published[350]	#OpBlitzkrieg[351]
March 13, 2012	Anons bring down the Vatican official Web site and centering in on Vatican Radio database[352]	In protest of Vatican Radio's use of repeaters with power transmission[353]
March 21, 2012	Anonymous publishes (PirateBay) 1.7 GB of data that Anons gleaned from the Web site of the U.S. Bureau of Justice Statistics[354]	#Op Monday Mail Mayhem; in support of freedom of speech and information[355]
March 23, 2012	Monsanto's Hungarian Web site experiences 1 week downtime due to DDoS attack[356]	#OpGreenRights; Hungary destroys all Monsanto GMO corn fields in late September[357]
March 28, 2012	Dominican Republic law enforcement arrests six alleged Anons [Cornille Milton Jimenez (Zerohack), Jean Carlos Acosta Leonardo (Nmap), Cristian de la Rosa de los Santos (Mot), Robert Delgado Reynoso (Frank_ostia), two minors are unnamed except by their hacker names, Xtreme and Alvin][358]	No statement of motivation found
March 20, 2012	#OpVatican launched in protest of latest, global wave scandals of the sexual abuse of minors by catholic priests and the Vatican's attempt to cover these up,[359] as well as the imprisonments of Paolo G abriele and Claudio Sciarpelletti who leaked documents uncovering corruption inside the Vatican (Vatileaks) to a journalist[a;360]	#OpVatican[361]
March 24, 2012	Contact information on the staff and donors of the Judge Rotenberg Educational Center in Canton, MA released (Pastebin)[362]	The special needs school is accused of medieval methods of punishment such as electric shock treatments, prolonged restraints, and the withholding of food[363]

Continued

Approximate date	Target, hacktivity, and modus operandi (where available)	Motivation as stated (where available)
March 30-April 5, 2012	Intrusion and defacement of between 327 and 485 Web sites associated with the national as well as regional governments and companies in China; theft and publication (on Pastebin) of personal data from some Web sites; "@Anonymous China" twitter account[364]	In protest against Chinese Internet censorship[365]
April 7, 2012	Anonymous launches *Operation Defense* (#OpDefense)[366]	Targets supporters of Cyber Intelligence Sharing and Protection Act (CISPA) thought to increase the abilities of government and private companies to monitor online activities of individual users[367]
April 9, 2012	DDoS attacks hit UK's Home Office Web site (www.homeoffice.gov.uk)[368] and other Web sites associated with the British government (www.number10.gov.uk,[369] www.justice.gov.uk)[370]	#OpTrialAtHome; in protest of the potential extradition of accused Anonymous hackers in order to stand trial in the United States[371,372] as well as in protest of suggested legislation (in the UK) that would increase Internet censorship and surveillance[373]
April 9, 2012	Intrusion and theft of 2725 e-mails pertaining to the government of Tunisia[374]	In protest of Internet censorship, demanding the Tunisian government to respect human rights and freedom of expression[375]
April 11, 2012	Boeing, TechAmerica, and U.S. Telecom Web sites experience DDoS attack[376]	#OpDefense, targeted companies are supporting CISPA legislation[377]
April 20, 2012	Anonymous launches new branch with *Operation Cannabis* (#OpCannabis), seeking public support for objective (support is shown by Cannabis-related avatar on individual social networking accounts) publication of reasons via video on Tumblr[378,379]	#OpCannabis, intents to further to end the cannabis prohibition and the legalization of marijuana for recreational and medical purposes[380,381]
April 21, 2012	Formula 1 Web site experiences downtime due to DDoS attack; information on ticket sales and attendees of the Grand Prix in Bahrain is redacted[382]	In protest of human rights violations of the al Khalifa government[383]
April 21, 2012	#Occupy Philippines defaces the China University Media Union Web site[384]	#Occupy Philippines; in response to Chinese hackers' territorial claim (Panatag Shoal/Huangyan Island)[385]
April, 27, 2012	#OpDefense Phase II launched; planned on-site protests target AT&T, IBM, Intel, verizon, CVS, Microsoft, Bank of America, Chase Bank, McGraw Hill, Pepsi, Coca-Cola, Target, Wal Mart, MasterCard, Visa, American Express on set dates over the coming 2 months[386]	#OpDefense Phase II; in response to CISPA legislation passing the U.S. House of Representatives[387]

Continued

Approximate date	Target, hacktivity, and modus operandi (where available)	Motivation as stated (where available)
May 9, 2012	UK Internet service providers, Virgin Media and TalkTalk, experience downtime due to DDoS attack[388]	In retaliation of blocking out The Pirate Bay[389]
May 17, 2012	14 Web sites affiliated or associated with the Indian government experience downtime due to DDoS attacks[390]	#OpIndia; in protest against Internet-filtering[391]
From May 20, 2012	#OpQuébec launched and brings down 13 Web sites affiliated or associated with the Quebec government and police[392]	#OpQuébec, in support of students' strike and in opposition to recent law (bill 78), which is intended to curb the right of assembly and free speech to undermine said student protest and the like[393]
May 25, 2012	KKK Web sites experience downtime via DDoS attack[394]	#OpBlitzkrieg[395]
May 31, 2012	Release of personal information of Grand Prix ticket holders[396]	#OpQuébec[397]
June 7, 2012	#OpColtanPress within OpGreenRights intrudes, garners and releases data on products as well as contact information on employees of Intel (intelconsumerelectronics.com)[398,399]	#OpColtanPress/OpGreenRights; in protest of the company's support of the conflict-perpetuating mining of Coltan in the Democratic Republic of Congo (DRC) through its persisting business relationship[400]
June 9, 2012	#OpIndia fields about 100 Guy Fawkes—mask wearing protesters on the ground in Mumbai[401]	#OpIndia[402]
June 21, 2012	Web sites representing the KKK and the American nazi party experience continued and repeated downtime due to DDoS[403]	#OpBlitzkrieg[404]
June 26, 2012	#OpJapan launched Web sites associated with the Japanese government experience DDoS attacks and defacements[405]	#OpJapan; in protest of copyright revision by the Japanese government, antipiracy law passed[406,407]
June 29, 2012	#OpParaguay is launched; Occu.Py Paraguay seeks to pursue justice for peasants, health services for landless peasants as well as the restoration of disowned land; like other Occupy movements, economic exploitation by large corporations is criticized and sought to be ended, while the federal government is seen as not representing the majority of the population, but as playing into the hands of the big companies[408]	#OpParaguay in protest of the plight of Paraguayan farmers[409]
July 25, 2012	Operation Anaheim launched, targets Anaheim police, publishes personal information on police chief[410] and mayor Tom Tait[411]	Operation Anaheim; following almost a week of protest against police brutality (unarmed Manuel Diaz was shot in the back of his head, followed by the fatal shooting of a man who was already handcuffed)[412,413]

Continued

Approximate date	Target, hacktivity, and modus operandi (where available)	Motivation as stated (where available)
July 25, 2012	#OpPedoChat and #OpDarkNet target Amy Lee (Evanescence), her manager, and the president of record company Wind Up Records[414]	Lee's lawyer prevented witness from reporting child pornography and other offenses
July 29, 2012	443,000 customer records of Australian telecommunications company, AAPT, are gleaned and partially published (Pastebin)[415]	In protest of a proposed law that would require telecommunication companies to track online behavior and store records thereof for 2 years[416]
August 9, 2012	Ukrainian Web sites of the Radio Broadcasting Council of Ukraine (nrada.gov.ua), Ukrainian Agency for Copyright and related Rights (uacrr.kiev.ua), and the Ukrainian Anti-Piracy Association (apo.kiev.ua) experience downtime due to DDoS attacks[417,418]	#OpDemonoid; in protest of Ukrainian crackdown on Demonoid[419–421]—a music-sharing Web site
August 14, 2012	Ugandan government Web sites are intruded upon and defaced[422]	In protest of the countries anti-homosexuality laws[423]
August 15, 2012	Anonymous presents measures against recognition by CCTV cameras/"TrapWire" a surveillance system employed by U.S. Department of Homeland Security[424,425]	With PLF; anti-surveillance, warning of Orwellian dimensions[426,427]
August 18, 2012	"Operation Free Assange" launched[428]	"Operation Free Assange" in support of WikiLeaks cofounder Julian Assange, demanding freedom[429]
August 20, 2012	DDoS attacks disrupts Web sites of and associated with the UK government, e.g., Ministry of Justice[430]	In protest of UK's plans to extradite Julian Assange to Sweden, #OpFreeAssange[431]
August 21, 2012	Defacement of Moscovian Khamovniki district court Web site[432]	AnonymousRussia; Court convicted three members of Russian punk band, Pussy Riot, to 2 years hard labor[433]
August 23, 2012	Local Anonymous group calls for real-world protests against CNMI—government (Northern Mariana Islands) on August 27, 2012, 9 a.m. in front of the CNMI Legislature[434]	Corruption of politicians, demanding the government step down[435]
August 27, 2012	#OpColtan-hacktivists exploit SQL vulnerability to extract and later publish data (privatepaste.com) from AVX Corporation[436]	#OpColtan seeks to expose and punish companies which purchase minerals extracted in war-torn countries; AVX is accused of fueling conflict in the DRC by supporting the exploitation of coltan[437]
August 27, 2012	Web sites of Interpol and SOCA (Serious Organized Crime Agecy) experience downtime due to DDoS attack[438]	#Op Free Assange; in support of Julian Assange[439]

Continued

Approximate date	Target, hacktivity, and modus operandi (where available)	Motivation as stated (where available)
September 3, 2012	AntiSec-hackers discover, glean 12 million, and publish redacted data of circa 1 million UDIDs from the laptop of a FBI agent[440]	#OpAntiSec, #FFF; Apple's UDIDs store personal information and technical behavior of the user; to find this kind of data on a laptop of a law enforcement officer is viewed as constituting a breach of individual privacy[441]
September 5, 2012	Call for fans to target Web sites associated with Evanescence's Amy Lee and the respective label, WindUp, with DDoS attacks, announcement of picketing concerts of the fall tour[442,443]	Anons found reportedly evidence that Lee and her lawyers forced Sam Smith into signing nondisclosure agreement, which prevented him from reporting cases of pedophilia on Evanescence-related online forums[444,445]
September 12, 2012	Barrett Brown (Zeta, Project PM) arrested on the charge of threatening a federal agent,[446] and later two charges of obstruction are added which his lawyer declares as "absurd and unnecessary" (Jay Leiderman)[447]	No statement of motivation found
Mid-September 2012	Publication of credit card details of 13 FBI agents[448]	#FFF, #AntiSec, in response to Barrett Brown's arrest[449]
September 14, 2012	Italian arm of Anonymous publishes (depositfiles. com) 2.5 GB e-mails of Italian priest arrested for alleged child abuse[450]	On endeavor to uncover information the Catholic church hides, in protest of the Catholic churches stance on gay rights[451]
September 15, 2012	#OpHKNEC is launched and targets the National Education Center in HongKong which set out to introduce classes to elementary school that encourage alignment with the Chinese government, evaluation, and grades in these classes that depend not on actually acquired knowledge, but on emotional attachment to the Chinese State/Central government[452]	#OpHKNEC (Hongkong govt. abandons plans to introduce mandatory Chinese civic education classes[453])
September 30, 2012	Protest of Philippines' Cybercrime Prevention Act of 2012[454] targeting government affiliated Web sites with DDoS attacks[455]	In protest of Philippines' cybercrime law[456,457]
October 5, 2012	Web sites of the Swedish government, the central bank, and others experience downtime due to DDoS attacks for the past week[458]	4chan coordinated protest against the shutdown of file-sharing Web site[459]
October 20, 2012	Announced: Global Protest against surveillance systems "TrapWire" and "INDECT"[460]; protest can be tracked on Google maps[461] and are coordinated thereon as well as on piratenpad. de,[462] Twitter, Facebook, YouTube, and Pastebin[463]	#OpNov5, #OpIndect, #OpTrapwire,[464] #OpBigBrother, Worldwide Day of Protest Against Surveillance; TrapWire, and INDECT utilize various surveillance technologies combining tracking of location data, image data analysis as well as social media and data mining for the drawing up of individual profiles[465]

Continued

Approximate date	Target, hacktivity, and modus operandi (where available)	Motivation as stated (where available)
October 31, 2012	#OpMyanmar launched in protest of human rights abuses, torture, forceful relocations by the Burmese junta[466]	#OpMyanmar[467]
November 15, 2012	Israeli government Web sites experience 44 million hacking attempts in just days targeting Web sites associated with the Israeli government, president, military, foreign ministry, aside from retail and business Web sites, most notable that of the Bank of Jerusalem.[468,469] Find a full list of 663 affected Web sites here: http://pastebin.com/Ms4nJSZx [last accessed January 19, 2013]	#OpIsrael, #OpGazaUnderAttack; In protest of Israel's air strike into Gaza, most hacks have been traced to Israel and Occupied Palestinian Territories[470,471]
November 15, 2012	87 Israeli Web sites are targeted in DDoS attacks and experience defacements; Anons provide information package for Gazans about alternative ways to communicate with the outside world[472]	#OpIsrael is launched as protest against the Israeli government's threat to cut Gaza's telecommunication connections[473]
November 28, 2012	#OpEgypt officially launched[474]	In protest to new constitution and Presidential decree that grants immunity and decisive powers to President Mohammed Mursi's[475] as well as violent crackdowns on protesters that left two dead and many injured[476,477]
November 29, 2012	#OpRevoluSec/Operation Syria launched[478]	In protest of the Assad-government shutting off the Internet[479]: Anonymous sets out to "keep open the lines of telecommunication with the free Syrian people" and to "be the voice of the voiceless in Syria"[480,481]
December 16, 2012	Publication (anonpaste) of personal data captured from the server of Israeli Musical Act Magazine (act.co.il)[482]	#OpIsrael (Twitter handle @OsamaTheGod)[483]
December 18, 2012	Intrusion, theft, and publication of personal information of members of Westboro Baptist Church,[484] defacement of church leader's personal computer,[485,486] hijacking of church leader's Twitter account,[487] filing death certificate for church leader causing her SSN to be blocked[488]	#OpWBC/#OpWestBor in cooperation with The Jester[489] and hacker Cosmo the God[490] Tax-exempt, hate clan, WBC, announced its intention to picket the funeral of victims of a Connecticut school shooting[491,492]
December 19, 2012	30 government Web sites DDoS-ed in #OpEgypt[493]	In protest to new constitution and Presidential decree that grants immunity and decisive powers to President Mohammed Mursi's[494] as well as violent crackdowns on protesters that left two dead and many injured[495,496]

Continued

Approximate date	Target, hacktivity, and modus operandi (where available)	Motivation as stated (where available)
December 19, 2012	Twitter suspends @YourAnonNews—account[497]	Apparently because the account was used to organize a human wall against WBC-picketing the funerals of Newtown, CT school shooting[498,499]
December 25, 2012	Names of 13 alleged gang rapists of a 16-year-old unconscious girl and parents accused of covering up the incident in Steubenville, Ohio, USA published while setting deadline for public apologies[500–502]	Anonymous-affiliated "KnightSec" in "Operation Roll Red Roll"[503,504]
December 25, 2012	Delhi police Web site taken offline[505]	In demand of investigation and persecution of perpetrators of the rape of a young woman on Delhi bus, who passed away later due to the severity of injuries inflicted[506]

[a]*The Pope pardoned Gabriele and Sciarpelletti, who were subsequently released from prison later in December 2012 (Edwards A. Pope's Christmas pardon for jailed former butler who stole documents alleging corruption in the Vatican. Daily Mail. Available at: http://www.dailymail.co.uk/news/article-2252190/Paolo-Gabriele-Popes-Christmas-pardon-jailed-Butler-stole-documents.html; December 22, 2012).*

References

1. Single R. Palin hacker group's all-time greatest hits wired. Available at: http://www.wired.com/threatlevel/2008/09/palin-hacker-gr/; September 19, 2008 [last accessed February 2013].
2. Single R. Palin hacker group's all-time greatest hits wired. Available at: http://www.wired.com/threatlevel/2008/09/palin-hacker-gr/; September 19, 2008 [last accessed February 2013].
3. Schwartz M. The trolls among us. *The New York Times*. Available at: http://www.nytimes.com/2008/08/03/magazine/03trolls-t.html?pagewanted=all&_r=0; August 3, 2008 [last accessed February 2013].
4. Schwartz M. The trolls among us. *The New York Times*. Available at: http://www.nytimes.com/2008/08/03/magazine/03trolls-t.html?pagewanted=all&_r=0; August 3, 2008 [last accessed February 2013].
5. Encyclopedia Dramatica. Hal turner. Available at: https://encyclopediadramatica.se/Hal_Turner; undated [last accessed February 2013].
6. Encyclopedia Dramatica. Hal turner. Available at: https://encyclopediadramatica.se/Hal_Turner; undated [last accessed February 2013].
7. Single R. Investigative report reveals hackers terrorize the Internet for LULZ. *Wired*. Available at: http://www.wired.com/threatlevel/2007/07/investigative-r/; July 27, 2007 [last accessed February 2013].
8. Kim L. Anonymous takes on child pornography. *IB Times*. Available at: http://www.ibtimes.com/anonymous-takes-child-pornography-sites-360614; October 24, 2011 [last accessed February 2013].
9. Singel R. War breaks out between hackers and scientology—there can only be one. *Wired*. Available at: http://www.wired.com/threatlevel/2008/01/anonymous-attac/; January 23, 2008 [last accessed February 2013].
10. Singel R. War breaks out between hackers and scientology—there can only be one. *Wired*. Available at: http://www.wired.com/threatlevel/2008/01/anonymous-attac/; January 23, 2008 [last accessed February 2013].
11. Reid S. Hip-hop sites hacked by apparent hate group; SOHH, AllHipHop temporarily suspend access. *MTVNews Top Stories*. Available at: http://www.mtv.com/news/articles/1590117/hip-hop-sites-hacked-by-apparent-hate-group.jhtml; June 30, 2008 [last accessed February 2013].
12. Reid S. Hip-hop sites hacked by apparent hate group; SOHH, AllHipHop temporarily suspend access. *MTVNews Top Stories*. Available at: http://www.mtv.com/news/articles/1590117/hip-hop-sites-hacked-by-apparent-hate-group.jhtml; June 30, 2008 [last accessed February 2013].

13. Rogers J. Teenage founder of No Cussing Club under siege. *The Associated Press/Ventura County Star*. Available at: http://www.vcstar.com/news/2009/jan/15/teenage-founder-of-no-cussing-club-under-siege/; January 15, 2009 [last accessed February 2013].

14. Rogers J. Teenage founder of No Cussing Club under siege. *The Associated Press/Ventura County Star*. Available at: http://www.vcstar.com/news/2009/jan/15/teenage-founder-of-no-cussing-club-under-siege/; January 15, 2009 [last accessed February 2013].

15. Anonymouszcvb19. Second Anonymous message to the 'New World Order'. *YouTube*. Aailable at: http://www.youtube.com/watch?v=Px_qNJ0KK0w; January 26, 2009 [last accessed February 2013].

16. Shachtman N. Iran activists get assist from 'Anonymous', Pirate Bay. *Wired*. Available at: http://www.wired.com/dangerroom/2009/06/iran-activists-get-assist-from-anonymous-pirate-bay/; June 18, 2009 [last accessed February 2013].

17. Fowler J. Anonymous joins fight against Tyranny in Iran. *BusinessPundit*. Available at: http://www.businesspundit.com/anonymous-joins-fight-against-tyranny-in-iran/; June 18, 2009 [last accessed February 2013].

18. Crawley K. A history of Anonymous. *InfoSec Institute*. Available at: http://resources.infosecinstitute.com/a-history-of-anonymous/; October 24, 2011 [last accessed February 2013].

19. Crawley K. A history of Anonymous. *InfoSec Institute*. Available at: http://resources.infosecinstitute.com/a-history-of-anonymous/; October 24, 2011 [last accessed February 2013].

20. Anonymous. 'Operation Didgeridie' and the 'war' on the Australian Government. *Anon SA*. Available at: http://www.anonsa.org/2009/09/operation-didgeridie-and-the-war-on-the-australian-government; September 9, 2009 [last accessed February 2013].

21. ABC News. Rudd website attacked in filter protest. Available here: http://www.abc.net.au/news/2009-09-10/rudd-website-attacked-in-filter-protest/1423834; September 10, 2009 [last accessed February 2013].

22. Zetter K. 'Anonymous' declares war on Australia over Internet filtering. *Wired*. Available at: http://www.wired.com/threatlevel/2009/09/anonymous-hacks-australia/; September 9, 2009 [last accessed February 2013].

23. Anonymous. 'Operation Didgeridie' and the 'war' on the Australian Government. *Anon SA*. Available at: http://www.anonsa.org/2009/09/operation-didgeridie-and-the-war-on-the-australian-government; September 9, 2009 [last accessed February 2013].

24. LeMay R. 'Anonymous' attacks Govt websites over filtering. *apc*. Available at: http://apcmag.com/anonymous-attacks-govt-websites-over-filtering.htm; February 10, 2010 [last accessed February 2013].

25. Moses A. Operation Titstorm: hackers bring down government websites. *The Sidney Morning Herald*. Available at: http://www.smh.com.au/technology/technology-news/operation-titstorm-hackers-bring-down-government-websites-20100210-nqku.html; February 10, 2010 [last accessed February 2013].

26. LeMay R. 'Anonymous' attacks Govt websites over filtering. *apc*. Available at: http://apcmag.com/anonymous-attacks-govt-websites-over-filtering.htm; February 10, 2010 [last accessed February 2013].

27. Dunn JE. Anonymous launches attack against Sony PS3 websites. *PC World*. Available at: http://www.pcworld.com/article/224360/sony_ps3_websites_attacked_by_anonymous.html; April 5, 2011 [last accessed February 2013].

28. Corrons L. 4chan users organize surgical strike against MPAA. *pandalabs*. Available at: http://pandalabs.pandasecurity.com/4chan-users-organize-ddos-against-mpaa/; September 17, 2011 [last accessed February 2013].

29. TheNewNewInternet. 'Operation Payback' results in 550 hours downtime, 742 interruptions. Available at: http://www.thenewnewinternet.com/2010/10/12/operation-payback-results-in-550-hours-downtime-742-interruptions/; July 1, 2012 [last accessed February 2013].

30. Rashid FY. PayPal, PostFinance hit by DoS attack, counter-attack in progress. *eWeek*. Available at: http://www.eweek.com/c/a/Security/PayPal-PostFinance-Hit-by-DoS-Attacks-CounterAttack-in-Progress-860335/; December 6, 2010 [last accessed February 2013].

31. Dunn JE. Anonymous launches attack against Sony PS3 Websites. *PC World*. Available at: http://www.pcworld.com/article/224360/sony_ps3_websites_attacked_by_anonymous.html; April 5, 2011 [last accessed February 2013].

32. Corrons L. 4chan users organize surgical strike against MPAA. *pandalabs*. Available at: http://pandalabs.pandasecurity.com/4chan-users-organize-ddos-against-mpaa/; September 17, 2011 [last accessed February 2013].

33. Lubin G. Check out the greatest hits of operation payback, the hackers that took down Mastercard. *Business Insider*. Available at: http://www.businessinsider.com/operation-paybacks-greatest-hits-2010-12?op=1; December 8, 2010 [last accessed February 2013].

34. Correll S-P. The 'Anonymous' cyber-protest group calls for an attack on Spain's copyright society (SGAE) to-night. *PandaSecurity*. Available at: http://press.pandasecurity.com/news/the-%E2%80%98anonymous%E2%80%99-cyber-protest-group-calls-for-an-attack-on-spains-copyright-society-sgae-tonight/; October 6, 2010 [last accessed February 2013].

35. eSecurity Planet. Hackers target Spain's SGAE. Available here: http://www.esecurityplanet.com/headlines/article.php/3907381/Hackers-Target-Spains-SGAE.htm; October 8, 2010 [last accessed February 2013].

36. Correll S-P. The 'Anonymous' cyber-protest group calls for an attack on Spain's copyright society (SGAE) tonight. *PandaSecurity*. Available at: http://press.pandasecurity.com/news/the-%E2%80%98anonymous%E2%80%99-cyber-protest-group-calls-for-an-attack-on-spains-copyright-society-sgae-tonight/; October 6, 2010 [last accessed February 2013].

37. eSecurity Planet. Hackers target Spain's SGAE. Available at: http://www.esecurityplanet.com/headlines/article.php/3907381/Hackers-Target-Spains-SGAE.htm; October 8, 2010 [last accessed February 2013].

38. Lubin G. Check out the greatest hits of operation payback, the hackers that took Down Mastercard. *Business Insider*. Available at: http://www.businessinsider.com/operation-paybacks-greatest-hits-2010-12?op=1; December 8, 2010 [last accessed February 2013].

39. Lubin G. Check out the greatest hits of operation payback, the hackers that took Down Mastercard. *Business Insider*. Available at: http://www.businessinsider.com/operation-paybacks-greatest-hits-2010-12?op=1; Decmeber 8, 2010 [last accessed February 2013].

40. Lubin G. Check out the greatest hits of operation payback, the hackers that took Down Mastercard. *Business Insider*. Available at: http://www.businessinsider.com/operation-paybacks-greatest-hits-2010-12?op=1; December 8, 2010 [last accessed February 2013].

41. Lubin G. Check out the greatest hits of operation payback, the hackers that took Down Mastercard. *Business Insider*. Available at: http://www.businessinsider.com/operation-paybacks-greatest-hits-2010-12?op=1; December 8, 2010 [last accessed February 2013].

42. Corrons L. 4chan users organize surgical strike against MPAA. *pandalabs*. Available at: http://pandalabs.pandasecurity.com/4chan-users-organize-ddos-against-mpaa/; September 17, 2011 [last accessed February 2013].

43. Tencer D. Hackers take down website of bank that froze WikiLeaks funds. *The Raw Story*. Available at: http://www.rawstory.com/rs/2010/12/06/hackers-website-bank-froze-wikileaks-funds/; December 6, 2010 [last accessed February 2013].

44. Tencer D. Hackers take down website of bank that froze WikiLeaks funds. *The Raw Story*. Available at: http://www.rawstory.com/rs/2010/12/06/hackers-website-bank-froze-wikileaks-funds/; December 6, 2010 [last accessed February 2013].

45. Pepitone J. Why attackers can't take down amazon.com. *CNN Money*. Available at: http://money.cnn.com/2010/12/09/technology/amazon_wikileaks_attack/index.htm; December 9, 2010 [last accessed February 2013].

46. Halliday J. Operation Payback fails to take down Amazon in WikiLeaks revenge attack. *The Guardian*. Available at: http://www.guardian.co.uk/media/2010/dec/09/operation-payback-wikileaks-anonymous; December 9, 2010 [last accessed February 2013].

47. Pepitone J. Why attackers can't take down amazon.com. *CNN Money*. Available at: http://money.cnn.com/2010/12/09/technology/amazon_wikileaks_attack/index.htm; December 9, 2010 [last accessed February 2013].

48. Halliday J. Operation Payback fails to take down Amazon in WikiLeaks revenge attack. *The Guardian*. Available at: http://www.guardian.co.uk/media/2010/dec/09/operation-payback-wikileaks-anonymous; December 9, 2010 [last accessed February 2013].

49. Stan. Watch: first interview with Mastermind of 'Anonymous' Hacker Group. *AlterPolitics*. Available at: http://www.alterpolitics.com/politics/watch-first-interview-with-mastermind-of-anonymous-hacker-group/; December 10, 2010 [last accessed February 2013].

50. Fuller E. WikiLeaks cyberattacks now involve Visa, Facebook, Twitter, Mastercard. *Christian Science Monitor*. Available at: http://www.csmonitor.com/Business/new-economy/2010/1208/WikiLeaks-cyberattacks-now-involve-Visa-Facebook-Twitter-MasterCard; December 8, 2010 [last accessed February 2013].

51. Fuller E. WikiLeaks cyberattacks now involve Visa, Facebook, Twitter, Mastercard. *Christian Science Monitor*. Available at: http://www.csmonitor.com/Business/new-economy/2010/1208/WikiLeaks-cyberattacks-now-involve-Visa-Facebook-Twitter-MasterCard; December 8, 2010 [last accessed February 2013].

52. AFP. Cyber attack takes out Visa.com, Palin also targeted. *The Independent*. Available at: http://www.independent.co.uk/life-style/cyber-attack-takes-out-visacom-palin-also-targeted-2155030.html; December 9, 2010 [last accessed February 2013].

53. AFP. Cyber attack takes out Visa.com, Palin also targeted. *The Independent*. Available at: http://www. independent.co.uk/life-style/cyber-attack-takes-out-visacom-palin-also-targeted-2155030.html; December 9, 2010 [last accessed February 2013].

54. Page L. Anonymous hackers' Wikileaks 'infowar' LATEST ROUNDUP. *The Register*. Available at: http://www. theregister.co.uk/2010/12/09/operation_payback_anonymous_wikileaks_infowar_latest/; December 9, 2010 [last accessed February 2013].

55. Page L. Anonymous hackers' Wikileaks 'infowar' LATEST ROUNDUP. *The Register*. Available at: http://www. theregister.co.uk/2010/12/09/operation_payback_anonymous_wikileaks_infowar_latest/; December 9, 2010 [last accessed February 2013].

56. Correll S-P. Operation: payback broadens to 'Operation Avenge Assange'. *pandalabs*. Available at: http:// pandalabs.pandasecurity.com/operationpayback-broadens-to-operation-avenge-assange/; December 6, 2010 [last accessed February 2013].

57. Correll S-P. Operation: payback broadens to 'Operation Avenge Assange'. *pandalabs*. Available at: http:// pandalabs.pandasecurity.com/operationpayback-broadens-to-operation-avenge-assange/; December 6, 2010 [last accessed February 2013].

58. CBS News. Twitter suspends account for organizing support for WikiLeaks. Available at: http://www.cbsnews. com/8301-501465_162-20025093-501465.html; December 8, 2010 [last accessed February 2013].

59. Wilson S. Twitter suspends account of pro-WikiLeaks hackers, 'Anonymous' opens new one. *L.A. Weekly Blog*. Available at: http://blogs.laweekly.com/informer/2010/12/twitter_censors_wikileaks_hack.php; December 8, 2010 [last accessed February 2013].

60. CBS News. Twitter suspends account for organizing support for WikiLeaks. Available at: http://www.cbsnews. com/8301-501465_162-20025093-501465.html; December 8, 2010 [last accessed February 2013].

61. Dugan L. WikiLeaks' defender "Anonymous" attacks MasterCard using Twitter; gets banned. *All Twitter*. Available at: http://www.mediabistro.com/alltwitter/twitter-suspends-wikileaks-defender-anonymous-account-after-attacking-mastercard_b933; December 9, 2010 [last accessed February 2013].

62. Dugan L. WikiLeaks' defender "Anonymous" attacks MasterCard using Twitter; gets banned. *All Twitter*. Available at: http://www.mediabistro.com/alltwitter/twitter-suspends-wikileaks-defender-anonymous-account-after-attacking-mastercard_b933; December 9, 2010 [last accessed February 2013].

63. Bryan-Low C, Grundberg S. Hackers rise for WikiLeaks. *Wall Street Journal*. Available at: http://online.wsj.com/ article/SB10001424052748703493504576007182352309942.html; December 8, 2010 [last accessed February 2013].

64. Bryan-Low C, Grundberg S. Hackers rise for WikiLeaks. *Wall Street Journal*. Available at: http://online.wsj.com/ article/SB10001424052748703493504576007182352309942.html; December 8, 2010 [last accessed February 2013].

65. Anon575. Anonymous—operation leakspin—a call to action. Available at: http://www.dailymotion.com/ video/xg3yxn_anonymous-operation-leakspin-a-call-to-action_people#.UQLK6Cf7Jja; December 13, 2010 [last accessed February 2013].

66. Cable Drum. Cable index. Available here: https://www.cabledrum.net/cables/; undated [last accessed February 2013].

67. Anon575. *Anonymous*—operation leakspin—a call to action. Available at: http://www.dailymotion.com/ video/xg3yxn_anonymous-operation-leakspin-a-call-to-action_people#.UQLK6Cf7Jja; December 13, 2010 [last accessed February 2013].

68. Bonner S. *WikiLeaks*: Anonymous stops dropping DDoS bombs, starts dropping science. *BoingBoing*. Available at: http://boingboing.net/2010/12/09/anonymous-stops-drop.html; December 9, 2010 [last accessed February 2013].

69. Quigley R. 4chan down due to DDoS attack Geeko. Available at: http://www.geekosystem.com/4chan-down-ddos/; December 28, 2010 [last accessed February 2013].

70. Quigley R. 4chan down due to DDoS attack. *Geeko*. Available at: http://www.geekosystem.com/4chan-down-ddos/; December 28, 2010 [last accessed February 2013].

71. Smith D. Anonymous hacker target Zimbabwe government over WikiLeaks. *The Guardian*. Available at: http:// www.guardian.co.uk/world/2010/dec/31/anonymous-hackers-zimbabwe-wikileaks; December 31, 2010 [last accessed February 2013].

72. Fogarty K. 'Anonymous' hactivists attack Zimbabwe. *IT World*. Available at: http://www.itworld.com/ internet/132245/anonymous-attacks-injustice-zimbabwe; January 3, 2011 [last accessed February 2013].

73. Ragan S. Anonymous targets corrupt Zimbabwean government. *The Tech Herald*. Available at: http://www. thetechherald.com/articles/Anonymous-targets-corrupt-Zimbabwe-government/12393/; December 30, 2010 [last accessed February 2013].

74. Crawley K. A history of Anonymous. *InfoSec Institute*. Available at: http://resources.infosecinstitute.com/a-history-of-anonymous/; October 24, 2011 [last accessed February 2013].

75. Crawley K. A history of Anonymous. *InfoSec Institute*. Available at: http://resources.infosecinstitute.com/a-history-of-anonymous/; October 24, 2011 [last accessed February 2013].

76. McDonald H. Fine Gael website targeted by Anonymous hackers. *The Guardian*. Available at: http://www.guardian.co.uk/technology/2011/jan/10/fine-gael-website-anonymous-hackers; January 10, 2011 [last accessed February 2013].

77. McDonald H. Fine Gael website targeted by Anonymous hackers. *The Guardian*. Available at: http://www.guardian.co.uk/technology/2011/jan/10/fine-gael-website-anonymous-hackers; January 10, 2011 [last accessed February 2013].

78. Halliday J. Police arrest five over Anonymous WikiLeaks attack. *The Guardian*. Available at: http://www.guardian.co.uk/technology/2011/jan/27/anonymous-hacking; January 27, 2011 [last accessed February 2013].

79. Halliday J. Police arrest five over Anonymous WikiLeaks attack. *The Guardian*. Available at: http://www.guardian.co.uk/technology/2011/jan/27/anonymous-hacking; January 27, 2011 [last accessed February 2013].

80. Hopkins K. Complete Internet blackout in Egypt (updated). *ReadWrite*. Available here: http://readwrite.com/2011/01/27/complete_internet_blackout_in_egypt; January 27, 2011 [last accessed February 2013].

81. Finley K. Egypt: Tor use Skyrocketing as users route-around Internet blocks. *ReadWrite*. Available here: http://readwrite.com/2011/01/28/egypt-tor-use-skyrocketing-as; January 28, 2011 [last accessed February 2013].

82. Hsu T. Egypt restores Internet access, Anonymous hackers get involved. *L.A. Times Technology Blog*. Available at: http://latimesblogs.latimes.com/technology/2011/02/egypt-restores-internet-access.html; February 2, 2011 [last accessed February 2013].

83. Johnson B. How Egypt switched off the Internet. *GigaOm*. Available at: http://gigaom.com/2011/01/28/how-egypt-switched-off-the-internet/; January 28, 2011 [last accessed February 2013].

84. Hsu T. Egypt restores Internet access, Anonymous hackers get involved. *L.A. Times Technology Blog*. Available at: http://latimesblogs.latimes.com/technology/2011/02/egypt-restores-internet-access.html; February 2, 2011 [last accessed February 2013].

85. Hopkins K. Complete Internet Blackout in Egypt (updated). *ReadWrite*. Available at: http://readwrite.com/2011/01/27/complete_internet_blackout_in_egypt; January 27, 2011 [last accessed February 2013].

86. eSecurity. Anonymous hacker target HBGary. Available at: http://www.esecurityplanet.com/headlines/article.php/3923906/Anonymous-Hackers-Target-HBGary.htm; February 8, 2011 [last accessed February 2013].

87. Bright P. Anonymous speaks: the inside story of the HBGary hack. *Ars Technica*. Available at: http://arstechnica.com/tech-policy/2011/02/anonymous-speaks-the-inside-story-of-the-hbgary-hack/; February 15, 2011 [last accessed February 2013].

88. Cringely RX. 2011: the year that hacking goes mainstream. *Infoworld*. Available at: http://www.infoworld.com/t/hacking/2011-the-year-hacking-goes-mainstream-255; February 11, 2011 [last accessed February 2013].

89. Jones G. *Anti-Berlusconi hackers block Italian government website. Reuters Canada*. Available at: http://ca.reuters.com/article/topNews/idCATRE7151XD20110206; February 6, 2011 [last accessed February 2013].

90. Jones G. Anti-Berlusconi hackers block Italian government website. *Reuters Canada*. Available at: http://ca.reuters.com/article/topNews/idCATRE7151XD20110206; February 6, 2011 [last accessed February 2013].

91. Mohit K. Operation Bahrain (#opbahrain)—Anonymous Press Release! *The Hacker News*. Available at: http://thehackernews.com/2011/02/operation-bahrain-opbahrain-anonymous.html; February 16, 2011 [last accessed February 2013].

92. Mohit K. Operation Bahrain (#opbahrain)—Anonymous Press Release! *The Hacker News*. Available at: http://thehackernews.com/2011/02/operation-bahrain-opbahrain-anonymous.html; Febraury 16, 2011 [last accessed February 2013].

93. AnonNews. OpWisconsin. Available at: http://www.anonnews.org/?a=item&i=585&p=press; undated [last accessed February 2013].

94. Greenberg A. Hackers vs. Billionaires: Anonymous takes down Koch-supported Websites amid Wisconsin Protests. *Forbes*. Available at: http://www.forbes.com/sites/andygreenberg/2011/02/28/hackers-vs-billionaires-anonymous-takes-down-koch-supported-websites-amid-wisconsin-protests/; February 28, 2011 [last accessed February 2013].

95. Greenberg A. Hackers vs. Billionaires: Anonymous takes down Koch-supported Websites amid Wisconsin Protests. *Forbes.* Available at: http://www.forbes.com/sites/andygreenberg/2011/02/28/hackers-vs-billionaires-anonymous-takes-down-koch-supported-websites-amid-wisconsin-protests/; Februry 28, 2011 [last accessed February 2013].

96. Greenberg A. Hackers vs. Billionaires: Anonymous takes down Koch-supported Websites amid Wisconsin Protests. *Forbes.* Available at: http://www.forbes.com/sites/andygreenberg/2011/02/28/hackers-vs-billionaires-anonymous-takes-down-koch-supported-websites-amid-wisconsin-protests/; February 28, 2011 [last accessed February 2013].

97. AnonNews. OpWisconsin. Available at: http://www.anonnews.org/?a=item&i=585&p=press; undated [last accessed February 2013].

98. Ragan S. Anonymous plans defense for Bradley Manning—promises media war. *The Tech Herald.* Available at: http://www.thetechherald.com/articles/Anonymous-plans-defense-for-Bradley-Manning-promises-a-media-war/12991/; March 4, 2011 [last accessed February 2013].

99. Greenberg A. Anonymous hackers target alleged WikiLeaker Bradley Mannings' Jailers. *Forbes.* Available at: http://www.forbes.com/sites/andygreenberg/2011/03/07/anonymous-hackers-target-alleged-wikileaker-bradley-mannings-jailers/; March 7, 2011 [last accessed February 2013].

100. Ragan S. Anonymous plans defense for Bradley Manning—promises media war. *The Tech Herald.* Available at: http://www.thetechherald.com/articles/Anonymous-plans-defense-for-Bradley-Manning-promises-a-media-war/12991/; March 4, 2011 [last accessed February 2013].

101. Crawley K. A history of Anonymous. *InfoSec Institute.* Available at: http://resources.infosecinstitute.com/a-history-of-anonymous/; October 24, 2011 [last accessed February 2013].

102. Crawley K. A history of Anonymous. *InfoSec Institute.* Available at: http://resources.infosecinstitute.com/a-history-of-anonymous/; October 24, 2011 [last accessed February 2013].

103. Stone M. Anonymous: operation Bahrain targets Formula 1 websites. *Examiner.* Available at: http://www.examiner.com/article/anonymous-operation-bahrain-targets-formula-1-websites; April 20, 2012 [last accessed February 2013].

104. Stone M. Anonymous: operation Bahrain targets Formula 1 websites. *Examiner.* Available at: http://www.examiner.com/article/anonymous-operation-bahrain-targets-formula-1-websites; April 20, 2012 [last accessed February 2013].

105. Couts A. Anonymous leaks 10,000 'top secret' Iranian gov't emails. *Digital Trends.* Available at: http://www.digitaltrends.com/computing/anonymous-leaks-10000-top-secret-iranian-govt-emails/; June 3, 2011 [last accessed February 2013].

106. Couts A. Anonymous leaks 10,000 'top secret' Iranian gov't emails. *Digital Trends.* Available at: http://www.digitaltrends.com/computing/anonymous-leaks-10000-top-secret-iranian-govt-emails/; June 3, 2011 [last accessed February 2013].

107. Nouveau T. Anonymous launches Operation Blitzkrieg. *TG Daily.* Available at: http://www.tgdaily.com/security-features/55690-anonymous-launches-operation-blitzkrieg; May 2, 2011 [last accessed February 2013].

108. Nouveau T. Anonymous launches Operation Blitzkrieg. *TG Daily.* Available at: http://www.tgdaily.com/security-features/55690-anonymous-launches-operation-blitzkrieg; May 2, 2011 [last accessed February 2013].

109. owi. Anonymous schiesst Neonazi-Seiten ab (Anonymous takes down Neo-Nazi Websites). *20 minuten ONLINE.* Available at: http://www.20min.ch/digital/webpage/story/Anonymous-schiesst-Neonazi-Seiten-ab-18914286; May 3, 2011 [last accessed February 2013].

110. owi. Anonymous schiesst Neonazi-Seiten ab (Anonymous takes down Neo-Nazi Websites). *20 minuten ONLINE.* Available at: http://www.20min.ch/digital/webpage/story/Anonymous-schiesst-Neonazi-Seiten-ab-18914286; May 3, 2011 [last accessed February 2013].

111. Sen0nymous. Anonymous—operation India. *YouTube.* Available at: http://www.youtube.com/watch?v=cYESlyheDCo; May 6, 2011 [last accessed February 2013].

112. Sen0nymous. Anonymous—operation India. *YouTube.* Available at: http://www.youtube.com/watch?v=cYESlyheDCo; May 6, 2011 [last accessed February 2013].

113. Sen0nymous. Anonymous—operation India engaged. *YouTube.* Available at: http://www.youtube.com/watch?v=D8H5Lp4ditE; May 15, 2012 [last accessed February 2013].

114. BBC News Technology. Anonymous attacks Indian government websites. Available at: http://www.bbc.co.uk/news/technology-18114984; May 18, 2011 [last accessed February 2013].

115. BBC News Technology. Anonymous attacks Indian government websites. Available at: http://www.bbc.co.uk/news/technology-18114984; May 18, 2011 [last accessed February 2013].

116. Cluley G. AnonPlus, Anonymous's social network, is hacked. *Naked Security*. Available at: http://nakedsecurity.sophos.com/2011/07/22/anonplus-anonymouss-social-network-is-hacked/; July 22, 2011 [last accessed February 2013].

117. Cluley G. AnonPlus, Anonymous's social network, is hacked. *Naked Security*. Available at: http://nakedsecurity.sophos.com/2011/07/22/anonplus-anonymouss-social-network-is-hacked/; July 22, 2011 [last accessed February 2013].

118. IBN Live. Anonymous India to use RTI in fight against Internet censorship. Available at: http://ibnlive.in.com/news/anonymous-india-to-use-rti-in-fight-against-internet-censorship/265823-11.html; June 13, 2011 [last accessed February 2013].

119. IBN Live. Anonymous India to use RTI in fight against Internet censorship. Available at: http://ibnlive.in.com/news/anonymous-india-to-use-rti-in-fight-against-internet-censorship/265823-11.html; June 13, 2011 [last accessed February 2013].

120. Couts A. Anonymous leaks 10,000 'top secret' Iranian gov't emails. *Digital Trends*. Available at: http://www.digitaltrends.com/computing/anonymous-leaks-10000-top-secret-iranian-govt-emails/; June 3, 2011 [last accessed February 2013].

121. Couts A. Anonymous leaks 10,000 'top secret' Iranian gov't emails. *Digital Trends*. Available at: http://www.digitaltrends.com/computing/anonymous-leaks-10000-top-secret-iranian-govt-emails/; June 3, 2011 [last accessed February 2013].

122. Stone M. Operation Malaysia: Anonymous DDoS attacks cripple gov websites. *Examiner*. Available at: http://www.examiner.com/article/operation-malaysia-anonymous-ddos-attacks-cripple-gov-websites; June 15, 2011 [last accessed February 2013].

123. Stone M. Operation Malaysia: Anonymous DDoS attacks cripple gov websites. *Examiner*. Available at: http://www.examiner.com/article/operation-malaysia-anonymous-ddos-attacks-cripple-gov-websites; June 15, 2011 [last accessed February 2013].

124. Stone M. Operation Malaysia: Anonymous DDoS attacks cripple gov websites. *Examiner*. Available at: http://www.examiner.com/article/operation-malaysia-anonymous-ddos-attacks-cripple-gov-websites; June 15, 2011 [last accessed February 2013].

125. Amped Status. A99 OpESR Communication #2: Ctrl+Alt+Bernanke. *YouTube*. Available at: http://www.youtube.com/watch?v=XySGw-g2tyk; June 14, 2011 [last accessed February 2013].

126. Schortgen Jr K. Hackers launch first operation of Empire State Rebellion. *Examiner*. Available at: http://www.examiner.com/article/hackers-launch-first-operation-of-empire-state-rebellion; June 11, 2011 [last accessed February 2013].

127. Amped Status. A99 Operation Empire State Rebellion—Communication #1. *YouTube*. Available at: http://www.youtube.com/watch?v=7D6neBzTnOQ; March 14, 2011 [last accessed February 2013].

128. Schortgen Jr K. *Hackers launch first operation of Empire State Rebellion*. *Examiner*. Available at: http://www.examiner.com/article/hackers-launch-first-operation-of-empire-state-rebellion; June 11, 2011 [last accessed February 2013].

129. Chapman S. Operation Anti-Security: LulzSec and Anonymous target banks and governments. *ZDNet*. Available at: http://www.zdnet.com/blog/security/operation-anti-security-lulzsec-and-anonymous-target-banks-and-governments/8812; June 20, 2011 [last accessed February 2013].

130. Albanesius C. LulzSec, Anonymous team up for 'Operation Anti-Security PCMag'. Available at: http://www.pcmag.com/article2/0,2817,2387264,00.asp; June 20, 2011 [last accessed February 2013].

131. A Guest. Operation anti-security. *Pastebin*. Available at: http://pastebin.com/9KyA0E5v; June 19, 2011 [last accessed February 2013].

132. McHugh M. LulzSec and Anonymous unite for operation anti-security. *Digital Trends*. Available at: http://www.digitaltrends.com/computing/lulzsec-and-anonymous-unite-for-operation-anti-security/; June 20, 2011 [last accessed February 2013].

133. Schonfeld E. Anonymous declares war on the city of Orlando. *TechCrunch*. Available at: http://techcrunch.com/2011/06/27/anonymous-declares-war-orlando/; June 27, 2011 [last accessed February 2013].

134. Ragan S. Anonymous defends the hungry—declares war on Orlando. *The Tech Herald*. Available at: http://www.thetechherald.com/articles/Anonymous-defends-the-hungry-declares-war-on-Orlando/13927/; July 7, 2011 [last accessed February 2013].

135. Anon6t7U. Anonymous operation Orlando press release. *YouTube video.* Available at: http://www.youtube.com/watch?v=yal7n1IrjSg; June 23, 2011 [last accessed February 2013].

136. Kumar M. Operation Intifada: Anonymous prepares For DDoS attack on Israel Parliament. *The Hacker News.* Available at: http://thehackernews.com/2011/07/operation-intifada-anonymous-prepares.html; July 26, 2011 [last accessed February 2013].

137. Kumar M. Operation Intifada: Anonymous prepares for DDoS attack on Israel Parliament. *The Hacker News.* Available at: http://thehackernews.com/2011/07/operation-intifada-anonymous-prepares.html; July 26, 2011 [last accessed February 2013].

138. Ragan S. Anonymous defends the hungry—declares war on Orlando. *The Tech Herald.* Available at: http://www.thetechherald.com/articles/Anonymous-defends-the-hungry-declares-war-on-Orlando/13927/; July 7, 2011 [last accessed February 2013].

139. Ragan S. Anonymous defends the hungry—declares war on Orlando. *The Tech Herald.* Available at: http://www.thetechherald.com/articles/Anonymous-defends-the-hungry-declares-war-on-Orlando/13927/; July 7, 2011 [last accessed February 2013].

140. Ragan S. Anonymous defends the hungry—declares war on Orlando. *The Tech Herald.* Available at: http://www.thetechherald.com/articles/Anonymous-defends-the-hungry-declares-war-on-Orlando/13927/; July 7, 2011 [last accessed February 2013].

141. Ragan S. Anonymous defends the hungry—declares war on Orlando. *The Tech Herald.* Available at: http://www.thetechherald.com/articles/Anonymous-defends-the-hungry-declares-war-on-Orlando/13927/; July 7, 2011 [last accessed February 2013].

142. Lee J. Florida court's tango down by Operation Orlando, Anonymous. *Cyber War News.* Available at: http://www.cyberwarnews.info/2011/07/06/florida-courts-tango-down-by-operation-orlando-anonymous/; July 6, 2011 [last accessed February 2013].

143. Lee J. Florida court's tango down by Operation Orlando, Anonymous. *Cyber War News.* Available at: http://www.cyberwarnews.info/2011/07/06/florida-courts-tango-down-by-operation-orlando-anonymous/; July 6, 2011 [last accessed February 2013].

144. Bright P. 'Military Meltdown Monday': 90K military usernames, hashes released. *Ars Technica.* Available at: http://arstechnica.com/tech-policy/2011/07/military-meltdown-monday-90k-military-usernames-hashes-released/; July 12, 2011 [last accessed February 2013].

145. Bright P. 'Military Meltdown Monday': 90K military usernames, hashes released. *Ars Technica.* Available at: http://arstechnica.com/tech-policy/2011/07/military-meltdown-monday-90k-military-usernames-hashes-released/; July 12, 2011 [last accessed February 2013].

146. Schertow JA. Operation Green Rights: Anonymous targets the Tar sands. *Intercontinentalcry.* Available at: http://intercontinentalcry.org/operation-green-rights-anonymous-targets-the-tar-sands/; July 13, 2012 [last accessed February 2013].

147. Anonymous. Operation Green Rights' project Tarmageddon. *AnonNews.* Available at: http://anonnews.org/?p=press&a=item&i=1021; July 12, 2012 [last accessed February 2013].

148. Schertow JA. Operation Green Rights: Anonymous targets the Tar sands. Intercontinentalcry. Available at: http://intercontinentalcry.org/operation-green-rights-anonymous-targets-the-tar-sands/; July 13, 2012 [last accessed February 2013].

149. Stone M. Anonymous hacks Monsanto: operation Green Rights begins. *Examiner.* Available at: http://www.examiner.com/article/anonymous-hacks-monsanto-operation-green-rights-begins; July 13, 2012 [last accessed February 2013].

150. Stone M. Anonymous hacks Monsanto: operation Green Rights begins. *Examiner.* Available at: http://www.examiner.com/article/anonymous-hacks-monsanto-operation-green-rights-begins; July 13, 2012 [last accessed February 2013].

151. AdBusters. #OCCUPYWALLSTREET. http://www.adbusters.org/blogs/adbusters-blog/occupywallstreet.html; July 13, 2011 [last accessed February 2013].

152. AdBusters. #OCCUPYWALLSTREET. http://www.adbusters.org/blogs/adbusters-blog/occupywallstreet.html; July 13, 2011 [last accessed February 2013].

153. Mills E. Monsanto confirms Anonymous hacking attack. *CNet News.* Available at: http://news.cnet.com/8301-27080_3-20079233-245/monsanto-confirms-anonymous-hacking-attack/; July 13, 2011 [last accessed February 2013].

154. Mills E. Monsanto confirms Anonymous hacking attack. *CNet News.* Available at: http://news.cnet.com/8301-27080_3-20079233-245/monsanto-confirms-anonymous-hacking-attack/; July 13, 2011 [last accessed February 2013].

155. Peckham M. Anonymous incurs Google + Ban, retaliates by launching own social network. *Time Tech*. Available at: http://techland.time.com/2011/07/18/anonymous-incurs-google-ban-retaliates-by-launching-own-social-network/; July 19, 2011 [last accessed February 2013].

156. Peckham M. Anonymous incurs Google + Ban, retaliates by launching own social network. *Time Tech*. Available at: http://techland.time.com/2011/07/18/anonymous-incurs-google-ban-retaliates-by-launching-own-social-network/; July 19, 2011 [last accessed February 2013].

157. Rodriguez S. FBI arrests 14 alleged members of hacker group Anonymous. *L.A. Times*. Available at: http://articles.latimes.com/2011/jul/20/business/la-fi-hacker-arrests-20110720; July 20, 2011 [last accessed February 2013].

158. Rodriguez S. FBI arrests 14 alleged members of hacker group Anonymous. *L.A. Times*. Available at: http://articles.latimes.com/2011/jul/20/business/la-fi-hacker-arrests-20110720; July 20, 2011 [last accessed February 2013].

159. Peckham M. Anonymous: hey, we just hacked NATO. *Time Tech*. Available at: http://techland.time.com/2011/07/21/anonymous-hey-we-just-hacked-nato/; July 21, 2011 [last accessed February 2013].

160. Zakalwe C. Turkish hacking group admits responsibility for Charlie Hebdo Website attack. *Islam versus Europe*. Available at: http://islamversuseurope.blogspot.com/2011/11/turkish-hacking-group-admits.html; November 5, 2011 [last accessed February 2013].

161. Cluley G. AnonPlus, Anonymous's social network, is hacked. *Naked Security*. Available at: http://nakedsecurity.sophos.com/2011/07/22/anonplus-anonymouss-social-network-is-hacked/; July 22, 2011 [last accessed February 2013].

162. Cluley G. AnonPlus, Anonymous's social network, is hacked. *Naked Security*. Available at: http://nakedsecurity.sophos.com/2011/07/22/anonplus-anonymouss-social-network-is-hacked/; July 22, 2011 [last accessed February 2013].

163. Wisniewski C. AntiSec movement continues to strike government security contractors. *NakedSecurity*. Available at: http://nakedsecurity.sophos.com/2011/07/30/antisec-movement-continues-to-strike-government security-contractors/; July 30, 2011 [last accessed February 2013].

164. Wisniewski C. AntiSec movement continues to strike government security contractors. *NakedSecurity*. Available at: http://nakedsecurity.sophos.com/2011/07/30/antisec-movement-continues-to-strike-government-security-contractors/; July 30, 2011 [last accessed February 2013].

165. VOICE. Shooting Sheriffs Saturday—official release statement. *Pastebin*. Available at: http://pastebin.com/iKsuRkUj; August 5, 2012 [last accessed February 2013].

166. Mills E. AntiSec hackers post stolen police data as revenge for arrests. *CNet News*. Available at: http://news.cnet.com/8301-27080_3-20089054-245/antisec-hackers-post-stolen-police-data-as-revenge-for-arrests/; August 6, 2012 [last accessed February 2013].

167. Stone M. Anonymous protests arrests with 'Shooting Sheriffs Saturday'. *Examiner*. Available at: http://www.examiner.com/article/anonymous-protests-arrests-with-shooting-sheriffs-saturday August 6, 2012 [last accessed February 2013].

168. Kremer A. Operation AntiSec: Neonazi-Netzwerk 'Blood and Honour' gehackt. *Gulli*. Available at: http://www.gulli.com/news/16792-operation-antisec-neonazi-netzwerk-blood-and-honour-gehackt-2011-08-06; August 6, 2011 [last accessed February 2013].

169. Kremer A. Operation AntiSec: Neonazi-Netzwerk 'Blood and Honour' gehackt. *Gulli*. Available at: http://www.gulli.com/news/16792-operation-antisec-neonazi-netzwerk-blood-and-honour-gehackt-2011-08-06; August 6, 2011 [last accessed February 2013].

170. Perlroth N. In attack on Vatican Web site, a glimpse of hackers' tactics. *New York Times*. Available at: http://www.nytimes.com/2012/02/27/technology/attack-on-vatican-web-site-offers-view-of-hacker-groups-tactics.html?pagewanted=all&_r=0; February 26, 2012 [last accessed February 2013].

171. Perlroth N. In attack on Vatican Web site, a glimpse of hackers' tactics. *New York Times*. Available at: http://www.nytimes.com/2012/02/27/technology/attack-on-vatican-web-site-offers-view-of-hacker-groups-tactics.html?pagewanted=all&_r=0; February 26, 2012 [last accessed February 2013].

172. Ragan S. Anonymous leaks BART data—prepares for a Bay of Rage. *The Tech Herald*. Available at: http://www.thetechherald.com/articles/Anonymous-leaks-BART-data-prepares-for-a-Bay-of-Rage; August 15, 2011 [last accessed February 2013].

173. Stone M. Operation BART 2: Anonymous protests—BART stations close. *Examiner*. Available at: http://www.examiner.com/article/operation-bart-2-anonymous-protests-bart-stations-close; August 23, 2011 [last accessed February 2013].

174. Jennings R. D'oh! BART hacked in censor furor; Anonymous unleash #OpBART. *Computerworld Blog*. Available at: http://blogs.computerworld.com/18797/doh_bart_hacked_in_censor_furor_anonymous_unleash_opbart; August 15, 2011 [last accessed February 2013].

175. Elinson Z, Shoshana W. Latest BART shooting prompts new discussion of reforms. *New York Times*. Available at: http://www.nytimes.com/2011/07/17/us/17bcbart.html?pagewanted=all&_r=0; July 16, 2011 [last accessed February 2013].

176. Kumar M. Vanguard Defense Industries (VDI) hacked for #Antisec operation. *The Hacker News*. Available at: http://thehackernews.com/2011/08/vanguard-defense-industries-vdi-hacked.html; August 16, 2011 [last accessed February 2013].

177. Kumar M. Vanguard Defense Industries (VDI) hacked for #Antisec operation. *The Hacker News*. Available at: http://thehackernews.com/2011/08/vanguard-defense-industries-vdi-hacked.html; August 16, 2011 [last accessed February 2013].

178. Adbusters. Anonymous Joins #OCCUPYWALLSTREET. Available at: http://www.adbusters.org/blogs/adbusters-blog/anonymous-joins-occupywallstreet.html; August 23, 2011 [last accessed February 2013].

179. Adbusters. Anonymous Joins #OCCUPYWALLSTREET. Available at: http://www.adbusters.org/blogs/adbusters-blog/anonymous-joins-occupywallstreet.html; August 23, 2011 [last accessed February 2013].

180. Kumar M. Texas law enforcement Hacked by #AntiSec and #FreeAnons—3 GB of data leaked. *The Hacker News*. Available at: http://thehackernews.com/2011/09/texas-law-enforcement-hacked-by-antisec.html; September 1, 2011 [last accessed February 2013].

181. Kumar M. Texas law enforcement Hacked by #AntiSec and #FreeAnons—3 GB of data leaked. *The Hacker News*. Available at: http://thehackernews.com/2011/09/texas-law-enforcement-hacked-by-antisec.html; September 1, 2011 [last accessed February 2013].

182. WeAreLegion1000000. Anonymous Operation Summerstorm gegen die NPD Webseite down ddos. *YouTube*. Available at: http://www.youtube.com/watch?v=NaVPLt4ZQX8; September 13, 2011 [last accessed February 2013].

183. WeAreLegion1000000. Anonymous Operation Summerstorm gegen die NPD Webseite down ddos. *YouTube*. Available at: http://www.youtube.com/watch?v=NaVPLt4ZQX8; September 13, 2011 [last accessed February 2013].

184. Crawley K. *A history of Anonymous. InfoSec Institute*. Available at: http://resources.infosecinstitute.com/a-history-of-anonymous/; October 24, 2011 [last accessed February 2013].

185. Crawley K. *A history of Anonymous. InfoSec Institute*. Available at: http://resources.infosecinstitute.com/a-history-of-anonymous/; October 24, 2011 [last accessed February 2013].

186. Gallagher S. Anonymous takes down darknet child porn site on Tor network. *Ars Technica*. Available at: http://arstechnica.com/business/2011/10/anonymous-takes-down-darknet-child-porn-site-on-tor-network/; October 23, 2011 [last accessed February 2013].

187. Gallagher S. Anonymous takes down darknet child porn site on Tor network. *Ars Technica*. Available at: http://arstechnica.com/business/2011/10/anonymous-takes-down-darknet-child-porn-site-on-tor-network/; October 23, 2011 [last accessed February 2013].

188. Kim L. Anonymous Takes on Child Pornography Sites. *IBTimes*. Available at: http://www.ibtimes.com/anonymous-takes-child-pornography-sites-360614; October 24, 2011 [last accessed February 2013].

189. Kim L. Anonymous takes on child pornography sites. *IBTimes*. Available at: http://www.ibtimes.com/anonymous-takes-child-pornography-sites-360614; October 24, 2011 [last accessed February 2013].

190. Kaelin L. Anonymous hacks Boston Police, publishes officer details. *TechSpot*. Available at: http://www.techspot.com/news/45975-anonymous-hacks-boston-police-publishes-officer-details.html; Oct. 24, 2011 [last accessed February 2013].

191. Kaelin L. Anonymous hacks Boston Police, publishes officer details. *TechSpot*. Available at: http://www.techspot.com/news/45975-anonymous-hacks-boston-police-publishes-officer-details.html; October 24, 2011 [last accessed February 2013].

192. Stone M. Anonymous takes down Muslim Brotherhood. *Examiner*. Available at: http://www.examiner.com/article/anonymous-takes-down-muslim-brotherhood; November 13, 2011 [last accessed February 2013].

193. Stone M. Anonymous takes down Muslim Brotherhood. *Examiner*. Available at: http://www.examiner.com/article/anonymous-takes-down-muslim-brotherhood; November 13, 2011 [last accessed February 2013].

194. Brodkin J. 4chan hit by DDoS attack, struggling to get back online. *Ars Technica*. Available at: http://arstechnica.com/business/2011/11/4chan-was-hit-by-ddos-attack-two-days-ago-still-struggling-to-get-back-online/; November 25, 2011 [last accessed February 2013].

195. Stone M. Anonymous targets top cops: Cabin Cr3w launches #OpPigRoast. *Examiner*. Available at: http://www. examiner.com/article/anonymous-targets-top-cops-cabin-cr3w-launches-oppigroast; November 22, 2011 [last accessed February 2013].

196. Stone M. Anonymous targets top cops: Cabin Cr3w launches #OpPigRoast. *Examiner*. Available at: http://www. examiner.com/article/anonymous-targets-top-cops-cabin-cr3w-launches-oppigroast; November 22, 2011 [last accessed February 2013].

197. Stone M. Anonymous hacktivists target UC Davis pepper spray cop Lt. John Pike. *Examiner*. Available at: http:// www.examiner.com/article/anonymous-hacktivists-target-uc-davis-pepper-spray-cop-lt-john-pike; November 23, 2011 [last accessed February 2013].

198. Stone M. Anonymous hacktivists target UC Davis pepper spray cop Lt. John Pike. *Examiner*. Available at: http:// www.examiner.com/article/anonymous-hacktivists-target-uc-davis-pepper-spray-cop-lt-john-pike;   November 23, 2011 [last accessed February 2013].

199. Stone M. Anonymous via TeaMp0isoN hacks UN, leaks email info. *Examiner*. Available at: http://www. examiner.com/article/anonymous-via-teamp0ison-hacks-un-leaks-email-info;   November   29,   2011   [last accessed February 2013].

200. Stone M. Anonymous via TeaMp0isoN hacks UN, leaks email info. *Examiner*. Available at: http://www. examiner.com/article/anonymous-via-teamp0ison-hacks-un-leaks-email-info;   November   29,   2011   [last accessed February 2013].

201. Stone M. Anonymous hacks Monsanto PR firm Bivings Group. *Examiner*. Available at: http://www.examiner. com/article/anonymous-hacks-monsanto-pr-firm-bivings-group; December 7, 2011 [last accessed February 2013].

202. A Guest. Bivings-Corp ended by Anonymous. *Pastebin*. Available at: http://pastebin.com/UZTcLMGT; December 5, 2011 [last accessed February 2013].

203. Zeigler T. Why we shut down Slurp 140. *The Brick Factory Blog*. Available at: http://blog.thebrickfactory.com/; January 9, 2013 [last accessed February 2013].

204. Stone M. Anonymous hacks Monsanto PR firm Bivings Group. *Examiner*. Available at: http://www.examiner. com/article/anonymous-hacks-monsanto-pr-firm-bivings-group; December 7, 2011 [last accessed February 2013].

205. A Guest. Bivings-Corp Ended by Anonymous. *Pastebin*. Available at: http://pastebin.com/UZTcLMGT; December 5, 2011 [last accessed February 2013].

206. Perlroth N. Hackers breach the web site of Stratfor global intelligence. *New York Times*. Available at: http://www. nytimes.com/2011/12/26/technology/hackers-breach-the-web-site-of-stratfor-global-intelligence.html; December 25, 2011 [last accessed February 2013].

207. Ball J. WikiLeaks publishes Stratfor emails linked to Anonymous attack. *The Guardian*. Available at: http://www. guardian.co.uk/media/2012/feb/27/wikileaks-publishes-stratfor-emails-anonymous; February 26, 2012 [last accessed February 2013].

208. Booth R. US Security firm Stratfor attacked by 'Robin Hood' hackers. *The Guardian*. Available at: http://www.guardian.co.uk/technology/2011/dec/27/security-stratfor-hackers-credit-cards; December 27, 2011 [last accessed February 2013].

209. Perlroth N. Hackers breach the web site of Stratfor global intelligence. *New York Times*. Available at: http://www. nytimes.com/2011/12/26/technology/hackers-breach-the-web-site-of-stratfor-global-intelligence.html; December 25, 2011 [last accessed February 2013].

210. Know Your Meme. Operation Megaupload. Available at: http://knowyourmeme.com/memes/events/ operation-megaupload; January 10, 2013 [last accessed February 2013].

211. Lennard N. Anonymous Reflects on a 'frantic and historic' year. *Salon*. Available at: http://www.salon.com/ 2012/12/27/anonymous_reflects_on_a_frantic_and_historic_year/; December 27, 2012 [last accessed February 2013].

212. Know Your Meme. Operation Megaupload. Available at: http://knowyourmeme.com/memes/events/ operation-megaupload; January 10, 2013 [last accessed February 2013].

213. Lennard N. Anonymous reflects on a 'frantic and historic' year. *Salon*. Available at: http://www.salon.com/ 2012/12/27/anonymous_reflects_on_a_frantic_and_historic_year/; December 27, 2012 [last accessed February 2013].

214. Lennard N. Anonymous reflects on a 'frantic and historic' year. *Salon*. Available at: http://www.salon.com/ 2012/12/27/anonymous_reflects_on_a_frantic_and_historic_year/; December 27, 2012 [last accessed February 2013].

215. Kirk J. Hacker billboard pastebin struggles with DDoS attacks. *PC World.* Available at: http://www.pcworld.com/article/250580/hacker_billboard_pastebin_struggles_with_ddos_attacks.html; February 23, 2012 [last accessed February 2013].

216. Kirk J. Hacker billboard pastebin struggles with DDoS attacks. *PC World.* Available at: http://www.pcworld.com/article/250580/hacker_billboard_pastebin_struggles_with_ddos_attacks.html; February 23, 2012 [last accessed February 2013].

217. Stone M. Anonymous joins Occupy Nigeria, warns Goodluck Johnson. *Examiner.* Available at: http://www.examiner.com/article/anonymous-joins-occupy-nigeria-warns-goodluck-jonathan; January 5, 2012 [last accessed February 2013].

218. Stone M. Anonymous joins Occupy Nigeria, warns Goodluck Johnson. *Examiner.* Available at: http://www.examiner.com/article/anonymous-joins-occupy-nigeria-warns-goodluck-jonathan; January 5, 2012 [last accessed February 2013].

219. Slyr0x. Anonymous hackers join 'arms' with Nigerians in the #occupynigeria protests. *Nairaland Forum.* Available at: http://www.nairaland.com/838582/anonymous-hackers-join-arms-nigerians; January 4, 2012 [last accessed February 2013].

220. Stevenson A. Elisagate: Anonymous hackers launch Finland cyber war. *International Business Times.* Available at: http://www.ibtimes.co.uk/articles/278887/20120109/anonymous-hackers-punish-finnish-court-s-pirate.htm; January 9, 2012 [last accessed February 2013].

221. Stevenson A. Elisagate: Anonymous hackers launch Finland cyber war. *International Business Times.* Available at: http://www.ibtimes.co.uk/articles/278887/20120109/anonymous-hackers-punish-finnish-court-s-pirate.htm; January 9, 2012 [last accessed February 2013].

222. AFP. Anonymous targets Finland over anti-piracy efforts. Available at: http://www.google.com/hostednews/afp/article/ALeqM5jvMa60BIl3pWs09v8h0U_HR15mXw?docId=CNG.95c30a89f1409b49ec29cd8739775a81.71; January 10, 2012 [last accessed February 2013].

223. AFP. Anonymous targets Finland over anti-piracy efforts. Available at: http://www.google.com/hostednews/afp/article/ALeqM5jvMa60BIl3pWs09v8h0U_HR15mXw?docId=CNG.95c30a89f1409b49ec29cd8739775a81.71; January 10, 2012 [last accessed February 2013].

224. Ernesto. Anonymous takes out Pirate Bay Nemeses. *TorrentFreak.* Available at: http://torrentfreak.com/anonymous-takes-out-pirate-bay-nemesises-120111/; January 12, 2012 [last accessed February 2013].

225. enigmax. Dutch ISPs ordered to block The Pirate Bay. *TorrentFreak.* Available at: http://torrentfreak.com/dutch-isps-ordered-to-block-the-pirate-bay-120111/; January 11, 2012 [last accessed February 2013].

226. Guest. Anonymous operation payback—media update. *Pastebin.* Available at: http://pastebin.com/m2P4sVK5; January 24, 2012 [last accessed February 2013].

227. Guest. Anonymous operation payback—media update. *Pastebin.* Available at: http://pastebin.com/m2P4sVK5; January 24, 2012 [last accessed February 2013].

228. Guest. Anonymous operation payback—media update. *Pastebin.* Available at: http://pastebin.com/m2P4sVK5; January 24, 2012 [last accessed February 2013].

229. Guest. Anonymous operation payback—media update. *Pastebin.* Available at: http://pastebin.com/m2P4sVK5; January 24, 2012 [last accessed February 2013].

230. BBC News. Polish site hit in Acta hack attack. Available at: http://www.bbc.co.uk/news/technology-16686265; January 23, 2012 [last accessed February 2013].

231. Bright P. ACTA on the edge in Europe? Poland suspends ratification, Greece gets hacked. *Ars Technica.* Available at: http://arstechnica.com/tech-policy/2012/02/acta-on-the-edge-in-europe-poland-suspends-ratification-greece-gets-hacked/; February 23, 2012 [last accessed February 2013].

232. BBC News. Polish site hit in Acta hack attack. Available at: http://www.bbc.co.uk/news/technology-16686265; January 23, 2012 [last accessed February 2013].

233. Guest. Anonymous operation payback—media update. *Pastebin.* Available at: http://pastebin.com/m2P4sVK5; January 24, 2012 [last accessed February 2013].

234. Guest. Anonymous operation payback—media update. *Pastebin.* Available at: http://pastebin.com/m2P4sVK5; January 24, 2012 [last accessed February 2013].

235. Guest. Anonymous operation payback—media update. *Pastebin.* Available at: http://pastebin.com/m2P4sVK5; January 24, 2012 [last accessed February 2013].

236. Guest. Anonymous operation payback—media update. *Pastebin.* Available at: http://pastebin.com/m2P4sVK5; January 24, 2012 [last accessed February 2013].

237. Russell J. Anonymous hacks into FTC online security site, warns of more protest action. *TNW (The Next Web)*. Available at: http://thenextweb.com/insider/2012/01/24/anonymous-has-just-hacked-into-the-ftcs-online-guardian-site/; January 24, 2012 [last accessed February 2013].

238. Bunn E. 'Anonymous' hackers target FTC, Sen. Grassley. *Medill*. Available at: http://news.medill.northwestern.edu/chicago/news.aspx?id=199000; January 24, 2012 [last accessed February 2013].

239. Russell J. Anonymous hacks into FTC online security site, warns of more protest action. *TNW (The Next Web)*. Available at: http://thenextweb.com/insider/2012/01/24/anonymous-has-just-hacked-into-the-ftcs-online-guardian-site/; January 24, 2012 [last accessed February 2013].

240. Bunn E. 'Anonymous' hackers target FTC, Sen. Grassley. *Medill*. Available at: http://news.medill.northwestern.edu/chicago/news.aspx?id=199000; January 24, 2012 [last accessed February 2013].

241. NewEurope. Anonymous hacks European Parliament website. Available at: http://www.neurope.eu/article/anonymous-hacks-european-parliament-website; January 26, 2012 [last accessed February 2013].

242. NewEurope. Anonymous hacks European Parliament website. Available at: http://www.neurope.eu/article/anonymous-hacks-european-parliament-website; January 26, 2012 [last accessed February 2013].

243. Anonymous-Operation Ethiopia. Facebook-page. Available at: https://www.facebook.com/pages/Anonymous-Operation-Ethiopia/357607667585625; January 28, 2012 [last accessed February 2013].

244. Anonymous- Operation Ethiopia. Facebook-page. Available at: https://www.facebook.com/pages/Anonymous-Operation-Ethiopia/357607667585625; January 28, 2012 [last accessed February 2013].

245. Kovacs E. UFC site hacked after Dana White threatens Anonymous. *Softpedia*. Available at: http://news.softpedia.com/news/UFC-Site-Hacked-After-Dana-White-Threatens-Anonymous-249073.shtml; January 27, 2012 [last accessed February 2013].

246. Kovacs E. UFC site hacked after Dana White threatens Anonymous. *Softpedia*. Available at: http://news.softpedia.com/news/UFC-Site-Hacked-After-Dana-White-Threatens-Anonymous-249073.shtml; January 27, 2012 [last accessed February 2013].

247. Lennard N. Anonymous Reflects on a 'frantic and historic' year. *Salon*. Available at: http://www.salon.com/2012/12/27/anonymous_reflects_on_a_frantic_and_historic_year/; December 27, 2012 [last accessed February 2013].

248. Lennard N. Anonymous reflects on a 'frantic and historic' year. *Salon*. Available at: http://www.salon.com/2012/12/27/anonymous_reflects_on_a_frantic_and_historic_year/; December 27, 2012 [last accessed February 2013].

249. AFP. 'Anonymous' hackers attack Brazilian bank websites. Available at: http://www.google.com/hostednews/afp/article/ALeqM5jyN0Fn4ZXfibMLdscIqXDnIXVDjw; February 1, 2012 [last accessed February 2013].

250. Kumar M. Citigroup sites hit by Brazilian Anonymous hacker. *The Hacker News*. Available at: http://thehackernews.com/2012/02/citigroup-sites-hit-by-brazilian.html; February 6, 2012 [last accessed February 2013].

251. Neugebauer C. Salt Lake City police website hacked; anonymous group takes credit. *The Salt Lake Tribune*. Available at: http://www.sltrib.com/sltrib/news/53417158-78/police-website-group-information.html.csp; February 1, 2012 [last accessed February 2013].

252. Neugebauer C. Salt Lake City police website hacked; anonymous group takes credit. *The Salt Lake Tribune*. Available at: http://www.sltrib.com/sltrib/news/53417158-78/police-website-group-information.html.csp; February 1, 2012 [last accessed February 2013].

253. Topping A. BNP links to US extremists revealed by Anonymous. *The Guardian*. Available at: http://www.guardian.co.uk/world/2012/feb/01/bnp-emails-far-right-anonymous; February 1, 2012 [last accessed February 2013].

254. Topping A. BNP links to US extremists revealed by Anonymous. *The Guardian*. Available at: http://www.guardian.co.uk/world/2012/feb/01/bnp-emails-far-right-anonymous; February 1, 2012 [last accessed February 2013].

255. Murphy D. Video: Boston Police fight Anonymous hack with Sarcasm. *PC Magazine*. Available at: http://www.pcmag.com/article2/0,2817,2400160,00.asp; February 12, 2012 [last accessed February 2013].

256. Murphy D. *Video*: Boston Police fight Anonymous hack with Sarcasm. *PC Magazine*. Available at: http://www.pcmag.com/article2/0,2817,2400160,00.asp; February 12, 2012 [last accessed February 2013].

257. Chen A. Anonymous leaks huge cache of emails from Iraq war crimes. *Case Gawker*. Available at: http://gawker.com/5882063/anonymous-releases-huge-cache-of-emails-related-to-iraq-war-crimes-case; February 3, 2012 [last accessed February 2013].

258. Chen A. Anonymous leaks huge cache of emails from Iraq war crimes. *Case Gawker*. Available at: http://gawker.com/5882063/anonymous-releases-huge-cache-of-emails-related-to-iraq-war-crimes-case; February 3, 2012 [last accessed February 2013].

259. CBS News. Anonymous hackers attack law enforcement sites. Available at: http://www.cbsnews.com/8301-201_162-57371325/anonymous-hackers-attack-law-enforcement-sites/; February 3, 2012 [last accessed February 2013].

260. CBS News. Anonymous hackers attack law enforcement sites. Available at: http://www.cbsnews.com/8301-201_162-57371325/anonymous-hackers-attack-law-enforcement-sites/; February 3, 2012 [last accessed February 2013].

261. RedOrbit. Swedish Government hit by hackers. Available at: http://www.redorbit.com/news/technology/1112468582/swedish-government-site-hit-by-hackers/; February 6, 2012 [last accessed February 2013].

262. RedOrbit. Swedish Government hit by hackers. Available at: http://www.redorbit.com/news/technology/1112468582/swedish-government-site-hit-by-hackers/; February 6, 2012 [last accessed February 2013].

263. Russia Times. Department of Homeland Security website hacked by Anonymous. Available at: http://rt.com/usa/news/homeland-security-website-anonymous-473/; February 4, 2012 [last accessed February 2013].

264. Russia Times. Department of Homeland Security website hacked by Anonymous. Available at: http://rt.com/usa/news/homeland-security-website-anonymous-473/; February 4, 2012 [last accessed February 2013].

265. Staff member. Anonymous hacks website of pro-ACTA group Prophon in Bulgaria. *Sofia Echo*. Available at: http://sofiaecho.com/2012/02/05/1759788_anonymous-hacks-website-of-pro-acta-group-prophon-in-bulgaria; February 5, 2012 [last accessed February 2013].

266. Staff member. Anonymous hacks website of pro-ACTA group Prophon in Bulgaria. *Sofia Echo*. Available at: http://sofiaecho.com/2012/02/05/1759788_anonymous-hacks-website-of-pro-acta-group-prophon-in-bulgaria; February 5, 2012 [last accessed February 2013].

267. Crum T. Hackers group posts chief's information online. *The Charleston Gazette*. Available at: http://wvgazette.com/News/201202070284; February 7, 2012 [last accessed February 2013].

268. Crum T. Hackers group posts chief's information online. *The Charleston Gazette*. Available at: http://wvgazette.com/News/201202070284; February 7, 2012 [last accessed February 2013].

269. The Moscow Times. United Russia Site hacked by Hacker Group Anonymous. Available at: http://www.themoscowtimes.com/news/article/united-russia-site-attacked-by-hacker-group-anonymous/452761.html; February 10, 2012 [last accessed February 2013].

270. The Moscow Times. United Russia Site hacked by Hacker Group Anonymous. Available at: http://www.themoscowtimes.com/news/article/united-russia-site-attacked-by-hacker-group-anonymous/452761.html; February 10, 2012 [last accessed February 2013].

271. Monsters&Critics. Hackers from Anonymous post classified German files online. Available at: http://news.monstersandcritics.com/europe/news/article_1689833.php/Hackers-from-Anonymous-post-classified-German-files-online; February 8, 2012 [last accessed February 2013].

272. Monsters&Critics. Hackers from Anonymous post classified German files online. Available at: http://news.monstersandcritics.com/europe/news/article_1689833.php/Hackers-from-Anonymous-post-classified-German-files-online; February 8, 2012 [last accessed February 2013].

273. Pavelic B. Hackers group targets Croatian president's Home Page. *Balkan Insight*. Available at: http://www.balkaninsight.com/en/article/anonymous-hackers-hacked-croatian-president-s-web; February 10, 2012 [last accessed February 2013].

274. Pavelic B. Hackers group targets Croatian president's Home Page. *Balkan Insight*. Available at: http://www.balkaninsight.com/en/article/anonymous-hackers-hacked-croatian-president-s-web; February 10, 2012 [last accessed February 2013].

275. Lennard N. Anonymous Reflects on a 'frantic and historic' year. *Salon*. Available at: http://www.salon.com/2012/12/27/anonymous_reflects_on_a_frantic_and_historic_year/; December 27, 2012 [last accessed February 2013].

276. Lennard N. Anonymous reflects on a 'frantic and historic' year. *Salon*. Available at: http://www.salon.com/2012/12/27/anonymous_reflects_on_a_frantic_and_historic_year/; December 27, 2012 [last accessed February 2013].

277. A Guest. WTF—FuckSOPA. *Pastebin* Available at: http://pastebin.com/qduWdS3y; February 10, 2012 [last accessed February 2013].

278. TheGift73. Anonymous start massive DDoS attack on sites in Mexico. *TechFleece*. Available at: http://techfleece.com/2012/02/11/anonymous-start-massive-ddos-attacks-on-sites-in-mexico/; February 11, 2012 [last accessed February 2013].

279. A Guest. WTF—FuckSOPA. *Pastebin*. Available at: http://pastebin.com/qduWdS3y; February 10, 2012 [last accessed February 2013].

280. TheGift73. Anonymous start massive DDoS attack on sites in Mexico. *TechFleece*. Available at: http://techfleece.com/2012/02/11/anonymous-start-massive-ddos-attacks-on-sites-in-mexico/; February 11, 2012 [last accessed February 2013].

281. Lee J. CAMIMEX, Mexican chamber of mines hacked and 700 mb+ of data leaked by Anonymous. *Cyber War News*. Available at: http://www.cyberwarnews.info/2012/02/11/camimex-mexican-chamber-of-mines-hacked-and-700mb-of-data-leaked-by-anonymous/; February 11, 2012 [last accessed February 2013].

282. Lee J. CAMIMEX, Mexican chamber of mines hacked and 700mb+ of data leaked by Anonymous. *Cyber War News*. Available at: http://www.cyberwarnews.info/2012/02/11/camimex-mexican-chamber-of-mines-hacked-and-700mb-of-data-leaked-by-anonymous/; February 11, 2012 [last accessed February 2013].

283. Moyer E. Anonymous invites CIA, others to its weekend party. *CNet*. Available at: http://news.cnet.com/8301-1009_3-57375923-83/anonymous-invites-cia-others-to-its-weekend-party/; February 11, 2012 [last accessed February 2013].

284. Moyer E. Anonymous invites CIA, others to its weekend party. *CNet*. Available at: http://news.cnet.com/8301-1009_3-57375923-83/anonymous-invites-cia-others-to-its-weekend-party/; February 11, 2012 [last accessed February 2013].

285. TheAnonMessage. A message to the state of Israel. *YouTube*. Available at: http://www.youtube.com/watch?v=X_6P5qAfUjg; February 11, 2012 [last accessed February 2013].

286. TheAnonMessage. A message to the state of Israel. *YouTube*. Available at: http://www.youtube.com/watch?v=X_6P5qAfUjg; February 11, 2012 [last accessed February 2013].

287. Moyer E. Anonymous invites CIA, others to its weekend party. *CNet*. Available at: http://news.cnet.com/8301-1009_3-57375923-83/anonymous-invites-cia-others-to-its-weekend-party/; February 11, 2012 [last accessed February 2013].

288. Moyer E. Anonymous invites CIA, others to its weekend party. *CNet*. Available at: http://news.cnet.com/8301-1009_3-57375923-83/anonymous-invites-cia-others-to-its-weekend-party/; February 11, 2012 [last accessed February 2013].

289. Stone M. Anonymous punishes Interpol after Saudi blasphemy arrest. *Examiner*. Available at: http://www.examiner.com/article/anonymous-punishes-interpol-after-saudi-blasphemy-arrest; February 11, 2012 [last accessed February 2013].

290. Stone M. Anonymous punishes Interpol after Saudi blasphemy arrest. *Examiner*. Available at: http://www.examiner.com/article/anonymous-punishes-interpol-after-saudi-blasphemy-arrest; February 11, 2012 [last accessed February 2013].

291. Winner D. About the ongoing hacking attacks in Panama. *Panama-Guide*. Available at: http://www.panama-guide.com/article.php/20120211123227309; February 11, 2012 [last accessed February 2013].

292. Winner D. About the ongoing hacking attacks in Panama. *Panama-Guide*. Available at: http://www.panama-guide.com/article.php/20120211123227309; February 11, 2012 [last accessed February 2013].

293. Venonymous. Operation Digiturk: Anonymous hacks Turkey's data authority. *Operation AntiSec*. Available at: http://operationantisec.com/tag/digiturk/; February 14, 2012 [last accessed February 2013].

294. Venonymous. Operation Digiturk: Anonymous hacks Turkey's data authority. *Operation AntiSec*. Available at: http://operationantisec.com/tag/digiturk/; February 14, 2012 [last accessed February 2013].

295. Kumar M. Anonymous leak 400 Mb documents from US Army Intelligence Knowledge Network. *The Hacker News*. Available at: http://thehackernews.com/2012/02/anonymous-leak-400-mb-documents-from-us.html#_; February 14, 2012 [last accessed February 2013].

296. Kumar M. Anonymous leak 400 Mb documents from US Army Intelligence Knowledge Network. *The Hacker News*. Available at: http://thehackernews.com/2012/02/anonymous-leak-400-mb-documents-from-us.html#_; February 14, 2012 [last accessed February 2013].

297. Kaelin L. Anonymous targets US ammunition supplier, combined systems. *TechSpot*. Available at: http://www.techspot.com/news/47458-anonymous-targets-us-ammunition-supplier-combined-systems.html; February 15, 2012 [last accessed February 2013].

298. Kaelin L. Anonymous targets US ammunition supplier, combined systems. *TechSpot*. Available at: http://www.techspot.com/news/47458-anonymous-targets-us-ammunition-supplier-combined-systems.html; February 15, 2012 [last accessed February 2013].

299. L0NGWAVE99. The 'L0NGwave99' cyber group presents: 'Operation Digital To'. *Pastebin*. Available at: http://pastebin.com/n3JXnHnn; April 25, 2012 [last accessed February 2013].

300. Schwartz MJ. Anonymous-backed attacks took NASDAQ website offline. *Information Week*. Available at: http://www.informationweek.com/security/attacks/anonymous-backed-attacks-took-nasdaq-web/232600975; February 16, 2012 [last accessed February 2013].

301. L0NGWAVE99. *The* 'L0NGwave99' cyber group presents: 'Operation Digital To'. *Pastebin*, Available at: http://pastebin.com/n3JXnHnn; April 25, 2012 [last accessed February 2013].

302. Schwartz MJ. Anonymous-backed attacks took NASDAQ website offline. *Information Week*. Available at: http://www.informationweek.com/security/attacks/anonymous-backed-attacks-took-nasdaq-web/232600975; February 16, 2012 [last accessed February 2013].

303. A Guest. FTC Jackhammerbuttraepd by Anonymous AntiSec. *Pastebin*. Available at: http://pastebin.com/2qfEqS1p; February 17, 2012 [last accessed February 2013].

304. Gallagher S. Anonymous Antisec hackers break into and bring down FTC website. *Ars Technica*. Available at: http://arstechnica.com/business/2012/02/anonymous-antisec-hackers-break-into-and-bring-down-ftc-website/; February 17, 2012 [last accessed February 2013].

305. A Guest. FTC Jackhammerbuttraepd by Anonymous AntiSec. *Pastebin*. Available at: http://pastebin.com/2qfEqS1p; February 17, 2012 [last accessed February 2013].

306. Gallagher S. Anonymous Antisec hackers break into and bring down FTC website. *Ars Technica*. Available at: http://arstechnica.com/business/2012/02/anonymous-antisec-hackers-break-into-and-bring-down-ftc-website/; February 17, 2012 [last accessed February 2013].

307. Kovacs E. Anonymous hacks Streetfightversand in OpBlitzkrieg. *Softpedia*. Available at: http://news.softpedia.com/news/Anonymous-Hacks-Streetfightversand-in-OpBlitzkrieg-253804.shtml; February 20, 2012 [last accessed February 2013].

308. Kovacs E. Anonymous Hacks Streetfightversand in OpBlitzkrieg. *Softpedia*. Available at: http://news.softpedia.com/news/Anonymous-Hacks-Streetfightversand-in-OpBlitzkrieg-253804.shtml; February 20, 2012 [last accessed February 2013].

309. Netburn D. Anonymous' flash mob targets Wall Street Journal's Facebook pages. *L.A. Times*. Available at: http://articles.latimes.com/2012/feb/21/business/la-fi-tn-anonymous-comments-flash-mob-wall-street-journal-20120221; February 21, 2012 [last accessed February 2013].

310. Netburn D. Anonymous' flash mob targets Wall Street Journal's Facebook pages. *L.A. Times*. Available at: http://articles.latimes.com/2012/feb/21/business/la-fi-tn-anonymous-comments-flash-mob-wall-street-journal-20120221; February 21, 2012 [last accessed February 2013].

311. Kovacs E. Spanish Police attacked by Anonymous after the arrest of six. *Softpedia*. Available at: http://news.softpedia.com/news/Spanish-Police-Attacked-by-Anonymous-After-the-Arrest-of-Six-255034.shtml; February 25, 2012 [last accessed February 2013].

312. Nouveau T. Anonymous pwns InfraGard yet again. *TG Daily*. Available at: http://www.tgdaily.com/security-features/61679-anonymous-pwns-infragard-yet-again; February 24, 2012 [last accessed February 2013].

313. Dotson K. InfraGard can't catch a break: Anonymous 0wns FBI-affiliate once again. *siliconAngle*. Available at: http://siliconangle.com/blog/2012/02/24/infragard-cant-catch-a-break-anonymous-wns-fbi-affiliate-once-again/; February 24, 2012 [last accessed February 2013].

314. AFP. 'Anonymous' hackers target private prison contractor. *The Raw Story*. Available at: http://www.rawstory.com/rs/2012/02/24/anonymous-hackers-target-private-prison-contractor/; February 24, 2012 [last accessed February 2013].

315. AFP. 'Anonymous' hackers target private prison contractor. *The Raw Story*. Available at: http://www.rawstory.com/rs/2012/02/24/anonymous-hackers-target-private-prison-contractor/; February 24, 2012 [last accessed February 2013].

316. Kovacs E. Spanish police attacked by Anonymous after the arrest of six. *Softpedia*. Available at: http://news.softpedia.com/news/Spanish-Police-Attacked-by-Anonymous-After-the-Arrest-of-Six-255034.shtml; February 25, 2012 [last accessed February 2013].

317. Kovacs E. Spanish Police attacked by Anonymous after the arrest of six. *Softpedia*. Available at: http://news.softpedia.com/news/Spanish-Police-Attacked-by-Anonymous-After-the-Arrest-of-Six-255034.shtml; February 25, 2012 [last accessed February 2013].

318. Sengupta S. Arrests sow mistrust inside a clan of hackers. *N.Y. Times*. Available at: http://www.nytimes.com/2012/03/07/technology/lulzsec-hacking-suspects-are-arrested.html?pagewanted=all&_r=0; March 6, 2012 [last accessed February 2013].

319. Geuss M. 25 alleged Anonymous members arrested internationally; hacker group retaliates. *Ars Technical*. Available at: http://arstechnica.com/tech-policy/2012/02/25-alleged-anonymous-members-nabbed-in-international-arrests-hacker-group-retaliates/; February 28, 2012 [last accessed February 2013].

320. Quinn B. Interpol website suffers 'Anonymous cyber-attack. *The Guardian*. Available at: http://www.guardian.co.uk/technology/2012/feb/29/interpol-website-cyber-attack; February 28, 2012 [last accessed February 2013].

321. Geuss M. 25 alleged Anonymous members arrested internationally; hacker group retaliates. *Ars Technical*. Available at: http://arstechnica.com/tech-policy/2012/02/25-alleged-anonymous-members-nabbed-in-international-arrests-hacker-group-retaliates/; February 28, 2012 [last accessed February 2013].

322. Quinn B. Interpol website suffers 'Anonymous cyber-attack'. *The Guardian*. Available at: http://www.guardian.co.uk/technology/2012/feb/29/interpol-website-cyber-attack; February 28, 2012 [last accessed February 2013].

323. Geuss M. 25 alleged Anonymous members arrested internationally; hacker group retaliates. *Ars Technical*. Available at: http://arstechnica.com/tech-policy/2012/02/25-alleged-anonymous-members-nabbed-in-international-arrests-hacker-group-retaliates/; February 28, 2012 [last accessed February 2013].

324. Espiner T. Vatican confirms second Anonymous hack. *ZDNet*. Available at: http://www.zdnet.com/vatican-confirms-second-anonymous-hack-4010025615/; March 13, 2012 [last accessed February 2013].

325. Batty D. Vatican becomes latest Anonymous hacking victim. *ZDNet*. Available at: http://www.guardian.co.uk/technology/2012/mar/07/vatican-anonymous-hacking-victim; March 7, 2012 [last accessed February 2013].

326. Batty D. Vatican becomes latest Anonymous hacking victim. *ZDNet*. Available at: http://www.guardian.co.uk/technology/2012/mar/07/vatican-anonymous-hacking-victim; March 7, 2012 [last accessed February 2013].

327. Espiner T. Vatican confirms second Anonymous hack. *ZDNet*. Available at: http://www.zdnet.com/vatican-confirms-second-anonymous-hack-4010025615/; March 13, 2012 [last accessed February 2013].

328. Pullella P. Hackers group Anonymous take down Vatican website. *Reuters*. Available at: http://www.reuters.com/article/2012/03/07/us-internet-vatican-idUSTRE82618620120307; March 7, 2012 [last accessed February 2013].

329. Boone J. Anonymous continues campaign against Monsanto. *Global Post*. Available at: http://www.globalpost.com/dispatches/globalpost-blogs/the-grid/anonymous-monsanto-campaign-dairy-farmers; March 1, 2012 [last accessed February 2013].

330. Boone J. Anonymous continues campaign against Monsanto. *Global Post*. Available at: http://www.globalpost.com/dispatches/globalpost-blogs/the-grid/anonymous-monsanto-campaign-dairy-farmers; March 1, 2012 [last accessed February 2013].

331. Benjamin M. 10 Reasons Why the Israeli Lobby AIPAC is so dangerous. *Anon Central*. Aavailable at: http://anoncentral.tumblr.com/post/18785495132/10-reasons-why-the-israel-lobby-aipac-is-so-dangerous; March 2012 [last accessed February 2013].

332. Stone M. Anonymous targets American Israel PAC: Operation Palestine. *Examiner*. Available at: http://www.examiner.com/article/anonymous-targets-american-israel-pac-operation-palestine; March 27, 2012 [last accessed February 2013].

333. Benjamin M. 10 reasons why the Israeli Lobby AIPAC is so dangerous. *Anon Central*. Available at: http://anoncentral.tumblr.com/post/18785495132/10-reasons-why-the-israel-lobby-aipac-is-so-dangerous; March 2012 [last accessed February 2013].

334. Sengupta S. Arrests sow mistrust inside a Clan of hackers. *New York Times*. Available at: http://www.nytimes.com/2012/03/07/technology/lulzsec-hacking-suspects-are-arrested.html?pagewanted=all&_r=0; March 6, 2012 [last accessed February 2013].

335. Winfield N. Anonymous hackers claim to bring down Vatican website, site inaccessible for hours. *Toronto Star*. Available at: http://www.thestar.com/news/world/2012/03/07/anonymous_hackers_claim_to_bring_down_vatican_website_site_inaccessible_for_hours.html; March 7, 2012 [last accessed February 2013].

336. Winfield N. Anonymous hackers claim to bring down Vatican website, site inaccessible for hours. *Toronto Star*. Available at: http://www.thestar.com/news/world/2012/03/07/anonymous_hackers_claim_to_bring_down_vatican_website_site_inaccessible_for_hours.html; March 7, 2012 [last accessed February 2013].

337. BBC News Technology. Hackers attack Panda Labs site after Anonymous arrests. Available at: http://www.bbc.co.uk/news/technology-17286690; March 7, 2012 [last accessed February 2013].

338. BBC News Technology. Hackers attack Panda Labs site after Anonymous arrests. Available at: http://www.bbc.co.uk/news/technology-17286690; March 7, 2012 [last accessed February 2013].

339. Oystan G. Anonymous talking about Kony 2012. *Pastebin*. Available at: http://pastebin.com/THmYgKRD; March 7, 2012 [last accessed February 2013].

340. TheAnonMessage. *Anonymous—KONY 2012 Warning*. *YouTube*. Available at: http://www.youtube.com/watch?v=qr1EdLzYz_M; March 8, 2012 [last accessed February 2013].

341. Oystan G. Anonymous talking about Kony 2012. *Pastebin*. Available at: http://pastebin.com/THmYgKRD; March 7, 2012 [last accessed February 2013].

342. TheAnonMessage. *Anonymous—KONY 2012 warning*. *YouTube*. Available at: http://www.youtube.com/watch?v=qr1EdLzYz_M; March 8, 2012 [last accessed February 2013].

343. Protalinski E. *Anonymous* hacks Panda Security in response to LulzSec arrests. *ZDNet*. Available at: http://www.zdnet.com/blog/security/anonymous-hacks-panda-security-in-response-to-lulzsec-arrests/10542; March 6, 2012 [last accessed February 2013].

344. Protalinski E. Anonymous hacks Panda Security in response to LulzSec arrests. *ZDNet*. Available at: http://www.zdnet.com/blog/security/anonymous-hacks-panda-security-in-response-to-lulzsec-arrests/10542; March 6, 2012 [last accessed February 2013].

345. Whittaker Z. Anonymous Leaks Symantec's Norton anti-virus source code. *ZDNet*. Available at: http://www.zdnet.com/blog/btl/anonymous-leaks-symantecs-norton-anti-virus-source-code/71183; March 9, 2012 [last accessed February 2013].

346. Whittaker Z. Anonymous Leaks Symantec's Norton anti-virus source code. *ZDNet*. Available at: http://www.zdnet.com/blog/btl/anonymous-leaks-symantecs-norton-anti-virus-source-code/71183; March 9, 2012 [last accessed February 2013].

347. Yin S. Anonymous attacks Symantec, New York Police supplier to protest LulzSec arrests. *PC Magazine Security Watch*. Available at: http://securitywatch.pcmag.com/none/295178-anonymous-attacks-symantec-new-york-police-supplier-to-protest-lulzsec-arrests; March 9, 2012 [last accessed February 2013].

348. Yin S. Anonymous attacks Symantec, New York Police supplier to protest LulzSec arrests. *PC Magazine Security Watch*. Available at: http://securitywatch.pcmag.com/none/295178-anonymous-attacks-symantec-new-york-police-supplier-to-protest-lulzsec-arrests; March 9, 2012 [last accessed February 2013].

349. Yin S. Anonymous attacks Symantec, New York Police supplier to protest LulzSec arrests. *PC Magazine Security Watch*. Available at: http://securitywatch.pcmag.com/none/295178-anonymous-attacks-symantec-new-york-police-supplier-to-protest-lulzsec-arrests; March 9, 2012 [last accessed February 2013].

350. Der Standard. *Anonymous* hackt Webshop der NPD und veröffentlicht Kundendaten (Anonymous hacks online shop of NPD and publishes customer data). Available at: http://derstandard.at/1331207056422/OPBLitzkrieg-Anonymous-hackt-Webshop-der-NPD-und-veroeffentlicht-Kundendaten; March 12, 2012 [in German] [last accessed February 2013].

351. Der Standard. Anonymous hackt Webshop der NPD und veröffentlicht Kundendaten (Anonymous hacks online shop of NPD and publishes customer data). Available at: http://derstandard.at/1331207056422/OPBLitzkrieg-Anonymous-hackt-Webshop-der-NPD-und-veroeffentlicht-Kundendaten; March 12, 2012 [in German] [last accessed February 2013].

352. Espiner T. Vatican confirms second Anonymous attack. *ZDNet*. Available at: http://www.zdnet.com/vatican-confirms-second-anonymous-hack-4010025615/; March 13, 2012 [last accessed February 2013].

353. Espiner T. Vatican confirms second Anonymous attack. *ZDNet*. Available at: http://www.zdnet.com/vatican-confirms-second-anonymous-hack-4010025615/; March 13, 2012 [last accessed February 2013].

354. Prince B. Anonymous hacktivists leak Bureau of Justice Statistics. *eWeek*. Available at: http://www.eweek.com/c/a/Security/Anonymous-Hacktivists-Leak-Bureau-of-Justice-Statistics-622457/; May 22, 2012 [last accessed February 2013].

355. Prince B. Anonymous hacktivists leak Bureau of Justice Statistics. *eWeek*. Available at: http://www.eweek.com/c/a/Security/Anonymous-Hacktivists-Leak-Bureau-of-Justice-Statistics-622457/; May 22, 2012 [last accessed February 2013].

356. Index. Biotechnológiai óriáscégnek üzent hadat a magyar Anonymous. Available at: http://index.hu/tech/2012/03/23/biotechnologiai_oriascegnek_uzent_hadat_a_magyar_anonymous/; March 23, 2012 [last accessed February 2013].

357. Gucciardi A. Hungary destroys all Monsanto GMO corn fields. *Natural Society*. Available at: http://naturalsociety.com/hungary-destroys-all-monsanto-gmo-corn-fields/; September 20, 2012 [last accessed February 2013].

358. HackRead. 6 Anonymous hackers arrested by Dominican Republic police. Available at: http://hackread.com/6-anonymous-hackers-arrested-by-dominican-republic-police/; March 28, 2012 [last accessed February 2013].

359. InformareXresistere. Anonymous—#Operation Vatican.va# Attaco al sito del Vaticano. Available at: http://www.informarexresistere.fr/2012/03/20/anonymous-%E2%80%93-operation-vatican-va-attacco-al-sito-del-vaticano/#axzz2J8xnZL54; March, 20, 2012 [last accessed February 2013].

360. Crypt0nymous. Anonymous—#Operation Vatican. *YouTube*. Available at: http://www.youtube.com/watch?v=OJ-M_M5fw_M; December 6, 2012 [last accessed February 2013].

361. Crypt0nymous. Anonymous—#Operation Vatican. *YouTube*. Available at: http://www.youtube.com/watch?v=OJ-M_M5fw_M; December 6, 2012 [last accessed February 2013].

362. Stone M. Anonymous targets child abuse at Judge Rotenberg Educational Center. *Examiner*. Available at: http://www.examiner.com/article/anonymous-targets-child-abuse-at-judge-rotenberg-educational-center; March 24, 2012 [last accessed February 2013].

363. Stone M. Anonymous targets child abuse at Judge Rotenberg Educational Center. *Examiner*. Available at: http://www.examiner.com/article/anonymous-targets-child-abuse-at-judge-rotenberg-educational-center; March 24, 2012 [last accessed February 2013].

364. BBC News Technology. Chinese websites 'defaced in Anonymous attack'. Available at: http://www.bbc.co.uk/news/technology-17623939; April 5, 2012 [last accessed February 2013].

365. BBC News Technology. Chinese websites 'defaced in Anonymous attack'. Available at: http://www.bbc.co.uk/news/technology-17623939; April 5, 2012 [last accessed February 2013].

366. TheAnonMessage. Anonymous—Operation Defense (CISPA). *YouTube*. Available at: http://www.youtube.com/watch?v=v8no3E0Hx7k; April 7, 2012 [last accessed February 2013].

367. TheAnonMessage. Anonymous—Operation Defense (CISPA). *YouTube*. Available at: http://www.youtube.com/watch?v=v8no3E0Hx7k; April 7, 2012 [last accessed February 2013].

368. Olanoff D. Anonymous takes down Home Office site in response to extradition practices. *TheNextWeb*. Available at: http://thenextweb.com/insider/2012/04/08/anonymous-takes-down-uk-home-office-site-in-response-to-proposed-email-surveillance/; April 8, 2012 [last accessed February 2013].

369. BBC News. Expect more online attacks, Anonymous hackers say. Available at: http://www.bbc.co.uk/news/uk-17648852; April 8, 2012 [last accessed February 2013].

370. Protalinski E. Anonymous hacks UK government websites over 'draconian surveillance'. *ZDNet*. Available at: http://www.zdnet.com/blog/security/anonymous-hacks-uk-government-sites-over-draconian-surveillance/11412; April 7, 2012 [last accessed February 2013].

371. Olanoff D. Anonymous takes down Home Office site in response to extradition practices. *TheNextWeb*. Available at: http://thenextweb.com/insider/2012/04/08/anonymous-takes-down-uk-home-office-site-in-response-to-proposed-email-surveillance/; April 8, 2012 [last accessed February 2013].

372. BBC News. Expect more online attacks, Anonymous hackers say. Available at: http://www.bbc.co.uk/news/uk-17648852; April 8, 2012 [last accessed February 2013].

373. Protalinski E. Anonymous hacks UK government websites over 'draconian surveillance'. *ZDNet*. Available at: http://www.zdnet.com/blog/security/anonymous-hacks-uk-government-sites-over-draconian-surveillance/11412; April 7, 2012 [last accessed February 2013].

374. Reuters. 'Anonymous' claim they've hacked Tunisian leaders' email. *Al Arabiya*. Available at: http://english.alarabiya.net/articles/2012/04/09/206477.html; April 9, 2012 [last accessed February 2013].

375. Reuters. 'Anonymous' claim they've hacked Tunisian leaders' email. *Al Arabiya*. Available at: http://english.alarabiya.net/articles/2012/04/09/206477.html; April 9, 2012 [last accessed February 2013].

376. Ragan S. Anonymous launches attacks against trade associations and Boeing. *SecurityWeek*. Available at: http://www.securityweek.com/anonymous-launches-attacks-against-trade-associations-and-boeing; April 11, 2012 [last accessed February 2013].

377. Ragan S. Anonymous launches attacks against trade associations and Boeing. *SecurityWeek*. Available at: http://www.securityweek.com/anonymous-launches-attacks-against-trade-associations-and-boeing; April 11, 2012 [last accessed February 2013].

378. YourAnonNews. #OpCannabis. *Tumblr*. Available at: http://youranonnews.tumblr.com/post/20852653732/opcannabis; April 20, 2012 [last accessed February 2013].

379. Webster SC. #OpCannabis: Anonymous hackers take up Marijuana Activism. RawStory/AlterNet. Available at: http://www.alternet.org/story/155092/%23opcannabis%3A_anonymous_hackers_take_up_marijuana_activism; April 20, 2012 [last accessed February 2013].

380. YourAnonNews. #OpCannabis. *Tumblr*. Available at: http://youranonnews.tumblr.com/post/20852653732/opcannabis; April 20, 2012 [last accessed February 2013].

381. Webster SC. #OpCannabis: Anonymous hackers take up Marijuana Activism. *RawStory/AlterNet*. Available at: http://www.alternet.org/story/155092/%23opcannabis%3A_anonymous_hackers_take_up_marijuana_activism; April 20, 2012 [last accessed February 2013].

382. Siddique H, Quinn B. Bahrain grand prix protests—Sunday 22 April. *The Guardian*. Available at: http://www.guardian.co.uk/world/2012/apr/22/bahrain-grand-prix-protests-live; April 22, 2012 [last accessed February 2013].

383. Siddique H, Quinn B. Bahrain grand prix protests—Sunday 22 April. *The Guardian*. Available at: http://www.guardian.co.uk/world/2012/apr/22/bahrain-grand-prix-protests-live; April 22, 2012 [last accessed February 2013].

384. Avendaño CO. Hackers bring PH-China dispute to cyberspace. *Philippine Daily Inquirer*. Available at: http://globalnation.inquirer.net/34379/hackers-bring-ph-china-dispute-to-cyberspace; April 23, 2012 [last accessed February 2013].

385. Avendaño CO. Hackers bring PH-China dispute to cyberspace. *Philippine Daily Inquirer*. Available at: http://globalnation.inquirer.net/34379/hackers-bring-ph-china-dispute-to-cyberspace; April 23, 2012 [last accessed February 2013].

386. Walton Z. Anonymous announces operation defense phase II in response to CISPA. *WebProNews*. Available at: http://www.webpronews.com/anonymous-announces-operation-defense-phase-ii-in-response-to-cispa-2012-04; April 27, 2012 [last accessed February 2013].

387. Walton Z. Anonymous announces operation defense phase II in response to CISPA. *WebProNews*. Available at: http://www.webpronews.com/anonymous-announces-operation-defense-phase-ii-in-response-to-cispa-2012-04; April 27, 2012 [last accessed February 2013].

388. Kim L. Anonymous targets Virgin Media, Talk Talk. *Digital Trends*. Available at: http://www.digitaltrends.com/computing/anonymous-targets-virgin-media-talktalk/; May 9, 2012 [last accessed February 2013].

389. Kim L. Anonymous targets Virgin Media, Talk Talk. *Digital Trends*. Available at: http://www.digitaltrends.com/computing/anonymous-targets-virgin-media-talktalk/; May 9, 2012 [last accessed February 2013].

390. BBC News Technology. Anonymous attacks Indian government websites. Available at: http://www.bbc.co.uk/news/technology-18114984; May 18, 2012 [last accessed February 2013].

391. BBC News Technology. Anonymous attacks Indian government websites. Available at: http://www.bbc.co.uk/news/technology-18114984; May 18, 2012 [last accessed February 2013].

392. Stone M. Anonymous: Operation Quebec supports students, opposes Bill 78. *Examiner*. Available at: http://www.examiner.com/article/anonymous-operation-quebec-supports-students-opposes-bill-78; May 24, 2012 [last accessed February 2013].

393. Stone M. Anonymous: Operation Quebec supports students, opposes Bill 78. *Examiner*. Available at: http://www.examiner.com/article/anonymous-operation-quebec-supports-students-opposes-bill-78; May 24, 2012 [last accessed February 2013].

394. Walton Z. Anonymous takes down KKK Web sites in #OpBlitzkrieg. *WebProNews*. Available at: http://www.webpronews.com/anonymous-takes-down-kkk-web-sites-in-opblitzkrieg-2012-05; May 25, 2012 [last accessed February 2013].

395. Walton Z. Anonymous takes down KKK Web sites in #OpBlitzkrieg. *WebProNews*. Available at: http://www.webpronews.com/anonymous-takes-down-kkk-web-sites-in-opblitzkrieg-2012-05; May 25, 2012 [last accessed February 2013].

396. Stone M. Anonymous hacks Canadian Grand Prix: Operation Quebec continuous. *Examiner*. Available at: http://www.examiner.com/article/anonymous-hacks-canadian-grand-prix-operation-quebec-continues; May 31, 2012 [last accessed February 2013].

397. Stone M. Anonymous hacks Canadian Grand Prix: Operation Quebec continuous. *Examiner*. Available at: http://www.examiner.com/article/anonymous-hacks-canadian-grand-prix-operation-quebec-continues; May 31, 2012 [last accessed February 2013].

398. A Guest. MexicanH Team Intel PWNED. *Pastebin*. Available at: http://pastebin.com/xfmfKdjk; June 7, 2012 [last accessed February 2013].

399. Lee J. Intel hacked by Anonymous for Operation Green Rights, #OpColtan. *Cyber War News*. Available at: http://www.cyberwarnews.info/2012/06/10/intel-hacked-by-anonymous-for-operation-green-rights-opcoltan/; June 12, 2012 [last accessed February 2013].

400. A Guest. OpColtan Press for Intel #OpGreenRights. *Pastebin*. Available at: http://pastebin.com/NDYG76Su; June 7, 2012 [last accessed February 2013].

401. Vaidyanathan R. Hacking group Anonymous takes on India internet 'censorship'. *BBC News Technology*. Available at: http://www.bbc.co.uk/news/technology-18371297; June 9, 2012 [last accessed February 2013].

402. Vaidyanathan R. Hacking group Anonymous takes on India internet 'censorship'. *BBC News Technology*. Available at: http://www.bbc.co.uk/news/technology-18371297; June 9, 2012 [last accessed February 2013].

403. Lee J. AmericanNaziParty.com & KKK.com under ddos attacks by #Anonymous. *Cyber War News.* Available at: http://www.cyberwarnews.info/2012/06/21/americannaziparty-com-kkk-com-under-ddos-attacks-by-anonymous/; June 21, 2012 [last accessed February 2013].

404. Lee J. AmericanNaziParty.com & KKK.com under ddos attacks by #Anonymous. *Cyber War News.* Available at: http://www.cyberwarnews.info/2012/06/21/americannaziparty-com-kkk-com-under-ddos-attacks-by-anonymous/; June 21, 2012 [last accessed February 2013].

405. Phneah E. Anonymous hacks Japanese govt. sites. *ZDNet.* Available at: http://www.zdnet.com/anonymous-hacks-japanese-govt-sites-2062305268/; June 28, 2012 [last accessed February 2013].

406. Phneah E. Anonymous hacks Japanese govt. sites. *ZDNet.* Available at: http://www.zdnet.com/anonymous-hacks-japanese-govt-sites-2062305268/; June 28, 2012 [last accessed February 2013].

407. Feit D. Japan passes Jail-for-Downloaders Anti-Piracy law. *Wired.* Available at: http://www.wired.com/gamelife/2012/06/japan-download-copyright-law; June 21, 2012 [last accessed February 2013].

408. Guri. #OpParaguay: Anonymous Hace Un Llamado Global Y Amenaza Al Gobierno Paraguayo Por lo Ocurrido en Curuguaty. *Dementes X.* Available at: http://www.dementesx.com/opparaguay-anonymous-hace-un-llamado-global-y-amenaza-al-gobierno-paraguayo-por-lo-ocurrido-en-curuguaty/; June, 17, 2012 [last accessed February 2013].

409. Guri. #OpParaguay: Anonymous Hace Un Llamado Global Y Amenaza Al Gobierno Paraguayo Por lo Ocurrido en Curuguaty. *Dementes X.* Available at: http://www.dementesx.com/opparaguay-anonymous-hace-un-llamado-global-y-amenaza-al-gobierno-paraguayo-por-lo-ocurrido-en-curuguaty/; June, 17, 2012 [last accessed February 2013].

410. Sweet D. 'Operation Anaheim' targets Anaheim Police Chief. *Occupy America.* Available at: http://occupyamerica.crooksandliars.com/diane-sweet/operation-anaheim-targets-anaheim-poli; July 27, 2012 [last accessed February 2013].

411. Stone M. Anonymous targets police brutality in Anaheim. *Examiner.* Available at: http://www.examiner.com/article/anonymous-targets-police-brutality-anaheim; July 25, 2012 [last accessed February 2013].

412. Sweet D. 'Operation Anaheim' Targets Anaheim Police Chief. *Occupy America.* Available at: http://occupyamerica.crooksandliars.com/diane-sweet/operation-anaheim-targets-anaheim-poli; July 27, 2012 [last accessed February 2013].

413. Stone M. Anonymous targets police brutality in Anaheim. *Examiner.* Available at: http://www.examiner.com/article/anonymous-targets-police-brutality-anaheim; July 25, 2012 [last accessed February 2013].

414. Zhao W. Anonymous targets Amy Lee and wind-up records in operation PedoChat. *Forbes.* Available at: http://www.forbes.com/sites/wenjiazhao/2012/07/25/anonymous-targets-singer-and-record-company-in-operation-pedochat/; July 25, 2012 [last accessed February 2013].

415. Colley A, Chris G. Anonymous hackers dump stolen data belonging to Australian telco AAPT. *The Australian.* Available at: http://www.theaustralian.com.au/australian-it/telecommunications/anonymous-hackers-dump-stolen-data-belonging-to-australian-firm-aapt/story-fn4iyzsr-1226437681976; July 29, 2012 [last accessed February 2013].

416. Colley A, Chris G. Anonymous hackers dump stolen data belonging to Australian telco AAPT. *The Australian.* Available at: http://www.theaustralian.com.au/australian-it/telecommunications/anonymous-hackers-dump-stolen-data-belonging-to-australian-firm-aapt/story-fn4iyzsr-1226437681976; July 29, 2012 [last accessed February 2013].

417. Protalinski E. Anonymous attacks Ukrainian government after Demonoid bust. *ZDNet.* Available at: http://www.zdnet.com/anonymous-attacks-ukrainian-government-after-demonoid-bust-7000002348/; August 8, 2012 [last accessed February 2013].

418. Kovacs E. Anonymous launches operation Demonoid after raid in Ukraine (updated). *Softpedia.* Available at: http://news.softpedia.com/news/Anonymous-Launch-Operation-Demonoid-After-Raid-in-Ukraine-285398.shtml; August 7, 2012 [last accessed February 2013].

419. Protalinski E. Demonoid busted by the police. *ZDNet.* Available at: http://www.zdnet.com/demonoid-busted-by-the-police-7000002208/; August 7, 2012 [last accessed February 2013].

420. Protalinski E. Demonoid owners under criminal investigation. *ZDNet.* Available at: http://www.zdnet.com/demonoid-owners-under-criminal-investigation-7000002297/; August 7, 2012 [last accessed February 2013].

421. Kovacs E. Anonymous launches operation Demonoid after raid in Ukraine (updated). *Softpedia.* Available at: http://news.softpedia.com/news/Anonymous-Launch-Operation-Demonoid-After-Raid-in-Ukraine-285398.shtml; August 7, 2012 [last accessed February 2013].

422. Jillian. LGBT Rights: Anonymous hacks Ugandan Government sites. *The Montreal Gazette*. Available at: http://blogs.montrealgazette.com/2012/08/15/lgbt-rights-anonymous-hacks-ugandan-government-sites/; August 15, 2012 [last accessed February 2013].

423. Jillian. LGBT Rights: Anonymous hacks Ugandan Government Sites. *The Montreal Gazette*. Available at: http://blogs.montrealgazette.com/2012/08/15/lgbt-rights-anonymous-hacks-ugandan-government-sites/; August 15, 2012 [last accessed February 2013].

424. Alisonerr. Anonymous: fighting Trapwire. *YouTube*. Available at: http://www.youtube.com/watch?v=Qg_9kF3ZkYs; August 20, 2012 [last accessed February 2013].

425. Huff S. TrapWire on notice: Anonymous says operation to disrupt surveillance are under way. *BetaBeat*. Available at: http://betabeat.com/2012/08/trapwire-on-notice-anonymous-says-operations-to-disrupt-surveillance-are-under-way/; August 15, 2012 [last accessed February 2013].

426. Alisonerr. Anonymous: fighting trapwire. *YouTube*. Available at: http://www.youtube.com/watch?v=Qg_9kF3ZkYs; August 20, 2012 [last accessed February 2013].

427. Huff S. TrapWire on notice: Anonymous says operation to disrupt surveillance are under way. *BetaBeat*. Available at: http://betabeat.com/2012/08/trapwire-on-notice-anonymous-says-operations-to-disrupt-surveillance-are-under-way/; August 15, 2012 [last accessed February 2013].

428. AnonLegionOps. Anonymous—message to UK Government (Free Assange). *YouTube*. Available at: http://www.youtube.com/watch?v=gq5D2NepOpo; August 18, 2012 [last accessed February 2013].

429. AnonLegionOps. Anonymous—message to UK Government (Free Assange). *YouTube*, available at: http://www.youtube.com/watch?v=gq5D2NepOpo; August 18, 2012 [last accessed February 2013].

430. Tomei L. 'Operation Free Assange': Tug-of-war takes to the web with a series of cyber attacks. *Global Post*. Aavailable at: http://www.globalpost.com/dispatch/news/regions/europe/120820/the-tug-war-over-assange-takes-the-web-series-cyber-attacks; August 20, 2012 [last accessed February 2013].

431. Tomei L. 'Operation Free Assange': Tug-of-war takes to the web with a series of cyber attacks. *Global Post*. Available at: http://www.globalpost.com/dispatch/news/regions/europe/120820/the-tug-war-over-assange-takes-the-web-series-cyber-attacks; August 20, 2012 [last accessed February 2013].

432. Baczynska G. Hackers target website of Russian court that jailed Pussy Riot. *Reuters*. Available at: http://www.reuters.com/article/2012/08/21/us-russia-pussyriot-court-idUSBRE87K0LS20120821; August 21, 2012 [last accessed February 2013].

433. Baczynska G. Hackers target website of Russian court that jailed Pussy Riot. *Reuters*. Available at: http://www.reuters.com/article/2012/08/21/us-russia-pussyriot-court-idUSBRE87K0LS20120821; August 21, 2012 [last accessed February 2013].

434. CyberWarZone. Anonymous Saipan: CNMI government step down. Available at: http://www.cyberwarzone.com/cyberwarfare/anonymous-saipan-cnmi-government-step-down; August 23, 2012 [last accessed February 2013].

435. CyberWarZone. Anonymous Saipan: CNMI government step down. Available at: http://www.cyberwarzone.com/cyberwarfare/anonymous-saipan-cnmi-government-step-down; August 23, 2012 [last accessed February 2013].

436. Kumar M. AVX Corporation hacked by Anonymous #OpColtan. *The Hacker News*. Available at: http://thehackernews.com/2012/08/avx-corporation-hacked-by-anonymous.html; August 26, 2012 [accessed February 2013].

437. Kumar M. AVX Corporation hacked by Anonymous #OpColtan. *The Hacker News*. Available at: http://thehackernews.com/2012/08/avx-corporation-hacked-by-anonymous.html; August 26, 2012 [last accessed February 2013].

438. Russia Today. 'Operation Free Assange'—Anonymous takes down Interpol website. Available at: http://rt.com/news/anonymous-interpol-free-assange-607/; August 29, 2012 [last accessed February 2013].

439. Russia Today. 'Operation Free Assange'—Anonymous takes down Interpol website available at: http://rt.com/news/anonymous-interpol-free-assange-607/; August 29, 2012 [last accessed February 2013].

440. A Guest. Special #FFF edition—Anonymous. *Pastebin*. Available at: http://pastebin.com/nfVT7b0Z; September 30, 2012 [last accessed February 2013].

441. A Guest. Special #FFF edition—Anonymous. *Pastebin*. Available at: http://pastebin.com/nfVT7b0Z; September 30, 2012 [last accessed February 2013].

442. 3News. Evanescence singer Amy Lee targeted by hackers. Available at: http://www.3news.co.nz/Evanescence-singer-Amy-Lee-targeted-by-hackers/tabid/418/articleID/268146/Default.aspx; September 5, 2012 [last accessed February 2013].

443. Giles J. Evanescence singer Amy Lee faces serious allegations from Hacker Group Anonymous. *Loudwire*. Available at: http://loudwire.com/evanescence-singer-amy-lee-faces-serious-allegations-from-hacker-group-anonymous/; September 5, 2012 [last accessed February 2013].

444. 3News. Evanescence singer Amy Lee targeted by hackers. Available at: http://www.3news.co.nz/Evanescence-singer-Amy-Lee-targeted-by-hackers/tabid/418/articleID/268146/Default.aspx; September 5, 2012 [last accessed February 2013].

445. Giles J. Evanescence singer Amy Lee faces serious allegations from Hacker Group Anonymous. *Loudwire*. Available at: http://loudwire.com/evanescence-singer-amy-lee-faces-serious-allegations-from-hacker-group-anonymous/; September 5, 2012 [last accessed February 2013].

446. Zetter K. Anonymous' Barrett Brown raided by FBI during online chat. *Wired*. Available at: http://www.wired.com/threatlevel/2012/09/barret-brown-raid/; September 13, 2012 [last accessed February 2013].

447. Zetter K. Feds pile on more charges against Anonymous agitator Barrett Brown. *Wired*. Available at: http://www.wired.com/threatlevel/2013/01/more-chargesfor-barrett-brown/; January 24, 2013 [last accessed February 2013].

448. CyberWarZone. #AntiSec releases creditcard details of 13 #FBI agents in retaliation for the arrest of @BarrettBrownLOL. Available at: http://www.cyberwarzone.com/antisec-releases-creditcard-details-13-fbi-agents-retaliation-arrest-barrettbrownlol; September 14, 2012 [last accessed February 2013].

449. CyberWarZone. #AntiSec releases creditcard details of 13 #FBI agents in retaliation for the arrest of @BarrettBrownLOL. Available at: http://www.cyberwarzone.com/antisec-releases-creditcard-details-13-fbi-agents-retaliation-arrest-barrettbrownlol; September 14, 2012 [last accessed February 2013].

450. Kumar M. Anonymous dump 2.5 GB data from email of priest accused for child abuse. *The Hacker News*. Available at: http://thehackernews.com/2012/09/anonymous-dump-25-gb-data-from-email-of.html?utm_source=feedburner&utm_medium=feed&utm_campaign=Feed%3A+TheHackersNews+%28The+Hackers+News+-+Security+Blog%29; September 13, 2012 [last accessed February 2013].

451. Kumar M. Anonymous dump 2.5 GB data from email of priest accused for child abuse. *The Hacker News*. Available at: http://thehackernews.com/2012/09/anonymous-dump-25-gb-data-from-email-of.html?utm_source=feedburner&utm_medium=feed&utm_campaign=Feed%3A+TheHackersNews+%28The+Hackers+News+-+Security+Blog%29; September 13, 2012 [last accessed February 2013].

452. A Guest. OpHKNEC. *Pastebin*. Available at: http://pastebin.com/ppNZdZ48; September 15, 2012 [last accessed February 2013].

453. CNN Wire Staff. Hong Kong abandons mandatory classes seen as pro-Beijing. *CNN*. Available at: http://www.cnn.com/2012/09/08/world/asia/china-hong-kong-education/index.html; September 10, 2012 [last accessed February 2013].

454. Anonphuser123. Anonymous Philippines message to Cybercrime Law supporters. *YouTube*. Available at: http://www.youtube.com/watch?v=QFBaapdoKrY; September 30, 2012 [last accessed February 2013].

455. Malig J. Global 'Anonymous' attack Philippine govt websites. *ABS-CBN News*. Available at: http://www.abs-cbnnews.com/lifestyle/10/02/12/global-anonymous-attack-philippine-govt-websites; October 3, 2012 [last accessed February 2013].

456. Anonphuser123. Anonymous Philippines message to Cybercrime Law supporters. *YouTube*. Available at: http://www.youtube.com/watch?v=QFBaapdoKrY; September 30, 2012 [last accessed February 2013].

457. Malig J. Global 'Anonymous' attack Philippine gov't websites. *ABS-CBN News*. Available at: http://www.abs-cbnnews.com/lifestyle/10/02/12/global-anonymous-attack-philippine-govt-websites; October 3, 2012 [last accessed February 2013].

458. Harper M. Anonymous attacks Sweden for taking away free music. *RedOrbit*. Available at: http://www.redorbit.com/news/technology/1112707906/anonymous-sweden-attack-ddos-100512/; October 5, 2012 [accessed February 2013].

459. Harper M. Anonymous attacks Sweden for taking away free music. *RedOrbit*. Available at: http://www.redorbit.com/news/technology/1112707906/anonymous-sweden-attack-ddos-100512/; October 5, 2012 [accessed February 2013].

460. 5had0w5. Defend your freedom—worldwide protest—TrapWire & Indect (worldwide). *WhyWeProtest*. Available at: https://whyweprotest.net/community/threads/nov-5-2012-defend-your-freedom-worlwide-protest-trapwire-indect-worlwide.105925/; October 21, 2012 [last accessed February 2013].

461. GoogleMaps. Part II World-wide Protests against #surveillance-Systems #Trapwire #INDECT Saturday. Available at: https://maps.google.com/maps/ms?ie=UTF8&oe=UTF8&msa=0&msid=200186625117421185333.0004c61615777b4f2813b; October 20, 2012 [last accessed February 2013].

462. 5had0w5. Defend your freedom—worldwide protest—TrapWire & Indect (worldwide). *WhyWeProtest*. Available at: https://whyweprotest.net/community/threads/nov-5-2012-defend-your-freedom-worlwide-protest-trapwire-indect-worlwide.105925/; October 21, 2012 [last accessed February 2013].

463. Blue V. Anonymous: anti-surveillance protest tomorrow. *CNet*. Available at: http://news.cnet.com/8301-1009_3-57535764-83/anonymous-anti-surveillance-protest-tomorrow/; October 19, 2012 [last accessed February 2013].

464. 5had0w5. Defend your freedom—worldwide protest—TrapWire & Indect (Worldwide). *WhyWeProtest*. Available at: https://whyweprotest.net/community/threads/nov-5-2012-defend-your-freedom-worlwide-protest-trapwire-indect-worlwide.105925/; October 21, 2012 [last accessed February 2013].

465. Blue V. Anonymous: Anti-surveillance protest tomorrow. *CNet*. Available at: http://news.cnet.com/8301-1009_3-57535764-83/anonymous-anti-surveillance-protest-tomorrow/; October 19, 2012 [last accessed February 2013].

466. AnonSirbu. Anonymous Burma-Myanmar. *YouTube*. Available at: http://www.youtube.com/watch?v=rgzxpdMs3E8; October 31, 2012 [last accessed February 2013].

467. AnonSirbu. Anonymous Burma-Myanmar. *YouTube*. Available at: http://www.youtube.com/watch?v=rgzxpdMs3E8; October 31, 2012 [last accessed February 2013].

468. Musil S. Israel government Web sites hit by hacker blitz. *CNet*. Available at: http://news.cnet.com/8301-1009_3-57551560-83/israel-government-web-sites-hit-by-hacker-blitz/; November 18, 2012 [last accessed February 2013].

469. Osborne C. Anonymous takes on Israeli websites, wipes Jerusalem bank. *ZDNet*. Available at: http://www.zdnet.com/anonymous-takes-on-israeli-websites-wipes-jerusalem-bank-7000007537/; November 16, 2012 [last accessed February 2013].

470. Musil S. Israel government Web sites hit by hacker blitz. *CNet*. Available at: http://news.cnet.com/8301-1009_3-57551560-83/israel-government-web-sites-hit-by-hacker-blitz/; Novemebr 18, 2012 [accessed February 2013].

471. Anon Relations. #opIsrael—Anonymous stands by Palestine in this time of war and grief. Available at: http://anonrelations.net/anonymous-opisrael-95/; November 15, 2012 [last accessed February 2013].

472. BBC News Technology. Anonymous hacker group attacks Israeli websites. Available at: http://www.bbc.co.uk/news/technology-20356757; November 16, 2012 [last accessed February 2013].

473. BBC News Technology. Anonymous hacker group attacks Israeli websites. Available at: http://www.bbc.co.uk/news/technology-20356757; November 16, 2012 [last accessed February 2013].

474. Kumar M. Anonymous hit Egyptian Government Websites as #OpEgypt. *The Hacker News*. Available at: http://thehackernews.com/2012/12/anonymous-hit-egyptian-government.html; December 19, 2012 [accessed February 2013].

475. BBC News. Egypt Crisis: Protesters maintain Mursi decree defiance. Available at: http://www.bbc.co.uk/news/world-middle-east-20521967; November 28, 2011 [last accessed February 2013].

476. Shenker J. Egypt: violent clashes in Cairo leave two dead and hundreds injured. *The Guardian (UK)*. Available at: http://www.guardian.co.uk/world/2011/nov/19/egypt-violent-clashes-cairo-injured; November 19, 2012 [last accessed February 2013].

477. Kumar M. Anonymous hit Egyptian Government Websites as #OpEgypt. *The Hacker News*. Available at: http://thehackernews.com/2012/12/anonymous-hit-egyptian-government.html; December 19, 2012 [last accessed February 2013].

478. AnonNews. Operation Syria—Anonymous/RevoluSec. Available at: http://anonnews.org/press/item/1117/; undated [last accessed February 2013].

479. Higginbotham S. Reports: Syria is cut off from the Internet and how it may have happened. *GigaOm*. Available at: http://gigaom.com/2012/11/29/reports-syria-is-cut-off-from-the-internet-and-how-it-may-have-happened/; Novemebr 29, 2012 [last accessed February 2013].

480. Stone M. Operation Syria: Anonymous fights for free Syrian people. *The Examiner*. Available at: http://www.examiner.com/article/operation-syria-anonymous-fights-for-free-syrian-people; November 30, 2012 [last accessed February 2013].

481. Musil S. Anonymous declares war on Syrian government Web sites. *CNet*. Available at: http://news.cnet.com/8301-1009_3-57556333-83/anonymous-declares-war-on-syrian-government-web-sites/; November 29, 2012 [last accessed February 2013].

482. Kumar M. Anonymous leaks database from Israeli Musical Act Magazine site #OpIsrael. *The Hacker News (THN)*. Available at: http://thehackernews.com/2012/12/anonymous-leaks-database-from-israeli.html?utm_source=feedburner&utm_medium=feed&utm_campaign=Feed%3A+TheHackersNews+%28The+Hackers+News+-+Daily+Cyber+News+Updates%29&_m=3n.009a.67.rn0aof3yo4.1t8#_; December 16, 2012 [last accessed February 2013].

483. Kumar M. Anonymous leaks database from Israeli Musical Act Magazine site #OpIsrael. *The Hacker News (THN)*. Available at: http://thehackernews.com/2012/12/anonymous-leaks-database-from-israeli.html?utm_source= feedburner&utm_medium=feed&utm_campaign=Feed%3A+TheHackersNews+%28The+Hackers+News+- +Daily+Cyber+News+Updates%29&_m=3n.009a.67.rn0aof3yo4.1t8#_; December 16, 2012 [last accessed February 2013].

484. Schwartz MJ. Anonymous posts Westboro Church members personal information. *Information Week*. Available at: http://www.informationweek.com/security/privacy/anonymous-posts-westboro-church-members/240144592; December 18, 2012 [last accessed February 2013].

485. LulzPirate. Westboro Baptist Church dox. *Pastebin*. Available at: http://pastebin.com/pCTSgLTJ; December 16, 2012 [last accessed February 2013].

486. Pavlo W. Anonymous' hackers target Westboro Baptist Church after protest plans. *Forbes*. Available at: http:// www.forbes.com/sites/walterpavlo/2012/12/18/anonymous-hackers-target-westboro-baptist-church-after- protest-plans/; December 18, 2012 [last accessed February 2013].

487. Thomas L. Anonymous versus Westboro, hactivists claim they won. *MYNorthwest.com*. Available at: http:// mynorthwest.com/646/2158623/Anonymous-versus-Westboro-Baptist-Church-hactivists-win; December 20, 2012 [last accessed February 2013].

488. Schwartz MJ. Anonymous Posts Westboro Church Members' personal information. *Information Week*. Available at: http://www.informationweek.com/security/privacy/anonymous-posts-westboro-church-members/240144592; December 18, 2012 [last accessed February 2013].

489. Twitter feed @th3j35t3r. I'm not trying to violate #WBC's civil rights. I'm just making best use of mine. And I'm non-violent. They hate that. Available at: https://twitter.com/th3j35t3r/status/281495612636139520; December 19, 2012 [last accessed February 2013].

490. Sweet, Hannah @CosmoTheGod. Tweet by @WBCSays: *"This account is now being ran by @CosmoTheGod #UGNazi #oops"*. Available at: https://twitter.com/CosmoTheGod; December 17, 2012 [last accessed January 19, 2012].

491. Pavlo W. Anonymous' hackers target Westboro Baptist Church after protest plans. *Forbes*. Available at: http:// www.forbes.com/sites/walterpavlo/2012/12/18/anonymous-hackers-target-westboro-baptist-church-after- protest-plans/; December 18, 2012 [last accessed February 2013].

492. Tenety E. Westboro Baptist Church to picket Sandy Hook funerals: 4 ways to respond. *Washington Post*. Available at: http://www.washingtonpost.com/blogs/under-god/post/westboro-baptist-church-to-picket-sandy- hook-funerals-4-ways-to-respond/2012/12/17/520a6ba0-488e-11e2-b6f0-e851e741d196_blog.html; December 17, 2012 [last accessed February 2013].

493. Kumar M. Anonymous hit Egyptian Government Websites as #OpEgypt. *The Hacker News*. Available at: http:// thehackernews.com/2012/12/anonymous-hit-egyptian-government.html; December 19, 2012 [last accessed February 2013].

494. BBC News. Egypt Crisis: protesters maintain Mursi decree defiance. Available at: http://www.bbc.co.uk/ news/world-middle-east-20521967; November 28, 2011 [last accessed February 2013].

495. Shenker J. Egypt: violent clashes in Cairo leave two dead and hundreds injured. *The Guardian (UK)*. Available at: http://www.guardian.co.uk/world/2011/nov/19/egypt-violent-clashes-cairo-injured; November 19, 2012 [last accessed February 2013].

496. Kumar M. Anonymous hit Egyptian Government Websites as #OpEgypt. *The Hacker News*. Available at: http:// thehackernews.com/2012/12/anonymous-hit-egyptian-government.html; December 19, 2012 [accessed February 2013].

497. Ferenstein G. Twitter suspends Anonymous account for Vigilantism, Breaking TOS for releasing Westboro Church Info [updated]. *TechCrunch*. Available at: http://techcrunch.com/2012/12/19/twitter-suspends- anonymous-account-for-vigilantism-breaking-tos-for-releasing-westboro-church-info/; Decemebr 19, 2012 [last accessed February 2013].

498. Roy J. Twitter Suspends Anonymous's Most Popular Account, @YourAnonNews; December 19, 2012 [last accessed February 2013].

499. Ferenstein G. Twitter suspends Anonymous account for Vigilantism, Breaking TOS for releasing Westboro Church Info [updated]. *TechCrunch*. Available at: http://techcrunch.com/2012/12/19/twitter-suspends- anonymous-account-for-vigilantism-breaking-tos-for-releasing-westboro-church-info/; December 19, 2012 [last accessed February 2013].

500. Russia Today. Anonymous takes on alleged Ohio gang rapists and their protectors. Available at: http://rt.com/ usa/news/anonymous-ohio-gang-rape-778/; December 25, 2012 [last accessed February 2013].

501. KnightSec. KnightSec + OpRollRedRoll. *Anonpaste.* Available at: http://www.anonpaste.me/anonpaste2/index. php?070961bcde7bf9d7#sObkWjsK+ZbV9PeupgZlNbJxqzROmyhDSNo2erqpU2M=; undated [last accessed February 2013].

502. Macur J, Schweber N. Rape case unfolds on Web and splits city. *New York Times.* Available at: http://www. nytimes.com/2012/12/17/sports/high-school-football-rape-case-unfolds-online-and-divides-steubenville-ohio.html?pagewanted=1&_r=5&smid=tw-share; December 16, 2012 [last accessed February 2013].

503. Russia Today. Anonymous takes on alleged Ohio gang rapists and their protectors. Available at: http://rt.com/usa/news/anonymous-ohio-gang-rape-778/; December 25, 2012 [last accessed February 2013].

504. KnightSec. KnightSec + OpRollRedRoll. *Anonpaste.* Available at: http://www.anonpaste.me/anonpaste2/index. php?070961bcde7bf9d7#sObkWjsK+ZbV9PeupgZlNbJxqzROmyhDSNo2erqpU2M=; undated [last accessed February 2013].

505. Russia Today. Anonymous takes down Delhi Police website over gang-rape case. Available at: http://rt. com/news/anonymous-delhi-police-rape-775/; December 25, 2012 [last accessed February 2013].

506. Russia Today. Anonymous takes down Delhi Police website over gang-rape case. Available at: http://rt.com/news/anonymous-delhi-police-rape-775/; December 25, 2012 [last accessed February 2013].

Glossary

A

API application programming interface
APT advanced persistent threat
ARPA Advanced Research Projects Agency (former name of DARPA)
ARPANET the precursor of the Internet developed by ARPA
AS Autonomous System

B

back door an unauthorized/unwanted connection from a system to an external machine, most likely under control
of an adversary
BGP Border Gateway Protocol
BOS Battlefield Operating System
botnet a "robot network" is a large group of infected computers who are under direct control of an adversary
through a "command and control" server. These compromised computers (termed "bots" or "zombies") can then
be directed by the adversary (often called a "botmaster" or "botherder") to do a number of activities—including
DDoS, CNE operations, and criminal activities such as phishing

C

C2 Command and Control (of a military unit)
C4ISR command, control, communication, computers, intelligence, surveillance, and reconnaissance
C&C Command and Control (i.e., command and control server of a botnet)
CCC Chaos Computer Club
CDN content delivery network
CIO Chief Information Officer
CJP Committee to Protect Journalists
CM collection management
CNA computer network attack
CND computer network defense
CNE computer network exploitation
CNO computer network operations
collection plan a plan by which intelligence professionals use to gather information requirements
COIN counter-insurgency
COMINT communications intelligence
COTS consumer off-the-shelf technology
CSIS Center for Strategic and International Studies
CYOP cyber psychological operations

D

DARPA Defense Advanced Research Projects Agency
DCS distributed control system

DDoS distributed denial of service

D.D.O.S. Destination Darkness Outlaw System—a botnet software package created by Russian criminal organizations

DNP distributed network protocol

DNS domain name server

DNS sinkholing often the C&C server of a botnet or other network of compromised computers is either shutdown or becomes abandoned. In the aftermath of such an abandonment, the compromised systems may still attempt to communicate with the server. With DNS sinkholing, a security professional registers a machine using the name of the C&C server. The compromised machines then connect to the server belonging to the security professional. The IP addresses of the compromised machines can then be identified in order to determine the extent of the spread of a given piece of malware for which a certain hacker group is responsible.

DOC the older file format for Microsoft Word that is susceptible to compromise

DOCTEMP doctrinal template

DoD U.S. Department of Defense

DoE U.S. Department of Energy

DoS denial of service

DSIE Defense Security Information Exchange

E

ECM electronic counter measures

EMS energy management system

EUCOM European Command

EW electronic warfare

EWS Engineering Workstation

F

FBI Federal Bureau of Investigation (FBI)

FEP Front End Processor

FEP Fuel Enrichment Plant

FSB the Russian apparatus for security and intelligence. The successor to the KGB

G

GCS Ground Control Station

GII Global Information Infrastructure

GSD General Staff Department (of the PLA)

H

HIC High Intensity Conflict

HMD Hardware Mitigation Device

HMI human-machine interface

honey pot a computer designed to appear vulnerable in order to lure hackers. Once the hackers gain access to the honey pot, their actions are then monitored by security professionals

HPT high-payoff target

HTTP Hypertext Transfer Protocol, the standard protocol computers use to interact with Web servers

HTTPS Hypertext Transfer Protocol—Secure

HUMINT human intelligence

I

IAEA International Atomic Energy Agency
ICA Iranian Cyber Army
ICCP Inter Control Center Protocol
ICT industrial control systems
IDF Israeli Defense Forces
IDS intrusion detection system
IEEE Institute of Electrical and Electronics Engineers
INEW Integrated Network Electronic Warfare
IO information operations
IP Internet Protocol
IP intellectual property
IR information requirements, pieces of information collected by intelligence professionals that are thought to have a significant impact on the success or failure of a military operation.
IRC Internet Relay Chat
IRGC Iranian Revolutionary Guard Corps
IRL In Real Life
ISP Internet service provider
ISR intelligence, surveillance, and reconnaissance
IT information technology
IW information warfare

J

JAM Jaysh Al-Mahdi

K

key logger malware designed to record all the keystrokes of the victim and report them to a third party
KH Kata'ib Hezbollah

L

LIC Low Intensity Conflict
LOIC Low Orbit Ion Cannon
LTG Lieutenant General

M

malware malicious software
MBR master boot record
MCO major combat operations
MeK Mujahedeen-e-Khalq
MITM Man-In-the-Middle
MTI moving target indicator
MTS multispectral targeting system

N

NATO North Atlantic Treaty Organization
NGO nongovernmental organization

NIST National Institute of Standards and Technology
NPD the (German) neo-NAZI Political Party
NSA National Security Agency

O

OB order of battle
OHHDL Office of His Holiness the Dalai Lama
OOP object-oriented programming
OPSEC operational security
OPT Occupied Palestinian Territories
OSINT open source intelligence

P

PDF Portable Document Format, a file format used by Adobe Acrobat
phishing social engineering attacks in which mass e-mails are sent out to a population in order to entice them to open an attachment or click on a link that causes a piece of malware to infect their system, often resulting in their computers falling under control of an adversary, often using a botnet.
PIR priority information requirements
PLA People's Liberation Army (of China)
PLC programmable logic controller
PLF People's Liberation Front
PMOI People's Mujahedeen of Iran
PoP Point of Presence
PPT the older file format for Microsoft PowerPoint that is susceptible to compromise
PRC People's Republic of China
PSYOP psychological operations

R

R&S reconnaissance and surveillance
RAM Random Access Memory (the temporary memory of a computer system)
RAT Remote Access Tool
RBN Russian Business Network
RDP Remote Desktop Protocol
RIM Research In Motion, makers of the BlackBerry mobile device
RMA Revolution in Military Affairs
RTU remote terminal unit
RUNET the Russian Internet

S

SACEUR Supreme Allied Commander of European Forces (the military commander of NATO)
SAR synthetic aperture radar
SATCOM satellite communication
SBU Sensitive But Unclassified
SCADA supervisory control and data acquisition
SCM Software Configuration Management system
script kiddies amateur hackers who merely follow instructions for a given hack or exploit—rather than using technology to fully understand or create their own exploits

security by obscurity the practice of relying on little known, but discoverable pieces of information as a means of security

SHAPE Supreme Headquarters Allied Powers Europe

SIGINT signals intelligence (i.e. radio intercepts)

smart grid a general term referring to the upgrade of communication systems in a power grid with the goal of obtaining improved monitoring, protection, and efficiency

social engineering attempting to manipulate a person to divulge certain information or perform a certain action

SEA Syrian Electronic Army

SMTP Simple Mail Transfer Protocol, the standard protocol used for e-mail on the Internet

SOPA Stop Online Piracy Act

spear phishing a phishing attack that targets specific users, often using information taken from CNE operations, social media, or open sources to appear legitimate and increase the likelihood of the user clicking on the malicious link or attachment

SQL structured query language

SQL injection an attack where an invalid SQL query is sent to a database with malicious executable code attached at the end. The system then fails to execute the invalid query and crashes, leading to the system executing the malicious executable code

T

TECHINT technical intelligence

TF-A two-factor authentication

TGIE Tibetan Government-in-Exile

TIA Total Information Awareness

Trojan see "Trojan Horse"

Trojan Horse a piece of seemingly innocuous software (i.e., a game, a pirated piece of commercial software) that has code that enables a hacker to obtain unauthorized access to the system that the software is running on

TTPs tactics, techniques, and procedures

U

UAV unmanned aerial vehicle

UCAV unmanned combat air vehicle

URL universal resource locator

USB Universal Serial Bus

V

VOA Voice of America

VPN virtual private network

W

WWW World Wide Web

Z

zero-day exploits a vulnerability to a piece of software that is currently unknown to the wider community (including major software vendors). All systems using that piece of software are generally regarded as being vulnerable to such an exploit

Index

Note: Page numbers followed by *f* indicate figures.

Printed and bound by CPI Group (UK) Ltd, Croydon, CR0 4YY

03/10/2024

01040327-0003